LIKE GOLD IN THE HANDS OF GOD

Bob Sutton

Published by New Generation Publishing in 2024

Copyright © Bob Sutton 2024

The author asserts the moral right under the Copyright, Designs and Patents Act 1988 to be identified as the author of this work.

All Rights reserved. No part of this publication may be reproduced, stored in a retrieval system or transmitted, in any form or by any means without the prior consent of the author, nor be otherwise circulated in any form of binding or cover other than that which it is published and without a similar condition being imposed on the subsequent purchaser.

Paperback ISBN: 9781835633380

New Generation Publishing
www.newgeneration-publishing.com

LIKE GOLD IN THE HANDS OF GOD

For the glory of God

Chapter 1

"For all have sinned and fall short of the glory of God."

Romans 3: 23

It was midnight and this was going to be my last night in Kirkham prison, in a few moments it would be the Queens official birthday, the 9th June 1988, a day that I thought would never arrive. As I lay on my prison bed waiting for morning to arrive and for the prison guard to unlock my door for the last time I felt like a little child waiting for Christmas morning to arrive with the excitement of waiting to see what presents would be under the Christmas tree. I would soon be leaving prison going back home to my wife and children, to start a new life and pick up all the broken pieces that I had left behind eight months ago when I was sentenced to 2 years in prison by the Judge. I wondered what my life would now be like as a Christian and I knew that I would not be on my own because God had promised to be with me every step of the way. As I waited for morning to come my mind flashed back over my life.

I was born on the 17th July 1951 to my mother Joyce and father Harold; I was the middle of three children, having an elder brother Arthur and a younger sister Diane. There were only a couple of years between all three of us and we were a very close family. My childhood was not very settled because my father changed jobs a lot and we moved all over the country. By the time I was 14 years old we had moved about fifteen times and we were living in Newport, South Wales. This was when I had my first bet on the horses and where I became addicted to gambling. It was my best friend Nick Cork who took me to the races with his family and from my first bet I experienced an excitement that I had never felt before. The horse that I had picked won and I thought this was a very easy way to get rich and make lots of money. If only I had known the misery that lay ahead of me I would not have been so keen to place another bet. Being young and carefree I was living for the here and now and the excitement of having a bet.

It was at this time that my parents announced that they were moving back to Manchester but as my school exams were only a few months away they agreed I could stay on in Newport at a friend's house until I had completed my exams. My parents had agreed to pay £4.10 shillings a week (£4.50p) as it was then for my board and 10 shillings a week (50p) for my spends. I lived with my friend Paul and his family right opposite the school I attended on Brynglas Hill. It was a very happy time for me as Paul and his family liked to have a bet on the horses and Saturday was the day we all looked forward to as we placed our bets and watched the horse races on television.

Within a few weeks of my family moving back to Manchester my gambling led me to commit my first crime. Nick had helped to convince me that a horse that was running was a cert and could not lose. "It could win on three legs" was the statement that convinced me we had to get hold of some money so that we could bet on this sure thing. I remembered that this was the day the postman delivered the letter with the £5 note that my father sent every week to the family I lived with. I convinced myself I was only borrowing the money as I intercepted the postman halfway up the driveway and signed for the registered letter addressed to Paul's parents. I planned to put the money back after the horse had won and no-one would be any the wiser of what had taken place. It never entered my mind that the horse could lose and my heart sank as the horse that I backed fell at the last fence when in the lead. My mind worked overtime trying to work out what I was going to say to Paul's parents and I decided not to say anything. After a few days had gone by Paul's mother told me she was going to telephone my father to ask why he had not sent my board money. I could feel my face going red as she spoke with my father who told her that he had posted the money. The following day the truth came out when the postman informed her that I had signed for the letter. I came very near to being sent back to Manchester but I was given a chance by my father who promised to send another letter with the money for my board. I promised that I would not do anything like that again not realising that the gambling had a grip of me and it was a promise I would not keep.

I started to steal money from the people in the house to feed my addiction and although it was never proven the fingers were pointing at me. When I was not gambling I went out with my best friend Nick who had two dogs. We would go for long walks by the canal with our air rifles and we also started to take an interest in girls. I had a few girl friends but nothing serious. I played football for the school team as a centre forward and for Newport Town as a goal keeper. I even went for trials to play for Wales youth team until the officials realised I was not qualified because both my parents were English. I was very involved in the drama classes at school and took a leading role in a play that won a drama competition. Some of my friends would bully other children at school but I was always sticking up for the underdog and telling my friends to leave them alone. The headmaster had a soft spot for me and made me a school prefect in charge of the school tuck shop. My last year at school must have been the only time the tuck shop lost money as I used a lot of the money to feed my gambling addiction. When a stock take was carried out I blamed the mice for the stock that was missing that could not be accounted for. One of the teachers did not like me after I made up a song about him having an affair with one of the other teachers. This teacher arranged for one of the biggest boys in the school to pick a fight with me.

The school had principals that if children wanted to fight they could fight wearing boxing gloves in the school playground supervised by a teacher with all the children allowed to watch. I had no reasons to fight this boy but if I backed down everyone would think I was a coward. This boy was so much bigger than me but I used my speed to keep out of the way of his punches for as long as I could. I managed to land a few blows but eventually he hit me with a blow that knocked me down. I could see this teacher smirking and I found the strength to get back up and land a few more blows myself. When the bell sounded for the end of the round I asked Nick to take my gloves off and I threw them at the teacher and told him that for me the fight was over as I had no reason to fight. The boy I was fighting was called Teggo and we became very good friends afterwards. It was Teggo who told me how the teacher had provoked him to start a fight with me.

After taking my exams in the summer of 1966 I had a holiday with Nick and his family before returning to Manchester to be with my family. It was a pleasant surprise to receive a letter from my school informing me that I had passed all nine of my exams with four distinctions. The only problem for me was my school report book where most of the teachers wrote negative comments about me. The one comment that stuck in my mind was the one made by the teacher who did not like me "Robert is a law unto himself". Those few words summed me up at fifteen years of age. Within a few weeks of arriving in Manchester I was given my first job as an apprentice engineer working with my father at the Sunblest Bakery in Stockport.

Chapter 2

"The righteousness of the upright delivers them, but the unfaithful are trapped by evil desires."

Proverbs 11: 6

It felt good starting my first day in work and it did not take me long to find out that there was a bookies runner who worked in the bakery. My luck was going well especially when I found a way of placing bets after the horse race was finished. I had noticed that the runner would write the time on the bets that were given to him by looking at the clock on the wall near to where he worked at the end of the oven. One Saturday morning when all the ovens had stopped working and no bakers were in sight I turned the clock back by one minute. I waited for Monday morning to arrive to see if my plan would work.

Monday arrived and at 2.30pm I wrote out my bet and I sneaked into the chief engineer's office to use his telephone so that I could listen to the live commentary of the 2.30 race at Newmarket that was a five furlong sprint. The race was over in less than a minute and Sweet Story romped home. I wrote its name down and ran with my bet to where the runner worked. He took my bet and looked up at the clock and remarked that I was just in time as he wrote 2.30pm on my bet. In fact the right time was 2.31pm and a few seconds but I was the only person in the place who knew what had taken place. It came as a pleasant surprise when I telephoned the bookies to find that the horse had won at the odds of 10-1 and I just hoped that I would be paid out without any problem.

The following day at lunch I joined the queue at the runners table to be paid out a total of £22. I was hoping my face would not give the game away when he said "that was a nice winner for you Bob, did you have some inside information?" I replied "it's a sweet story I might tell you about one day". I was walking on air with the equivalent of four weeks wages in my pocket as I joined the queue for lunch. I asked the girl in front of me if she would pass me the menu and she replied "anything for you love" I just smiled at her as I took the menu out of her hand.

For the next few weeks I placed bets on a regular basis making sure that I placed some losing bets as well so that I would not draw attention to myself. The mistake I made was letting a friend in on my secret and we got greedy. After having a winning streak that the bookie had never experienced before the runner was told not to take any more of our bets but we enjoyed the run while it lasted.

The works social club organised a works outing to Blackpool for the illuminations in September 1966 and it was on this outing that I met my wife Janice. I was with four other lads from the bakery who were deciding what girls each lad was going to link up with. It turned out that a girl called Lynn was left over and they asked me if I would link up with her. I did not fancy Lynn but one of the lads said "don't worry Bob, as soon as we leave the Islander bar you can dump her and go your own way". We all left the Islander in pairs and as soon as I went to hold Lynn's hand she said "what do you think you're doing?" I let go of her hand in a flash and within seconds I was 3 metres in front of everyone else and about to do a disappearing trick when one of the lads grabbed me from behind and said "you can have Janice and I will have Lynn". Before I could say anything he had placed the hand of Janice into my hand, when I looked at her face I realised that this was the girl from the dining room lunch queue at work who had said "anything for you love".

Janice and I walked off along the prom at Blackpool and we went for a game of ten pin bowling. It was love at first sight for both of us and I wanted the night to last forever. When it came for time for the coaches to leave I boarded the same coach as Janice that was going to Stockport and not the coach with my mum and dad that was going to Manchester. My parents thought I was mad getting the coach to Stockport because it would mean I would have about a ten mile walk from Stockport to my home in Manchester. All I cared about was being on the back seat of the coach with the girl of my dreams in my arms. The coach stopped at Brinnington in Stockport and Jan got off to be met by her sister on the street corner. I carried on to the centre of Stockport where I got off and skipped the ten miles to where I lived in Manchester. I was wondering if Jan would go out with me again and I did not have a long wait to find out.

It was the following week at work when Jan's best friend Lynn did a bit of match making and arranged for Jan and I to go on another date. We did not need anyone to do any more match making after our second date as we fell madly in love with each other. We spent every day with each other and my parents only saw me when it was my bed time as I caught the last bus from Stockport to where I lived. I could not wait for the day we could get married as I knew that Jan was the girl I wanted to spend the rest of my life with. After we had courted for about six months we made love for the first time. We were both virgins and it happened in a very natural way as our feelings for each other was growing stronger every day. After a year of courting we both changed jobs so we could earn more money and save up to get married. I was 16 and Jan was 18 but I had to lie about my age to get a job in the local brewery. I started to earn a good wage compared to what I was earning as an apprentice engineer but the problem was that I started gambling again so I was never able to save up any money. I thought I could win the money I needed by gambling but it never worked that way.

One day while I was at work I decided that I was going to have an industrial accident so that I could get some compensation to get married. I very nearly lost my life as the large chain conveyor got hold of my finger and dragged me towards the large chain cog. I screamed for help and it was the quick thinking action of a work mate who saved me from losing more than a finger. I was in a great deal of pain for the next two months as surgeons tried everything to save my finger but in the end they had to amputate it completely.

Jan and I were married on the 1st February 1969 when I was seventeen and Jan was nineteen years of age. The money I had received from the government in compensation was enough to get married with even though later on I lost my claim for compensation against the Brewery I worked for because I had lied about my age when applying for the job. My gambling was getting worse and on the day of our wedding I was in the bookies putting my last £2 on a horse. On this occasion the horse won and I had enough money to buy the first round of drinks for about sixty guests who had attended our wedding. I did not win enough to pay the landlord of the pub for providing all the food for our guests and he was not a happy man when I told him I did not have enough money with me to pay his bill. I told the landlord I had not taken enough money from the bank to pay him and I would come in the following week to settle the bill. The truth was I had gambled his money weeks before and had lost all the money I had trying to win it back.

For a gambler it is always "One more bet and when it wins I will stop" but the reality is that when I won I thought my luck was in so I carried on gambling until the bookies shut or I had lost all my money. My father convinced the landlord that I would pay the bill for the reception and he let me leave the pub in one piece although at one stage I thought he was going to hit me. Jan and I went back to our first home at Stockport, a small two rooms up and two rooms down terraced house that we were buying on a private mortgage. The house cost £650 and we agreed to pay £75 deposit and the balance at £2 per week. Our first night of married life together was something I had looked forward to since the first day I had fallen in love with Jan. To hold Jan in my arms and know that we were married was a very special feeling, when Jan fell asleep I lay looking at her beautiful face knowing that I was a very lucky young man.

Chapter 3

"You shall not make for yourself an idol I the form of anything in heaven above or on the earth beneath or in the waters below. You shall not bow down to them or worship them; for I, the Lord your God, am a jealous God, punishing the children for the sin of the fathers to the third and fourth generation of those who hate me, but showing love to a thousand generations of those who love me and keep my commandments."

Exodus 20: 4-6

Within a few weeks of being married Jan told me the great news that she was expecting our first child. We were both excited and could not wait to tell our family and friends. We would sit up in bed at night picking names for a boy or girl. We decided on Mark Anthony for a boy and Donna Marie for a girl. Within a few months of being married we started to argue a lot. It was always over my gambling because I was now going to the local pub on a regular basis to play cards for money. Jan hated my gambling because I neglected her and also lost money I could not afford to lose. Jan's own father was a heavy drinker and gambler and left her mother to bring up thirteen children by herself. Jan was determined that her marriage was not going to be the same as her parents but the more that Jan had a go at me the more we argued. To try and keep the peace I would try and gamble behind Jan's back but this led to more rows when she found I had lied to her.

The time came for Jan to go into Stepping Hill Hospital to have our baby. Jan gave birth to our first son Mark Anthony on the 23rd September 1969 after having a normal delivery. Mark was perfect in every way and had beautiful blond hair. We were both thrilled to be parents for the first time and I was a very proud dad. While Jan was in hospital I sold all our furniture to bet with and told Jan we had been burgled and all our furniture had been stolen. By now I had become a convincing liar and Jan never once suspected what I had done. I had to buy some more furniture on credit before Jan came out of hospital and the furniture arrived just one hour before Jan and Mark arrived home.

With Jan not working I was the only one earning any wage and I was working at the dye works opposite our home. I would lie about my wages so that I could keep some back for gambling with. At one stage I only had one shirt to my name and I would dye it different colours to make people think we were not as poor as we was. I would rather spend money on gambling than on clothes and during this period we never had enough money to pay our bills. I did have a small win when Mark was nine months old that was enough to go on our first holiday to Cornwall with my parents, brother and sister. We were so happy and it was during this holiday that Jan stopped breast feeding Mark and put him on solid foods. Jan and I spent hours walking along the beach and cliff tops at Portreath and we both fell in love with Cornwall wishing that one day we could live there.

This was a time when we had put all our cares behind us and we wanted the holiday to last forever. It did not rain once and our guest house overlooked the beach and sea at Carbis Bay. The owners of the Blue Dolphin guest house made a big fuss of Mark and they offered to look after him so we could go for a drink in the evening. We would walk arm in arm to St. Ives and walk around the harbour together. I loved to be near the sea to watch people fishing from the harbour wall and the fishing boats returning with their catch. Jan was happy because we were together and I was not leaving her to go gambling. The second week of our holiday we spent touring the country and when we arrived near London I persuaded everyone to go to the evening horse racing at Alexandra Park.

It was a beautiful evening as we parked up our car to go into the races and a man at the gate gave us a tip for two horses. I never liked backing other people's tips since I lost my board money in Newport so I relied on my own fancies and placed my bets. My mum was very excited when the tips we had been given both won but not as much as the man in front of her because my mum was jumping all over his back to cheer her horses past the winning post. We all had a good laugh when my mum asked what horse had won the race. On the fourth race I picked the winner at 8-1 and also got the forecast up by naming the first two in correct order. At that point the heavens opened and it rained so much that the meeting had to be abandoned. We all left the races in a happy mood because we had all won and for once Jan was not complaining about my gambling. It was a holiday we would never forget but like all good things it came to an end and we returned to our home at Stockport.

Within a few weeks from coming off our holiday Jan found out she was expecting our second child. By now my credit rating was very bad and we had to leave our house and rent a furnished flat in one of the roughest areas of Manchester. We had only been in the flat for a few days when I had to force open the electricity meter to use the contents to buy food because I had lost all my money gambling. The flat was a dump and I came home from work to find Jan in tears, she cried, "Get an ambulance Rob I think I'm losing the baby". I ran to the telephone and called the emergency services and Jan was rushed into Withington Hospital where she lost the baby the same day. I had never seen Jan look so unhappy and I promised her that we would move away from Manchester and have a fresh start together.

Chapter 4

"The wages of the righteous bring them life, but the income of the wicked brings them punishment."

Proverbs 10: 16

Within a few days of Jan coming out of hospital I had found a job at a sweet factory in Blackpool as a maintenance engineer. My parents took us in their car to Blackpool to help us find a place to live and we soon found a furnished flat to rent. The flat was nothing special and we had to live, eat and sleep all in one room. I started work at my new job and we looked forward to what we were going to do with my first week's wages. While I was at work Jan would take Mark out in his trolley for walks along the front at Blackpool near to where we lived. We had borrowed enough money from my parents to help get us through the first two weeks until I was paid my wages. We did not have a lot but Jan did a good job of making the money spin out.

Pay day soon came around and I was given my first wages of more than £40. It was a lot of money and I felt pleased with myself as I counted out the money from my wage packet to make sure it was all there. It was during the last tea break of the day when one of the other engineers shouted over to me, "hey Bob you like to have a flutter don't you, there's a dog running tonight and it can't be beaten, it's been running under a false name and its better than any other dog at Blackpool". The mere talk of gambling got my adrenaline running and the thought of winning a lot of money so we could move to a better flat would not leave my mind. I normally finished work at 5.00pm but at 4.00pm I telephoned the flats and asked the lady in the flat next door to give Jan a message. I told her that I had to work late on a breakdown at work and would be home for about 8.30pm.

I knew that I would have enough time to go to the greyhound track and place my bet, collect my winnings and be home for 8.30pm. The dog track was only a few hundred metres from where we lived and I waited excitedly for the race where this cert was running. I looked at the dog I was going to back with the number three on its back as it paraded past where I was standing wondering if it was going to win. I put my hand on my wages that were still in my pocket trying to make my mind up on what to do. The dogs were being loaded in the traps and the hare was running as I found a bookie offering odds of 4-1. I handed him the £40 and pointed to the number three on his board. As soon as the bookie gave me my ticket the traps lifted and I ran to the fence to watch the race. I reached the track fence as the dogs were running around the first bend; my heart sank as the dog that I backed was knocked over the running rail by another dog and was out of the race. The track officials carried the dog that I had backed on a stretcher near where I was standing. As it passed the dog lifted its head up and looked straight at me as if to say "I tried".

I walked away from the dog track with empty pockets and I felt very hollow inside. I wondered what I was going to tell Jan because she had looked forward to having enough money to take Mark out along the front at Blackpool and buy him an ice cream. I arrived home and I said "Jan, I've got some bad news for you, my wages have been stolen out of my jacket at work". I tried to look sad but Jan was having none of it and said as she started to cry, "You've blown them at the bookies". I would not admit what I had done and I had to take her engagement ring to sell it at the second hand shop so we had money for food for the weekend. I even told Jan I had sold it for less than I received so that I could try my luck on the horses Saturday afternoon.

I was able to talk Jan around once again by promising her that my wages would go direct into her hands the following Friday. For two days before I got paid our food had run out and when I came home from work Jan had to put salad cream on a round of bread so that Mark had something to eat. It hurt me to hear Mark was crying because he was hungry and I knew it was all my fault. I wanted to be a good husband and father by doing what was right but when it came down to it I always failed. I loved my wife and son so very much and yet I did things that caused them so much pain. If I won at gambling I would spend my winnings on Jan and Mark but I always lost more than I won. I knew in my heart that my gambling was affecting our relationship but the gambling was controlling my life.

I made sure that my wages went into Jan's hand for the next few weeks and I was given some money back so that I could have my bet on Saturdays. I started to go for a drink with some of the lads from work but Jan would not accept this and made me stop. As the summer season of 1971 approached our landlord told us we would have to leave our flat because he wanted to rent it out for the summer season at a higher rent than we were paying. I had to give up my job and we moved back to Manchester to look for a place to live and a job. As usual we turned up at my parent's home but they were on holiday and we ended up staying with my sister Diane and her husband Barry for a few nights. They had a daughter Samantha who was a year younger than Mark and although they only had a small house they agreed to let us stay for a few nights. Within a few days of moving in Diane asked us to leave because their gas meter had been broken into. Although Diane could not prove it she knew it was me, I hoped that I could win some money, put the money back in the gas meter and get a home to rent but as usual the horse I backed lost. We now found ourselves homeless on the streets of Manchester with no-one to turn to for help.

Chapter 5

"My sheep wandered over all the mountains and on every high hill. They were scattered over the whole earth, and no-one searched or looked for them."

Ezekiel 34: 6

We walked the streets of Manchester all day trying to find somewhere to stay for the night. The only accommodation we could find was a refuge for battered wives in Fallowfield where Jan and Mark were allowed to stay but I had to sleep on the park benches in the centre of Piccadilly Gardens. I picked the bench that was going to be my bed for the night and I was looking around at all the other people who were homeless and sleeping rough like me. Many of them were drinking alcohol and I knew that I did not want to end up like them. I found it impossible to sleep because an alarm bell had been set off in Woolworths Store that seemed to get louder and louder. I thought of Jan and Mark all alone in that hostel and I was determined to get myself out of the mess I was in. I put my hands in my pockets to keep them warm as I waited for morning to arrive.

    I was startled by a man aged about thirty five who sat down on the bench next to where I was lay. As I sat up he started to ask me how I had become homeless so I shared the details of my predicament with him. I was then informed that I could spend the night at his house and he would help me in lots of ways. I thought my luck was changing as I got into a taxi with him and headed towards Cheetham Hill where he lived. I was led upstairs to the attic of the house into a small bedroom with a single bed in it. This man then asked me to get into bed with him as he started to walk towards me pulling the zip of his trousers down. My heart started to beat very fast as I realised that I had been picked up by a homosexual. I ran towards the doorway and knocked the man out of my way with all the strength I could muster. As he fell backwards I ran through the doorway and jumped down the stairs ten at a time. I slammed the front door shut behind me and I did not stop running until I was back in Piccadilly Gardens. I knew that I had escaped from a situation that could have turned out much worse and the sound of the alarm bell ringing did not sound as bad as it had a short time before. It was a very long night and at 6.00am the town started to come alive with the early morning workers and buses. I had arranged to meet Jan at 9.00am outside of the hostel where she was staying. As I walked to meet Jan I was determined that things were going to change for the better.

I could not wait to tell Jan how I was going to change and when we met up I could see the tears in her eyes as Jan told me how bad the hostel was. We decided to try my parent's house again and we were both pleased to find that they had returned from their holidays and back at home. We were able to stay with my parents for a few days until we found a furnished flat to rent. Within two weeks we had both found a job but it was not long before I started gambling again.

We ended up losing the flat because of my gambling and my parents let us buy their house on a private mortgage as they had bought a small cottage in Todmorden, Yorkshire. We were both very happy to move into my parents house as it was in a good condition then Jan found out she was pregnant again. Our daughter Donna was born of the 13th June 1972 and we were both very happy to have a beautiful sister for Mark. I felt that the birth of Donna helped to take away some of the sadness from our lives when Jan had lost the other baby she had been carrying.

Our lives carried on in much the same way with much of my time spent gambling and my wife and children coming second best all of the time. It was when Donna was born that I met up with some of the local criminals in the pubs of Stockport near to where we lived. I found myself spending more time with them than I had with my family and this led to endless rows with Jan. They would burgle houses and I soon became a member of their gang. I was the one who had the nerve to go into banks with the stolen cheque books and cash cheques for large amounts of money. I became well liked by other members of the gang when on one occasion I cashed a cheque for £1000. We split the money four ways and I thought that this was much better than working for a living.

We had to move home again when our parents decided to move back to Stockport from Yorkshire. My father had offered to pay us £500 in cash if we let him have the house back. The thought of having that much cash in my hands was difficult to resist. Jan did not want to move but I convinced her that we would be better off in a council house. We ended up homeless for a short period of time and the council provided us with accommodation in a local bed and breakfast hotel. By the time we had been offered a council flat we had used up the money my parents had given us and we had to start from scratch all over again. It was not long before we had the flat looking very nice and in our own ways we were very happy. We would sit on the balcony of the flat at night talking about how nice it would be for our children to have a house with a garden to play in. Our wish soon came true when the council offered us a house with a garden a few hundred metres from where we lived. We moved into our new home and we soon had it looking nice. On the 8th August 1975 our Son Robert was born and we were both very proud parents.

Within a few weeks of Robert being born I was arrested by the police and charged with several burglaries. The police would not give me bail and I was sent to Risley remand Centre to await my court appearance. I hated it in Risley and while I was there some prisoners tried to kill themselves. It has the nickname "Grisley Risley" and I soon realised why it had such a name. Within a few days of being sent to Risley my leg was broken by one of the other prisoners and the doctor said it was just badly bruised. At night time all I could think about was my wife and children at home alone and I was missing them very much. The tears just rolled down my cheeks as I thought about them and each day at Risley was like a month.

After being on remand for three weeks my solicitor convinced Stockport Magistrates to grant me bail and I was so thankful to be back with my family again. The same day I was given bail I went to Stockport Infirmary to find my leg was broken and required putting into plaster. I tried everything I could think of to get a job before appearing at Crown court for sentence. I wanted to plead not guilty because I had never entered any of the houses that had been burgled; all I had done was cash cheques from the cheque books that had been stolen. My solicitor convinced me to plead guilty and he tried to persuade the judge not to send me to prison. My barrister tried his best but I was given a twelve month prison sentence in February 1976 when Robert was only six months old.

This was my first experience of prison and I was taken to Strangeways Prison in Manchester to serve my sentence. I tried to act hard on the outside but inside of me I was hurting. I wondered if Jan would still be waiting for me when I came out and I longed to hold her and my children in my arms. I hated every moment that I spent in prison and I promised Jan on her first visit that things would change for the better when I was released. Jan promised that she would stand by me and I was happy to believe her. After two months at Strangeways I was transferred to Appleton Thorn open prison. It was during my time at Appleton Thorn that I ended up in a fight with another prisoner. This prisoner had been bullying me for weeks with some of his mates and I was not going to take any more and gave him a good beating. I was placed in the punishment block of the prison because all his mates lied about what had taken place and I was moved to Walton prison in Liverpool to complete my sentence and wait for a trial by Jury for assault. When the date came for me to be released from my prison sentence I was taken direct to Risley Remand Centre to await a Crown Court trial. I was back where I had started out even though I had completed one prison sentence and now I had another one staring me in the face. After three weeks on remand my barrister convinced me to put my trust in him. He told me that if I pleaded guilty to assault I would be back with my family that day. I would have pleaded guilty to anything if it meant I could go home to me family. The crown Court Judge listened to my barrister plead on my behalf and made the following remarks. "I am giving you a chance to do what is right with your life. Your son Mark is being affected by you not being at home and your behaviour is going to have a bad affect on him unless you change your ways. You have a good wife who is prepared to stand by you even though you have neglected her. You are sentenced to six months in prison but I am going to suspend the sentence for twelve months, you are free to go.

It was a dream come true to hold Jan in my arms once more and to be heading back home together. Jan had come to court to speak up for me and we were back as a family again.

Chapter 6

"He who scorns instruction will pay for it, but he who respects a command is rewarded."

Proverbs 13: 13

I had written countless letters to Jan whilst I had been in prison and each letter contained the promise that I would look after her and our children when I was released from prison. I had promised to give up my gambling and be a good husband and father. Within two weeks of being released from prison I had found a job and I worked all the hours that I could so that I could provide good things for my family. I had realised when I was in prison that the people I had been calling friends were not the friends I thought them to be. When Jan was in need no-one came to visit her or see if she needed any help. I was determined that I would say goodbye to these so called friends and put my family first.

We had started to save up so we could buy our own house again and we found a house that was being built on a new housing development at Davenport in Stockport. We had paid our initial deposit and had nine months to save up the balance of our deposit. We would go along to the building site and watch our house being built brick by brick and dreaming of the day when we could move into it.

I was working for a company as a maintenance engineer and I worked seven days a week to earn as much money as I could so that we could build our banking account up. Then one day my boss told me that I was being passed over for promotion and that one of the other workers was being promoted to foreman. Everyone believed that I should have been given the job and I went out from work and got drunk. I then ended up in the casino where I lost all the money I had on me. From the casino I went to where I worked and broke into my boss's office and wrecked it. I was caught by the police and taken to the local police station and placed in a cell. When my boss came to the police station I begged him to forgive me and not to press charges against me. I explained that I was on a suspended prison sentence and that it could result in me being sent back to prison. It made no difference to my boss as he told the police to charge me.

That one night of madness resulted in me losing my job and also the means of obtaining a mortgage for our new house. I was given a fine by Stockport Magistrates and ordered to pay compensation for the damage I had caused. Thankfully they had not activated the suspended prison sentence that was still hanging over me. I then started gambling again and within a week I had lost all the money we had saved up. As usual I promised Jan that I would make things up to her and I formed my own company and started to work for myself. I started to earn good money and this meant that I could gamble for higher stakes. After working for one full month I received a cheque for over £600 that was double what I had normally earned. In one day I had lost all the money I had worked for. I decided that I would not do that again and I promised Jan that she would get her money before I went gambling with what was left.

Our life started to settle down and for once I made sure that my family did not go without because of my gambling. When I had a good win I made sure that I treated Jan and our children to something nice and this helped to keep the peace. The next few years were very good for us all and in 1978 we moved to another council house in Offerton, Stockport. By this time I employed several people and I was earning good money. I became well known in the local social club as a gambler and this was where I spent most of my time when I was not working. It was also a place where I could find the workmen that I needed from time to time. On the 25th July 1979 our daughter Michelle was born and we now had four children to look after.

My gambling had become very heavy by now and my business started to suffer because of the amounts of money I was losing. I hit on a plan to defraud the banks out of a lot of money and I let one of my workmen in on the plan. Everything would have worked out if my friend and employee had not been greedy but he decide to empty all the money that was in the bank account while the bank was waiting for a cheque to clear that we knew would bounce. I was upset when the police were called in and they started to investigate all areas of my business including every bank account I had opened. I had signed Jan's name on a mortgage application form stating that she worked for my company when we applied for a mortgage to buy our house from the council under the right to buy. I was charged with several offences and bailed to appear at the Crown Court in Manchester for a trial. I decided that I was going to leave England before my case came to court. I talked with Jan at length about having a fresh start in another country. I went for a job interview in London and I was offered a job as chief engineer of a sweet factory in Kano, Nigeria in West Africa.

    I thought that if I was in another country far away from England we would be able to have a fresh start with our lives. I knew that I was at fault for the situation that we found ourselves in and I should not have involved Jan like I had done. It was a very big step for me to take because I did not like being apart from my family. When I saw how wealthy the owners of the sweet factory were I had visions of becoming wealthy myself by working for them. I wanted the best for my family and I made the mistake of thinking I could win lots of money by gambling but always ended up making our situation worse. When I was offered the job I made it clear that I would only be going on a trial basis and if I did not like it in Nigeria I would return back to England. I asked them to buy me a return ticket because I knew I did not have any money of my own to buy a flight ticket if I did settle in Nigeria. They agreed with my request and after agreeing what my starting salary would be and conditions of employment I signed a contract. After the interview I returned back home to Stockport and within a week I received the return flight tickets from my employers. I only had seven days to wait before my flight was due to leave from Gatwick Airport and I had lots of butterflies in my stomach wondering what I had let myself in for. In my heart I did not want to leave my family behind but I did not see any other way out of the situation we were in.

Chapter 7

"The sorrows of those will increase who run after other gods."
Psalm 16: 4

We had agreed that I should go to Africa by myself to see what it was like and then after a few months I could send for Jan and our children. I had made arrangements for my wages to be paid into a bank account in Jan's name so she would not be without money. I felt very alone as the jumbo jet I was travelling in took off from Gatwick airport and headed towards Africa. I counted only twenty people on the plane and I wondered what Africa would be like when we arrived. We were given free drinks by the stewardesses because the plane had been delayed for takeoff due to a problem with the engine cowling. After several shorts I was feeling a little drunk and this helped to take away some of the fears that I had.

It was an experience I would not recommend to anyone as the plane was diverted to Lagos airport because of being late. The lights had been turned off at Kano airport and that was why we were being diverted. It was a relief when we landed safely but a further shock awaited me when I was informed by the stewardess that a private aeroplane had been provided to fly me back to Kano. If I had not been drunk I don't think wild horses would have been able to drag me onto the plane. It was like something out of the "flying doctor" and I had to climb a ladder to get into the plane. There were only two other passengers and two black stewardesses. I swallowed hard when I heard an Irish accent come over the speaker who introduced himself as the pilot. He sounded as drunk as I felt and my mind conjured up all sorts of reasons why an Irish pilot would end up flying an aeroplane that looked like it was ready for the scrap yard, thousands of miles from Ireland.

It was pitch black as I looked out of the window and I hoped that the pilot knew where he was going. One and a half hours later we landed safely at Kano airport and I was greeted by a black man with a piece of cardboard with my name on it. I was not allowed to take the spare parts through customs I had brought with me for the repairs to some of the machinery because they wanted a bribe. I was surprised at the open way in which they asked me for money. Eventually I had to agree for them to keep the parts until the owners of the company I was going to work for had paid the customs officers some money.

The man who met me was called Danlide and he explained in broken English that he was my driver and the boss of the company had left him to wait for me when they found out that my plane had been diverted to Lagos. We left the airport and Danlide carried my cases to the car. We had only travelled about four miles when our car was stopped by four men in army uniforms waving guns around. At first I had only seen the flash light they were waving and they told us to get out of the car. I was not sure what was happening as they only looked young boys to me but the guns they were waving around looked very real and menacing. Danlide explained that I was from England and what I was doing in Africa and where we were heading, he then told me to give them the bottle of Jonnie Walker that I had brought from England that he had seen in my duty free bag. When I gave the bottle of whisky the soldier's attitude changed completely and they put their arms around me patting my back. They were all smiling and laughing as they thanked me for my gift. I was soon to find out that bribery and corruption was common place in Nigeria at that time.

I had never experienced anything like I found in Africa, with the red hot days that lasted from 6.00am to 6.00pm. Kano was a large town and nearly everyone I met was black. I had never been prejudiced against colored people and I got to like Danlide and also the young house boy called Sabu who looked after my apartment. I did not like the way my bosses treated the workers in the factory and I would stick up for them on lots of occasions. Within a few days of arriving in Africa I knew that Jan would not be happy if I sent for her and I thought often of returning home to England. After two weeks of wondering what to do Danlide told me that I would be better off back in England with my wife and children. I had spoke about my family on lots of occasions as Danlide drove me around. It was only a week from Christmas and I bought a tape from the local market that had a record on it titled "I'll be home for Christmas". When I listened to the words of the song I knew that I had to do all that I could to be home for Christmas.

I told Danlide to keep it secret as I went to the local airline agents to enquire about my ticket back to England. My bosses had given me a return ticket that was not valid as it had been bought as a return from Kano rather than the other way round. I realised that my bosses had done this to keep me trapped in Africa. Over the next few days I sold all my possessions to raise the money I needed for the ticket and I ended up buying the last seat on the aeroplane that would be leaving Kano airport four days before Christmas. When I arrived at the airport I did not have enough money to buy a drink but I was happy to know that I would soon be back in the arms of my wife and children who I loved very much. Just before my plane was due to take off my boss turned up and tried to stop me leaving. He offered to pay me double my wages and wanted to know how I had managed to get a ticket. This confirmed that he only ever intended to get me a one way ticket even though they had promised me a return ticket and that I could leave if I did not like it in Africa. No amount of money could have got me to stay a moment longer in Africa away from the ones I loved and I moved into the departure area where only those with a valid ticket were allowed to go.

Jan was very surprised when I telephoned her from London to inform her that I was back from Africa and would soon be back home with her and my children. The day after I arrived home it was on the evening news that there had been a revolution in Nigeria and the army had put the president in prison and had taken over the running of the country. Kano airport along with all the other airports had been closed down and no-one was sure when they would re-open or what was taking place. I had caught the last plane out of Africa and I thought for a moment that someone was looking after me. We did not have a lot of money at Christmas but the fact that we were together as a family meant a great deal for us all. With Christmas over we faced the Crown Court trial together but Jan was angry for being roped into something she had not known anything about. It was the summer of 1984 when we were both convicted by the jury even though Jan was completely innocent. My friend and his daughter were cleared by the jury even though they were guilty. I think the judge knew the truth because he gave Jan a conditional discharge for the one charge she had been convicted of and I was given a suspended prison sentence for the four charges I had been convicted of. I had expected to be sent to prison and no-one was more surprised than me when the judge gave me a chance to get my life together. I think that the fact I had a probation officer who gave me an excellent report plus my own father speaking up for me helped convince HHJ Wood to give me a chance. I was determined to make the most of the chance I had been given.

Chapter 8

"Unless the Lord builds the house, its builders labour in vain."

Psalm 127: 1

I lost my business shortly after the court case when I had to declare myself bankrupt due to all the money I owed to different banks. I was able to carry on working when Jan and my father opened a business account in their names so they could look after the money side of the business. It was about this time we found out that our son Mark had problems with glue sniffing so we tried to get him help from Stockport social services. It was clear that no-one knew what to do for the best so we decided to move house away from the people Mark was going around with. We had wanted to move to Cornwall into a beautiful house we had found for sale overlooking Carbis Bay. We decided against this due to it being a big gamble with the limited amount of money we had from the sale of our ex-council house. Instead we bought a three bed roomed semi-detached house in Hazel Grove with a large plot of land at the side and the rear.

 I shared a dream with Jan of turning the house into a five bed roomed luxury house with a detached games room at the back where we could invite all our family and friends. It would also give Mark an interest with plenty of work to keep him occupied. We moved into the house in 1985 and the plans were drawn up and passed by the council to turn the house into our dream home. We had never worked so hard in our lives and all the profits from the building business were used in our dream home. I cut back on my gambling and although I still had a bet it was not as heavy as in the past. We had it rough for the first few months because all the main services had to be disconnected while I installed the foundations and services for the new building and extension to the property. We spent much of our time eating out in the pub opposite our home due to not being able to cook with all the building work that was taking place. It was a large project and we worked seven days a week and late into the night with everyone playing their part. Mark and I would go for a drink and a game of snooker together and he was now much taller than me. Mark worked for me and I paid him a good wage for his age. One night in 1986 Mark was arrested by the police for breaking a shop window when he was drunk. I went to see the owner of the shop and asked him not to press charges and told him that I would replace the broken window the same day. The owner refused my request and insisted that Mark was charged with criminal damage. This was the first time that Mark had been in trouble with the police and I felt they took delight in charging Mark because he was my son. At court Mark was fined and ordered to pay one hundred and fifty pounds in compensation for the shop window.

We put this incident behind us and carried on with our lives and then in November of 1986 I went into a betting shop to place a ten pound bet, a bet that was going to have dire results for our family. I had placed bets on thousands of occasions in the past but on this occasion I was given both parts of my betting slip back. I knew right away that I had been presented with a golden opportunity to take a lot of money from the bookies by altering the bet. After my bet had been put through the till where it was time recorded it should have gone through the security camera with the top copy being kept by the betting shop staff. The lady who took my bet forgot to photo copy it and gave me the part she should have kept. I was able to alter the £10 win to a £1.00 win by adding a dot and a zero that left me with £9 to bet with. I picked our four good priced horses after they had won and added them to the betting slip. I them threw the top copy away and acted out the plan I had formulated for getting the winnings from the bookies.

I knew that I would not be paid out immediately because the winnings came to over £40,000 but I was convinced they would be forced to pay me out as they had no proof of what I had done. William Hill brought in their own investigators some of whom were ex-police and they put enough pressure on the police to charge me. I was not worried when the police charged me with attempting to obtain £40,000 by deception because I was convinced that I would be cleared by a jury when it came to court and the bookies would be forced to pay me out. I paid to have a large sign made and put it up outside of my home stating that the bookies had robbed me of £40,000. I issued a high court summons against the bookies for damages in the belief that I would be cleared by the jury.

As usual the police roped my wife in and charged her to put pressure on me to plead guilty. Then a few days after we were charged by the police Jan and I were assaulted by a police officer a few hundred yards from our home in Hazel Grove. We were then both charged with police assault to cover up for what the police had done to us. We had to go through Christmas of 1986 with a great deal of pressure on both of us. We tried to put our worries behind us and invited all our family and friends for Christmas diner in our new home. We had a great time and I cooked dinner for twenty two people on Christmas day. January 1987 started off in a bad way when we heard the news from Jan's sister Carol that her husband Alan had died of a heart attack. We had all been together on Christmas day laughing and joking and now he was dead. We were just coming to terms with the death of Alan when another tragedy struck our family. It was the 27th January and we had arranged to meet Mark at the Blossoms pub where we were playing darts and crib for the Bulls Head. Mark did not turn up and we thought that Mark had met up with some of his mates and gone off with them.

We had planned to go for a meal to the Bamford Arms but Jan said she wanted to go home when the match was finished and we arrived home at about 10.00pm. We had only been home for a few minutes when the door bell sounded. I opened the door to be met by three police officers and a police inspector. I thought they had come to arrest me over something else but their attitude was very somber as they asked to come in. The police inspector then asked us a lot of questions concerning Mark over his identity. After answering his questions he then informed us that a boy answering those descriptions had been found dead on the railway line near our home and they believed it was Mark.

Jan started to cry and hit the police inspector on the chest with both of her hands screaming at him to tell her it was not true. I was in a daze and I thought I was having a nightmare that I was going to wake up from at any moment. I soon realised that it was not a nightmare that I was going to wake up from as Jan's sister Dot arrived followed by my parents. Soon the house was full of people and Donna, Robert and Michelle got out of bed to find out what was going on. I remember asking my dad if he would identify the body for the police because I did not feel strong enough to undertake that task. I broke down in tears as my dad held me close to him and said he would do it for me. After a few hours everyone had gone and Jan and I held each other close as we lay down on the settee waiting for morning to arrive. We did not sleep and our tears mingled together as they ran down our cheeks. Our children joined us on the settee and we all held each other very close afraid of letting go. In my mind I was thinking about Mark being on the railway line and wondered what he was doing there. I knew that my parents lived on the other side of the railway track near to where he had been found and wondered if he had been taking a short cut. I started to get severe chest pains and I thought I was going to have a heart attack so Jan called out the emergency doctor.

After the doctor checked me over he gave us both sleeping tablets but we did not take them. We lit up cigarette after cigarette to help calm our nerves and by morning we both had bad headaches due to all the stress and smoke. I was supposed to pick my workmen up for work but I telephoned one of my workmen telling him what had happened and asked him to carry on without me. My mind flashed back to a few days before when I had shouted at Mark for doing something wrong at work. I started to feel really bad about all the things I had said or done that may have hurt Mark over the years. For some reason my mind started to bring up all the events where I had caused Mark to cry and I could not get them out of my mind. I thought about the time when he was only two years old and I had smacked him for peeling off the wallpaper as soon as I had decorated. I then thought about the time I had left Mark at the social security office when they had refused to give us any money when he was only three. I could picture Mark crying and wondering why I was leaving him behind. I knew there were also lots of happy memories but my mind kept thinking about the ones I wished I could have changed.

I wanted to turn the clock back and alter many of the things I had done but I knew it was too late for that. I knew that as Mark's father I should have been the one to go and identify his body but I was not strong enough to see my son who I loved so very much lying dead in a mortuary. My dad was just as heartbroken and yet he found the strength to do what I could not do. The policeman who had been on the scene of where Mark had been found came to see us. Nothing seemed to make any sense on why Mark should have been on the railway line. The policeman stated that he had found a small bag of glue a few yards from where Mark's body had been found but did not know if it belonged to Mark. We were informed that there would be an inquest due to the mystery of Mark's death but it would not take place for a few months.

Chapter 9

" But if from there you seek the lord your God, you will find him if you look for him with all your heart and with all your soul. When you are in distress and all these things have happened to you, then in later days you will return to the Lord your God and obey him. For the Lord your God is a merciful God; he will not abandon or destroy you or forget the covenant with your forefathers, which he confirmed to them by oath."

Deuteronomy 4: 29-31.

The vicar from the local church at Norbury came to see us to talk about the funeral arrangements for Mark. The church was only fifty yards from where we lived and it was the church where my parents attended. Mr. Barton asked if we had any favourite hymns that we would like during the service but we did not know of any with not going to church. The only times we had been to church was to get married and when our children were Christened so we asked if we could have two records played. Jan and I had a favourite record by Simon and Garfunkle called "Bridge over troubled waters" and the words of the song spoke what was in our hearts. Mark was a Madonna fan and we asked for "True Blue" to be played as we knew he would have wanted that to happen.

A few days before the funeral I started to question in my mind if God was real. I was not able to sleep at night so I sat up and wrote Mark a long letter and poured out all the feelings from my heart. I asked Mark to forgive me for anything I may have done wrong as a father and for anything I had ever done to hurt him. I asked Mark if he could let me know if he was in heaven if it existed. I let Mark know how much I loved him and how much I was missing him. I talked with Jan about going to see Mark at the funeral directors before he was buried as the funeral director told us that we might regret it at a later stage if we did not go and see him and say goodbye. I was really frightened of what we would see if we went to see Mark as I pictured a body cut up very badly by the train. We were then informed that Mark only had a back and foot injury and we would only see his face.

On the night before the funeral Jan and I plucked up the courage to go and see Mark and say goodbye. (This was something I would never regret doing as I looked back years later). I took the letter with me that I had written and some of Mark's favourite things. Donna, Robert and Michelle all gave something to be placed in Mark's coffin. Jan took off her gold chain and pixie that I had bought her many years before in Cornwall that had never left her neck. When we arrived at the funeral directors it was about 8.00pm and when we were ready the curtain was drawn back to reveal Mark in his coffin. We both sobbed our hearts out seeing our son who we loved very deeply in his coffin. We talked to Mark as though he could hear us and we both gave Mark a kiss. I was not sure what to expect when I kissed Mark but his skin felt cold and hard. I read the letter to Mark I had wrote as tears streamed down my face so that I could not see the writing on the letter.

The undertaker had placed Jan's gold chain around Mark's neck and this gave us both some comfort. I was pleased with the way the undertaker allowed us to place some of Mark's personal things, those from his parents, brother and sisters in his coffin to be buried with him. My father who had taken us to see Mark also said his goodbye and we left the funeral directors together. Jan and I were pleased we had been to see Mark and we were very grateful to the funeral director for helping us to do so.

On the day of the funeral it was raining very hard and there was some concern about the grave flooding with water. We had picked a headstone for Mark's grave in the shape of a heart and with the words engraved "To live in the hearts you leave behind is not to die". I knew that Mark would always be alive in our hearts and be a part of us. When we arrived at the church I was surprised at how many people were present. The church was full of many young people that Mark had known and when I saw how many friends he had I knew that he had a lot to live for. After the service we followed Mark's coffin to the graveside. It was when the covers of the grave were removed and I looked into the hole that had been dug that I thought "There has got to be more to life than this" I wished that it had been me being buried in that grave in place of Mark. If this was what life was about then for me it was not worth living.

As Mark's coffin was lowered into his grave we made our way towards the funeral cars to leave. Jan noticed Kevin a good friend of Mark crying by the side of the church. We both took hold of him and asked him to get into the car with us. We then made our way to the Bulls Head pub where the Landlord and Landlady had made some refreshments for everyone. After everyone had left we crossed over the road to our home to carry on with our life and all the problems that we had to face. When we arrived in the house it was Jan who noticed a single red rose that had fallen onto the floor. Jan bent down to pick it up and placed it inside a bible that had been given.

Mark had only been buried for about three days and I woke up screaming in the middle of the night. I had dreamed that Mark was at the side of my bed talking to me and when I woke up Jan, Donna, Robert and Michelle were all trying to calm me down. It was so real and our children had come running into our room to find out what the screaming was all about.

Chapter 10

"I tell you, my friends, do not be afraid of those who kill the body and after that can do no more. But I will show you whom you should fear: Fear him who, after killing the body, has the power to throw you into hell. Yes, I tell you, fear him."

Luke 12: 4-5.

Everything became an effort after the death of Mark and we still had many problems to overcome. In March 1987 Jan and I were both convicted of the false police charges brought against us at Stockport Magistrates Court. We wondered if things would ever go right for our family and it felt like everything was against us. I talked with Jan about putting in an appeal against the conviction and taking it to the Crown Court but we both wondered if we could go through all the pressure again. We then had Mark's inquest to attend but Jan did not feel strong enough to go. I said I would go for both of us and it was held in front of a jury. After listening to various witnesses give evidence it was still not clear why Mark had ended up on the railway line. The train driver stated that Mark was lay across the tracks and yet the doctor who examined Mark stated that this was not consistent with the injuries he had received. Mark could not have been lay across the tracks when the train hit him because the injury that killed him was to his back and the doctor stated that he thought it was a glancing blow from the train. It was a very distressing inquest to sit through and when it was my turn to give evidence I broke down in tears. The coroner had to finish reading my evidence for me that I had wrote down in a statement. The jury were not sure of the circumstances surrounding mark's death and they recorded an open verdict.

With the inquest out of the way I persuaded Jan that we should appeal against the Stockport Magistrates decision to find us guilty for police assault as it was a wrong decision. Reluctantly Jan agreed and I asked our solicitor to lodge an appeal. We tried to continue with our lives as before for the sake of our children but it was not easy with all the problems we had to face. We decided to have a week's holiday at Butlins for Donna's birthday and to get a break from everything. All I could think about was the appeal against the police and the William Hill bet that was still waiting to come to trial. I had won the money for the Butlins holiday gambling on the horses with a 50p win yankee. Even though I had won over £1000 I felt like I had been robbed of over £10,000. Even with what had happened to Mark I did not stop gambling and this was where I retreated from reality. I picked four horses and when I went into the bookies the first two had won at odds of 10-1 and 9-1. I knew I had a good bet going and so did the bookie as he ran up the road to William Hill and lay the bet off. Carol Ann who I had placed the bet with placed two £50 singles and a £100 double on my other two selections that both won at 12-1. I calculated my winnings at over £12,000. I was soon sickened when it was announced that my 9-1 winner had been disqualified after a steward's enquiry that had lasted over half an hour. Carol Ann only had to pay me £1000 and they made over £18000 from the bet they had placed at William Hill for the two selections that had won.

I felt that our luck was changing after we returned from holiday to find that our appeal against the police was to be heard. We were both thrilled when the Crown Court Judge and Magistrate that heard our appeal found in our favour and overturned the verdicts of the Stockport Magistrates. My faith in British justice was now restored and this meant we could take Greater Manchester police to court for what they had done to us. We instructed our solicitor to issue a summons against the police and Jan won over £1500 in damages for what the police had done to her.

We now only had the William Hill trial that was listed for the first week of October 1987. Within the first two days of the trial the Judge ordered the Jury to find Jan not guilty of any involvement over the bet I had placed. It was clear to the Judge that the police had roped Jan in to put pressure on me and I felt it would only be a matter of days before I was cleared. Even though I was guilty I did not believe that the police had enough evidence for me to be found guilty. The prosecution had finished putting their theory and evidence to the jury and the following day it would be my turn to give evidence. I left court at 4.00pm with Jan and we made our way home to Stockport.

Jan asked me how I thought it was going and I told her that I was convinced I would be found not guilty. We arrived home at about 5.0pm and I went to the off licence to buy a bottle of Pernod that we both liked to drink. It was raining very heavy and it was dark and I decided to go to Mark's grave. I sat down on Mark's grave and I started to talk with him. I told Mark how much I was missing him and that I wished he was back at home with us all. I did not care that I was soaked through to the skin and I looked up through the rain to where I though heaven would be if there was a heaven. I did not know if there was a God but I said "God if you are real, I need a break in my life. You know how much money I have lost to the bookies over the years and I have lost my son Mark. Life has been cruel and I need to be with my family who need me and not in prison. Please help me to be found not guilty so that we can start to re-build our lives."

I left mark's grave and returned home to Jan and our children where I spent the night holding Jan in my arms waiting for morning to arrive. I arrived at Crown court on the 9th October 1987 full of confidence that I was going to be found not-guilty. If God was real I convinced myself I had nothing to fear because he would make sure that I won so I decided to put my trust in God. I told my barrister that I was not going to give any evidence because the prosecution had not proven my guilt. He agreed with me that I did not have to give any evidence but I had not told him that I did not want to pick up a Holy Bible and swear to tell the truth and then tell a pack of lies.

By 1,00pm all the summing up had been done and the jury went out to consider their verdict. The judge continued my bail and I took Jan and my supporters out for lunch to the Grand Hotel nearby. We all knew that very soon the jury would return with their verdict and twelve months of suffering was about to come to an end….or was it?

Chapter 11

"Come to me, all you who are weary and burdened, and I will give you rest. Take my yoke upon you and learn from me, for I am humble in heart, and you will find rest for your souls. For my yoke is easy and my burden is light."

Matthew 11: 28-30

The jury had been out for two hours and we were informed they had reached a verdict. The foreman of the jury was asked to stand up and he was asked for the verdict, "Guilty" he replied, and when I heard that word my heart sank. I could not believe that I had been found guilty and I kept my fingers crossed hoping the judge would not send me to prison. The judge stated "You have been found guilty of a very serious attempt to obtain £40,000 by deception from William Hill. In view of the tragedy that you have suffered in the loss of your son I am going to treat you leniently and send you to prison for two years."

I felt that my nightmare was continuing and I wondered if the judge had a heart in sending me to prison for two years. It felt like a life sentence to me and no-one seemed to care how I was hurting inside. I was convinced at that moment that God did not exist as I was taken down the steps into the cells below to begin a two year prison sentence. Jan was allowed to come and see me for a few minutes in the cells below the court and I asked my best friend Steve to take care of her for me. I could see that Jan was hurting just as much as I was by looking into her eyes and Jan promised that she would stand by me and wait for me. I was then taken off to Strangeways Prison to serve my prison sentence as the nightmare continued.

The coach I was in drove through the large gates of Strangeways Prison and I was led into the reception area of the prison. I had been handcuffed to another prisoner and these were taken off and I was given a cardboard box to place all my clothes and belongings in. I was given a set of prison clothes that had been worn by many prisoners before me where even the underwear was badly soiled. After being in the reception area for about four hours I was taken with the other new intakes into the main part of the prison. I was placed in a cell with two other prisoners where we were given a plastic bucket which was going to be our toilet for the night.

The cell consisted of a set of bunk beds and a single bed and I ended up on the top bunk. The prisoner in the bottom bunk was an alcoholic and he was in and out of bed all night with the runs. The smell was appalling and made me feel sick. I had to put my head under the blanket to try and keep out the smell and the sound of him using the bucket. The tears started to run down my cheeks as I thought of my wife and children at home. I needed their love so badly and I wanted more than anything to be at home with them. The following morning I was given a cell on "C" wing of the prison that I had to share with one other prisoner who was being released in two days time.

Chapter 12

"The spirit of the sovereign Lord is on me, because the Lord has anointed me to preach good news to the poor. He has sent me to bind up the broken-hearted, to proclaim freedom for the captives and release from darkness for the prisoners, to proclaim the year of the lord's favour and the day of vengeance of our God, to comfort all who mourn, and to provide for those who grieve in Zion - to bestow on them a crown of beauty instead of ashes, the oil of gladness instead of a spirit of despair. They will be called oaks of righteousness, a planting of the Lord for the display of his splendour."

Isaiah 61: 1-3

Saturday night I could not get any sleep for wondering how the jury had reached a guilty verdict. I wondered if they had been bribed by William Hill because I was convinced that I should have been found not guilty through lack of evidence. Sunday morning at 7.00am the cell door was unlocked and I was allowed out of the cell to "slop out" (empty contents of bucket and go to toilet). On the landing I looked right into the eyes of a prison guard who was a double of the foreman of the jury. I was convinced it was the same man and ran away from him down the stairs trying to get some help. I was really desperate as the prison guards ran after me shouting at me to come back. I was on the ground floor where all the wings of the prison meet at the centre of the prison. I was standing on the centre grate where no prisoner was allowed to stand. The more the prison guards shouted at me to come off the more I went into the middle of the grid.

In no time at all four prison guards had grabbed hold of me and started to carry me off holding me by my legs and arms. I was terrified of what they were going to do to me and although I tried to fight them off I had no chance as I was completely overpowered. I was carried down some more stairs into the lowest depth of the prison, all my clothes were ripped off me and I was thrown completely naked into an empty cell known as a strip cell. I believed that I was going to be killed and I cowered in the corner of the cell like a frightened animal waiting to be attacked. I could hear the prison guards laughing and I thought they were laughing because they knew I was soon to be killed. The door opened and a hand pushed in some food and water in a plastic cup and dish. I was convinced that it was drugged so I would not eat or drink anything that was offered. I thought that I would be hung up when I was unconscious and the guards would say I had committed suicide. I knew that people would accept this with what I had gone through in the past year alone but I was determined to go down fighting.

After two days of being in this strip cell where I refused to eat or drink anything offered to me I became very weak. It was my third night in this strip cell that I started to choke. My throat was all dry and I felt like I was being strangled and when I tried to swallow I found my throat had closed up. I knew that if I did not get a drink of water I would die anyway. I did not know what time it was but guessed it was about 2.00am because of the quietness of the prison also it was pitch black outside my cell window. I had refused all food and water from being placed in the strip cell because of the fear of it being drugged but now I knew the only hope I had of staying alive was to get a drink of water.

I wanted the prison guard to see how desperate I was for a drink of water after I had pushed the emergency bell on the wall so I got down on my knees in a begging position and waited for him to come. I could hear his footsteps getting nearer to my door and then he was outside of my door lifting the spy hole cover in the solid door to look inside the cell at me. All I could see was his eyeball as I pleaded, "Please can I have a drink of water I am choking to death".

The door vibrated as he kicked the bottom of the door and replied in a very gruff voice, "Get your fucking head down and get to sleep". The prison guard walked away and his footsteps got fainter until there was no sound to be heard.

I had reached the stage where I could not take any more and I did not want to live. I now understood how Mark must have felt all alone on that railway line waiting for that train to come. I wanted my life to end there and then; if this was life I did not want any part of it. I then started to think of my wife and children all alone at home in Hazel Grove. Jan had been a good wife and mother but I had let her down time and time again. I thought about all the times I had neglected them to do the things that I had wanted to do. All I had cared about much of the time was me, I realised that they were hurting just as much as I was and yet all I was thinking about was how much I was hurting. I had not considered their feelings in any way and I knew that I should have been with them at home to help support them through the death of Mark. I started to cry and the tears started to drop on the cell floor where I was still in a kneeling position. I cried out to God, "Oh God, please help me, I don't want to die I want to live".

Within a few seconds of crying out to God for help in the quietness of that strip cell I heard a voice speak to me very clear and in a soft tone. "Robert you are not going to die, forget you can't swallow, lie down and breathe through your nose". It was a voice that I obeyed even though I could not see anyone else in the strip cell with me. I lay down and started to breathe through my nose and a quiet peace came over me that I had never experienced before. I closed my eyes and fell asleep; this had been the first deep sleep I had experienced since Mark had been killed.

When I woke up it was morning and the light from the sun was shining through my cell window directly into my face where I was lay. Even though I felt weak I was happy to be alive and I was thinking about what had taken place in the early hours of the morning when suddenly the cell door opened. I could see a man in a light brown suit and two prison guards beside him. I was sat on the cell floor resting on my elbow when the man in the brown suit crouched down next to me and put his hand on my shoulder and spoke to me in a very gentle voice, he asked if I would like my clothes back and to move into a cell with a bed in it. I answered, "Yes please I would not treat an animal like you are treating me."

I was helped up off the floor and this was the first bit of compassion that I had been shown since arriving in the prison five days before. The man in the suit explained that he was the prison doctor and that I was suffering from a nervous breakdown. I was led into a cell opposite the one I had been in and I was pleased to see a bed with some cupboards in the corner. One of the prison guards instructed one of the other prisoners to go and get me some clothes. I was given some clothes and I felt a lot better not being naked any more. No sooner had I dressed when the cell door opened once more and this little man with a dog collar on his neck walked in and introduced himself in the following way. "Hello young Sutton, my names Noel Proctor and I am the prison chaplain, your father has written me a letter and I'd like to read it to you if you don't mind."

As soon as I looked at Noel I could see something different about him. He was smiling and happy, something that I was not used to seeing in the prison. I asked Noel to read me the letter from my father.

"My son Robert who I love very much has been sent to prison for trying to obtain some money from the bookmakers by deception. God knows if Robert is guilty or not but regardless of that I know that Robert suffered greatly with the death of his eldest son and my grandson Mark who was killed on the railway line in January. Robert will be in need of a friend and I would be very grateful if you could look in on Robert and let him know we love him very much."

Noel could see the tears running down my cheeks as he read out the letter that my father had wrote to him. I was thinking about all the pain I had caused my parents over the years by doing all the things that were wrong and for the first time I realised how much my parents loved me.

Noel asked, "would you like to have a New Life right here and now?" as I was thinking about what had taken place in the early hours of the morning and the voice I had heard, Noel continued, "Jesus Christ died for all the sins you have committed, He died so that you can be forgiven and be reconciled to God. He died so that you can have a New Life and live eternally in Heaven with God. Jesus loves you and wants to take away all the pain in your heart. You can have a new start here and now if you want it."

I knew that my life was in a mess and that I had hurt many people especially those who had loved me the most. I decided that I was being offered a free bet, something where I had nothing to lose but everything to gain. I said to Noel, "Yes please, I would like a New Life."

I knelt down on my knees and Noel placed his hands on my head and asked me to repeat after him,

"Dear Lord Jesus, I realise that I am a sinner, I know that I cannot live the Christian life in my own strength, but I come to you now Lord and ask you to come into my life, I ask you to take away my sin, I ask you to give me the power to live for you day by day, I give my life to you Lord, take me now in Jesus name, Amen."

As soon as I had repeated that prayer the tears started to flood out and run down my cheeks onto the cell floor. I could feel a burning sensation inside of my head where Noel had placed his hands on top of my head to pray. I could feel all the hurt, bitterness and bad leaving me as I cried like a little child. Noel then helped me to my feet and gave me a mint, "that's an anti-swear tablet to help you stop swearing, as soon as you're back on a wing and out of the hospital I'll put your name down so you can come on the Bible classes and prayer groups." He gave me a hug and said "welcome into the family of God, brother Bob."

Noel gave me a copy of a book he had written called "Cross behind bars" and some other leaflets about being a new Christian then left my cell. Within a few minutes of Noel leaving, my cell door opened again and a prison officer said, "you can come out for fifteen minutes recreation to get a book out of the library if you like," I was not much of a book reader but I relished the thought of leaving my cell even if it was only for fifteen minutes and I was not letting the opportunity pass me by. I soon found out that I was in the hospital on "A" wing. I started to exchange information with the other prisoners about what had happened to me and why they were in the hospital. The library consisted of about three book cases and my eyes were drawn to a dusty book on the top shelf of the first bookcase I looked at. When I looked at the title it read "New Testament" and at the bottom, "placed by the Gideon's." I decided to take this book back to my cell to give me something to read.

Chapter 13

"For God so loved the world that he gave his one and only Son, that whoever believes in him shall not perish but have eternal life."

John 3:16

In prison you have lots of time on your hands and each day is like the day before. The hardest thing is finding something to occupy your time because when the cell door shuts at night after the last meal it is a long time until morning. I was given a meal to eat and I took it back to my cell and started to eat. I then opened the New Testament I had taken from the library and started to read about Jesus. The words came alive to me and I was able to understand for the first time in my life all about Jesus. I knew that this was the Jesus I had asked to forgive me and to come into my life. Every spare moment that I had was used for reading the New Testament and after a few days I reached the gospel of John. I read the words at John 3:16 and put the book down. I got down on my knees to thank God for loving me enough to send Jesus to die in my place. That was the moment when I understood for the very first time the love of God for each and every one of us.

I knew what it was like as a father to lose a son you loved very much and for him to die in a tragic way. God decided of his own free will to send his one and only son to die in our place because he loved us so much. God only had Jesus and yet I had three other children and I would still not have done what God did for me and for you. I made a promise to God that I would serve him for the rest of my life and even though I had given God a pile of rubbish with my life it was his forever.

I knew that God understood how I was hurting inside at the loss of Mark and the separation from my family because God had suffered in the same way. I could feel God very close to me and I knew that I was starting my life afresh in Strangeways prison. I talked with God a lot and asked him to take away the shaking of nerves in my body. I had been in the hospital wing for about a week and I still refused to take any medication that was offered to me. One of the reasons for this was the state that some of the other prisoners were in and I was frightened of ending up like a zombie. During the day I was let out of my cell to have an hour's recreation with the other prisoners. This consisted of watching TV for an hour or having a cigarette and listening to the other prisoners talk about how they were going to kill themselves. I talked with them about the experience I had with God and how I had asked Jesus to come into my life. I explained that God was going to help me sort out all the problems in my life and God would help them if they asked him.

I felt that I would end up crazy if I did not get out of the hospital and I asked the doctor if he would discharge me so that I could go back onto a normal wing of the prison. The doctor stated that I had made myself well and it had nothing to do with him. I told the doctor that God had healed me and the doctor smiled at me as he signed the note stating I was fit to re-join the main prison from Monday. I thanked the doctor for his kindness and left his office to go back to my cell. I heard a voice call out "727 Sutton, visit."

My heart started to beat very fast with the excitement of having my first visit. I was praying that it would be Jan so that I could tell her everything that had happened. I was so happy when I got to the visiting room and Jan was waiting for me with one of our friends Steven Mair who also had also worked for me.

Jan asked me how I was and Steven said that he wished he could serve my prison sentence in my place. I started to tell Jan and Steven about my experience with God and how I had given my life to Jesus, but the pair of them looked at me as though I was crazy. I told them about the experience that I had with the prison guard who was the double of the foreman of the jury and that I thought I was going to be killed. I promised Jan that God was now on our side and everything would work out. I was going to appeal against my conviction and sentence and trust in God to give me my freedom. I wanted to hold Jan close to me but the visiting room was not private enough for that. I promised Jan that our lives would change for the better and from now on I would be the husband and father that I should have been a long time ago. Jan promised me again that she would wait for me and that I was the only one for her. All the children sent me their love and said they were missing me. I wanted the visit to last forever but the half hour passed by as if it was only seconds.

Chapter 14

"Therefore, if anyone is in Christ, he is a new creation; the old has gone, the new has come."

2 Corinthians 5:17

I was very happy after I had seen Jan and she reassured me that she was coping with things back at home. The hardest part for me was having to say goodbye to Jan knowing it would be another month before I would be able to see her again. I told Jan that I would leave it up to her if she felt it was right to bring our children to see me. We both felt that it might upset the children to see me in a closed prison with bars at all the windows.

After the visit I was moved back into the main part of the prison on "wing C4" and was given a job working in the boiler house for a wage of £3.50p per week. I was allowed out of my cell for about six hours a day now that I had a job and I started to build up my strength again. At night I would lie on my bed, close my eyes and think of my wife and children at home. I was missing them so very much and I counted the days to when my next visit was due. After I had been back in the main prison for about three days Noel Proctor came to see me and asked me if I wanted to attend the Wednesday night Bible study group with Lionel Cook and also the Friday night fellowship meeting. It was a meeting where about twenty other Christian prisoners attended and I enjoyed learning all about God.

On the Friday night I joined the fellowship meeting that was held in the chapel of the prison. The chapel was very big and held about eight hundred prisoners when it was full. I was offered a chair that was in a circle of about fifty chairs at the front of the chapel. I noticed there were several men and women who were wearing civilian clothes and the rest of the circle was made up of prisoners in the same uniform that I was wearing. Noel led the meeting in singing a few songs and then some members of the group started to pray. I had never heard prisoners praying for one another's needs before and when some of them started to pray for me I could feel a lump rising in my throat. I bowed my head as a prisoner started to sing the chorus "I love you Lord" then other people in the group started to sing and I could feel the love of God so very special in that chapel. The tears started to roll down my cheeks onto the floor and I felt very close to God as I started to sing from my heart the words of that chorus.

I went back to my cell that night feeling a lot better than I had felt before. Even though I knew that I was guilty of trying to obtain that money by deception from the bookies I carried on with my appeal against conviction and sentence because I felt that many underhanded things had taken place between William Hills and the police. Now that I had given my life to Jesus I believed that God would help me win my appeal and that I would soon be freed from prison. Every day I would pray for God to let me back home with my family and each time my name and number was called out I expected it to be over my appeal. I had been in Strangeways for about six weeks and my cell mate was short of money to buy some tobacco. I was doing my best to live the life of a Christian and I told him that he could have my imitation Rolex watch to sell so that he could buy some tobacco. The watch had only cost me ten pounds and I felt that I was doing what God wanted me to do. My cell mate sold the watch and he gave me one ounce of tobacco and told me we would receive the rest in a couple of days.

The following day I returned from work at tea time to find that my cell mate had been moved out of the prison. I knew that I could say goodbye to the rest of the tobacco that was owed for the watch and I did not give it another thought. That was until I was confronted on the landing outside of my cell by two other prisoners who said "you owe us a lot of money and if we don't get it we are going to do you." I was very frightened and I soon found out that my cell mate had sold the Rolex as a genuine Rolex watch and he had been given drugs, money and tobacco for the watch. My cell mate had asked to be moved from the prison because he knew what was going to happen. I tried to convince these other prisoners that I knew nothing about what my cell mate had done but they did not believe me. After enduring a few days of being constantly threatened I stood my ground against them and told them that I would do to them what they were threatening to do to me. The prison officer on the landing came to break up what nearly ended up in a fight and I was pushed back into my cell and the door was locked.

I felt that things were getting worse for me since I had become a Christian and I prayed to God for help. I knew that God did not want me to fight but I was not going to let these prisoners threaten me any longer. I was not expecting God to answer my prayer in the way that he did and as soon as my cell door was opened in the morning the prison officer said "Sutton report to the wing officer after your breakfast." I wondered what I was wanted for thinking it was over my appeal but I was informed that I was being moved to Kirkham prison near Blackpool that very day. I was informed that Kirkham was a low category prison where prisoners who could be trusted were sent. It did not have closed doors, bars or high walls like Strangeways and would be much easier than Strangeways. I thanked God for answering my prayer so quickly and I was taken to reception with some other prisoners where we were given our civilian clothes to wear for the coach journey to Kirkham.

It felt really good to be leaving Strangeways prison behind and the prisoners who were after my blood, but I was sad at leaving Noel and the fellowship that I had grown to love. Everyone on the coach was in a happy mood and I was excited to be moving to a prison where I could have a visit every two weeks that lasted two and a half hours. I could buy telephone cards to use on the telephones; there were also no prison walls, closed doors and steel bars.

My first sight of Kirkham reminded me of an army barracks with just a ten foot high wire fence around the perimeter of the prison and rows of brick huts. We were informed that all new intakes into the prison had to go through an intake programme where we would learn all we would need to know about the prison including the rules. During the first part of the programme we were taken to see the chaplain of the prison where each prisoner in turn went into his office. When it was my turn to go in I was expecting to meet another chaplain like Noel Proctor who was warm and full of love. I was interviewed by a Methodist minister who worked part time in the prison and he was very quiet except for asking me a few questions. I had been told by Noel that I would meet a chaplain who used to work with him at Strangeways by the name of Jeff Lynn who in Noel's words was "On fire for Jesus" but it was Jeff's day off when I was interviewed by the chaplain.

When I arrived at Kirkham it was the first week of December and although I did not relish the thought of spending Christmas in prison apart from my family I was thankful that I was in Kirkham and not Strangeways. I was given a job working in the boiler house and I was thankful for the job because I knew that I would be warm throughout the winter months. The hut that I was placed in contained eight rooms on either side of a corridor with two beds in each room. At one end of the hut were two baths and two toilets between the thirty two prisoners who lived in the hut.

I could not wait to obtain my first telephone card so that I could surprise Jan by giving her a call. I had only been in Kirkham for four days when a prisoner called Joe had a go at me over some sugar. Joe was upset that I had offered my sugar to another prisoner when Joe shared the same room as me. Joe went to hit me but I pushed him towards the wall in the corridor and held him tightly so that he could not hit me. The old me would have hit him but I went back to my room and got out my bible and started to read from Matthew chapter 5 verses 43 to 48. When I read verse 44 "But I tell you: Love your enemies and pray for those who persecute you." I knew that Jesus was telling me to love Joe but I did not know how. I prayed to God for him to help me and then Joe came into my room. I put my hand out towards him and opened my mouth, "I'm sorry if I have done anything to hurt you Joe, will you please forgive me?" Joe took hold of my hand and shook it and we became very good friends after that. I could not believe that I had spoken those words and it was clear that God was doing something very special with my life.

Prison was a very lonely place and it was full of people who had lots of character defects. It did not take much for a fight to break out as lots of the prisoners had a very short fuse. Lots of the prisoners were bored so they would find ways of breaking up the boredom. Some of them would get family or friends to smuggle in drugs or money during the visits. The drug barons made lots of money by selling the drugs to prisoners who were desperate to feed their addiction. I made my mind up that I was going to try and live my life as a Christian and not get involved in anything that would bring me down.

Chapter 15

"If you believe, you will receive whatever you ask for in prayer."

Matthew 21: 22

I had my first meeting with the chaplain Jeff Lynn and he was very much like Noel with a love for Jesus and the prisoner that was so real. I had my first visit from Jan at the end of the first week at kirkham and I was thrilled to see her with my children and best friend Steven Lamont when I walked into the visiting room. It was a lot more relaxed than Strangeways and I was able to hold my family and friend very close to me. Steven used to go out with Mark and I to have a drink and play snooker, Steven was as devastated as we were when Mark was killed. Steven had been working in Saudi Arabia and he had lent me over ten thousand pounds while I had been working on our dream home. Steven informed me that he was going to pay two hundred pounds a month into my bank account whilst I was in prison to stop the bank from taking the house from Jan and me. On top of the money I owed to Steven I had a bank overdraft of twelve thousand pounds and a mortgage of twenty five thousand pounds on our home. Jan was claiming social security benefits and they had agreed to pay the interest on our mortgage so that the house would not be repossessed by the building society.

It did not help being in prison and having so many problems to try and sort out. At least our financial problems were going to be put on ice until I was back at home and could sort them out myself. I was eager to tell my family and Steven about Jesus but in the next breath I was asking Jan to sneak me some money in. I was not thinking about Jan needing the money at home except that I needed to buy some telephone cards so I could keep in touch with my family. Jan passed me a ten pound note wrapped in tape and I swallowed it and waited for nature to take its course.

It was a good visit and I felt really happy after seeing all my family in one go. The next few weeks passed by and I could not keep my thoughts away from my wife and children. This was going to be our first Christmas apart since we had met and I was not looking forward to spending Christmas without them. The day before Christmas Eve the chaplain came to see me where I was working and informed me that Jan had been rushed into Stepping Hill hospital for an emergency operation and would have to undergo a hysterectomy. Jeff led me back to his office and he prayed with me and asked God to heal Jan and for me to be allowed out of prison to see her in hospital. I went in to see the Governor of the prison and asked him if I could have a day's parole to go and see Jan in hospital. The Governor informed me that I could go and see Jan in hospital. On the 24th December at 2.00pm I was at Jan's hospital bed as she was waking up after her operation. Jan started to cry as she saw me next to her bed and within a few minutes she had regained consciousness and was sitting up. I learned that our three children had been taken in by Steven and Pam Mair and were going to spend Christmas with their three children. For the first time in my life I realised that it was the devil who wanted to make my life a misery but in God I could put all my trust. My prayers had been answered yet again and my faith in God was getting stronger as each day passed.

On Christmas Eve I was back at kirkham prison knowing that God was going to take care of my family and all my problems. It was 8.00pm and I was in the chapel sat around the piano with five other prisoners. The chaplain and the visitors had gone home and the six of us started to sing Christmas carols. I could feel the presence of God right next to me and for the very first time I understood what Christmas was all about. I thought again about how Jesus had come into the world as a gift from God for all the world. I had always used Christmas as a time for celebration but only now did I fully understand what I should have been celebrating all those past Christmases. For once I was able to celebrate Christmas in a way that I knew would make God happy.

On New Year's Eve Jan was allowed out of hospital for her birthday and she was happy to be back at home with our children once again. I had been allowed a special visit from Jan and I used this visit to smuggle in thirty pounds in fifty pence pieces. I knew that it was wrong to ask Jan to bring in this money but the prison barons were making life hell for lots of the prisoners. They would lend the new intake prisoners tobacco and then charge them 100% interest each week until it was repaid. If they failed to pay it back on time they would be beaten up and another 100% interest added on top until eventually they had to be moved to another prison for their own protection. With the money that Jan brought in I was able to buy enough tobacco to lend it interest free to anyone who had a need. It also left me enough to buy a two pound telephone card each week. I had made a decision to stop smoking at this time so that I could buy telephone cards with my wages and keep in regular contact with my family. I also shared the thirty pounds with Joe as he helped me to smuggle the money in.

Life in the boiler house was becoming very difficult because the prison officer in charge hated the fact that I was a Christian. I had asked him for paint so that I could clean up and paint all the workshops in the boiler house. He would sit down most of the day talking and smoking with two other prisoners whilst I carried on working. When I was working in one of the out buildings I noticed ten gallons of home brew wine that had been placed there by the prisoners I worked with. I knew that if it was found that I would be blamed and I asked them to move it. They told me that it would be moved within a few days and I asked God to help me out of the situation.

The following day Jeff Lynn said that he was looking for a chapel orderly to replace Tony who was going home. I was asked to pray about working for the chaplain but I knew it would not be easy getting a transfer out of the boiler house. The prison officer I worked for told me that he would keep me in the boiler house forever, I replied, "If God wants me to stay in here with you I will stay, if God wants me working in the chapel that is where I will go." For the next few days I prayed about the situation and I carried on living my life for Jesus. I carried on being nice to the prison officer I worked for even when he made some nasty comments to me saying I was using God to get parole. I felt that I would be nearer to God if I could work in the chapel for the chaplain and I asked God to give me the job. I was given the news the following day that I had been given the job as the chaplains orderly and all the objections put up by the prison officer to keep me in the boiler house had been overcome. I was transferred immediately and the first thing I decided to do in my new job was clean the church like it had never been cleaned before. I got down on my hands and knees and scrubbed the floor with scouring pads getting into all the corners where years of dirt had built up. When it was finished everyone noticed the difference and I did the same in the Catholic Church for the glory of God. I had scrubbed that hard my skin at the end of my fingers had rubbed off but I felt that God was happy to have a very clean church for His people to worship him.

Chapter 16

"Cast your cares upon the Lord and he will sustain you; he will never let the righteous fall."

Psalm 55: 22

My faith was growing daily and a very special relationship was forming between God and me. In my new job I was able to spend much more time studying Gods word and God was opening my mind to many things. I had started to understand how Jesus lived without sin on this earth and the love that he had for our Father God. It was a great feeling to know that I could call God my Father because Jesus had died for me on that cruel cross for all the sins I had ever committed, past present and future. I knew that I had received the Holy Spirit of God into my life because other people had started to notice the changes in me.

I had been in my new job for about two weeks when I was given the news by Jeff that my daughter Donna had been rushed into Stepping Hill hospital for an emergency operation. I had been reading the book of Job in my bible and I knew that the devil was having another go at me through my family. Jeff prayed with me and we both asked God to heal Donna. I asked the Governor if I could have a day's parole to go to the hospital and see Donna but this request was turned down. I was upset about this and I spoke with Mrs. Cove an elderly Christian visitor who helped me to understand that God was in complete control of the situation.

Mrs. Cove was a real blessing to many of us prisoners and she was in her late seventies. Every Thursday night she would come into the prison and run a bible class where she would help us understand Gods word. Mrs. Cove had a love for Jesus that was evident to all of us. I had many questions that needed answering and she always had the answer. I felt her love for us prisoners in a very special way and she would refer to us as "my boys". I am sure she loved us as if we were her own sons. At about the same time I received a letter from another elderly lady called Kathleen Hardman also in her seventies who lived very near to my home in Hazel Grove. I had never met Kathleen before but she explained that she knew my parents and had heard about my conversion to God in the prison, she continued to explain how she was calling in to see my wife and children from time to time and that they were coping well. I felt much better to know that a Christian lady was calling in to see my wife and children because I wanted my family to accept Jesus into their own lives so that we could start a new life together.

After many people had prayed for Donna the news came in from the hospital that she had a burst appendix and after an emergency operation she was back in a ward recovering well to all the doctors satisfaction.

I went into the chapel by myself and got down on my knees to thank God for answering my prayers yet again. I also thanked God for the love and concern that was being shown to me by many Christians that I was meeting. It was never a dull moment in the chapel because Jeff had Christian activity on every night of the week, I was starting to understand why God had allowed me to be sent to prison when I had asked God to let me be found not guilty so that I could be with my family. God knew that I was searching for the meaning of life and in prison of all places God was showing me what we had been created for and the true meaning of life. God was giving me time to get to know him in a very special way and I could hear Jesus speaking into my heart saying "follow me". I realised for the very first time that even though I was in prison I was free.

I knew that I did not have to wait for my release from Kirkham before I started to serve God but that I could serve him here and now. I asked God for him to help me live my life in a way that would please him and I knew that I had to turn away from many of the things I had done in the past. The devil started to attack me through some of the other prisoners because I was living my life for God. One night I found that the wires from my radio had been pulled out from the inside. I enjoyed listening to my radio at night time because it gave me a great deal of comfort. I shouted out, "if I catch the person responsible for ripping the wires out of my radio I'm going to break their legs and then their arms". It went very quiet for about thirty seconds and this voice called back, "that's not very Christian of you, is it Bob?" I thought about what I had just shouted out for all the prisoners to hear and realised that I had not responded in a way that Jesus would have wanted me to, so I replied, "no it isn't so I will forgive whoever you are this time but don't do it again".

I found that for most of the time the other prisoners left me alone because I think they were frightened that I would inform on them to the prison officers about some of the things they were doing. It would have been very easy to have let the prison officers know about the drugs and alcohol that was being brought into the prison and they would have all been moved back to a closed prison. This was something I could not do but I made it very clear that if anyone put any drugs or contraband in my room I would shop the lot of them.

During the month of February Jeff came to see me to inform me that my youngest daughter Michelle had been rushed into Stepping Hill hospital with a mystery virus. Jeff made the comment "I have never known a family go through what your family is going through in such a short period of time." We prayed together and by now I was getting wise to what the devil was up to. I knew that the devil wanted to take away from me the peace that God had placed in my heart but nothing was going to take me away from God and the peace he had given to me. After we had prayed I believed that Michelle was going to be healed and I asked the Governor for a day's parole to go and see her. I thanked God when the Governor agreed to my request and made arrangements for me to have a day's parole the following day.

I arranged for my friend Steven Mair to pick me up at the gate so that I did not waste any time waiting for trains and buses. I asked Steven to drop me at the cemetery so that I could have some time alone at Marks grave before going home. I stood over Marks grave and I prayed that Jesus would be holding him very close. I knew that Jesus had a deep compassion for people with a broken heart and I pictured Mark in heaven waiting for the day when we would all be together again. Thinking of Mark made me realise just how much I was missing him and I just wanted to be back with my wife and children. I could see the back of my house from the cemetery and I made my way home where Jan was waiting for me.

We went together arm in arm to Stepping Hill hospital to see Michelle, the hospital was only a mile away from where we lived and just walking down the street was a strange and exciting feeling. I told Jan that many people were praying for Michelle just as they had in the past for her and Donna. When we arrived in the children's ward at the hospital Michelle was sat up in bed with a big smile on her face. The nurse came and spoke to us, We have not been able to find what was wrong with Michelle but this morning Michelle made a remarkable recovery and if she is this well tomorrow she can go back home.

I knew that God had healed Michelle and I threw my arms around her to give her a big hug and a kiss. I told Michelle that God was watching over her and I looked forward to the day when I could go to church and worship God with all my family. After spending an hour with Michelle Jan and I went home to spend a few hours in each other's arms making love to each other. It was a day that I did not want to end and it was a very special to know that God had blessed me with a very special day with my wife and daughter. I had missed not seeing Donna and Robert as they were at school but they would be coming to see me at weekend on a visit. I got the train back to Kirkham and on the train God spoke very clearly into my heart.

I had trusted God with the lives of my wife and two daughters and each time God had answered my prayers in a very special way. I understood that God wanted me to trust him with my life and I withdrew my appeal against conviction and sentence. I had been in prison for four months and if I was given parole I could be freed in another four months. If I was not given parole I would have to spend at least another year in prison. I had clung on to the hope for the past four months that any day I could be freed on appeal and now God was asking me to let go and trust in Him. I realised that God had brought me through a situation where I had wanted to die and now I had a life that was very special to me. I knew that I had to put all my trust in God and when I arrived back at kirkham I asked to see the senior prison officer and informed him that I wanted to withdraw my appeal.

Chapter 17

"I waited patiently for the Lord; he turned to me and heard my cry. He lifted me up out of the slimy pit, out of the mud and mire; he set my feet on a rock and gave me a firm place to stand. He put a new song in my mouth, a hymn of praise to our God. Many will see and fear and put their trust in the Lord".

Psalm 40: 1-3

The time at kirkham was going by very quickly and I had made some very good friends at the fellowship meetings organized by Jeff. I had even met Christians from Stockport who had a music ministry who were invited in on a Friday night fellowship to minister to us all. I became very friendly with Eric, John and Ray and it was good to make many new friends. One couple in particular played a very important part in my Christian growth and they were Jeff and Cathy Hammond. Jeff was an officer in the Salvation Army and Jeff and Cathy would come into the prison every Friday night without fail to share fellowship with us all. We had something in common because they had lost one of their sons in a tragic accident and they had experienced what Jan and I had suffered. They lived in Blackpool but they had lived in Stockport for many years before moving to Blackpool and it was good to talk with them about places I was familiar with.

It was soon the month of May and my friend Joe heard he had been given parole and would be leaving kirkham at the end of the month. I was wondering why I had not heard if I had been given parole and by the 20th May I thought that I was going to be refused parole. My daily reading was from the book of Hebrews chapter 12 verses 1 -11 and I read about God disciplining his sons because he loved them. I wondered if God wanted me to stay longer in prison because I needed more discipline or because he wanted me to serve him in the prison. I had looked forward to getting parole because with parole you were given four days home leave before you was released to spend some time getting used to your home surroundings again. You had to have at least three weeks of your sentence left after your home leave to qualify for the four days at home. The parole date I had been given if I was granted parole was the 9th June and when the 20th May had come and gone I knew that even if I was given parole I would not qualify for the four days home leave.

On Monday 23rd May my daily reading was psalm 40: 1-11 and I wrote in my diary "Be patient for the Lords help it is on its way". I went to work as normal and then a prisoner came to see me to inform me that I was wanted in the Governor's office. My heart started to beat very fast and I was praying that I would be granted parole. I was told to go into the Governor's office and I stood very still in front of his desk praying silently all the time. It was Mr. Balantine and I had cleaned his office regularly over the past few months. I also noticed that Mr. Balantine attended church on a regular basis and on many occasions we had knelt side by side to share Holy Communion together. He spoke the words that I had waited to hear for so many months, "I'm very pleased to inform you that you have been granted parole and you will be released on licence from the 9th June 1988".

I breathed a sigh of relief and I asked the Governor if it would be possible for me to have four days home leave. Mr. Balantine informed me that I did not have enough days left of my sentence to qualify for home leave. I left his office thanking God that I had been granted parole knowing that in less than three weeks I would be back home with my family for good. I went into the chapel and I prayed to God over my home leave and I accepted that God probably had his own reasons why I was not having any home leave. I thought about the days I had with my family during my sentence when they had been in hospital and how God had given me so many good things. As I was leaving the chapel a prisoner shouted over to me that I was wanted in the Governor's office.

I was wondering what I was wanted for and was hoping that he had not made a mistake about my parole. As I reached his office the door was opened by Mr. Balantine who started to speak. "It has been brought to my attention that under certain conditions the Governor has the right to grant home leave to prisoners even if they do not have three weeks of their sentence left to serve. Of all the prisoners who have been granted parole and home leave none have been more deserving than you. I take great pleasure in informing you that I am granting you four days home leave from Monday 30th May until Thursday 2nd June".

    I left the Governor's office walking on air knowing that other people had started to see something good in my life. My God had undertaken for me yet again in a way that I could not have expected. The 30th May arrived and I spent four wonderful days with my family. I had not smoked a cigarette since the 31sy December and I started to smoke again on my home leave. I had given up smoking cigarettes so that I could use the money on telephone cards and I was sorry that I had started again after giving it up for five months. I went swimming with my wife and children and did a lot of things that I had not had time for in the past. The four days went by very quickly and I returned to kirkham to complete the last week of my prison sentence.

    The other prisoners had given me a good last night party and one of them in particular had moved me to tears when he played his guitar and sang "Bridge over troubled waters". Taffy had a wonderful Welsh voice and he knew that it was a very special song for me and my wife. I had prayed for another prisoner who had given his life to Jesus after hearing my testimony. As I was leaving the chapel for the last time one of the hardest prisoners in the prison came up to me and said, "Bob I really admire you for the way you have stood your ground as a Christian and put up with all the abuse and threats you have received, you are a far harder man than me and I believe that you have found something very special to you. I want to wish you luck as you leave the prison tomorrow". I replied, "Its Jesus in my life that has given me all the strength and courage that I need but above all else I now have a love for everyone that I never had before, Jesus will do for you what he has done for me if you will ask him into your life".

    It was now the 9th June as the prison officer shouted out my name and brought my mind back to the here and now. It was a wonderful experience to make my way to reception for the very last time and put on my civilian clothes once again. I was given twenty eight pounds in cash and told this was to last me one week until I had time to sign on and make a claim for income support. I had to report to my probation officer on my arrival at Stockport as a condition of my parole. I was grateful to be met at the gate by one of my ex-employees Les Jones.

I felt like a man who had just won the pools as I travelled in Les's van back to my home in Stockport. I looked back on the past eight months and realised that I was now living in the day that I thought would never arrive. Time does move very quickly when we look back but when we look ahead time seems to move slower. Les gave me thirty pounds so that I could take Jan out for a meal and give her a treat. I felt very well off to have over fifty pounds in my pocket after having a wage of less than four pounds a week for the past eight months.

Les pulled up right outside my front door and said goodbye as I thanked him for being so kind. I walked into the house to find a big message in the front room with "welcome home dad and Rob, we love you" wrote on it and balloons all over the place. Jan took me in her arms and said, "This is to make up for the Christmas we never had together".

We had a good party and Jan and I talked well into the night. I talked about my plans to turn what was going to be my own private pub into a day nursery for children. This would provide Jan with a job and I was going to start up my building business again so we could get back on our feet.

Chapter 18

"Love your neighbour as yourself".

Luke 10: 27

I made a point of calling round to see my next door neighbour's to thank them for the way they had been a friend to Jan while I had been in prison. It was not easy for me because my neighbour's had not been speaking to me for many months before I had been sent to prison. They had fallen out with me because I had refused to sign a petition they were taking around to have a roller ring extension at the back of our house refused planning permission. I told them of my plans to turn the games room at the back of our house into a day nursery for children. Everything was starting to work out for us as my bank manager agreed to give me a further overdraft of fifteen hundred pounds to enable me to buy a van and start up my business again.

Within a few weeks I was back at work earning good money again. It felt good to have my freedom and I started to attend Heaton Chapel Christian Church where the pastor Gordon Wright had come to see me when I had been at Kirkham. I found the people to be very friendly and it was not long before we were all going as a family. By the end of September 1988 we found out that our neighbour's had objected to our plans to turn our games room into a day nursery and they had stopped speaking to us again. The council refused our planning application and when we took it to appeal we lost that as well. Work was starting to pick up for me and I found that I had to employ people again to keep up with the work coming in. It was during this period that we decided to take out a second mortgage on our house so that we could repay all the money we owed to various people.

I borrowed enough to repay our major creditors and then I borrowed some more money to complete the building works on our house. The interest rate then doubled and I now found myself paying over twelve hundred pounds a month on our mortgage and second mortgage. We decided that we would turn our games room into living quarters and rent out the main house to help us through our financial crisis. We had no sooner moved into the bungalow at the back of our house when our neighbours started taking photographs of us from their bedroom window. They had brought in the planning officer who informed me that we would need to put in a planning application if we wanted to use the bungalow for living accommodation. We had been able to let our house out to five people and this was bringing in an income of nearly eight hundred pounds a month and we prayed everything would work out.

Then one day our Robert came home from school with a busted nose, his teacher informed us that our next door neighbour's eldest son had hit Robert on the nose at school. Their son was two years older than Robert and much bigger. We went and spoke with our neighbour's who assured us it would not happen again. Life was becoming very difficult living next door to a woman who would grin and smirk all over her face every time she saw me. The straw that broke the camel's back was when our daughter Michelle came home from school in tears because our neighbour's daughter had taunted her over the death of Mark. I had been out playing snooker with my friend Steven Lamont when we arrived home to find Michelle in tears. We both went round to their house to speak with our neighbour's. They did not have any bell or letter box on their front door. As we lived on a very busy main road that was noisy both Steven and I kicked the bottom of the front door so they would hear us. The glass at the bottom of the door was accidentally broken and our neighbour's took great delight in telephoning the police and blamed me for the broken window.

It was a case of hear we again as I was charged and ended up at Stockport Magistrates Court. The police wanted me to agree to be bound over to keep the peace and I could not believe what I was hearing. I had tried to keep the peace with my neighbour's since leaving prison but they had been very devious and sly in what they had been doing. I was convicted by the magistrates even though Steven admitted he had broken the glass. I wondered if it had anything to do with the fact that we had taken the police to court for what they had done before I got sent to prison. I was very upset about being convicted of causing criminal damage to my neighbour's window and I appealed against conviction to the crown court where my pastor Gordon Wright spoke on my behalf. It made no difference and I lost my appeal and had to pay legal costs of over one thousand pounds for a piece of glass that cost five pounds.

I was very upset about what had taken place and I felt than an injustice had been done to me. I wondered why God had let my neighbour's win when they had been the ones causing all the problems. The old Bob Sutton would have done much more than smash a window and yet I had to endure the grins and smirks of neighbour's who were full of evil intentions. I thought back to a prisoner in Kirkham called Kit who had driven a bus through his neighbour's house because they had made his life hell. I advised Kit that he would have to hand his anger over to God and then pray for them. I knew that the advice I had given was something that I would now have to take on board for myself and that night I asked all our house group to pray for our neighbour's.

I thanked God for taking away the anger and I carried on with the plans to turn our games room into living accommodation. In the spring of 1989 the council turned down our planning application because of our neighbour's objections and when we appealed we lost that as well. This was the time I started to gamble again and for once I had a lucky streak and won over two thousand pounds. I took all the family on holiday to Cornwall and we stayed in a beautiful hotel overlooking St. Ives bay. I spent most of the days in the bookies while Jan was alone with the children on the beach. I won over a thousand pounds but it was not money that Jan wanted but my company.

Chapter 19

"It is for freedom that Christ has set us free, Stand firm then, and do not let yourselves be burdened again by a yoke of slavery."

Galatians 5 : 1

I had been out of prison for just over a year and I had slowly started to drift towards my old way of life. The trouble with me was that I enjoyed having a bet but I did not know when to stop. In other words I was an addict. I knew that God did not want me to gamble because every time I had a bet I felt that my relationship with God became distant. Each time that I slipped up and had a bet I would ask God to forgive me and I would try again to leave my gambling alone. I had a love for Jesus that was very special and nothing was going to take that love away. Soon after we had returned from Cornwall I was given a leaflet inviting me to Stockport Prison Fellowship at Greek Street Baptist Church in Stockport.

I had not intended to go to the meeting on the Monday night but as I passed the Town Hall at Stockport God spoke into my heart and I decided to go along just to see what it was all about. I was surprised to meet three people that I knew and one of them in particular I had known many years before. Brian Griffiths shared how he had been led by God to Stockport Prison fellowship not knowing how God was going to use him. It was a real friendly fellowship and I soon warmed to all of the people who were present. After attending the fellowship for a few months I started to get dissatisfied because no one did anything practicable for the prisoners or prisoners family. In November of that year I had been invited by Jeff Lynn to speak at a rally being held at the Salvation Army citadel in Blackpool. I asked Jan if she would come with me and we decided to make a weekend of it and go and stay with her sister Carol at Cleveleys.

We had a great time and we met up with Jeff and Cathy Hammond who we had become very friendly with. Jeff and Cathy had been very kind towards us and I remembered that on my release from prison a letter had been waiting for me at home to encourage me with my walk with God. We had even been invited to the wedding of his son Glynn to Samantha and made me feel very special. Jeff had played a big part in the Rally on the Saturday night and we had arranged to meet on the Sunday morning at the citadel so we could have a good talk before we returned to Stockport. I was devastated when Jeff did not turn up and the Major announced that Jeff had been involved in some form of accident in his car on his way to the citadel. We all prayed for Jeff and as soon as the service was over I rushed to Victoria Hospital to be given the sad news that Jeff had died of a heart attack.

I went back to Carol's to tell Jan the sad news and we returned to Stockport. I wondered why God had taken someone who was working really hard for him in the prisons and I was very confused. Jeff was not very old and he had a love for God that was very special and I knew that I was going to miss him very much along with many other people. On the Monday I had decided that I was not going to go to the prison fellowship meeting because nothing really happened. At 7.00pm I received a telephone call from the leader of the prison fellowship who made the following statement, "I have decided to step down as the leader of the prison fellowship and after praying and speaking with Brian Stephenson we both believe that you are the man God wants to be the new leader of the fellowship, if you are willing I would like to hand over the leadership to you at this evenings meeting".

I believed that God was ready to do something very special for the prisoner and I knew in my heart that much more could be done for the prisoner and prisoner's family than was being done at that moment. I knew that Jesus was alive and that our God was a God of miracles. I had a faith that was very strong and at our first meeting I challenged the members of the fellowship with the words from James 2 : 14 - 17.

It was amazing that God had given me the responsibility of leading our fellowship when I was only a baby Christian but I knew that God would give me all the wisdom that I needed. If God had given me a job to do the future would hold the answer.

The last place that I wanted to go when I left prison was back to prison and I now found myself helping people who were in prison or who had just left prison. With what God had done for me I had a very special love for all kinds of hurting people. This was a work that Jan started to get involved with and she worked with some of the prisoner's wives and children. Things were really starting to happen and our fellowship also grew in numbers. On many occasions some of the prisoners we were trying to help let us down but I understood that this was something that we would have to give to our Lord.

One Wednesday afternoon I was doing some paperwork in the bungalow at the rear of our house and the news came over the radio that several prisoners in various prisons throughout England had tried to kill themselves. Four of the prisoners had died and certain people were demanding that a special inquiry be set up. My mind went back to the time I wanted to die in the strip cell of Strangeways prison and I understood how each and every one of them had felt. I started to pray for the families of the dead prisoners and for the prisoners who had been saved by the prison officers who had found them. I cried out to God, "There must be something that you can do for the prisoner". I picked up my bible and started to read from psalm 37: 4 "Delight yourself in the Lord and he will give you the desires of your heart".

My heart's desire at that moment was for God to do something very special for the prisoner, to give them light in their darkness and a hope for the future. I believed that God was going to do something because He had just told me through his word that if I delighted in Him he would give me my heart's desire. The following day God gave me the first piece of a very big jigsaw picture. It was a Christian friend called Rickie who gave me a copy of a book by Frank Costantino titled "More than a miracle" and told me that he believed God wanted me to read it.

I took the book home with me and that night I started to read the book and before I had read the first chapter I knew that God was showing me something very special. I stayed up all night to finish the book and I woke Jan up with my excitement and told her that God had just shown me what was needed in this country. Only God could change a person from the inside and I was reading about a Christian aftercare centre in America called "The Bridge" where ex-prisoners and people who had committed crimes could go and get their lives together, either as an alternative sentence to prison or during the last six months of their prison sentence.

As the leader of Stockport Prison fellowship I believed in leading from the front and I started to employ some ex-prisoners within the family building business. Many of the people we had employed were not ready for work because they had never dealt with the problems in their lives. At the Bridge all the residents worked on a programme that would help them deal with all the major problems in their lives and prepare them for release back into the community. I looked back at the time I had been released from prison and if it had not been for God taking hold of my life I dreaded to think of where I would be.

At the next meeting of our Prison fellowship group I shared about The Bridge in America and how I believed we needed something like that in our country. I told them I had wrote a letter to Frank Costantino asking if it would be possible to visit The Bridge and see for ourselves what God was doing. I asked them to pray over the letter and for God to confirm if it is His will to have a similar rehabilitation centre here in England.

It was several weeks later when our P.F. group had shared fellowship with Ackroyd Evangelical Church that God answered our prayers. I returned home at 10.00pm feeling very drained after sharing my testimony. It was a surprise for Jan to tell me that Frank Costantino had telephoned from America giving us an open invitation to pay a visit to The Bridge in Orlando, Florida.

At this time I was working very hard to keep up our mortgage payments that had increased to over twelve hundred pounds a month due to the interest rate rising to over 15% and we had five thousand pounds in the bank. It was not a lot of money with the overheads that we had of running a business and paying our way. We shared the vision of The Bridge with Rickie and Pat and they both said that they would like to go to America and see it for themselves. Our minds were made up very quickly and my faith was strong enough to know that God would undertake for us. I had experienced the miracles from God on a few occasions and it was very exciting as we prepared to put our trust in God and go to America. As I was about to book the air tickets for America Rickie informed me that Pat and himself would not be going. We had to decide if we were to go by ourselves and we decided that we should take our three children and our new grandson Steven who was six months old.

Jan and I were thrilled when Donna had informed us that she was expecting a baby even though she was not married to Steven Lamont at the time. We both told Donna that she did not have to marry Steven but they got married when Donna was three months pregnant. It was another answer to prayer when Donna was about to have a caesarean section. Donna was on the operating table and the surgeon was preparing for the operation. Jan and I prayed and Jan went to the hospital to be with Donna. As Jan was with Donna the baby turned and she gave birth without requiring any stitches at all. We both felt that God had given us a grandson who looked very much like Mark when he was a baby and we could feel the love that God had for us all.

The fact that Donna, Robert, Michelle and our grandson Steven were coming to America with us made us feel less afraid of going without Rickie and Pat. The same day we booked our flights to America we had our P.F. meeting and shared that we were going. It was a bit upsetting when the founder of the P.F. group stated that what we were going to see could not happen in this country because of Home Office rules and regulation. I could not believe what I was hearing and I asked my Christian brother if he had taken God into account before making his remarks. I knew that God was going to bring about a miracle to make it possible to have something similar to The Bridge here in England.

It came as no surprise the following Sunday to hear on the news that a riot had started at Strangeways Prison and that the prisoners had taken over parts of the prison. It was a riot that attracted front page headlines throughout the world and it started in the prison chapel when the chaplain Noel Proctor was leading the service. It was April 1st 1990 and I believed that through this riot God would bring about the vision he had given to me. Within a few days of the riot many people connected with the prisons and penal reform was talking about alternative ways of dealing with criminals in our country. A public inquiry was set up headed by Lord Justice Woolfe who was to look into every aspect of the riot and why it had taken place.

Three weeks after the riot had started the prisoners were still on the roof of the prison. Just before we left for Manchester Airport to catch our aeroplane to Orlando I took some video film of the prisoners and Strangeways to include on a video we were going to make about The Bridge "An alternative to prison". The Governor of Strangeways prison, Brendon O'Friel described the riot as an "Explosion of evil". God promised us that he would work for good through all things and as we left for America it was in the knowledge that God was in control and reigning on the throne. This was the first time that Jan, Robert, Michelle, Donna and baby Steven had flown in an aeroplane and to be going to America was something that dreams were made of. It was going to take all our money to go to America but I was going to trust God to provide for us when we returned to England and our mortgage was due. As the aeroplane took off for America I knew that there could be no turning back.

Chapter 20

"I know that you can do all things; no plan of yours can be thwarted".

Job 42 : 2

Flying at over thirty thousand feet and looking down on the earth gave me some idea of the view that God had from Heaven. I looked at my family and it was good to see them so excited as we made our way towards America. Both Jan and I had a fear of flying but God had now taken that fear away as we both trusted in our Lord to take care of us all. We arrived at Orlando airport at 3.00am and we felt very honored when Frank and Bunny Costantino were both at the airport to meet us in person. It came as a very pleasant surprise to find that Frank and Bunny was down to earth people and not stuck up in any way. Frank helped us to load all our suitcases into his car and we headed towards the car hire firm where Frank arranged for us to hire a car.

I think that Frank was very surprised when I informed the man at the counter that I did not have any credit cards and that I wanted to pay in cash. I explained to Frank that no bank would let me have a credit card due to my exploitation of the banks when I was a criminal. Frank had to hire the car on his credit card and I paid Frank the money in cash. I had never driven an automatic before or on the right hand side of the road and I started to pray that God would help me make the adjustment.

Frank and Bunny led the way to the furnished bungalow they had arranged for us to rent for the three weeks we were staying in Orlando. It was still dark when we arrived at the bungalow and Frank said he would call us in a couple of days when we had adjusted to the time difference between our two countries. The bungalow was beautiful and it did not take our children long to find a bedroom and fall into bed. We were soon in bed ourselves and fast asleep.

I was woken by the sun shining in my eyes through the bedroom window. I jumped out of bed put on a pair of shorts and started to explore the bungalow. It had three bedrooms all en-suite, a fully fitted kitchen, dining room, lounge and a garage with washing and drying machines. On the outside I found a swimming pool and a sauna. Frank and Bunny had picked a beautiful place for us to stay and I was wondering how much it was going to cost us. The owner of the bungalow called to say that Frank and Bunny were good friends of his and that we would only be charged $300 a week for the rent. I was expecting to pay double that amount and I knew that we were in the will of God.

All the family loved the bungalow and we spent the next two days getting used to our new surroundings and exploring Florida. I then received a telephone call from Frank to say that he would be picking us up to take us to The Bridge. I had formed a picture in my mind of what the Bridge would be like but from arriving at the entrance it was better than anything I had imagined. Frank introduced Jan and me to all the staff and made arrangements for one of his employees to give us a full tour of The Bridge.

We were informed about all aspects of The Bridge and how men and women came into the centre as an alternative to prison or during the last six months of their prison sentence. From that first moment I arrived at The Bridge I knew that this was what was needed in England. I believed that God was going to bring about a miracle in England and that I was going to be involved in a very big way. Jan and I were given permission by Frank to make a video and speak to any of the staff and residents that were present at that time. We interviewed both male and female residents asking them lots of questions. They all agreed that at The Bridge they had a real chance of dealing with the deep rooted problems in their lives and being prepared for release back into society. Many of the residents had a drug or drinking problem and this was one of many issues that the residents had to face up to whilst resident at The Bridge. The thing that impressed me the most was that they were all there because of their own free will and a determination to get their life together. Many of the people we interviewed had not been a Christian when they first entered The Bridge but they had found Jesus whilst they had been working through the programme.

I was very impressed with the hand of friendship we had received from everyone at The Bridge and it was a time of great learning. We were able to interview Frank for a full half hour on video and ask him many questions that we needed answers for. I spent many days at The Bridge over the next few weeks sitting in on the counselling classes and soaking up all the information that I could. Frank and Bunny made sure that I spent some time taking in the sights of Florida and we went to Disney, Daytona Beach and many other places. The highlight for us all was when we went to Sea World. Looking at the whales I was reminded of the greatness of our God and the story of Jonah in the Bible.

The time came for us to leave America and on our last night Frank and Bunny invited us to their home where they had prepared a wonderful Italian meal for us. We were given an open invitation to return to The Bridge for training when we were ready and we had a facility in England. In my heart I was hoping that Frank would open a centre in England and let me be involved in some way. I could see that Frank had a great deal of experience and also many important contacts. It was at that moment that God reminded me that I could have no greater contact than almighty God Himself. We had all fallen in love with Florida and the many people we had met. We prayed that one day we would be able to return as we packed our suitcases and headed for the airport to return to England.

When we returned from America I found out that a job I had left two men working on was not finished. It was clear that I had been taken advantage of and the money that I had left behind for wages and materials had been spent. One of the men I had employed was an ex-prisoner and he had started to take drugs again while I had been away. I was suffering from jet lag and the last place I wanted to be was on a roof thirty feet above ground. My heart was no longer in my business and I felt that now was the time to give it all up and concentrate on the vision that God had given to me.

I shared the vision of The Bridge with the Stockport Prison fellowship at our next meeting and I asked them to pray for me as I looked to God for the way forward. I was given a great deal of help by David Burgin who helped me to edit the video so that it could be prepared in a professional way for sending out to various people connected with the prisoner. We spent £250 having over 25 videos made and then I received a cheque for £250 from an anonymous person. I felt that God was confirming that I was in His will and then I received a cheque for £500 to help me with the vision. I called the video "The Bridge, an alternative to prison" and I sent it to many people including Her Majesty the Queen and Lord Justice Woolfe.

I made arrangements for the director and area leader of Prison fellowship England and Wales to make a visit to Stockport so that I could share the vision with them in more detail. I was expecting them to get behind the vision and I was very disappointed with the negative response that I received. I was informed that I would need to form a separate charity and that the work could not be undertaken as part of Prison Fellowship England and Wales. I prayed to God for direction in the way forward and it was then that I was led to form a charity in the name of "The New Life Centre". God had put it on my heart to ask certain people if they would be a Governor of the charity. I knew that God was with me when Noel Proctor and the Bishop of Stockport Frank Sargeant agreed to be joint presidents of the charity. I was a little nervous when I contacted the Bishop of Stockport for the first time to tell him that God had told me to ask him if he would support the vision of The New Life Centre.

I was not even sure how I was to address a Bishop and I was made to feel at ease with the warm welcome I received from Bishop Frank as I shared the vision with him. My own Pastor Gordon Wright agreed that I could use the church for having a meeting where Bishop Frank would be the main speaker. I invited over two hundred churches in the Stockport and Greater Manchester area and was a little disappointed when only about thirty people turned up. I realised it was quality that counted and not quantity and at that meeting were people who had a real heart for the prisoner. A free will offering on the night raised over £200 to pay towards the cost of forming the charity.

Chapter 21

"If you can"? said Jesus, "everything is possible for him who believes".

Mark 9 : 23

Word about what God was doing in my life started to spread and I was getting invitations to share my testimony in many places. It was also an opportunity to share about the vision of The New Life Centre to anyone who was prepared to listen. I had received some very encouraging letters including one from The Queen and Lord Justice Woolfe. I had been tempted to form the charity with my own family as Governors so that I would be able to make sure that I went the way that God wanted me to go. God made it very clear to me that I was to ask people from outside of my family so that The New Life Centre would never belong to any individual and that no Governor could ever make any financial gain from the charity. The New Life Centre was to belong to God and if I did everything His way then God would bring about the vision he had given to me.

I was obedient to God and after asking Bishop Frank and Noel Proctor to be joint presidents I asked David Burgin, Brian Griffiths, Cathy Hammond, Marjorie Wright and my wife Jan to be Governors of The New Life Centre. The solicitors that I had instructed informed me that it would be better to form a company and also apply for charitable status. I was expecting God to do everything overnight and now I was going to learn about being patient. We started to meet once a month at our home so that we could pray about the vision and it was a time of getting to know each other a lot better. Jan and I started to take ex-prisoners into our home as we waited on God to provide a suitable building. At one of our meetings I shared how we were in danger of losing our home because we had fallen behind with our mortgage payments. It was decided that if we could obtain planning permission for our home to be used as a Christian hostel, The New Life Centre would purchase the house at an amount set by an independent house valuer. Jan and I had left the meeting at the time the vote was taken concerning our home. God had made clear to me that Jan and I were to have no dealings with any finances of The New Life Centre.

David Burgin arranged for a valuation and a figure of £125,000 was given as a fair price for the value of our house. At the time we owed a total of £80,000 so after the sale we would have been left with around £40,000 after paying all legal costs. By now I was getting an expert at putting in planning applications and we felt that this time we would obtain planning permission. From all accounts it was the ideal home with five bedrooms and a detached bungalow at the rear that would have been ideal for an office and counselling purposes. It was August of 1990 and we were given the news that our planning application had been turned down yet again. The local papers had got hold of the news and did a story about an ex-con trying to help offenders. At this time we had three ex-prisoners living in our home. I had been signing on as unemployed now for about three months and we were getting further into arrears with our mortgage payments.

We prayed about the situation and believed that God had everything under control. It was September 1990 that I was asked by some Christian friends if we could drive a van to Romania with some supplies for the orphans. I asked Jan if she would like to go with me. We had time on our hands se we decided that we would drive the van and help in any way that we could. We had seen the slides that Billy Hough had brought back from Romania and our hearts were touched by God.

It was a very exciting journey to Romania and I knew that God was with us in a very special way. I believed in praying about every situation and we had some very special prayer times along the way. Keith Dalzell had made arrangements for us to collect over one thousand Romanian bibles in Germany as we travelled to Romania and it was a time of great blessings. When we arrived in Romania it was like going back in time as we made our way to our destination of Hateg.

What we witnessed in the handicapped children's orphanage was worse than anything we had seen on the TV or slides. The first thing that hit us was the smell and then we witnessed the appalling conditions that the children had to endure. We all ended up in tears and I wondered what more we could do to help their desperate situation. We were invited to speak at the local Baptist church and our hosts daughter Elena translated for us. When it was my turn to speak I shared how God had rescued me from a pit of despair and the love that God had given to me was the love I was sharing with them. I shared about my work with the prisoners and I asked them to pray for the prisoners in their own country.

After the service was over I was met outside by a Romanian who introduced himself as Renato Falticska. I listened intently as Renato shared how God had put it on his heart to help prisoners in Romania but he did not know what to do. Renato had always been frightened of the police since being a little boy and even though he had this fear of the police and prisons he felt that God wanted him to do something for the prisoner. Renato could speak only a little English when we had arrived but now God had given him the power to speak almost perfect English. We sat up through the night as I shared with him about my ministry with the prisoners and the vision that God had given to me.

The next day Elena introduced us to a Pastor at Hunedoara who went into the prison on the odd occasion. Pastor Elisa could speak some English and he shared about his ministry and work in the prisons. Jan and I were taken to the orphanage at Hunedoara where we were introduced to a little boy called Daniel who was two years old. We were asked if we would like to adopt the boy and give him a new life back in England. As soon as Jan had picked Daniel up and held him in her arms I knew that Jan wanted to offer him a home with us. We both had a lot of love to give and we learned that Daniel had come from a broken home where the parents were not married and no one wanted him. Pastor Elisa said he would help us with the paperwork and get permission from the parents for us to adopt the child.

From the orphanage we went to Hunedoara prison where I was praying we would be allowed in to speak with the prisoners about Jesus. The guard at the gate said that we could not go in without a special invitation but he agreed to take bibles from us to give to all the prisoners. I felt that this was an achievement even though we had not been allowed in ourselves. The most important thing was that the word of God was going into the prison. From the prison we were taken to see an old man called Sigusmund who lived by himself in a small wooden shack. The sight that greeted me will live with me forever.

I noticed a man crippled with arthritis and lay in a bed with rags as blankets. I had never seen a deformed body like he had and the smell in the room was appalling. In one corner was a log burning fire that had not been lit for a long time and next to the fire was a rusty wheel chair with only one wheel. The flies were everywhere and Sigusmund just lay there helpless. My heart started to break and I wondered why God had allowed this man to be in this situation. It was then that God spoke into my heart and told me to look more closely. I noticed a bible that was on a stand that was on a small table next to the bed. Pastor Elisa helped to prop Sigusmund up so that he could have a drink. We had brought some cans of coke with us and some still orange juice. Elisa put a rubber tube in the can and placed it in the mouth of Sigusmund who sucked out every drop without pausing for breath.

It was clear that Sigusmund had not even had a drink for many days and he had to rely on people coming in to help him all the time. After Sigusmund had a drink he moved his head towards the bible and I understood why the bible pages had swelled when I watched Sigusmund turn the bible pages with his tongue. Sigusmund asked us to sing some songs with him as we prayed and praised Jesus together. I realised that I had met a man who was nearer to God than anyone I had ever met before. Sigusmund had worn out his bible from reading it from cover to cover and he had a joy in his heart that I also not seen before. I had met a man who had nothing in the eyes of the world and yet my new friend had everything.

We returned to our host's house George and Elizabeth Simondroni where we were made to feel part of the family. We had only been in Romania for five days and yet we had made so many friends. It was going to be hard to say goodbye but I knew that we would be returning in the very near future. Keith, Jan and I were the last to leave and we headed for home after saying goodbye to our new family.

We arrived in Hungary and our eyes lit up when we saw a McDonalds sign above the road. We followed the sign until it led us to a McDonalds restaurant in the town centre. We only had enough currency to buy a hamburger each and a cup of coffee for Jan but it was like eating fillet steak after what we had been eating for the past week. From McDonalds we headed towards Austria and we knew that we only had enough money for one hotel stop. We had given away most of what money we had and we had left ourselves short for going home. We decided that we would have a hotel stop in Austria with a good meal, a good sleep and then we would sleep rough in the van the following night in Germany. We could not have picked a nicer hotel and the log fire was burning up the chimney when we arrived very cold, tired and hungry at 9.00pm.

Jan and I shared a room and Keith had a single room all with excellent facilities. We decided that we would have a steak that night for our evening meal and make the most of our one night of luxury. After our meal we went straight to bed as we were very tired. In the morning we woke up early and made our way to the restaurant for our breakfast. Keith had met three men from Switzerland who were on their way to Romania, taking out aid for the poor just as we had done. We were invited to join them for breakfast and we shared all about what we had found in Romania. I asked if we could pray for their journey into Romania and we all linked hands as I prayed for them. Our three Swiss friends left the table as we continued to finish our breakfast. When I went to pay the hotel bill with the last of the money that we had I was informed by the manager that our bill had been paid. He pointed to the van with our Swiss friends that were just leaving the car park.

I knew that God had used our brothers from Switzerland to meet our needs so that we would not have to sleep rough the following night in Germany. As we reached Germany and slept in a nice warm bed I knew that we had a God who we could put all our trust in. At breakfast Keith gave me a business card with the name and address of one of our Swiss brothers and I knew that when we returned home I was going to write and thank them for what they had done for us. At the same time I was pondering in my heart what I could do to help those helpless children in the handicapped children's hospital in Hateg. Being a builder I knew what could be achieved and if God wanted me I was prepared to return and refurbish the hospital.

The day after we returned from Romania I was given a copy of the local newspaper with the front page headlines "Beds Without Bars". The vision I had been given for The New Life Centre had made front page headlines and I had not had anything to do with it. We then received the news that our planning application had been refused and the building society was going to apply to the courts for possession of our home. We decided to appeal against the planning refusal to an inspector from the department of environment but this was going to take six months to be heard.

Chapter 22

"Whoever acknowledges me before men, I will also acknowledge him before my Father in heaven. But whoever disowns me before men, I will disown him before my Father in heaven".

Matthew 10 : 32-33

I could not get the young helpless children we had seen in Romania out of my mind and I tried to picture the handicapped children's hospital refurbished. I wrote to thank our Swiss friends for paying our hotel bill and shared how we had been blessed by their kindness. I received an invitation from Billy Hough to attend a meeting at Poynton Baptist Church where everyone who had been involved with Romania had been invited. I felt that this would be a good time to share the vision I had of returning to Romania in time for Christmas to refurbish the handicapped children's hospital.

It was the first week of October 1990 and I shared the vision with about forty people who were present. I was expecting everyone to be for the vision and I was shocked when person after person gave reasons why it would not be possible. "You will have no where to stay, it will be minus 20, the roads will be blocked off" were just some of the comments that were made. I could not believe that I was in a room full of Christians and after all the negative statements had finished I spoke up. "I have listened to you give reasons why I should not go but not one of you have taken God into account. My Lord undertakes miracles and if I was thinking like you do tonight I would not be here or contemplating returning to Romania".

As I was leaving the meeting Billy Hough came up to me and said he would give me all the help he could if I decided to return to Romania. I went home feeling that most of the people in that room did not know Jesus Christ. I asked Jan if she would be willing to return to Romania at Christmas time if God confirmed we were to go. Jan told me that she would only go if Robert and Michelle came with us. We prayed that night over the situation of returning to Romania and the adoption of Daniel. In the morning I received a telephone call from Rickie who told me that God had given him a word to share with me from Judges 18 :5-6. Then they said to him, "Please enquire of God to learn whether our journey will be successful". The priest answered them, "Go in peace. Your journey has the Lord's approval".

I thanked Rickie for the word and I prayed to God and asked him to confirm if that word was from Him. I had just said "Amen" when the telephone started to ring. I picked up the telephone and it was Cyrill on the line from Switzerland who said, "I have been given five thousand Swiss Francs for your next journey to Romania, I will be posting it off today". There was no way that Cyrill could have known what was on my heart and I knew that God was giving me the go ahead to return to Romania. I shared with Jan that God was going to provide everything we needed for refurbishing the children's hospital and that we would have to work very hard to get everything ready that we needed. When the cheque from Cyrill arrived it had increased to six thousand Swiss Francs in the post and it was worth nearly two and a half thousand pounds sterling.

The local newspapers got hold of the story and printed an appeal for everything that we would need. Our telephone was red hot and people were very generous. From a building point of view I had the experience to make a list of every item that would be needed to undertake the refurbishment and it was a very long list. The newspapers asked me when we would be going and I gave them a date of November 18th 1990. I decided to hand all the monies to Billy Hough so that no one could accuse me of taking any money for myself. While we were getting everything ready for the refurbishment of the children's hospital Jan and I also had to get all the paperwork together for the adoption of Daniel.

Everything was going well until we had a meeting with Stockport social services who stated that they did not consider us to be suitable parents for adoption because of my past criminal convictions. It was clear they were looking at the old Bob Sutton and not the new creation in Jesus. We decided that if God wanted us to adopt Daniel then everything would be overcome.

By the 18th November we had two seven and a half ton wagons and my own Sherpa van loaded with everything that we were going to need. At the last moment a police mechanic who had volunteered to drive my Sherpa van backed out because he thought my van was not roadworthy. I telephoned the AA and asked them to do an emergency inspection on the van. After undertaking the inspection the AA informed us that in his opinion the van was in a sound mechanical condition and if driven carefully it would make it to Romania and back. This was still not good enough for our police mechanic who refused to go.

The team that I was leading consisted of Rickie, Keith, Peter, Gordon, Jan and Michelle. Robert had decided that he did not want to go so we made arrangements for him to stay with his friends parents until we returned to England after Christmas. We left Larkhill Baptist Church at 10.00am after Pastor Gordon Wright and Martin Graty prayed us on our way.

As we set off towards the ferry at Ramsgate I thought about the way that God had provided everything that we had needed. Billy and his wife Doreen along with Martin, Eric and Chris were to leave for Romania a week before Christmas and meet us all in Hateg. They were going to bring all the food and toys for the children's Christmas party that we had planned for them. This was going to be a Christmas that no-one would forget for a very long time.

We called at Gummersbach in Germany to collect over one thousand bibles and we were given accommodation and food for the night. This was where I started to experience problems with members of the team and Rickie stated he was upset because I had my wife and daughter with me and he was by himself. Rickie and Keith were from the Pentecostal church, Peter a Catholic, Gordon had been a Monk, Jan, Michelle and I attended an Evangelical church. We were a real mixed bag but I knew that in Jesus Christ we were all one. Before we had left for Romania I explained that we would be going the long way round via Switzerland so that we could meet up with Cyrill, Eugen and Josef to let them see what we had done with the money they had sent.

When we stopped for a short break in Germany Keith and Rickie were complaining about us going to Switzerland. I was already upset with Keith because he had slapped Michelle across her face a few hours before and I shouted at the pair of them. I threatened to send them home in the Sherpa van if they did not stop acting like little children. It was clear that I was not getting the support that I should have received as leader of the mission and things started to get worse.

We met up with our three friends in Switzerland and they had made arrangements for us all to stay in a hotel near Basel. They would not let us spend the money that we had and we had a wonderful meal in a nearby restaurant. In the morning our three friends met us at the hotel to have breakfast with us and see us on our way. As we were leaving Cyrill gave me five hundred Swiss Francs to help us on our way through Austria. As we drove through Switzerland into Austria the snow covered the mountains and by the time we found a hotel to stay in the snow was falling very heavy. We had a wonderful rest and when we woke up in the morning I was met by Peter who complained that Gordon had made sexual advances towards him during the night. This was another situation that I had to deal with and it seemed one thing after another.

It was only God that was keeping us together and without God we would have turned back. We arrived at our destination of Hateg on the 23rd November and we all stayed at the home of George and Elizabeth Simondroni for the first night. On the following day we unloaded one of the big vans as Peter was going to take it back to England on the 25th November as the company that had loaned it for the mission needed it back. Rickie and Keith went to stay with a family from the Pentecostal church and Gordon went to stay with a family from the Baptist church. I was given the bad news that we would not be allowed to refurbish the handicapped children's hospital because it was going to be closed down. I met with leaders of the government but nothing was going to change their minds about the hospital closing down.

We prayed about this situation and Keith suggested that we give the building supplies to the Pentecostal Pastor who was building a new church. I shared that I did not feel that this was right because we had collected all the supplies for the benefits of the children. We asked God to lead us to another building and the following day Elena took us to a school/orphanage at Pestianna about ten miles from Hateg.

It was a place where over one hundred children lived in very poor conditions. Most of them had come from broken homes or from large families that could not afford to look after them. The children were crying out for love and affection and our hearts went out to them. I met with the director of the orphanage and he pleaded with us to undertake the building works at Pestianna. The bedrooms were very cold and I had never seen so many beds in one room. The toilets consisted of two holes in the floor and there was no hot water or central heating. I shared with our team that this was the place for us to undertake the works. The director of the orphanage employed some Romanian workers on our behalf and work started on the refurbishment of the orphanage. The children were really excited when the two holes in the concrete floor were capped off and we installed two toilets complete with seats. I watched some of the children lifting the seats up and down wondering what it was for.

We then set about installing central heating, hand basins and showers in the bathroom, tiling, cleaning and painting. We had brought clothes for the children, toiletries, medicines and food. Everyone was excited as we unloaded the supplies that we had brought and placed them in the cellars underneath the building. When we attended the Baptist church on the Sunday morning I thanked God for undertaking for us yet again. As I was praying I heard God speak to me, "I want you to go to the president of Romania and get permission to go into the prisons to share the good news with the prisoners".

I was going to Bucharest the following day to pick up a couple who had flown out from England with the intention of adopting a Romanian child. I told God that I was willing to be obedient if He would provide me with an interpreter. After the service I went up to a Romanian lady called Fenela and asked her if she would be willing to come to Bucharest the following day to translate for me. I knew it was of God when she agreed even though she said she was frightened. We decided to leave Hateg at 1.00am in the early hours of Monday morning to travel overnight to the capital city of Romania. Rickie agreed to share the driving with me and Jan and Michelle came along for the ride. It was a journey I had never experienced before as we drove over three hundred miles through mountain roads that were covered in ice without any lights at the side of the road. We could all feel the presence of God as a very bright moon lit up the dark sky and the road ahead. The van just stuck to the road as if it was a normal dry day and fears that we had disappeared.

We arrived outside of the Presidents palace at 9.00am after driving nonstop through the night. I was beginning to wonder if I had got it wrong when a palace guard holding a machine gun barred our entrance at the gate. I spoke to him in English and Fenela translated into Romanian. I asked to see the President and explained that I wanted permission to go into the prisons to share the good news of Jesus Christ. The guard spoke in Romanian and told us to follow him where we were led into an office building at the front of the palace. After an hour I spoke with a man in a dark suit who explained that I needed to see the Minister of Justice to obtain the permission I required and not the President of Romania. We were given the name and address of the official we needed to see and a half hour later we were in the court building waiting to see the official.

After a short time I was informed that I needed to see the director of the prisons at an address that Fenela had never heard of. It was now lunch time and everyone in the van was asking for something to eat. We asked many taxi drivers if they knew where the building was that had been wrote down for us and yet no-one we asked had any idea. We had arranged to meet the couple from England in the Continental hotel at 3.00pm so we decided that we would go there early and have something to eat. After waiting ages in the restaurant to be served we were informed that they did not have a menu to choose from and when they described the food to us we decided to give lunch a miss.

It was at this point that God gave me the heart to ask another taxi driver the way to the building we needed to find. I was almost ready for giving up but because we had given lunch a miss we had a little more time on our hands. The taxi driver nodded his head to say he knew where the building was and Fenela and I got into the taxi and asked him to take us there. After a fifteen minute drive he pointed to a building that was surrounded by police with machine guns. It was now nearing the anniversary of the revolution that had taken place less than a year ago and there was still a lot of unrest between the Romanian people and their government. We got out of the taxi and asked the driver to wait for us to return. We made our way through the police guarding the building to the main entrance. Fenela explained why we were there and the policeman asked for our passports and led us into the building.

We were shown into a room about twenty feet square that was filled with policemen all with guns. The chairs were all around the perimeter of the room and everywhere we looked our eyes met those of the policemen who were looking at us. I felt sorry for Fenela because she was the only female in the room and some of the policemen started to chat her up and her face started to go red. I started to pray that God would protect Fenela from any embarrassment and then the policemen started to talk amongst themselves leaving Fenela alone. It was a very long hour that we waited in that room and then our names were called out to go into another office. The official I met was the director of all the prisons in Romania and I started to explain why I wanted to go into his prisons. I told him that Jesus Christ had the power to change lives and that the men in prison needed to hear the good news of Jesus Christ.

I was pleased that he could speak good English and I gave him a copy of the bibles that I wanted to give to the prisoners. I shared how I was a member of Prison Fellowship and that it would benefit his prisons if he allowed Prison Fellowship into his prisons. After talking with him for half an hour he spoke the words that I longed to hear "How many prisons would you like to visit and which ones"? I informed him that I did not know where his prisons were but I would like to visit six prisons in the time we had and stated he could chose the prisons that we were to visit. I asked if Martin, Eric and Renato could be included on our invitation.

We were asked where we were staying and the director informed us that he would contact all the prisons we were to visit so that we would be allowed in. The prisons that he selected were spread all around Romania at Deva, Arad, Oradea, Aiud, Gherla and Timisoara where the revolution had started. I thanked Colonel Chris for his help and although I had not seen the President of Romania I had the permission that God had sent me for. I told Fenela that God would bless her for what she had done and gone through. As we left the building I noticed a man in a long black leather coat follow us out. We got into our taxi and returned to the Continental hotel to meet up with Jan, Michelle and Rickie who had waited patiently for us. We waited another hour and we were joined by Keith and his wife Janet who had flown from England with the intention of adopting a Romanian child.

We made the return journey to Hateg and it was a very long drive because Keith and Janet were being sick every half hour and we had to stop the van each time. They had eaten a meal in the restaurant that we had refused and the smell was that bad we had to drive with the windows open even though it was very cold. We arrived safely back in Hateg in the early hours of Tuesday morning some thirty hours after we had first set out. We all went to bed for a few hours to catch up on some of the sleep we had lost.

The following day Jan and I took Michelle to meet up with Daniel the little boy we had returned to adopt. We met up with Pastor Elisa at Hunedoara but when we arrived at the orphanage we were told that Daniel had been given up for adoption to a couple from Canada. Daniel was still at the orphanage and he was brought out for Jan and Michelle to hold. Elisa was able to find out that the doctor at the orphanage had been given $1000 bribe by the Canadian couple so they could adopt him. The doctor was classing Daniel as having no parents so that the Canadian couple would not need the parents consent to adopt Daniel. We had all the paperwork that was required to adopt Daniel and in our eyes he had been sold to a couple from Canada. The doctor was very embarrassed that we had returned with the paperwork and brought two other children for us to choose from. Jan and I both said that we would not choose and we left the orphanage feeling very sad. In one way we were pleased that Daniel was going to a home where he would not go short of anything but I also knew that we had a great deal of love to give that money could not buy.

The snow was falling very hard now and it was getting very difficult to drive around. We called to see Sigusmund and gave him a wheel chair we had brought from England, also some food and money. His face lit up as we went into his room especially when he saw the wheel chair and he started to cry. This made all of us cry and Eric got his guitar out of the van so that we could have a time of praise and worship together. The joy in Sigusmund face was evident to us all and if we had just gone to Romania for that act alone it would have been worthwhile. I felt God so near to me and each day had blessings of its own. It was true that the devil kept on having a go but God always had the last word.

It was a blessing to take the word of God into prisons and share my testimony with the prisoners of how God had saved me when I did not want to live. I knew the conditions that they had to endure were worse than anything I had gone through. I knew that I was preaching and sharing with the power of God in my life because all around the room were prison guards with guns. When I saw one of the prison guards pick up a bible I knew that I was to share about the conversion of the prison guard from the book of Acts. Jesus Christ died for the sins of the whole world and this included prison guards as well as the prisoners. I knew that I was preaching on the right subject when Renato who was translating for me started to sweat buckets.

When Renato and I left the prison to return to Hateg I was met by Keith and Janet who were very angry. They had offered to buy a baby from a couple a few houses away from where we were staying. The family consisted of four children and a new born baby. The father was unable to work and the mother was too ill to cope due to the pressure of having another baby. They had no money or food and the mother was only letting Keith and Janet adopt the baby because she knew the baby was in danger of dying. I had shared the story the day before with Janet from 1 Kings 3 : 16 - 28 where one prostitute was prepared to let another prostitute keep her baby so that it would not be cut in half and killed by the King. God had put it on my heart to share with Janet in love and in truth that what they were doing was wrong. The money Keith was flashing around was a big temptation to a family that had nothing and I believed that they should have used their money to help keep the family together and not to split them up. Janet had gone crying to Keith and he was not a very happy man when I saw him. I spoke the truth to Keith but he told me to mind my own business and leave him to do what he was doing. Keith and Janet were not Christians and they looked at things through the eyes of the world. I wondered if it was a couple like them who had bought Daniel.

It was good to be able to go to the prison at Timisoara with Eric and Martin before they returned back to England. Eric had wanted to play his guitar but the guards refused to let him take it into the prison. It did not stop Eric singing Amazing Grace to the prisoners with a little help from Martin and myself. We gave the prisoners and guards bibles and chocolate covered biscuits with our love. Martin was given the badge out of the Captains hat as a token of his appreciation. When we left the prison Martin and Eric headed back to England as Renato and I made our way back through the night to Hateg. By now Renato and I were becoming very close friends and I realised that God had his hand on Renato in a very special way.

Chapter 23

"Again, I tell you that if two or you on earth agree about anything you ask for, it will be done for you by my Father in heaven. For where two or three come together in my name, there am I with them".

Matthew 18 : 19 - 20

The work was progressing really well at the orphanage and it was very exciting to work with Romanian workmen who were using methods we had used over fifty years ago. Although we had a language barrier it was amazing how we managed to communicate through sign language and drawing pictures of what we were trying to get across to each other. I had made arrangements with the director of the orphanage to put on a Christmas party for all of the children and staff for the 20th December. Doreen had made a Father Christmas outfit to fit Billy and we had brought enough presents from England for everyone at Pestianna. We had decided to have the party before Christmas because Doreen, Billy and Chris had to return to England for Christmas day. While Jan, Michelle, Billy, Doreen, Chris and our Romanian friends prepared for the Christmas party Renato and myself headed for the prison at Aiud over one hundred miles away. Rickie and Keith had already left for England because Rickie wanted to be with his family in time for Christmas.

   We had left for the prison at 6.00am because we wanted to be back at Pestianna for the start of the Christmas party at 2.00pm. As we left Hateg it was snowing and after we had been travelling for about two hours the engine in my Sherpa van seized up and we came to a standstill. I checked the engine and found that there was no oil registering on the dip stick. Renato asked me what we should do and I told him that we should pray. In Romania they only had filling stations in the main towns and we were in between towns where we had broken down. I knew that only God could help us out of this situation and if God wanted us to preach His word at Aiud we needed his help. After we had finished praying together I looked in the back of the van and found some bottles of oil that I had not given away. I put the oil in the engine, got back into the van and turned the ignition key. The van started first time and we both started to praise God. Renato felt that we should turn around now the engine was running and head back to Hateg just in case God did not want us at the prison. I told Renato that if God did not want us at the prison we would still be at the side of the road.

It was the right decision to go forward to Aiud in faith because the prisoners and prison guards responded to what we shared in a remarkable way. I shared that Jesus Christ could set them all free right there and then if they would ask Him into their lives. I shared how I became a free man in prison even though I was still locked up behind prison bars. How in the depth of my despair Jesus Christ had come into my strip cell and had given me a new life. Renato translated for me and I could see the prisoners and guards with tears rolling down their cheeks. I knew that God was working in their hearts and that souls had been won for Jesus that day. It was good to see Renato speaking with the power of the Holy Spirit and overcoming the fear he had of prison. We were both given an open invitation from the director to return at any time and he told us that we would not require permission to enter. We made our way back to Pestianna rejoicing in what our Lord had done for us.

We arrived at Pestianna at 2,00pm just in time for the start of the Christmas party. Jan had brought our Christmas tree and decorations from home to decorate the dining room and make it special for everyone. One of the children held his hands out towards the tree with sheer delight when he saw it all lit up. The tables had been placed in a big rectangle around the room with the children sat down. Behind every child was a member from the choir at the Baptist church and they started to sing Christmas carols to the children. It was like listening to Angels sing and the faces of the children said it all. They were so excited as we placed sandwiches, fruit, chocolate cakes and biscuits in front of them to eat. Then it was time for each of them to receive a present from Father Christmas. The children formed a line and waited eagerly for their turn to receive a present and what I was witnessing had made everything so worthwhile. The children were no different than other children around the world as they ripped off the wrapping paper to see what God had brought them. We had explained to the children the real meaning of Christmas and that it was God who gave the very best gift of all in His one and only son Jesus Christ.

When we left Pestianna that day we all left a piece of our heart behind and I knew that we would be returning at some date in the near future. On the 21st December Billy, Doreen and Chris headed back to England but we could not leave with them because I had one last prison to visit at Gherla the following day. It was not possible for Renato to come and translate for me at Gherla because he had to be in work but Elena offered to stand in for him. It was a two hundred mile drive to Gherla and as we passed through Romanian towns Elena gave me a history lesson. In the four weeks we had been in Romania I had travelled over two thousand miles visiting six prisons and I had seen at firsthand what a beautiful country Romania is.

When we arrived at Gherla it was the largest of all the prisons in Romania. It was as big as a town and it housed thousands of prisoners. As we were introduced to the director of the prison he asked me if I had a bible for him. I only had one full bible left as all the other bibles I had were new testaments. I wrote in the scripture from John 3:16 and I replaced where it read "the world" with his name. I think the director was pleased that I had brought an attractive young girl to translate for me as he made a big fuss of Elena. It was a very overwhelming prison and the sheer size of the place took some getting used to. We could see guards with machine guns everywhere we looked and the prisoners were dressed the same as we had seen at previous prisons we had visited. They all wore a dark and light brown striped sack cloth uniform, their hair was shaved very short and I noticed that some of them had marks on their wrists where they had obviously been shackled with chains.

We were led into a large room full of chairs and three tables at the front of the room. Elena and I were at the tables with prison guards either side and the director was sat at the side of the room on a separate table. Prison guards with machine guns were standing up all around the room and I was informed that what I said would be taped. I could sense that Elena was getting a bit nervous and I told her that God would protect her and fill her with His Holy Spirit. After a few minutes about one hundred prisoners were marched into the room with guards at the front and the back of them.

The prisoners sat down and then I stood up and started to share my testimony with them. It was amazing how God had helped both Elena and I to talk in turn so that Elena could translate what I was sharing and at the same time keep everything flowing smooth. I shared from John 3:16 and I led everyone through a prayer of repentance and salvation that I had been led through by Noel Proctor over three years before. I gave every prisoner and prison guard a new testament and a packet of chocolate biscuits before saying goodbye to all our new friends at Gherla prison. We left with another open invitation to return at any time we wanted. We then started to make our way back to Hateg as the night closed in on us. As Elena covered herself with a blanket and fell asleep I felt God so near to me and marveled at the way that God had undertaken for us yet again. This was going to be our last day in Romania and a great part of me did not want to return to England. I had witnessed a great need in Romania of people who needed to hear the good news of Jesus Christ.

We said our goodbyes to George and Elizabeth and set off for England in the early hours of the morning on the 23rd December with Elena for company because she wanted a lift to Timisoara on our way to the border. The snow was starting to fall as we left Hateg and make our way to the border crossing at Nadlac. We said our goodbyes to Elena as we dropped her off at Timisoara and by 6.00pm we were at McDonalds in Hungary having a Big Mac and chips. We had made arrangements with Cyril to return via Switzerland so we made our way through Austria towards Switzerland. The weather had turned very bad and the snow was falling very heavy as we travelled through Austria. Our van was the only vehicle on the roads and at times I found it hard to tell if I was on the road or not because everything was covered in snow. The road had many winding turns and Jan had her hands clasped very tightly together in prayer as we continued on our way. Michelle was fast asleep in a makeshift bed at the back of our seats covered in blankets to keep her warm. Jan and I had our legs covered in blankets to keep us warm from the cold draft that was finding its way through from the front of our van. At times I had to slow right down as we approached bends in the road to prevent the van from going into a skid and just as the van was about to stop it picked up speed again. I knew that if the van stopped we would not be able to carry on because I had no snow chains in the van.

After travelling for many miles without seeing any other vehicles we neared a tunnel that was over 15 miles long. We were both praying that we would reach this tunnel to give us a break from the snow. We all cheered as the mouth of the tunnel was in sight and when we reached the other end of the tunnel a snow plough was in front clearing away the snow. We did indeed have a God who looked after us in more ways than we could ever imagine. We made our way to Innsbruck and we found a beautiful hotel half way up a mountain where we were going to spend Christmas Eve and Christmas day. This was something I had only ever seen on post cards and it was something I had always wanted to do. The mountains were all around us covered in snow, the hotel was like a big log cabin with a log burning fire in the lounge. We were the only guests and from our bedroom we had a wonderful view of the town and also the mountains with all the skiers on them. Everything was covered in snow, the sky was blue and the sun was shining down.

Our hotel was reached by a railway track where one train going down helped to pull the other train coming up the mountain. At the rear of our hotel were the ski lifts that took skiers to the top of the mountain. Jan and I went into the town centre on Christmas Eve to look around the shops and we bought a statue of Jesus for Cyril and his wife Claudine in Switzerland. Michelle was not feeling very well and she started to come out in red spots all over her body. We both prayed for Michelle and on Christmas day Jan stayed with Michelle while I went to a nearby church to spend some time in God's house thanking him for Jesus. We had never spent a Christmas day like it and Michelle said she felt well enough to accompany Jan and me to the top of the mountain. It was a wonderful experience as we looked down from the top of the mountain. I felt that I had experienced what Moses had experienced when Moses had spoken with God on the mountain at Sinai. It felt like I was looking out on the whole world from where I was standing and I marveled at the beautiful world our God had made.

As we made our way to Switzerland on the 26th December the front tyre on our van had a puncture as we were travelling at 65 mph and we had to stop and put on our spare wheel. We were driving through torrential rain unlike anything we had experienced before. I thought about what our friend the police mechanic had said about our Sherpa van and I wondered what he would say if he could have seen some of the conditions our van had made it through. I realised that it was not the van that had brought us through but our wonderful Lord. We arrived at Basel at 7.00pm on the 26th December where Cyril and Claudine had made arrangements for us to stay in a beautiful hotel with everything provided. After we had freshened up we were taken out for a wonderful meal to a restaurant that our hosts had chosen. Michelle decided she would rather have a Big Mac than a steak so after we had eaten our steak Michelle was taken for her hamburger.

We were treated like royalty by Cyril and Claudine and the following day Cyril took Michelle to see a doctor of the hospice he had founded where she was diagnosed as having German measles. The hospice was like a first class hotel and we were given a guided tour by Cyril. I was so impressed with everything I saw and it even had a chapel where people could spend time alone with God. In the garage they had the facility for storing and sorting aid they were going to be taking to Romania very shortly. After we left the hospice Cyril took Jan and Michelle shopping while one of Cyril's office workers took me to the garage to have two new tyres fitted on our van. The man at the garage found it hard to believe that the tyres had been driven through the conditions that we had gone through. Cyril and Claudine did everything they could to help us and they even bought Jan some tights because Jan had given away her last pair to a poor Romanian woman. I did not know if Cyril and Claudine knew we were short of money but they would not let us spend any money whilst we were with them. It was now our turn to receive from two loving people who wanted to share what God had blessed them with. We set off for England at 12.00pm on the 27th December and we arrived safely back home on the 30th December in time for Jan's birthday on the 31st December.

We had all looked forward to seeing our loved ones while we had been away and we spent a few hours on the telephone letting them know we had arrived home safely. I was met by a mountain of mail behind the front door and the first letter I opened was from a solicitor informing us that our mortgage lender was taking us to court because they wanted possession of our home. I felt upset by the letter but with what I had just experienced with God I knew that our lives and future could not be in better hands. I believed that God had everything under control and that everything would work out for us.

We started the new year of 1991 with high hopes that things would work out for us as a family. It was soon to take on a different picture when we found out that our daughter Donna was going through a very difficult time with her husband Steven who had started drinking again. I then had to appear at the high court where I asked the registrar to give us two months to clear our mortgage arrears so that our home would not be taken away from us. I asked our house group and Pastor at church to pray about our situation as we neared the time for our appeal against the planning refusal to turn our home into a Christian hostel.

The day came when we met with the inspector from the department of environment and as usual our next door neighbours were present to do everything they could to stop us winning our appeal.

Chapter 24

"Do not fret because of evil men or be envious of those who do wrong"

Psalm 37:1

We entered the room at Stockport Town Hall that had been set aside to hear our appeal. Our next door neighbours sat facing Jan and I as we presented our case. The reasons for refusing our planning application were read out and I was given an opportunity to question those who opposed our application. The hearing lasted for almost four hours and at the end of it the inspector for the D.O.E. stated that he wanted to visit the site. After spending a short time looking at our home the inspector stated that we would receive his decision within the next few weeks. We did not have long to wait before the letter arrived stating that we had lost our appeal.

    I was very confused and wondered why God had allowed us to lose when we had been prepared to use our home for the Lord. It was clear that we were now in danger of having our home taken away from us by the building society and a few weeks later we received a notice from Stockport County Court informing us that they had granted the building society possession of our home and we had twenty eight days to leave. When we went to see Stockport housing to enquire if we could rent a council house we were informed that we would have to go into a hostel. This was a time of testing for my faith and I wondered why we had lost everything we had worked for during the past ten years. I wondered why my church had not rallied round to help us considering that we had taken in people from our church that were homeless. With the last bit of money that we had we rented a house in Bramhall still hoping that a miracle would happen. We knew that we could only afford to stay in Bramhall for a few months because the rent was £150 a week and I did not have any income coming in except unemployment benefit.

After spending a great deal of time in prayer we received a letter informing us that the council was prepared to offer us a council house in Adswood. If we refused their offer we would not be offered anything else. When we viewed the house our hearts sank, it had all the windows and doors covered with steel shields to prevent people from breaking in. Adswood had a reputation of being one of the worst areas of Stockport in which to live and I felt very sad that I had allowed my family to reach a situation where they had to move into one of the worst areas of Stockport. Even so I felt that God had a reason for allowing this to happen and in many ways it made me to seek God for the reasons why.

I promised Jan that I would make the house as nice as I could and I returned to our old home to take out the fitted kitchen, bathroom and central heating system to install into our council house. I had spent more than £50,000 in five years trying to build a dream home and now I had to take out some of the things I had spent a lot of time installing. I had to store things I had removed from our old home into what was going to be our new home and hoped that they would be safe. I wanted to make the house as nice as I could before moving my family into it. We still had three weeks left at Bramhall before we had to leave and I worked twelve hours a day working on our council house to make it as nice as possible. The house started to take shape and the fitted kitchen and bathroom made a big difference. After I had been working on the house for about two weeks Jan and I went to pick something up on our way to church on a Sunday morning. As soon as we opened the door we knew that we had been robbed as the back door was open and the kitchen window was broken. Everything of value had been stolen including all my tools. I went to telephone the police and found that the telephone had been taken as well. We both broke down and started to cry. I could not take any more and I told Jan that I wanted to make a fresh start in Cornwall and walk away there and then.

It was Jan's turn now to be strong and she told me to put a nail in the door to lock it and carry on with her to church. I poured my heart out to God and the tears rolled down my cheek as I thought of the pain that Jesus had gone through for me. I pictured Jesus nailed to the cross and looking down on me with love in his eyes and pain in his face. I felt that God was speaking right into my heart and telling me to trust in him. As we left church I knew that we had to carry on and finish the work we had started. As we walked away from church our Pastor came up to remind me that I had promised to share my testimony at a church he was speaking at in the evening. I did not feel like going but I knew that God had given me a testimony that might lead other people to believe in Jesus. If it was the devil's plan to stop me from going then he had not succeeded.

On the Monday morning I carried on with my work that I had started even though most of my tools had been stolen. I could not help thinking that the people who had broken into our home to steal from us were the people that God had called me to help. I knew that we had moved into a human jungle where only the strong would survive. I knew that with the Holy Spirit working in our lives we would succeed. We were praying that God would send some help to us and we expected brothers and sisters from our own church to come and help us. I think that this hurt us more than anything when our own church did nothing to help us. In fact it was a brother from the local Baptist church who called round to offer us some help. I had first met Eric Want when I was serving my prison sentence at Kirkham prison. Eric had come into the prison on a Friday evening with a gospel group and I remembered being so pleased to meet a Christian from my own town. Eric had been a member of Heaton Chapel Christian Church in Stockport and when he returned to Stockport he told everyone about his meeting with me. This resulted in me joining H.C.C.C. when I was released from prison. Eric was led by God to leave H.H.C.C. and help build the new Larkhill Baptist Church about half a mile from where we now lived. This was the same Eric who had come into the prisons with me in Romania and had met Sigusmund.

Eric shared how they had been praying for someone like me to join their church to help them reach out to those that were lost who did not know Jesus. I had wondered why God had allowed us to lose our home and felt that God wanted to use me for reaching the lost sheep where we now lived. Jan and I prayed together and we were both hurt at the lack of support we had received from our own church. We both felt it was right to leave H.C.C.C. and join Larkhill if the elders of Larkhill were prepared to accept us and our vision for reaching those that were lost. First I wanted to start a youth club on a Tuesday and Friday evening for children aged between ten and sixteen years of age. From the children we would be able to reach other members of the family and the church would grow. It was going to be hard work and we would need the help of other members in the church. Eric felt that I would make an ideal Pastor for Larkhill and I knew that I had a heart and love for people just like Jesus.

The Pastor at Larkhill Martin Graty shared that he intended to make way for a full time Pastor and he was happy for me to become assistant Pastor to him with the backing of the elders. At an elders meeting they decided that it was a big step for them to make me assistant Pastor right away and they would like me to be co-opted onto the elders for a six month period. I did not see myself as an elder but agreed to give it a six month trial to see how things worked out. Within a few weeks we had more than fifty children attending our youth clubs and we started to share the love of Jesus with them. It was clear that they were not used to listening about God although some of the children had learned a few things at school. The children we worked with all lived within walking distance from the church and we started to build a bond with the children.

They were soon sharing things that they felt they could trust us with and I believed that these children would be the future church. We soon found out that all the elders from the church lived outside of the area and in many ways they did not relate to a church on a council estate. Even the children of our church members could not relate to children from the local area and it was not long before our church member's children stopped attending the youth club. In some ways I believed that our church children looked at our church as their own private club. All the children we were working with were street wise children as they had to be where they lived. These were the children that would end up on the wrong side of the law if they were not reached by others who could show them a better way. I knew that as Christians we had a lot to offer in Jesus Christ and we continued working with the children.

One Sunday morning I had been asked to lead the service at Larkhill and just as I started to speak ten of the older children we had been working with walked into the church for the first time and sat on the back row of the church. This was what we had been praying for and they all looked at me and started to smile. I felt my eyes well up with tears and I choked up. After about a minute although it seemed like ages I asked God to help me continue with the message I had prepared in my heart. I was sharing on the lost sheep and how the good shepherd would go out and search for any that were lost. God had given me a living example of what this message was about as ten lost sheep came into our church.

It was not long afterwards that it became clear that the elders of Larkhill were not ready for the challenge of working with the children from the area and I was given orders by the elders to close down the Friday youth club for the 13 to 16 year olds and just work with the younger children on a Tuesday. I told the elders that if the children went then so would we. Eric and his family had moved to another church as we joined Larkhill and now we were moving on. It would have been easier to follow Eric to where he had gone but Jan felt that it would be better for us to return to H.C.C.C. until God made it clear of the way forward.

During our time at Larkhill we had been able to plant many seeds and one family in particular had benefited from our help. We had only just joined Larkhill when a young man was killed on a pedestrian crossing near to the church. He had left a young widow with five young boys to look after all under the age of eight. When Jan and I first called to see Diane we were able to meet her where she needed help the most. The end result was that Diane gave her heart to Jesus and started to attend church on a regular basis with her five children in tow.

At about the same time we had been able to put in a planning application for a house that was owned by one of the elders of Larkhill for the New Life Centre to have a Christian rehabilitation centre. This was something that had come under a great amount of opposition from the local neighbours in Offerton and we were turned down yet again by the local council. We appealed to the secretary of state as before and the month of March 1992 was the date set to hear our appeal.

When we re-joined H.C.C.C. it was January 1992 and at about this time I was led by God to go back to The Bridge in America for three months training. I had shared with Jan about how I felt that God wanted us to be trained up and I would only go if Jan agreed to come with me. After praying Jan said that she would come with me and I asked Brian Griffiths and Archie Barr if they would pray about coming as well. When they agreed I believed that it was of God and I made arrangements with Frank Costantino for us all to go. I asked Frank if he could find a school for Michele to attend but a few weeks before we were due to leave Jan informed me that she would not be going. We both prayed that if there was someone else that God wanted to send in place of Jan that it would be confirmed. We had just said Amen to our prayers when the telephone rang and it was David McEvoy who we had never met before. David shared how he had read about our plans to open a Christian rehabilitation centre for ex-prisoners and addicts and that he would like to help us. We now had our fourth member that we had just prayed for.

Just before we left to go to America I represented The New Life Centre at Stockport Town Hall where our appeal was taking place. The local council had a solicitor working for them and even the local neighbours had employed a solicitor to work for them. I knew that I had God on my side and that he would give me the words to speak. In many ways the previous planning applications and appeals that we had gone through at our old house had given me a great amount of wisdom. I was able to question some of the witnesses who were against us and point out time and time again that the objections were not reason enough to refuse planning permission. The council produced a file containing over five hundred written objections but I pointed out that not one of the objections contained a lawful reason that should affect a planning decision. After the first day at the Town Hall I went home and fell asleep in a chair exhausted. I knew that I should have been preparing my closing statement for the appeal hearing but my mind could not take any more pressure. I prayed that God would give me the words to speak for the following day.

When morning arrived I knew that God would put the words into my mouth and when it was my turn to give a closing speech I just spoke from my heart. I shared how the work of The New Life Centre would benefit our town and that it was not something that people should be afraid of. I shared the words from Luke 4: 18-19 and used the occasion to be a witness for Jesus Christ. When we left the Town Hall we knew that we had done all that was within our own power. Now it was up to God what the end result would be. We were informed that we would be notified within two months of the outcome of our appeal.

I did not like the thought of leaving Jan by herself for three months but trusted in God to watch over my family whist I was away. At the same time Brian was leaving his wife and children behind and they had never been separated in the past. Archie was single and so was David who took the place of Jan. we left for America on the 31st March 1992.

Chapter 25

"If I rise on the wings of the dawn, if I settle on the far side of the sea, even there your hand will guide me, your right hand will hold me fast".

Psalm 139 : 9-10

It was the last day of March and I picked David, Archie and Brian up at 4.30am. We stopped at the end of the road where Brian lived and asked God to bless our journey to America. We arrived at Heathrow airport at 10.00am and just before we boarded our plane we were all offered £500 if we gave up our seats on the 757 plane and waited for a later flight. It was a tempting offer that we refused and we continued on the journey that our Lord had mapped out for us. We arrived at Newark airport in New York on time and after passing through customs and immigration we made our way across town to Le Gardia airport. I said a prayer for all the families of the people who had lost their lives in the aeroplane crash at Le Gardia a week before we had arrived. We were met by American Airline officials who checked in our cases and we only had a two hour wait before our aeroplane left on time for Orlando Florida. We made a stop on route at Raleigh Durham to drop off some passengers before flying on to Orlando. We arrived at 10.50pm American time some twenty five hours after leaving Stockport. We were met at the airport by a lovely Christian called Rego who held up a board in front of him with my name on it. We were all pleased to be met by a smiling face and two hours later we were unpacking our cases at The Bridge. We were all tired but we thanked God for our safe journey and had a time of prayer before going to bed. We drew lots for our bedrooms, Archie and Brian drew the single bedrooms and David and I ended up sharing the twin bedroom.

It was the first day of April and we got out of bed at 7.00am. We started the day in prayer as we would do every day of our stay in America. We met with Frank Costantino at 9.0am where we all had breakfast together in his office. Frank shared that he had a vision to open other centre's and that he might open one in England if he had a favourable response from a meeting he was going to have with Joe Pilling who was the director of prisons for England in July. I told Frank that he could open a centre and let us run it on behalf of The New Life Centre. After being introduced to all the staff Gee Lee was assigned by Frank to look after us. It was good to be back at The Bridge and this was going to be our home for the next three months. Our apartment had been well furnished by Frank he also went to a lot of effort to make us feel at home. Frank let us all telephone our families so that we could let them know we had arrived safely. At night time we attended our first service at church where we met the Pastor B.G. and his wife Diane.

It was what was called a "Care Night" and we met many of the church members and residents. It was good to see their wives, girl friends and other family members allowed in for the service. When we arrived back at our apartment Brian found himself locked out of his bedroom but we had no trouble finding an expert lock picker amongst the one hundred residents at The Bridge. After having a short time of praise and prayer together we went to bed at 11.00pm.

Our days at The Bridge started very early and we were all having breakfast together by 6.00am. Archie was always first up and many a time I found him reading his bible at 3.00am. At first it felt a little strange to be living amongst the residents but we soon settled in. The Bridge contained over eighty males and twenty females and was separated by the main office building. The residents all wore badges with their names on them and one of the residents made badges for us and asked us to wear them. I think that this helped them accept us even more when we wore the same badge. We spent a great deal of time learning all aspects of the rehabilitation programme and we decided that the best way of learning the programme was to go through it ourselves.

We were invited to an "Overcomers" meeting at the alternative sentence house half a mile away. This was where up to sixteen men lived together in a Christian environment and worked through a twelve step programme using the Holy Bible for guidance. It was good to meet Mark who had started this facility and Gerry who had been one of the residents at The Bridge the last time I had been there. Gerry had relapsed going back on drugs but Mark had taken him back in to give him another chance of getting his life together. We walked back to The Bridge at 9.00pm where the moon lit up the dark night sky. I thought of my family back at home who should have been fast asleep in bed and said a silent prayer for them.

Everyone at The Bridge warmed to us and it was not long before many of the residents were sharing their problems with us. It was clear in many cases that the drugs and alcohol were used to block out many sad memories in their lives. The problem was that they soon became addicted and all their lives had taken a downward spiral. I knew this to be true for many people in the prisons of England and they needed a facility where they could deal with the problems in their lives and make a start on the road to recovery. I believed that God was going to give us a facility in England where we could do a similar work. Only God knew when that would come about but in the meantime I knew that we had to learn as much as we could about the way The Bridge was run. So we would be ready when that time came.

We started to work in every job position at The Bridge from the director's office to cook in the kitchen. It was during our time in the kitchen where we went to the Swan hotel at Disneyland to pick up leftover food that had not been eaten from a banquet that had taken place. The Bridge was a registered charity and had joined the "Food Surplus Harvest" where they were given unused food from many of the top hotels. I was amazed at the quality of the food that we were given and I had never seen a hotel like this one in my life. I was going into places that not many people would have been able to go all because I had stepped out in faith and followed Jesus.

Brian, Archie and I had settled down very well but not so with David. Many Christians worked at The Bridge and David was forever telling us that we were all strange people. David had started to withdraw from everything and I had to have a quiet word with him about his attitude. I think that it worked because he started to join in with things. We all surrounded David with prayer and it was not long before he started to open up and share with the other residents. It was clear that each of us had different personalities and that the residents could relate to us all in different ways. I noticed that certain residents who did not open up with Archie, Brian or I could speak with David and this was the same for us all. It was also evident that not only had we come to The Bridge to learn but we had also come for God to do a work in our own lives.

We had been at The Bridge for two weeks and we were invited to a Full Gospel Businessmen's Fellowship at the American Legion. It was during our prayer time that God spoke to me, "Trust in the Lord, I am the good shepherd who looks after my sheep, I call you by name, do not worry but trust in the Lord your God". I was then given a vision of a cheque being made out but could not see the amount. The word from God continued, "I am the truth and the light the only way to the Father is through me". I felt refreshed to feel the presence of the Holy Spirit and I believed that God was going to bless us in a mighty way. It was also good to meet the Christian who travels all around the world with the banner "JOHN 3:16".

The following morning I was woken up by Archie who was full of the Holy Spirit saying, "we can fly, we have wings of an eagle and we can fly, we have new life through Jesus Christ and we can fly". In many ways I was expecting Archie to take off and I thanked him for sharing that word with me even if it was only 4.0am. I could see God at work in everything we were involved with and during that afternoon we were given the sad news that one of the residents Rapheal Parez had been confirmed of having AIDS. Rego who was one of the workers brought Raphael to our apartment for prayer and Rego anointed him with oil. We all placed our hands on Rapheal and I spoke in tongues. Rego translated in Spanish for Raphael and then I shared what God had given to me. "I am the Lord your God who heals thee, the ground you are standing on is Holy ground" I could feel the heat coming up from the souls of my feet and I shared this feeling with Archie, Brian, Rego and Raphael. I was then led by God to open my bible and guided by the Holy Spirit to Malachi 4:2, "But for you who revere my name, the sun of righteousness will rise with healing in its wings. And you will go out and leap like calves released from the stall". I knew that we had a God of miracles and that nothing was impossible for those who believed. Rapheal left our apartment that night with bounce in his step and a smile on his face. When we got up for breakfast the following morning the first person we met was Rapheal who still had a big smile running across his face, this was God at work and it was a good start to our day.

We decided to have a short break half way through our stay to break up the time for us. I had made friends with some Christians who lived in South Carolina and I wrote to them to see if we could make a visit. We were all looking forward to the break, then we received a telephone call from Bob and Frankie Tiedaman inviting the four of us to stay with them between the 8th and 10th of May. We made arrangements to hire a car from that date until the time came for us to return back to England. Bob and Frankie were members of a fellowship group called "Liberty Ministries" and the Pastor was called Roy Porter who was married to Jeanette. We had met them in England a few years before when Jan and I put up the entire fellowship group for the night. We had a great time of fellowship with them and I was looking forward to meeting up with them again.

I started to get home sick and in many ways I felt at times that I was back in prison but realised that I had come to serve God and must not look at things that way. I think that the devil was having a go at me when I was feeling a bit weary. I prayed that God would make it possible for Jan to come to America and I told God that I did not like to be separated from her and our children. I always felt better when I had poured out my heart to God because God knew what was on my heart before I brought it to Him in prayer.

After we had been at The Bridge for three weeks we decided to take a day off and go to Daytona Beach. Both Brian and I were missing our wives and children and it was good for the four of us to relax. We spent the day fishing from the pier and sun bathing, having a laugh about the fish I caught that was swallowed up by a Pelican after the fish had bit me causing me to drop it whilst taking out the hook. One of the locals joked that this Pelican sat on the pier all day waiting for that to happen so it did not have to do any fishing for itself. We returned to The Bridge refreshed and ready to carry on with our mission. I went to bed early and played the Christian music tape that Michelle had given to me on our mission to Romania. I was wishing that I was with them and said a prayer for Brian, Archie and David who were also missing loved ones in different ways. The following morning I telephoned Jan who informed me that no-one from our church had been to see her. This hurt me very much and when I spoke with Brian he told me that Pam had not received any support from her church. We both prayed about the situation and we asked God to forgive our Pastors, elders and church members for the way they had neglected our wives who were all alone. I think what hurt me the most was that many members of my own church fellowship had promised to look in on Jan and I realised they were just empty promises. I tried to put angry thoughts to the back of my mind but I knew that God understood how Brian and I were both feeling.

Brian and I had been invited by B.G. to go into Orlando County Correction facility with him to give our testimonies. We were very surprised to find that it was very much like "Cell block H" from the television programme and full of female prisoners. We all praised God when six of the prisoners gave their lives to Jesus. We returned to The Bridge after having a hamburger and a cold drink with B.G. We then found that Tony Costantino the son of Frank had moved into our apartment. Tony had been to another Christian rehabilitation centre to receive help and now Frank was asking us to help Tony in any ways that we could. For all that Frank had done for us we were pleased to help and welcome Tony into our apartment. At night time I went for a drive and parked up near International Drive. I walked around watching couples walking arm in arm and I thought back to the time two years before when Jan and I were doing the same thing. I thought about all the times Jan had taken second place and I prayed that God would soon unite us together again. I arrived back at The Bridge at 10.00am and went straight to bed where I had a dream that I was holding Jan in my arms.

It was a great day for us all when the 7th May arrived and we picked up our hire car and set off for South Carolina over six hundred miles away. We set off at 6.00pm and as we left Orlando we could see the Space Shuttle take off leaving a large vapor trail behind as it soared into the sky. We must have been one hundred miles away and yet I could feel the excitement for those on board and also on the ground. We drove through the night and took it in turns to drive. The lights of the motels flashed by as we made our way to South Carolina. After a short time it started to rain very heavy but we continued through driving rain to meet our brothers and sisters. The miles went by very quickly and at 8.30pm we stopped at Shoney's restaurant for a meal that Archie paid for. We all felt good as we made our way through the night to Greenville, South Carolina. We arrived safely at 6.00am and after having two hours sleep in the car we went into the town centre to look around. Archie bought us all a silver dollar and I felt that this was the token we could give for all the people who completed six months in the rehabilitation centre we planned to open in England. The words on the coin that spoke to me were "In God We Trust" plus it was something that would link us with America. We then went to meet our hosts at Liberty Ministries where we were all made to feel at home. We sat up until the early hours of the morning sharing what God had been doing in all our lives for the past few years. Roy and Jeanette had enough room for all four of us to stay with them but it meant that Brian and I had to share a bed together. We both had a good laugh about this and when we went to sleep we had our backs to each other with a good gap between us. When we woke up in the morning we had our arms and legs around each other like a loving couple.

Arrangements had been made for all our brothers and sisters from Liberty Ministries to meet up with us all at 9.0am for breakfast. We went to a local restaurant to have a typical American breakfast. It was good to meet up with our American friends that we had first met over two years before when they had visited England. We shared about all the things we had been doing since we last met. After breakfast we were taken for a ride into the Blue Ridge Mountains and the border with North Carolina. The views were breath taking, when we arrived back at our host's home we were all ready to eat again. We had a great time of fellowship and the four of us were prayed for. Bob and Bill shared that I had a deep wound that God wanted to heal.

I knew that I had always blamed myself over the death of Mark and I sat down on the chair to be prayed for. Within a few minutes I found myself sobbing as the Lord opened up the wound that had been covered over. God was now healing me from within and I knew at last that God had removed the guilt once and for all. Roy asked me if I would lead the service at their church on the Sunday morning so I went to bed early to spend some time alone with my heavenly Father. I felt the presence of God so very near to me and I was led to pray for all the lost souls that everyone at church would know about.

On the Sunday morning I was up at 7.00am and after having a shower I spent some time with God and prayed for Him to fill me with the Holy Spirit and bless everything that was undertaken that day. The service went very well and it was good to listen to Brian, Archie and David share. After sharing my testimony God led me to ask everyone to write down two names on a piece of paper of people they knew who needed saving by our Lord. The sheet of paper was soon full of names and then I prayed over all the names and asked God to show each and every one of us what we could do to help the people we were praying for come to know Jesus. Roy asked for a free will offering to be given towards our work and we were blessed with a gift of $240. After diner we were invited by Bob and Frankie to speak at their church fifty miles away where again we were filled with the Holy Spirit to serve our Lord. I was led to pray for three people who needed a touch from our Lord and Roy's daughter Rhoda who had problems with her internal organs. I believed that God was answering my prayers because God wanted Rhoda fit and well to work for him with the orphans in the Dominican Republic.

On the Monday morning we had breakfast together and after we had prayed with our hosts we got ready to return to Orlando. We were all given a packed lunch including a gift for our wives and family. We were all overcome with the love and kindness we had been shown. It was our prayer that we would all meet again in England. We were then led by Roy and Bob to highway 395 where we made our way back to Orlando.

Chapter 26

"Accept him whose faith is weak, without passing judgement on disputable matters".

Romans 14 : 1

We arrived back at The Bridge at 9.15pm and we were met by lots of people who were happy to see us back. It was clear that lots of things had been going wrong while we were away. Two of the residents had done a runner after taking cocaine and two more residents had tested positive for drugs. I received a letter from Jan where she told me she had not seen anyone from church while I had been away and I felt hurt that my family had been neglected. Before we left for America many people had promised to look in on Jan and yet after six weeks she had not had one visitor.

I shared my feelings with Brian and asked him if he wanted Pam and his children to have a short holiday in Orlando during the last few weeks of our stay. Brian informed me that Pam was content to wait for him to return but I believed that God was going to make it possible for Jan to come to Orlando. Just before leaving for America I had undertaken a job where I had earned £2000 and I was prepared to use that money to give Jan and our children a holiday. I telephoned David Burgin and asked him if he could try and get three air tickets for Jan, Robert and Michelle to come to Orlando and I would repay him on my return to England.

It was back to the grindstone as Archie and I got up at 4.00am to cook breakfast for one hundred residents. I had prayed about Jan coming out for a holiday as I thought back to all the sacrifices my family had made. I did not believe it was wrong to want them with me and I felt that David Burgin understood how I felt. It was great news for me when Jan telephoned me to say that David had booked them on a flight for the 21st May for a three week stay. It was going to take all the money that I had to give them this holiday but I believed God would take care of all our needs for the future. I believed I had our Lord's blessing when David was able to obtain air tickets and insurance for £199 each. I was also able to book the same holiday bungalow that we had stayed in two years before when we had first come to visit The Bridge. I prayed that our young nephew Carl would also be able to come as he had lost his dad a few weeks before Mark had been killed and he had never really come to terms with it. Within a few hours I received another call from Jan to say Carl was also coming with her and our children.

I thanked God for answering my prayers and it felt like a big burden had been lifted from my shoulders. I felt sad that Pam and her children would not be coming out with Jan as I had offered to pay for their holiday as well. I knew that Brian was missing his family just as much as I was missing mine and I prayed that God would take away all his heartache. We carried on with our mission that we had come to The Bridge to undertake. I was upset to be told by David Burgin that Pam had telephoned him to say she was very upset that Jan was coming to America for a holiday. I spoke with Pam on the telephone and she was very angry accusing me of being selfish. As far as Pam was concerned if Brain could not have her company then I should not have Jan's company.

I thought about the times when we had lost our home, when we had been broken in at Adswood, when we had opened our home to prisoners, when we had given up our Christmas to help orphans in Romania, when we had given up our time to speak in churches to start The New Life Centre and when my family had done without because I had put other people before them. I went and shared with Brian about the situation and we prayed together. I believed that God was answering the prayer I had made to him five years before when I was still in prison. I had prayed for God to include Jan in his plans wherever I was sent in the world to serve him. I had made it clear from day one that if it was possible I would try and get my family out for a holiday during our three month stay at The Bridge. I was surprised that Brian had never told Pam that at first Jan was going to The Bridge for training until she changed her mind. Brian assured me that he would speak with Pam and let her know that nothing underhanded had taken place stating he was at peace knowing that

Jan was coming out. After praying about the situation we all felt better and carried on with the work we had to do.

The following day we decided to take a break from things, Archie decided to go for a round of golf as Brian, David and myself headed for Daytona Beach. We spent the day fishing and sun bathing and I enjoyed going for a swim with Brian. We all returned to The Bridge feeling more relaxed after a wonderful day out. It was good when the mail arrived with Archie receiving eight letters. I thanked God that people had responded to the telephone call I had made asking people from our church to write to Archie. I felt the happiness that Archie was feeling opening all his mail also for Brian who as usual had a sack full. I thanked God for the peace we had been given and as a team we were united.

On Wednesday 20th May it felt good to get up at 4.00am as this was my last day in the kitchen. I had always been confident about cooking food as I had lots of practice at home cooking plenty of meals. One of the greatest things about working in the kitchen was to witness the behaviour of our residents. After work Archie went for a round of golf while the rest of us went for a drive to Cocoa beach for a few hours sun bathing. I did not like this beach as much as Daytona but we could get a good view of Cape Kennedy Space Centre. When we arrived back at The Bridge Archie was waiting for us with a big smiling face. After we had cooked diner Frank came in to say "hello" as he had just returned from Russia. As I was getting ready for church B.G. came in and asked me to lead the service the following Wednesday as he was going to be away that day. We were also given two board games that Sugar had bought for us to take back to England.

Thursday morning I was up early in anticipation of Jan and the children coming out from England. After dropping Archie off at the golf course I went to the holiday bungalow to make sure it was ready for Jan's arrival. I then made my way to the airport to meet Jan, after trying to find the right terminal for half an hour I eventually found the right one. It was so good to see Jan and the children coming down the stairs at the airport and holding them in my arms again. I thanked God for bringing them safely to America. I got a big kiss from all the children and I could see the excitement on their faces being in Florida. After settling in at the holiday bungalow we went for a drive to the local shops to buy in some supplies. It felt good to be together again and it felt right for Jan and the children to be with me.

I moved into the holiday home with my family, Jan and I both felt sad for Brian and Pam that they were not together. Jan had brought some mail from England so we drove to The Bridge to deliver the mail. I carried on working through the programme at The Bridge learning everything that God wanted to teach me. I tried to make sure that having my family with me would not interfere with the work that I had to do. B.G. had made arrangements for Archie, Brian, David and myself to take a look at another Christian rehabilitation centre called Dunklin Memorial Camp where they had been helping people for over twenty five years. It would mean being away from my family for a couple of days because Dunklin was over one hundred and fifty miles away in the middle of the swamps. We would need to spend a few days learning how things were done plus meeting some of the staff. Frank's son Tony agreed to be our driver and take us to Dunklin.

The lads picked me up at 4.00am at our holiday home and we made our way to Dunklin. When we arrived it was a wonderful feeling to see what God had provided for people to get their lives together. It was at least a three hundred acre farm with various buildings scattered around the place. Buildings for sleeping in, eating in, working in, various workshops, offices and even guest quarters. In the two days we spent at Dunklin I learned so much about what God wanted me to do for the prisoners in England. This was where I learned that without the power of the Holy Spirit working in a person's life it would not be possible for anyone to have a new life. God made it very clear to me that if we wanted to succeed then we would have to trust in him completely.

I spent a lot of time with Micky Evans who had started the work over twenty five years ago. Dunklin had started in a small way and over the years had grown in size and stature. Some of the counsellors had overcome their own addiction problems and were now helping people do the same. It was clear to me that to be involved in this kind of ministry you needed people who had a real love and heart for those we would be trying to help. While we were present a young man had sneaked away to obtain some alcohol and had been caught by a member of staff. All the residents were present at a meeting as a decision was reached to ask the man to leave Dunklin.

I was a bit shocked by this decision as it would mean that this man would be returned to prison and serve a sentence of six years. It was explained to me that this man knew what the outcome would be if he took any drugs or alcohol whilst going through the programme at Dunklin. Even though Dunklin was fifteen miles from the nearest town some of the residents were prepared to make that long walk to satisfy the cravings of the flesh. Micky Evans gave us a lot of the material they had been using in their programme for us to use when we started our work back in England. We returned back to Orlando much the wiser and we thanked God for the hospitality we had been given and for all that we had learned.

Chapter 27

"You my brothers were called to be free. But do not use your freedom to indulge the sinful nature; rather serve one another in love".

Galatians 5 : 13

After spending three weeks with my family they returned back to England and I moved back to The Bridge with Brian, Archie and David. It was good for the four of us to be back together again as we started to prepare for our return back to England. I felt that we had learned a great deal during our time at The Bridge and wondered how long it would be before God provided us with our own facility back in England. We had made many friends while we had been in America. B.G. put on a party for us at the church just before we returned to England. It was hard for us to say goodbye because we had become very close to so many people.

I received a telephone call from Jan just before we were due to return to England to say that we had lost our appeal to turn the house in Offerton into a Christian rehabilitation centre. I felt like a boxer who had just been knocked down yet again. We took our frustrations to our Lord in prayer. We returned to England in June 1992 after being away from home for almost three months.

I had only been at home for a few hours when I started to read the mail that had accumulated whilst I had been away. The first letter that I read was from the Secretary of State concerning our appeal against the council's decision to refuse our planning application for the house in Offerton. As I read the letter I realised that Jan had made a mistake and that we had in fact won our appeal. I was very excited as I shouted to Jan that we had won. Jan had seen the word refuse and thought we had lost but it was a long letter explaining all about the appeal and the sentence stating we had won was contained at the end of the letter. It was a very exciting time for us all as I shared with everyone that we had won our appeal. The question now was if God would provide the means of buying the house owned by Steven Hough.

I spoke with Steven on the telephone and explained that we had won our appeal and would like to buy his house if the price was right. I was a bit shocked when we received a letter informing us that he wanted £120,000 for the house. When we did not receive any money to buy the house we took it as an indication from God that we were not to buy it. The newspapers got hold of the story that we had won our appeal and it made front page headlines. We continued to meet regularly for prayer and by chance David Burgin was informed about a big detached house that was for rent in Marple.

It had been used as a care home for elderly people and had planning permission for ten people. David and I went to look at the house and we both felt it was ideal for what we wanted to do. It was in its own grounds with large gardens and out building. We could see it had a great deal of potential. We spoke with the estate agents who informed us that some other people had made an offer for the building but if they dropped out we would be considered for taking over the lease of the property. From our point of view the building was ideal and it was purpose built for what we required. It was ready to move into and start our work if we could obtain the lease. We prayed about the situation and then a few days later we received a telephone call to say that the other people had dropped out and we could go in for the lease. We then received another telephone call informing us that some other people had offered £4,000 a year more than what we had agreed to pay but the owners were still prepared to let us have the lease for the price we had agreed if we could complete within two weeks.

The rent was £14,000 per year and the owners wanted £3,000 for fixtures and fittings. We were £5,000 short of what we needed and on the Sunday evening I asked my church to pray for £5,000. On the Tuesday morning the postman called to my house with the mail. The first letter I opened contained two cheques, one for £1,000 and the other for £4,000 giving the exact amount we had prayed for. They were building society cheques and it was impossible to find out who they were from. There was a card enclosed with the words from Jeremiah 29 : 11 "I know the plans I have for you, says the Lord, plans to give you hope and a future".

I knew that this was an answer to our prayer and God was giving us the go ahead for the house in Marple. We contacted the estate agents to say that we would be ready to complete within the time limit and we thanked God for providing for us. As we waited to complete the legal formalities God put it on my heart to hand over the leadership of Stockport Prison Fellowship to Brian Griffiths so that I could concentrate on The New Life Centre. I had no sooner handed over the leadership to Brian when I received an invitation to be part of a live program called "This is the day" that was going out live from Onlee prison during prisoners week. It was an opportunity to share my faith with hundreds of thousands of people live on the B.B.C. and I felt God working in my life in a special way.

The day before I appeared live on the B.B.C. I was handed the keys to our first New Life Centre at Marple. It was November 1992 and at long last we had the keys to our first residential facility. I was able to share with everyone on live T.V. why our country needed a facility like The New Life Centre. The house was known as "Ivydene" but I knew that the name for our first house had to be " Proctor House" in memory of Noel's wife Norma who had died of cancer a short time before and also Noel Proctor who had led me to Jesus Christ.

In America the facilities that we had been to see helped prisoners who had committed crimes due to their addiction to drugs and alcohol and we believed that Proctor House would be a similar facility. We put in our planning application to turn Proctor House into a "Christian counselling and residential rehabilitation centre" for up to ten residents. We met with the same opposition that we had suffered in Offerton but we knew that this time the council would not be able to refuse our planning application in light of the victory we had won in Offerton. This time the opposition was more intense and some councilors tried to use our application for political purposes. I found that my name was in many newspapers and even the Bishop of Stockport came under a lot of fire as did Noel Proctor. I was still referred to as an "Ex-con" and all my past was being raked up by the media and local residents opposed to our plans.

The social services came on the scene and informed us that we would require their approval before we could work with people who had a past or present dependency on drugs or alcohol. At the same time we met with a Christian called David Linnington who had a heart for addicts and we felt that he would be the ideal person to be house manager and in charge of the counselling. In December 1992 I took on the position of executive director on a salary of £15,000 per year and David Linnington was appointed house manager on the same salary. As I concentrated on our planning application and social services registration David Linnington started to train up Christians who felt they were being called to be Christian counsellors for those with addiction problems.

I soon became aware that we were meeting a lot of unfair opposition from those in authority and that many underhanded things were taking place. The so called "independent inspection unit" belonging to the social services were supposed to help us with our registration but in fact they were looking for anything they could find to refuse our registration. In March 1993 we were refused registration by the councilors who sat on the social services committee. We had seen a letter that had been circulated by the Tory party stating that they would close our centre down using any means that they could. The reason that they had given for refusing our registration was that David Linnington was not a proper and fit person to be Manager of Proctor House. This was because David had not managed a care home before even though he had been recommended by the director of social services in Lancashire.

It was clear to me that the councilors realised that they could not stop us on planning grounds so they were going to use the social services as a means of stopping our work. We decided to appeal against their decision and a few weeks later we attended an appeal hearing with our solicitor. It was a newspaper reporter who telephoned me to inform me that we had lost our appeal even though we were informed that the appeal hearing was private and confidential. They had now included me as another reason for refusing our registration saying I was an unfit person because of my past criminal convictions. The fact that someone connected with that appeal hearing had leaked the outcome to the press confirmed that we were dealing with people who had very little integrity. David Linnington suggested that we call a meeting of all concerned to decide on the way forward. At this meeting it was decided that I should step down as executive director and David Linnington take over the running of Proctor House. We had taken legal advice about appealing against the social services committee but our advice was that it would be better if I was not included on any application form for registration. From all the people present only my wife was in favour of appealing.

In many ways I felt that what we were doing was not right because if I was not considered a fit person because of my past crimes it would make a mockery of what we were all about. It was clear that worldly people did not understand about New Life in Jesus Christ and if we did not make a stand for what we believed in then who would. I had received a gift of £5,000 from my Christian brother in Switzerland that I handed over to The New Life Centre to help pay our wages. After the decision was made for me to stand down I went and signed on as unemployed to save The New Life Centre from paying me any wages. David Linnington started to deal with the social services to see if he could obtain registration.

I concentrated on the New Life Ministry with Ian Reynolds who had a vision of making music tapes with testimonies. We made our first tape with Ian's music on one side with my testimony on the other containing a challenge from Noel Proctor to become a Christian. We had hoped to sell five hundred tapes to break even but we only managed to sell three hundred. We had hoped that profits we made would help The New Life Centre to continue but at least some people would hear the gospel message of New Life in Jesus Christ. In April 1993 God put it on my heart to return to Romania with some more aid. At the same time it was an opportunity to gather my thoughts concerning Proctor House.

It was good to meet up with Renato again and to see the children at Pestianna orphanage. We had a successful mission and we returned to England after being away for two weeks. I was not surprised to find that David Linnington had got no further in trying to obtain our registration. It was clear to me that God was not opening the door for us to be an addiction treatment centre and money had stopped coming in for us to pay our way. For the very first time we found ourselves without money to pay important bills. We had a meeting where we decided not to continue with our plans for social services registration. David Linnington resigned stating that he would not work with us if I was involved with the work. We decided to go back to the start of the vision and work with ex-prisoners who were leaving prison. It was clear that the social services could not prevent us from working with people who did not have a drug or alcohol dependency problem. A few days later David Linnington and Ian Reynolds sent out letters attacking me that contained many hurtful comments, I took it to God in prayer.

Chapter 28

"Trust in the Lord with all your heart and lean not on your own understanding"

Proverbs 3 : 5

In June 1993 it looked like we were going to lose Proctor House because we had no money in the bank to pay the rent. We all believed we were back on the right track by not proceeding as a rehabilitation centre for addicts but we needed God to undertake a miracle for us to pay the rent. I carried on working at Proctor House in faith and Jan had started a paid job making rubber stamps to help out with our finances. Jan had hoped to save up for our silver wedding anniversary due in February 1994 but all her wages were being used just to pay our way. It was a time when I felt that we had been left all alone and that other Christians were standing by watching us go under.

The day that the rent was due I woke up at 3.00am and I drove to Proctor House to spend time in prayer, expecting a miracle from God. I poured my heart out to God telling him how I felt with all the battles we had gone through in trying to open Proctor House. I knew that God had seen everything that had taken place and if we had made any mistakes we had made them without knowing. After pleading with God to keep Proctor House open I then told God that if it was his plan to close Proctor House it was a decision that I would accept. I loved God enough and knew enough about God to know that His way would always be the best way and I wanted to be in His will. I watched the postman walk towards the front door and push the letters through the letter box. I caught the letters before they hit the floor and took them into my office. I opened the letters and one of them contained a cheque. As I folded the cheque back to read it I was praying that it would be enough to pay our rent. It was only a cheque to pay for some New Life challenge tapes and at that moment I thought that the miracle I had prayed for was not to be.

It was at that moment that I decided to start back at work and try to pick up the pieces of my own life. I knew that I had neglected my family on more than one occasion and maybe God wanted me to concentrate on them. I had no sooner thought about starting back in work when the telephone rang and I was offered a small building contact at Thornton near Blackpool. It was for about five weeks work but I would earn about £2,500 profit when it was finished. The only problem was the money I needed to start the job and I prayed that God would supply for our needs. I walked away from Proctor House knowing that I had done everything in my power to keep it open. If God wanted a Christian rehabilitation centre in Stockport then only God could work everything out. I felt very sad as I closed the door but maybe God had better things in store.

Two days after closing the doors to Proctor House I received a telephone call from Archie who was desperate to find accommodation for a young lad called Paul who had just given his life to Jesus Christ. Paul had been sleeping rough on the streets of Manchester and he needed the help that The New Life Centre was started for. Even though we did not have the rent money for Proctor House I knew that David Burgin and I had given a personal guarantee for the rent so the owners would expect us to pay the rent even if The New Life Centre had no money. I made a quick prayer to God and felt it was right to tell Archie he could take Paul to Proctor House on condition that Archie moved in with him.

I had made a commitment to start the building contract at Thornton so it was not possible for me to help in any way. As Archie and Paul moved into Proctor House I started my work at Thornton, then Archie telephoned to inform me he now had three residents at Proctor House who had all been ex-prisoners. I believed that God was going to provide the means to keep Proctor House open because we had now started the work that The New Life Centre had been formed for. Paul and Paddy had been in and out of trouble with the police for many years and they both had very sad stories to tell about their lives from a very early age. I sent out a newsletter explaining that we could not pay our rent and taking our supporters through my last night at Proctor House. Archie had been living at Proctor House for a week and then he received a telephone call from my friend Cyril in Switzerland saying, "Tell Bob that the rent is on its way".

Cyril was a man of very few words but his actions spoke greatly about his love for God and compassion on those in need. Archie telephoned me to give me the good news and I cried tears of joy and praised God from deep within my heart. Everyone connected with the New Life Centre was happy to hear the good news that the rent was on its way. We all rejoiced in the knowledge that we had been provided for. I felt that in many ways we had been tested by God to see how we reacted under pressure and to make sure that we understood that The New Life Centre belonged to God. Many people had attacked me personally for trying to open Proctor House and even some Christians had attacked me unjustly for speaking what God had put on my heart. David Linnington and Ian Reynolds had written to many people telling them that I was an unhealthy driving force behind The New Life Centre and it was not of God. If anyone had any doubts about The New Life Centre being a vision from God they were now going to be cleared up. I had been very tempted to answer the unjust letters wrote by David and Ian but God had told me that he would deal with it and for me to remain silent.

In the midst of all that had been taking place I had a joy and peace in my heart that could have only been put there by God. I wrote to my Pastor and elders of my church asking them to lend me £1000 so that I could complete the building contract I had started at Thornton. They all agreed to lend me this money and I was handed a cheque for £1000. The following day I was given some letters by Archie that had been sent to Proctor House. One of the letters contained a cheque for £1000 made out in my name. The lady who sent the cheque told me that God had put it on her heart to send me the money and I could use it for myself or The New Life Centre. I decided to give the money to The New Life Centre because my own church had loaned me the £1000 that I needed. I knew I could repay my church when I had been paid for the work I was doing but for a short moment I was tempted to keep the money for my own needs. Over the next few days many of our supporters sent gifts and then we received the cheque from Cyril for almost £5,000. We had been sent enough money to pay the rent and all outstanding invoices. We now had about £2000 in the bank after paying our bills and for a short time the financial pressure was taken away.

Many of us were concerned for Archie and felt that he had been doing more than his fair share of work at Proctor House. Archie had a heart of gold and it was clear the residents were taking advantage of him. We agreed that we needed someone who had experience of running a residential facility and our chairman David Burgin shared about this couple he knew who had just returned from Spain. Roy and Brenda Taylor were very well known in and around the Stockport area and we all believed they were an answer to our prayers. They were prepared to work by faith and move into Proctor House to help get it up and running on a trial basis.

They had only been working at Proctor House for a few weeks when I made a visit during evening meal. Roy and Brenda were eating steak and our residents were eating sausages. This was the first time I had a very uneasy feeling in my spirit concerning Roy and Brenda and it was the first of many such feelings. Roy and Brenda brought in two friends of theirs to help at Proctor House called Cyril and Breeda and they confirmed that what was taking place was not of God. I had a confrontation with Roy where I rebuked him in the name of Jesus because of accusations he had made. I had found out that Roy had opened an illegal bank account in the name of The New Life Centre and he had taken in an alcoholic called Richard who was still drinking. From what I had learned in America I knew that Richard was not getting the expert help he needed and that we were in danger of having a tragedy on our hands if drastic action was not taken. I wrote letters and called an emergency meeting of the Governors to ask them to dismiss Roy and Brenda before we had a serious incident take place. My views were backed up by two very experienced counsellors in the area of addictions.

My letters were not acted upon because I turned up at the meeting to find it had been cancelled by other Governors who had been taken in by Roy and Brenda. The fears that I had listed in my letter became a reality when Richard almost died due to drinking large quantities of vodka. It was only the quick thinking of Cyril and Breeda that saved his life by calling for an emergency ambulance. It was a few days before I found out what had taken place and I informed David Burgin that if he did not use his powers to dismiss Roy and Brenda from all responsibility at Proctor House that I would resign from The New Life Centre.

Jan agreed that I could move into Proctor House for a short period to get it up and running and install some discipline. Roy had put Richard out on the streets before I moved into Proctor House. It was agreed that Roy and Brenda could stay on for a short period of time while the house they were buying was completed. I found myself under attack again as Roy and Brenda wrote letters to all the Governors that contained many untrue statements. I asked David Burgin to find out why Roy and Brenda had left Spain and word came back that left many of the Governors speechless. Everything that I had felt in my spirit had been confirmed by other people but I felt sad that people who professed to be Christians could behave in such a way. The fact that they were involved in starting a new church in Marple left me with some very unhappy thoughts.

It was confirmed at the next Governors meeting that I would take over the running of Proctor House without pay until we found the right person to take over. I tried to find out where Richard had gone to see if he wanted to come back to Proctor House and receive the help that he needed. I then received a telephone call from his dad informing me that Richard had been found dead in a hostel in Manchester. It was a very sad time for us all and in many ways I felt that I had been prevented by Roy from helping Richard when he was a resident at Proctor House. This was something that I would have to leave with God. It was only a short time later that Roy and Brenda made front page headlines for smuggling their dog through customs where they were fined £500 and had to pay court costs. This affected one of our residents in a bad way who had been attending their church. Bill felt betrayed as he had put a great deal of trust in Roy and Brenda. I explained to him that we are all capable of letting Jesus down and that is why we must look to Jesus and not mankind.

In my walk with Jesus I had been hurt more by Christians than any other people and yet God was teaching me how to forgive and to keep my eyes on Jesus. I started to put into place the programme that I had learned in America and I felt that at last we were getting somewhere. I missed not being at home with my family and I prayed that God would provide the right person to manage Proctor House. Paul and Paddy realised that they could not get away with the things that they had in the past as I started to challenge them about their behaviour.

Bill was a real asset to me and he had spent twenty seven years of his life in and out of prison. Thomas another of our residents was brought to Proctor House after other Christians had found him sleeping rough on the streets of Stockport. I was not sure about taking Thomas in because he was drunk but God put it on my heart to take him in. I wondered what the social services inspector would have done if he had found out about me taking Thomas in but realised that if we were ever taken to court I could plead guilty to being a Christian. I realised that I had to try and be like Jesus if I was to make progress at Proctor House. Jesus had all the qualities that I needed but I knew that in many ways I fell far short of my Lord. The comfort for me was that God was the potter and I was the clay.

For three nights running I sat up with Thomas, held his hands, prayed with him, cried with him as he went through withdrawal from the alcohol in his body. On the second night I tried to get a doctor to come out to see him because he was in a bad way but no doctor would respond to my call for help. It was at this moment of despair that God took over and helped Thomas through his withdrawal without any more discomfort. Once again I had left my building business and my family to help others overcome the problems in their own lives and I prayed that God would unite me with my family. I had prayed that Jan would move into Proctor House with me but I knew she was right not to bring our fourteen year old daughter Michelle into a situation with many young lads not much older than her.

By working at Proctor House I realised that it might not be a couple that we required but a single man who had many of the qualities of Jesus Christ. God had put it on my heart to return to Romania in time for Christmas and at the same time he reminded me of a man called Roger Paddock that I had met several months before. Roger had been introduced to me by a Christian brother called Joe Whelan who worked for the Langley House Trust. Roger also worked for the same trust but he was looking to work in a Christian rehabilitation centre, where he could use the gifts that he believed God had given to him. I telephoned Roger to see if he was still available and if he was prepared to come to a meeting with the board of Governors. When I had first met Roger it was over diner in the prison officer's mess at Strangeways prison with Noel Proctor and Joe Whelan present. At the time I was uneasy because Roger was single as we all believed we were looking for a married couple. I might have felt uneasy because I was eating a meal surrounded by people who were once my jailers but them only God can bring about situations like that. Now God was telling me that Roger was going to be the next Manager at Proctor House. It I was right and it was the will of God I would soon be back home with my family and also able to return to Romania in time for Christmas.

At our Governors meeting Roger came across as the person we were looking for and it was agreed that Roger be appointed as house manager on a three month trial period. This was good news for Jan and me because we could be together again and go to Romania. We decided to go to Romania with Robert and Michelle and use it as our family holiday. The money that we would have used going on holiday we decided to put towards the cost of making the journey. We had hoped to go at Christmas with other members from our church but Jan's boss would not let her have any extra time off over the Christmas period so we decided to go out earlier. We set off for Romania on the 29th October 1993 with our van loaded with medical supplies and food for the poor families of Romania. It was good to be back with Jan, Robert and Michelle and for the four of us to be going as a family.

Robert could not wait to get behind the wheel to drive the van and I let him drive on the motorway where it was easy for him to drive. We had to compromise over the music that we played because all our tastes in music were different. It was the prayer of Jan and I that our children would move close to God as we made our way to Romania. We made our first overnight stop at Gummersbach where we picked up over 1000 Romanian bibles. We were all very tired because we had travelled over eight hundred miles without a break and we were all thankful of a good night's sleep. We had breakfast in our van and then we continued on our way and arrived in Romania four days after leaving Stockport.

It was good to see our Romanian brothers and sisters again and we were made very welcome. We distributed the supplies that we had brought between lots of poor families. We knew that what we was doing spoke much about the love of our Lord Jesus Christ. After spending four days in Hateg it was time for us to return home so that Jan could be back in time for work. As we were leaving Hateg our exhaust pipe broke in two pieces and it sounded like a motor boat engine. After a quick prayer God gave me the wisdom to carry out a repair. We had a tin of fruit cocktail that Jan opened and I cut it into a tube to form sheet metal. I was able to wrap this around the broken pipe and secure it in place with two jubilee clips. We thanked God that it worked as we continued on our way back to England.

Chapter 29

"I tell you the truth, anyone who has faith in me will do what I have been doing. He will do even greater things than these, because I am going to the Father"

John 14 : 12

We had almost reached Trier when Jan noticed that the rear wheel was red hot. I had thought the smell of burning rubber was coming from the diesel pump and was ready to drive on. We were thankful for the man at the filling station who could speak English as we telephoned for the German equivalent of our A.A. Within an hour the A.D.A.C. had arrived and found the wheel bearing had seized up and cut into the rear axle. We had taken out five star insurance with the A.A. before we left for Romania and now we were thankful for our Pastor who had paid this for us. When the breakdown truck arrived he placed our van on his truck and then demanded six hundred German Marks from us (£200). We did not have that amount of money left and I tried to explain that the A.A. would pay for all our costs incurred through our breakdown insurance. It started to turn into an ugly incident and I made a telephone call to John Miles in England to ask him to pray for us. I had to call out the police because at one stage the breakdown truck driver started to drive away with our van leaving us behind at the filling station on the motorway.

After the police had arrived an agreement was reached for us to travel with our van to this man's garage where we could contact the A.A. and sort out how he would be paid. The A.A. in England was fantastic and even though it was Sunday they were able to provide the help that we needed. We were put up in a hotel for the night whilst arrangements were made to hire us a mini bus to get us back to England. The A.A. had agreed to cover all the costs and arrange for our van to be taken back to England. We were able to continue on our way after a delay of about twenty four hours. We were thankful to God that we were all safe because the rear wheel could have broken off the axel at any moment. We were sad to leave our van behind and we prayed that Ian and Myra who had let us borrow their van would understand when we returned without it. It was good for us to be back in England where I telephoned Ian to give him the news about his van. We knew that God had prepared his heart for the news because of the calm way he accepted it. I telephoned some garages to get a rough estimate of what it would cost for the repairs and was shocked to find out that it would require a new back axle. It was going to cost over one thousand pounds for the van to be repaired and I was looking to God for this need. Jan started back at work and I continued to work at Proctor House and do any building jobs that came my way. After we had been home for a week I received a telephone call to say Ian's van was on its way back to Stockport. I asked for the van to be taken to Proctor House so that it could be repaired on the large car park.

It was God who gave me the ability to undertake the repairs with the help of a mobile mechanic. I was able to obtain a rear axle from a scrap dealer near Sheffield from a van that had been involved in an accident. It was as good as new and within a few days the repairs had been undertaken for a total outlay of £300. Included in this price was a full service for the van and I returned it to Ian and Myra in first class condition. I think they were impressed with what was done because they both agreed that the van could be used to make another journey to Romania in December when other members from our church would be going.

Our life was very full and there was never a dull moment. With Roger Paddock starting work at Proctor House it gave me the opportunity to take a break from everything and spend some time with my family. In many ways I felt that I was at burn out stage and I knew that I also needed to spend more time with God as well as my family. I wanted to serve my Lord Jesus with all my heart and yet I knew that I did not have the support from within my own church to do so. I had neglected my business to concentrate on the vision of The New Life Centre and my wife had been the bread winner for almost a year. It was our silver wedding anniversary on the 1st February 1994 and if it was not for Jan working we would not have been able to plan a holiday.

Just before Christmas 1993 I received a letter from our dear friend Cyril in Switzerland with a gift of £2000 to use on replacing my van and £1000 for Jan to use on anything that she wanted. I could not wait to meet Jan at work to tell her the good news. We had only prayed a few days before for the means to replace my Sherpa van and to be able to give our children a nice Christmas. Jan had been informed by her boss that she would lose her Christmas bonus for good time keeping because she had half a day off work in the last year. This was the day that Jan had finished work at dinner time so that we could catch the ferry to France while it was still light as we took aid to Romania. It made me realise that we could never out give God. When I read the letter to Jan she burst into tears to think that someone cared enough about her to send her money. God spoke to my heart through this gift because I had been very upset with my own church for their lack of support. I felt God was telling me to keep my eyes on Him and not to look to anyone else. God had used our friends in Switzerland to meet our needs yet again and we thanked God for their loving support. I told Jan that she might have lost her Christmas bonus from her worldly employers but she had been given one from God that came with a blessing.

    I am sure that I would have given up with the vision of The New Life Centre many months before if it had not been for the handful of brothers and sisters who wrote letters of encouragement. Some of them contained personal gifts for Jan and I knowing that some of them had given out of the little that they had. Frank Costantino had warned me that it would be a hard road but I am not sure if Frank encountered the hard times that we had encountered. It was the thought of Jesus suffering on the cross for me and the rest of mankind that helped me to keep going. I had this vision for a real live church in Adswood where we lived that would not leave my mind. Every day I passed people that were heading towards hell and my heart cried out to God for them. Jan had become upset with the work I was involved with and I'm sure that it was because she could see paid leaders of God doing very little to extend the kingdom of God. Jan had witnessed the opposition that I had suffered and I could feel Jan hardening towards God's church. I could also feel my own heart hardening and I prayed that God would forgive us and give us a heart like his own.

    We tried to involve the four local churches in Adswood in starting a youth work and a Sunday night service aimed at reaching out to all the lost sheep. We had eight people turn up at our first meeting who agreed that none of the local churches were meeting the needs of the local people. Not one church was prepared to let its building be used for a Christian youth club or a Sunday evening service to reach the lost sheep. My experience at Larkhill Baptist church had taught me a very valuable lesson. I knew it was a waste of time trying to change a church set in its ways and it would be easier planting a new church. I wanted to be more like Jesus but in many ways I found I soon lost patience with other Christians who tried to stop the work of the Holy Spirit.

As I spent time with God in prayer I could see where the church of God was going wrong. Many Christians were content to live a quiet life and stay in shallow water. I had met many church leaders who could quote from the word of God but I had not met many who lived by what they preached. If the church leaders were not setting an example it was clear that the church members would not grow as they should. My own church leaders were planning a building extension when most of our church members wanted to be involved in planting a church. God had made it very clear on the way forward but our church leaders were being blinded by worldly passions.

It was good for Jan and I to have a two week holiday for our silver wedding anniversary but for a while I questioned if it was right for us to go with all the poverty we had witnessed in Romania. The fact that we had received that gift from Cyril convinced me that we had God's blessing to go. We arrived in Tenerife on the 29th January 1994 and on the 1st February I was able to take Jan for a candle light dinner at a restaurant overlooking the beach where we celebrated our twenty five years of married life together. We both exchanged rings that we had bought for each other and I thanked God for giving me such a loving wife. Two days later Jan became very ill and I had to telephone for an emergency doctor. It was confirmed that Jan had two burst ear drums through some infection causing a great deal of pain. We both prayed for God's healing touch and although Jan's hearing did not get any better God gave her the grace to cope with the pain and discomfort. We also had to put up with our apartment that had very little furniture and overlooked a very noisy building site. It was during our holiday to Tenerife that I received a vision concerning my own church.

It concerned a shepherd who had lots of sheep in his care. The shepherd was not able to notice the sick sheep in his care but he had decided to build his sheep pen bigger so that he could put more sheep in it. When he had done this more sick sheep came in and this resulted in most of the sick sheep dying. I was then given another vision of a shepherd who decided to build another sheep pen and put another shepherd in charge of this sheep pen. The first shepherd then placed some of his strong sheep with this new shepherd so that the first shepherd could spend more time looking after the sick sheep. The new shepherd was able to take in sick sheep that had been waiting to come into the sheep pen and both shepherds worked together to look after the sheep in their care.

I prayed that God would give this vision to someone else in our church so that I was not the one to speak out. When we returned from Tenerife I waited for someone to share this word with our church. After we had been back for two weeks I was convicted by God to share this vision during open worship. I informed the congregation that another person had been given this vision to share but this person had not been faithful to God. I asked that if this other person was present that they would make themselves known. I knew that what I shared would not go down well with my Pastor or church leaders who had made up their minds on what they were going to do. Never the less I was faithful to share the vision that God had given to me.

At The New Life Centre things started to go wrong with Roger our house manager. I had been popping in and out and I had noticed a few things about Roger that did not make me feel very happy. At the same time our financial situation had started to get worse as we found ourselves with a cash flow problem. We had four residents at this time and they all shared they were not happy with Roger. It was decided that we would have no alternative but to make Roger redundant and let our residents take on the responsibility of running their own home with lots of support from the volunteers. One of our residents called Don wanted to take on responsibility as house group leader with the backing of our other residents. We agreed to give it a trial period to see how things worked out.

At first things seemed to be working out well and our volunteer counsellors continued to work with our residents on a regular basis. From a financial point of view we had never more than we needed but now we were in a bad way. This was when I was given the vision to open a charity shop and after praying with Jan we both agreed that it could help keep Proctor House open. Jan was willing to work in the shop as a volunteer if we opened one. Jan had to have an operation on her ears and while she was off work sick she was sacked. I shared the vision with the Governors at a meeting and everyone agreed that it could be good for The New Life Centre. We prayed about the vision and started to look for a shop in the Stockport area. When we called to see Jan's sister in Thornton Cleveleys we shared our vision with her. To our surprise Carol shared that she wanted to give up the lease on her shop and that if we wanted it we could have the lease for nothing and all the shop fittings. The fact that Carol could not make a profit in her shop did not put us off and we believed that this was the shop that God had prepared for us to start our first charity shop. At about the same time we were given an invitation to spend some time at a Carmelite Monastery in North Wales. The sisters had collected some goods for us to sell in our charity shop and we were invited to stay overnight.

We used this time to seek confirmation concerning the charity shop. The first book I picked up out of the book case to read was containing information about a charity that had hundreds of charity shops to support its ministry. First thing was to find a house for Jan to rent in Cleveleys and within one day of looking she had found a house that was suitable. It was a house that had been completely refurbished and everything in it was new. This would mean that Jan and I would be separated as Michelle wanted to finish her schooling and take her exams. I had started up my building business again dividing my time with working at Proctor House and working with the youth in Adswood. We decided that we would give it a year to see how things worked out. I was not in a position to support Jan in Cleveleys and she was able to make a claim for income support including housing benefits. Michelle was able to spend her holidays and weekends with her mother with the rest of the time living with me. I wanted to be able to support Jan in Cleveleys but only time would tell if I was going to be in a position to do so. At about the same time Jan moved to Cleveleys I had to move back to Proctor House as we were concerned at the way things were going. One of our residents had brought cannabis into the house and this was something we could not tolerate.

Chapter 30

> *"See I am setting before you today a blessing and a curse, the blessing if you obey the commands of the Lord your God that I am giving you today; the curse if you disobey the commands of the Lord your God and turn from the way that I command you today by following other Gods, which you have not known"*
>
> Deuteronomy 11 : 26 - 28

Our eldest daughter Donna had moved back with me with her two children as she was not happy where she lived in Manchester. Donna agreed to look after Michelle whilst I moved into Proctor House knowing that I was only a fifteen minute drive away if I was needed. Within a few days of moving into Proctor House I could sense that something was not right. I believed that one of our residents was doing something wrong with the money and I tried to find something that would give me the proof that I needed. The same resident had a love bite on his neck and I knew that no females had been around so that led me to believe that something of a homosexual nature was taking place between some of our residents. Archie had also moved back into Proctor House with me and we shared a room together on the ground floor.

    I was able to spend my weekends at Cleveleys with Jan and during the week live in at proctor House. We had made plans to have a family holiday in Cornwall on the 9th July and this was something we were all looking forward to. I would take my grandchildren Steven and Melissa with me every other weekend to Cleveleys and Michelle when she wanted to go. Michelle was courting a young lad called John so she spent most of her spare time staying at the home of John's grandmother. My own Pastor called me into his office to tell me that he was unhappy about one of the newsletters I had sent out where I shared that we had received no support from within our own church. I told my Pastor that I was sorry if what I had written hurt him but my letter was the truth. Not long after this meeting I had another meeting with my Pastor where he agreed to back a church plant in Adswood. At long last I felt that the vision that God had given to me would come about but we still had a long way to go.

John and Elizabeth Miles had been a real encouragement to me and they had spent much time in prayer over the meeting I had with my Pastor. I felt like a boxer who was being attacked from all sides and yet none of the blows were hurting me. I knew that God had put a shield around me and felt that I was being given divine insight into many things. Just before we were to go on our family holiday to Cornwall three of our residents were arrested on suspicion of shop lifting in the local supermarket. They were all protesting that a mistake had been made but I had witnessed with my own eyes the trolley full of food being unloaded at Proctor House. They had filled the trolley up with food that they paid for and then went back round with another trolley filling it with the same items. I shared with our counsellor Irene Walker what I had witnessed and that I was convinced that other serious things were taking place. I used the opportunity whilst our residents were in the police station to search their bedrooms inch by inch. Even though the police had searched their bedrooms and found nothing I was convicted by God that I would find something. I was only searching for a few moments when I found the evidence I was looking for. One of our residents had opened a bank account in the name of The New Life Centre and he had been paying in cheques sent in by our supporters and also housing benefit cheques. The amount paid in was almost £2000 and I knew that I had to inform the police. At the same time I informed the police that the three of them could not use Proctor House as a bail address.

The following day I met with Ron who had made a full confession to the police about the things he had done. Ron explained about his gambling problem and asked for forgiveness. I was able to forgive him but I told him that he would have to face up to the things he had done. I was not prepared for him to live at Proctor House until I had returned from Cornwall and had met up with the other Governors. While I was on holiday the other Governors had a meeting and decided that the three of them could return to Proctor House on a trial period. Archie had moved in to supervise them but I knew that it was not a good decision. On my return from holiday we had a Governors meeting to decide on the way forward.

We had been praying about the money for the down payment for the charity shop because we had to find six months rent in advance. At the same time we wanted to employ Irene Walker on a part time basis. I represented The New Life Centre at a rent appeal tribunal that God had put on my heart to fight for. We won the appeal and our rent was increased from £61 per week to £85 per week for each resident in our care. I was informed that this would be back dated from the date we took in our first resident and we received a cheque for over £4000 in back payment. I took this as a sign from God that we were to open our charity shop. It would also be possible to employ Irene on a part time basis.

At about this time I found myself having a bet again and I believed that God did not want me to gamble. It would be easy to make excuses and say that it was because of all the pressure that I had been under but I knew that it was an evil desire of my flesh. I knew that I did not want to gamble because when I did have a bet I felt bad about it afterwards knowing what God had done for me. I asked my Christian friends to pray for me to overcome the desires of my flesh and for God to give me the strength that I needed.

When I was given the vision for The New Life Centre God gave me the wisdom to set up the charity so that I was never in a position to obtain any monies from any of our bank accounts. I was very upset when Brian and Pam started to have doubts about my honesty. It hurt me very deeply because of all that my family and I had given up to help bring about the vision of The New Life Centre. The following night I was unable to go into our healing service meeting at Proctor House until this issue had been resolved with Brian and Pam. I asked Irene to come into the kitchen with Brian, Pam and myself where I asked everyone to speak the truth in love.

I think that what had been taking place at Proctor House had affected everyone to some extent. I think that in some ways Brian and Pam had been taken in by our residents who had stolen money believing that I would be capable of doing the same things. I explained that it would be wrong for us to stop trusting in people because of the failings of a few. I asked Brian to pray about the things he had said to me because I did not believe they were of God. It was a meeting where Jesus Christ was present because we all spoke the things that had been on our hearts and at the end of the meeting we were able to hug and forgive each other for anything we had done to hurt one and other.

Chapter 31

"If we deliberately keep on sinning after we have received the knowledge of the truth, no sacrifice for sins is left, but only a fearful expectation of judgement and of raging fire that will consume the enemies of God"

Hebrews 10 : 26 - 27

I was now fully aware that for the time being at least I would have to be a "tent maker" just like St. Paul. Jan and I decided that it would be better for me to start my building business back up in the hope that it would bring in the income we needed to support our family. By working for myself I would be able to have the time off that was needed to work at Proctor House and anything else that God wanted me to do. I knew that God knew what was on my heart and I trusted that God would give me what he wanted me to have. Things were working out very well with Jan at Cleveleys also with me living at our council house in Adswood plus Proctor House. Donna then informed me that she wanted to move into a council flat she had been offered in Adswood so this meant I had to move back home with Michelle to look after her. I was very concerned about the way things were at Proctor House and at a management meeting it was decided that Ron should be asked to leave. Irene and I were to break the news to Ron but we believed that he already knew.

    We decided to leave speaking with Ron until the following day and before the meeting I had to travel to Leicester prison to interview a prisoner who had requested to reside at Proctor House. When I arrived back at Stockport it was time to meet with Ron. It was at this meeting that we found out about the homosexuality that had been taking place between some of our resident. One of our younger residents had been selling his body for money so that he could buy drugs. Ron and George had been tempted by Steven to give him money for the use of his body. Steven was twenty one and yet he only looked like a fourteen year old boy. It was at this meeting that we also found out that George had just served a five year prison sentence for having unlawful sex with young boys. Steven had been blackmailing Ron to give him money and this played a big part in why Ron was stealing money. Everything that had been happening in the dark had now been brought into the light and Ron broke down in tears and asked God to forgive him for everything that he had done. Irene and I decided to confront Steven and George about what had been taking place to see what their reaction would be. Both of them said that they wanted to repent and receive help for the problems that they had.

Irene shared the words from Hebrews 10 as a warning to them not to do the things that they had been doing. The following day Steven and George spent time with their counsellors. After their sessions were over George asked me if he could take Steven with him to the public telephone box down the road as George wanted to speak with his family. I was sat on the rear steps eating a round of toast and drinking a cup of coffee. I said it was alright for George to take Steven with him and carried on eating my toast. This was when Harold came up to me and said that he felt that God was telling him to read Ephesians 6 : 10 - 20 to me. I sat very still as I listened to Harold read from God's word to me. As Harold read verse 12 the Spirit of God within me told me that George and Steven had gone to use the telephone to order drugs from a drug dealer. I waited for Harold to finish reading and I told him that I had to go right away. I got into my van and drove to where the telephone box was situated. If I was right it would be Steven with the telephone in his hand and not George.

Sure enough when I arrived at the telephone box it was Steven holding the phone. I was surprised that they did not hear my van approaching them because it had a very noisy diesel engine. Even when I stopped my van and walked up to the telephone box they did not see me. It was like I was invisible as I put my ears to the glass panel to listen to what Steven was saying. It was very clear that Steven was ordering his drugs supply and asked George where they were going to pick them up. They were both shocked as I opened the door and I told them that they could not keep anything hidden from God. I knew that they had to leave Proctor House and I told them both to return, pack their bags and leave. They both returned to

Proctor House and tried to convince Irene and Pam that I had wrongly accused them of something they had not done. For a few moments I think Irene and Pam were half convinced that I had got it wrong. This was when Irene asked Steven to let her speak to the person he had just been speaking with. I thanked God when Steven confirmed that I was right and that George let him make the call for drugs so that he would continue to have sex with him.

Chapter 32

"Blessed are the merciful, for they will be shown mercy"

Matthew 5 : 7

The months that followed at proctor house were very turbulent with many new residents coming in search of a new life. In the winter of 1994 we met with some people who worked with the homeless in Manchester at a night shelter. On the face of it they seemed to be very caring people and they told us that the council was forcing them to close the night shelter putting fifty more people back onto the streets of the city. Since opening Proctor House we had never run at full capacity and at a Governors meeting we decided to open the doors wider and take in homeless people direct from the streets. As we were short of workers we asked the people we had met in Manchester if they would like to run Proctor House with their staff and volunteers under the authority of our board of Governors.

Within a few days Proctor House was a hive of activity with every bed full and lots of workers helping with the work. This allowed me to move to Cleveleys on a permanent basis to be with Jan as Michelle had decided to leave home to live with her boyfriend's grandmother. I signed our council house in Adswood over to our son Robert and with mixed emotions made the move to Cleveleys. One part of me wanted to stay in Adswood to carry on working with the youth but I knew it was impossible without the support of other Christians. The charity shop at Cleveleys was doing very well and within a few months God had blessed Jan through all the hard work she had put in. The shop was full of donated items but it did not make a great deal of profit for the charity because of where it was situated. What it did do was bring in lots of good quality clothing for homeless people and poor people in Romania that we helped. We had that much donated clothing during Christmas 1994 that we decided to make another mission to Romania. Jan had been very busy sorting the donated clothing and packing it into boxes ready for going to Romania. We made our Christmas appeal for shoe boxes filled with goodies for children and we soon had enough goods to fill a twenty ton wagon.

It was amazing to see how God blessed our efforts and provided everything we needed yet again. On this mission we decided to send the aid overland with an experienced wagon driver so that we could fly to Romania and meet up with the aid when it arrived in Hateg. It was a very successful mission where we experienced the blessings of God on many occasions. This surely was what Christmas was all about as we shared the love of Jesus with our brothers and sisters in Romania in a very real way. We were able to bring joy into the lives of over 2000 people on this mission but we received back more than we ever gave. Much of the satisfaction came in knowing that all the donated aid was reaching the poor people and children it was meant for. As we waited on the railway platform for the overnight train to take us to Bucharest to catch our flight back to England I thanked God from my heart for the privilege of being part of this mission. I did wonder why people were so willing to give to our missions to Romania and yet very few people would give to our ministry at Proctor House.

The new year of 1995 had now started when Jan and I were told about a new church in Blackpool that had just opened who was working with all the homeless in Blackpool. We decided to take a look and it was good to see a lot of Christians working with those who had fallen upon bad times. We started to go along to the Monday night outreach at this church and within a few months we had started to attend the church services and house group at one of the elders house.

Jan and I both wanted to be part of a church that was caring and loving as Jesus taught us to be and for a short time we thought we had found that church. It just goes to show how first impressions are not always what they seem to be. Some of the elders had been influenced by attending a well known church in Florida and others had been influenced by what was happening in Toronto and Sunderland. We were open to whatever God wanted to do but we were not going to be part of anything that was manmade. I was asked to become an elder of the church and after praying about the offer I decided to accept knowing that I would be involved in the leadership and decisions that were made. At my first elders meeting I knew that the people I had joined were very much of the flesh. The way that they decided to dismiss an elder of the church was one of the most ungodly things I had ever experienced from people who professed to be Christians. I shared from the word of God how they should have been dealing with the situation and had it noted in the minutes that I could not be part of what was taking place. It was very clear that one family had overall control of the church and what they wanted would be what took place. Some of the elders owned hotels in the Blackpool area and they were exploiting some of the homeless people we were trying to help. Many of them had addiction problems and were receiving state benefits. This did not prevent some of the elders from employing them on a casual basis and giving them money to feed their addictions.

We were very sad to leave the church but had become very disappointed with many of the Christians we had met. We had become very dissatisfied with the church and we stopped attending church for quite a while. We carried on with the work that God had given us to do and it was a full life with never a dull moment. The staff we had taken on at proctor House soon proved to be wolves in sheep's clothing and we had to dismiss them for what they had been doing. False bank accounts had been opened in the name of our charity by one of the managers and fraudulent applications had been made too many charitable trusts using our charity number. Some of them had been sleeping with prostitutes they had taken in while pretending to help them. This was a time that I was beginning to lose heart with people who professed to be Christians. God did not leave us downhearted for long because at the same time we dismissed the management staff we met up with Janice and Barry who proved to be very real Christians.

They moved into proctor House and were thrown in at the deep end of things. We also had a clear out amongst the residents because over half of them were just using Proctor House as a doss house with no intention of doing anything about the problems in their lives. We were still finding it very hard to receive any help from the local churches in Marple even though we prayed constantly over this situation. Janice and Barry settled in very quickly and they put Jesus at the centre of all that took place. We were given an old caravan to start an outreach in Manchester. Our residents and staff worked hard in preparing the caravan ready for going out on the streets of Manchester to feed the homeless and share the love of Jesus in a practical way.

It was a blessing to see our residents helping out other people who were in the place where they had been only a short time before. We went into Chinatown in Manchester on a Sunday evening after our church service had finished until the early hours of Monday morning. It did not take long for us to build good relationships with the homeless community where we had the privilege of leading many men and women to Jesus Christ. For those who wanted the help we were able to take them back to Proctor House and give them the help and support that they needed. Most of the people that we helped had been in prison at some time in their lives and it was clear we were helping people that had been completely rejected by society. Because of the need that we had seen we decided to put a planning application in to the local council to extend Proctor House by nine more bedrooms. We were very excited about the prospect and I applied to lots of charitable trusts for grants towards the building costs. The plans were passed by the council without any objections from the local community and we praised God for this. The time was passing by very quickly as we helped lots of people through our ministry.

We decided to undertake another mission to Romania at Christmas 1995 because of all the donated goods that Jan had collected at the Charity shop. We also felt it would be a good experience for some of our residents to be involved with the mission. We left for Romania on the 19th December with a fully loaded twenty ton wagon plus two mini buses full of volunteers and residents from Proctor House. It was a very successful mission where we touched thousands of orphan children and poor families with the love of Jesus.

Chapter 33

"What good is it, my brothers, if a man claims to have faith but has no deeds?
Can such faith save him? Suppose a brother or sister is without clothes and daily food. If one of you says to him, "Go, I wish you well; keep warm and well fed," but does nothing about his physical needs, what good is it? In the same way, faith by itself, if it is not accompanied by action, is dead"

James 2: 14 - 17

Back in England we prayed about opening another hostel in Blackpool because of the growing homeless situation. It was February 1996 and we signed a three year lease for Springfield House in Blackpool that had previously been used as a guest house. It had eight separate bedrooms and at £10,000 per year in rent it seemed ideal for our work. Within a few days of signing for the lease we had taken in our first residents and the opposition from local hoteliers started. It was like the opposition we had experienced in Stockport when we first started out but this time it was more organized and vicious.

The social services at Stockport had started to take an interest in what was happening at Proctor House and they advised the social services at Blackpool to do the same. The housing benefits at Stockport without any reason reduced the amount of housing benefits we received from £85 per week to £49 per week putting us under severe financial pressure. We had been sending out newsletters to our supporters informing them of what was taking place and one Christian Brother who was a senior probation officer at Stockport was handing them to his superior who in turn was handing them to the social services inspection unit. In our newsletters we shared about the loving care that we gave to our residents but the social services and probation services were trying to make a case that what we was providing was personal care. This put me under a great deal of pressure because I found myself having to deal with attacks from every agency that we were dealing with. Not once did they offer any help or advice but it was clear they wanted to shut us down at all costs. It was hard enough trying to help the damaged people that we were taking in without having to defend ourselves against all the agencies that came against us. Blackpool council were put under pressure by the hoteliers to issue an enforcement order against us even though other hotels were providing homeless people with bed and breakfast accommodation without having any planning permission. We decided after much prayer that we would stand our ground and carry on with the mission we had been given to undertake.

Jan and I carried on at Springfield House trying to help the people we had taken in but we were coming under a great deal of pressure. Our daughter Michelle came to live with us at Springfield House because of problems she had living with her boyfriend's grandmother. We were pleased to have her back with us and we explained to her about our ministry with advice not to get involved with any of our residents. We had mixed sexes at Springfield House because of the number of females we had met crying out for help. It was a bad mistake because some of our residents started to form relationships with each other when we were not present. Our own daughter Michelle started to get over friendly with one of our residents Jason who was trying to overcome his addiction to drugs. We decided to close Proctor House for six weeks so that Janice and Barry could move to Blackpool to work with Jan and myself so we could work as a team. The idea of this was for both houses to have the same working timetable and house rules so that it did not matter where a resident lived as they would experience the same conditions in Blackpool and Stockport.

Janice and Barry had not been involved with running a hostel before and they were being taken advantage of by many of the residents. The people we were trying to help were very street wise and they were experts at getting their own way. The people we were taking in had been drug addicts, alcoholics, prostitutes, ex-prisoners and in care, some had been abused by family members. They all stated that they wanted a new life and were willing to turn away from their old way of life. Many of the people we helped we had met on our outreach work in Manchester and Blackpool. We had been donated a mini-bus and caravan by Ian and Myra Fallows so that we could reach out to people in need where we shared the love of Jesus in a very practical way. It was amazing how many opportunities we had to share the good news of Jesus Christ as many homeless people flocked to our caravan outreach for food and hot drinks. The need of what we were doing seemed to be great because some nights we would meet in excess of thirty people who were sleeping rough on the streets of Manchester and Blackpool.

We were desperate for more help and we placed an advertisement in local and national Christian magazines for volunteer workers to give up twelve months of their time and help us with the work. Janice and Barry were forced to give up working for The New Life Centre because Barry had a breakdown due to the pressure of the work. This put even more pressure on Jan and me who found ourselves on duty twenty four hours a day and seven days a week. The newsletters we sent out on a regular basis kept our supporters informed of our situation with a prayer list that was very long. Our residents had lots of problems to overcome in their own lives and the ongoing problems of the ministry seemed to be increasing.

It was during March of 1996 that we were joined by Frank and Kathleen who had been gifted with a wonderful healing ministry and had spent many years working at Ellel Grange. Christine Fontain who had been a member of our management committee had agreed to take over the running of Proctor House with the help of Nigel who was three years into his sobriety. Things seemed to be coming together as we prayed to God for direction and to help us find a loving church in Blackpool where our residents would be accepted. We tried a few churches to test the water and when we entered Blackpool Christian Centre we all felt that this was the church where we would have fellowship. We found the Pastor Jim Thompson to be a wonderful man of God where the Spirit of God was allowed to move. On Easter Sunday it was a special day when two of our residents, Lisa and Claire were baptized. It had been my pleasure to lead them to Jesus and the glow on their faces was evident for all to see. It was an added bonus when one of our other residents went forward to give his life to Jesus when the Pastor leading the meeting made an appeal. Earlier that day Jan and I had prayed with John that he would be able to receive the new life that Jesus wanted to give him. It was very clear that God was blessing our ministry as we witnessed lives that were being snatched from the flames.

It did not take long before the devil hit back at us through the local council who served an enforcement order on Springfield House stating that we were in breach of planning regulations. It appeared that other hoteliers were allowed to take in residents on housing benefits without being in breach of regulations as long as they also took in holiday makers. The fact that we only concentrated on homeless people made us different from other hotels. The local neighbours were up in arms and we were accused of many untrue things. It was another case of the NIMBY syndrome with some very influential people in Blackpool deciding that they did not want any hostels in what they considered to be a holiday area. The only way that I would have described Blackpool was like a modern day version of Sodom and Gomorrah. It was a place where everything was allowed, sex shops, gay bars, night clubs, casinos, drugs dens with pubs on every corner but a Christian home trying to help people get their lives together was not wanted. The hotel owner at the side of us was opposite a house dealing in drugs where up to fifty young people a day would go to buy drugs. He was that blinded by the devil he could not see what was going on under his nose and concentrated his efforts on doing all he could to close something down that was good. We decided to appeal against the enforcement order as this would enable our work to continue for the time being.

 David Burgin worked with me to put together a profile of the work of The New Life Centre so we could apply to charitable trusts for some financial help for our ministry. This put extra work load on my shoulders but I seemed to be coping very well with the pressure. Jan was working very hard at the charity shop with some of our residents helping out as part of their rehabilitation.

Chapter 34

"The Lord will guide you always; he will satisfy your needs in a sun-scorched land and will strengthen your frame. You will be like a spring whose waters never fail"

Isaiah 58 : 11

It was during May of 1996 that things started to get very difficult for Jan and myself. Our advertisement for volunteer workers did not bring in much response but the local Blackpool Prison Fellowship responded by getting involved with our ministry. Alec and Joyce were a real answer to prayer and although they did not have a lot of time to spare what they gave was a blessing. It was evident that active Christians were already committed to other works of God and that was why we found it hard to get volunteers. The charity shop started to become a burden to Jan because of the lack of volunteers to help run it. Jan found herself running the shop on a full time basis and having our residents help out in the shop was not working out. We had one incident where one of our residents ran off with the shop takings after being placed in a position of trust. Jan's mum Ada had also been diagnosed as having cancer and Jan had to go and spend some time looking after her after the operation to remove the cancer.

As we came under more pressure God used some of our supporters to bless and encourage us. We felt let down by church communities but God was showing his love for us through a handful of people who showed they cared. The amazing thing was that almost all the people who seemed to really understand what we were going through were getting on in years. Arthur and Gladys who lived in Burton-on-Trent had encouraged and helped us time and time again when we were at our lowest. The same could be said for Grace and Mabel who lived in Cornwall, Ellen who lived in Teddington, Dorothy who lived in

Ireland, Colin who lived in Stockport, John who lived in Leominster plus Noel Proctor and David Burgin who were a constant tower of strength. It seemed that every time we were ready for giving up our ministry a word or letter of encouragement would arrive from one of these dear friends.

In spite of our own personal family circumstances we tried with all our heart to continue with the ministry we had been given. Our list of supporters on our mailing list was over three hundred and fifty people but in my heart I knew that most of these people had stopped supporting our work a long time ago. God spoke to me through the story of Gideon and I wrote to all our supporters giving them the opportunity of coming off our mailing list. At least this way we would know how many Christians we could rely upon to support our work through prayer. It did not come as any surprise when only thirty five people requested to be kept on our mailing list. At least we knew how many men and women of God were praying for our needs and all the opposition we were facing.

After Jan had returned from looking after her mother we were given the news by Michelle that she was expecting a baby and the father was one of our residents. Jan and I both felt that we had failed Michelle by letting her live in an environment like Springfield House where she could be influenced by young men who were experts at manipulation. We had trusted our resident's friendship with our own daughter and we felt that our trust had been misplaced yet again. We needed lots of grace from God to deal with this situation and Jan decided to move back to our rented bungalow with Michelle. I still tried to help the father of Michelle's baby overcome his addiction to drugs but after two weeks I asked him to leave because he started taking drugs again. Michelle decided that she wanted to have the baby so Jan and I both supported Michelle with her decision promising that we would do all we could to help her.

We then had the sad news that two of our supporters Arthur and Norman had both died within a week of each other. They had both been a source of blessing and encouragement to all of us and they would be sadly missed. Arthur and his wife Gladys supported The New Life Centre and my family for a long time. They worked so hard to collect things for our charity shop and the many missions we undertook for Romania. Every time we went to their home in Burton-on-Trent we received a loving welcome and we always took away a good supply of homemade jam for our residents as well as a van full of supplies for Romania. Norman was seventy five years of age but he spent his time teaching our resident's wood working skills, he came on our last mission to Romania where he was Father Christmas to hundreds of orphaned children. They both brought love and laughter to all of us and they would be sadly missed.

We continued our outreach work in Manchester and Blackpool but came under increasing financial pressure. Jan and I did not receive any financial reward for the work that we undertook and our only source of income was my unemployment benefit. Sometimes we would receive a love gift from one of our supporters that always came when we needed help the most. In spite of our difficulties we decided to go ahead with our Christmas mission to Romania. We also decided to take our residents on a weekend camp to North Wales where we could also pay a visit to our sisters at the Carmelite Monastery at Dolgellau. Our sisters had been a source of blessing to us over the years where they prayed for us on a regular basis. All of our residents were excited about the thought of going camping and it was like watching little children going away on their first family holiday. It was a wonderful weekend as we all sang Christian songs as we travelled on our way. Our sisters at Dolgellau provided tea and homemade cakes as we shared with each other what God had been doing in all our lives. Each evening Michelle helped me prepare and cook a barbecue for all our residents. It was good watching them play football and rounders in the open fields of the camp site where we stayed. The views were breathtaking as we looked out over the countryside and hills that reminded us all about the beauty of God's creation. One of our residents remarked that this was what life was all about, so simple and yet so special. I had also taken our young grandson Steven who enjoyed playing with our residents who all made a fuss of him. The weekend camp had set many of our residents thinking about what they had been missing out on in life making them realise that not everything centered around drugs and alcohol.

Chapter 35

"I have told you these things, so that in me you may have peace. In this world you will have trouble. But take heart I have overcome the world"

John 16 : 33

August 1996 was a month of blessing with Ted and his wife Maureen agreeing to take over the running of Proctor House with another volunteer Brian who had responded to our advertisement in a Christian magazine. Ted had been a Pastor of a church at one time and together with his wife Maureen they provided a very stable Christian home at Proctor House. More and more of our residents were making a decision to accept Jesus Christ into their hearts as we did everything to encourage them with their walk with God. The more successful we were in helping people the more under attack we came from the local authorities. The housing benefits at Stockport had applied new housing benefit legislation to our charity that we should have been exempt from. This put us under severe financial pressure because of the low level of housing benefits we had been reduced to. At the same time I received a letter from the head of the charity commission stating that they had been informed of my past criminal convictions before I became a Christian in 1987. They informed me it was illegal for me to continue as a trustee of the charity I had formed. This came as a complete shock because I believed that the Charity Commission was informed about my background when The New Life Centre was formed as a charity. The only way that I could continue as a trustee was if I received a Royal pardon or a waiver of disqualification from the Charity Commission. I wrote a letter to the Queen and the head of the Charity Commission and left everything in the hands of God.

Our plans to send aid to Romania continued and by October we had collected over twenty tons of aid. We sent the aid overland with Bill Taylor again. Jan and I flew out to meet up with the wagon in Romania because our time was limited due to our commitments in England. God had provided everything that we needed for the mission through caring people who were prepared to share with those in need. We witnessed God working for our good when the paperwork allowing us to travel to Romania was delayed by two weeks. Jan had an operation on a burst ear drum that would have prevented her from flying on the original date we had booked to go but the two week delay gave her ear time to heal. It was a very successful mission where Jan and I enjoyed the time we had together.

We stayed with our friends George and Elizabeth Simondroni who we had first met six years before. They had loved us as one of their own family and we always enjoyed staying with them. From the safety of their home we were able to distribute aid that had travelled overland with Bill Taylor. We visited the orphanage at Pestianna, the mentally handicapped children's hospital at Paclisa where we put on a party for all the children. We distributed Christmas shoe boxes to all the children filled with goodies by caring people in England. The hugs and kisses from all the children made it clear how happy the children were to see us making all the effort worthwhile. We were able to visit many poor families around Hateg and a small village at Pretesti about sixty miles from Hateg where many poor families lived. We were able to distribute donated aid consisting of food, clothing, medicines and money to many of the families. We were also able to pray for many of the families we visited where we could feel the presence of God in a mighty way. One of the families that I had helped over many years was the Hulei family. On this visit we prayed for a young boy called Dorin who had an eye infection and gave money for medicines and shoes for some of the children who had no shoes to wear for school. This family like many others we helped shared what little food they had with our team and the love they showed us was very great.

Over the years we had become very good friends with Renato Falticska who we supported on a regular basis. Renato was someone we trusted with all our hearts and we would leave the aid we did not have time to distribute with him so he could help many poor families long after we had returned to England. It was good to be able to buy a disc for the tractor we had brought him out the year before and to leave him enough money to buy twenty piglets. We also prayed for his wife Anca who had suffered two miscarriages during the past year that she would receive a healing touch from God and be able to give birth to a healthy baby.

We were able to have a day out in the mountains of Romania with Renato's father who took us to a place that could only be described as beautiful and breathtaking. It was a time to relax and reflect on the Majesty of God and the beauty of his creation. I also thought about my situation with the Charity Commission I had left behind in England with the problems we had with all the authorities who were against us. I knew that God had changed me into a loving caring person and yet I was still being judged on my past. On the last Sunday we were in Romania I was invited to preach at the Pentecostal church by Pastor Mercia where I spoke from Isaiah 58. We had been a living witness in Romania for the past six years and I believed that God spoke to his church through his word and through the work we had been doing. It was clear the church in Romanian was neglecting many of the social needs of its people due to many mitigating factors. God confirmed his word through verses 6 and 7. "Is not this the kind of fasting I have chosen: to loose the chains of injustice and untie the cords of the yoke, to set the oppressed free and break every yoke? Is it not to share your food with the hungry and to provide the poor wanderer with shelter, when you see the naked to clothe him, and not to turn away from your own flesh and blood?" I was able to share about our work with homeless people in England as well as Romania and the amount of times we had cried out to God for help. As in verse 9 our Lord always answered our prayers by saying "Here am I".

On the Sunday evening after services at the Baptist church we waited at our host's home for Renato to pick us up to take us to the railway station to begin our long journey back to England. Many people called to say goodbye and to pray with us. We were given a prophetic word by a young gypsy girl that a big problem we had left behind in England was going to work out in our favour and to trust in God. I believed that this concerned the Charity Commission and that I would be vindicated. The love that we received was much more than we had ever given out. We felt that our mission had been blessed by God from start to finish.

It was a long tiring journey back to England but the joy we felt in our hearts made everything worthwhile. We arrived back at Proctor

House on the 4th November to pick up the mini bus we had left behind so we could drive back to Blackpool. As we entered the car park we could hear the sound of people praising God coming from inside of the house. It was music to our ears as we joined the fellowship inside of the house to join in praising our Lord. We had only been away for ten days and it was surprising how much had happened in that space of time. We received a mixture of good and bad news. We had lost four residents in the space of one week because they had decided to go their own way. It was good to see a new resident called Mark who we had met on our outreach in Chinatown before we had left for Romania. Mark was the result of our faithfulness before we had left for Romania. We were parking our caravan outside H.C.C.C. for the evening service before going into Chinatown to feed the homeless when a car crashed into the back of it. Even though the back was crushed in we decided to continue with our journey to feed the homeless. Ted gave us the good news that someone had read the article in the newspaper about the crash and had donated a caravan so our outreach work could continue. It needed some work doing on it and another charity had donated £1000 towards our outreach work that would help towards the cost of repairing the donated caravan.

On the 5th November canon Noel Proctor M.B.E. and our chairman David Burgin, the head of the Charity Commission and I met at Proctor House to discuss if I was to be allowed to continue as a trustee of The New Life Centre. It was a very long meeting and we were all interviewed separately by the Charity Commission. I was informed that someone had written an anonymous letter to the Charity Commission enclosing an old newspaper cutting about my past criminal convictions. I was given an opportunity to share about the new Bob Sutton and why I should not be judged on my past life before becoming a Christian. I could feel the presence of God in a mighty way as I believed that the head of the Charity Commission was listening with a very open heart. I knew that I also had Noel and David on my side because they had supported me from day one. On the 7th November I received a personal telephone call from the head of the Charity Commission who spoke the following words. "I have listened very carefully to all the evidence put before me and I would like you to know that it is my opinion that you should be given a waiver of disqualification and be reinstated as a trustee of The New Life Centre. I wish you every success with the work you are doing and hope you can continue doing what is right. It is very rare for someone to be given a waiver of disqualification and I hope my trust in you is not misplaced".

After thanking the head of the Charity Commission for allowing me to continue with the mission God had given me to do I put the telephone down. I put my head in my hands and cried tears of joy with thankfulness to God for vindicating me. I felt the love of God so very close to me and could actually feel God holding me in His arms and letting me know how special I was to him. At least for now I was going to be able to continue with the work God had given me to do but did not know for how long. The following day I received a letter from the social services inspection unit at Stockport stating that they were going to prosecute The New Life Centre if we did not register Proctor House as a care home. We knew that this would have massive implications for our charity because to staff a registered care home to the satisfaction of the social services would have meant we would have to charge in excess of £300 per week for every resident at Proctor House. Before the social services would pay that amount of money a person would have to be diagnosed as being in need of or requiring personal care. It was clear that the social services inspection unit at Stockport were working with the housing benefits section in a bid to close Proctor House down. Letters I had wrote in confidence to the housing benefits section in a bid to have housing benefit restored to its proper level had been handed over to the head of the inspection unit. I knew that the people we were dealing with were very underhanded and sly. It was clear that the devil was using them to attack us from all directions. I was informed by Ted that the inspection unit had waited for me to go to Romania and had made a number of visits to Proctor House in my absence. When Ted and Maureen gave me a detailed report of the two people who had made the visits I knew right away who they were. We had nothing to hide and they were given full access to Proctor House and all their questions were answered. It was not long before David Burgin was asked to attend a formal meeting at the offices of the inspection unit with the head Mike Jobbins and his assistant Janet Ranson. When Mike Jobbins saw me at the interview the first words out of his mouth were, "What's he doing here?" It was made very clear to Mike Jobbins that if he did not agree for me to be present we would be leaving the interview room. Mike Jobbins agreed for me to be present but stated I must remain silent. The interview had only been in progress for a couple of minutes when I could not contain myself any longer because of the malicious things that Mike Jobbins was putting to David. I interrupted the interview to correct Mike Jobbins and he rose from his chair like a wild animal shouting and screaming that I had to leave the meeting. We left the meeting with our solicitor who advised us that it would be better to continue but I had to keep my mouth shut no matter what was spoken by Mike Jobbins. After agreeing to keep silent I was allowed to be present at the interview so that it could be concluded. I found it very difficult to keep silent because I could see the evil forces at work in Mike Jobbins and he knew that I knew.

Chapter 36

"They will fight against you but will not overcome you, for I am with you and will rescue you," declared the Lord"

Jeremiah 1 : 19

It is a wonderful thing when we are given a word from God that we can stand on if we believe it is for us. We needed that word more than ever because now we were being attacked on all sides. Even within my own family we had serious problems to deal with. Our experience was that when the devil attacked he threw everything at us. Just after the interview with the social services we received a telephone call from our son Robert informing us that he had been petrol bombed out of his home in Adswood. Robert was living with his girlfriend Samantha who was expecting a baby. Robert had seen burglars breaking into a house next door and had telephoned the police. It turned out that the burglars had a police radio and intercepted the message and were able to escape before the police arrived. In revenge they petrol bombed Robert's car that was parked outside of the front door. The fire almost killed the next door neighbour's baby and the father of the child broke his arm in four places trying to break out of the back of the house. Robert and Samantha were very fortunate to escape with their own lives due to the intensity of the heat. We picked them both up to come and stay with us but within twenty four hours of leaving local thieves in Adswood had broken into their home, completely ransacking it stealing everything of value that they could carry. Even the things they had been buying for the baby were stolen and it was heartbreaking to see what they were going through. We helped Robert and our daughter Michelle find suitable rented accommodation in the Cleveleys area praying that God would undertake for them. We had lots of residents who had many problems to overcome plus with the opposition from the local authorities to deal with I was coming under increased pressure.

It was a big answer to prayer to see Robert and Michelle settle into nice rented houses. We were also overjoyed when Samantha gave birth to a beautiful healthy baby and they named him Anthony Mark in memory of Robert's older brother Mark Anthony who had been killed in 1987. The bad memories of what had taken place in Adswood were soon behind as we looked into the eyes of our latest grandchild. It was a case of onward Christian soldiers as we continued with the work we had been called to do. At about this time we started to receive applications from Christians in Uganda to come and work as volunteers for The New Life Centre. The situation was so bad with the local authorities that I was forced to make an official complaint to the local government ombudsman. They found in our favour and awarded us £150 in compensation for the way they had been delaying paying housing benefits to our charity. This made the council more intent on attacking our finances. Even though they had to accept they had unlawfully applied new housing benefits to our charity they refused to put them back to their proper level. One of the senior probation officers at Stockport continued to give our newsletters to the social services inspection unit in the hope that they could use some of the details of our work against us. I would give our supporters details of some of our residents so that they could pray for their needs but this was now being used against us.

Our residents at both houses were making life very difficult for the staff because of the constant lying. We had residents who on the face of it gave the impression that they were walking with Jesus and overcoming the problems in their lives. When staff were in bed some of them were sneaking out of the house to obtain drugs and alcohol. When the drugs and alcohol were offered to other residents who were still weak it brought them down as well. At Proctor House the residents were stealing each other's medication and because they shared rooms we were forced to buy a strong medicine cabinet to keep the medicines in. At Springfield House I went into one of our resident's room and caught two of the residents dividing some heroin. The thing that shocked me the most was the fact they had the powder on the top cover of a Holy Bible. It was an opportunity to share about the life and death they had in front of them. I explained that on one hand the devil was offering them a life of misery and death through the heroin. Underneath the heroin was the new life that was being offered through the word of God found in the Holy Bible. Both of these residents had made a commitment to Jesus Christ and I explained that God was not a God who would be mocked.

They were both given a choice to throw the heroin down the sink or to leave Springfield House with the heroin and not to come back. I prayed for God to undertake a miracle in their lives and waited to see what would happen. Jason made a decision to stay but John decided to leave with the heroin. As John left Springfield House to take the heroin I thought that was the last I would see of him. Within a couple of minutes he had returned telling me that he had walked right into a police officer and had thrown the heroin away. I told John that the only way I would accept his story was if he took me to the police officer he had bumped into. John led me to the hotel where the police officer had called and she confirmed that she had spoken to John about the suspicious way he was acting. I believed that God had intervened in this situation to give John another chance to get his life together. I thought back to the night when Jan and I had been with John to Victoria hospital and sat with him all night. This was the same John who a few months before had been brought back from the brink of death after taking a large drugs overdose. John had taken drugs since the age of fourteen and it resulted in him being forced to leave home by his mother and father. After ten years of drug abuse John had started to get close to his family again when his mother who he loved very much died of cancer. This led to a few more years of drug abuse trying to cover up the pain and hurts in his life. Without the drugs John was a loving and caring person and in his own words he said the following, "You don't know what it is like for me being a prisoner to the drugs that control my life. I have hurts and pain that the drug takes me out of while I have the drug the pain disappears. It's like being in another world and my life stopped when I got hooked on drugs at fourteen years of age. I do want to sort my life out but I need help. I am starting to get something out of going to church and reading my bible but at times I feel so alone".

I knew that John needed a lot more help than we could give him and I spoke to him about going to Yeldall Manor a Christian addiction treatment/rehabilitation centre where he could receive the help he needed. I made enquiries and obtained the application forms for John to obtain funding to be admitted into Yeldall Manor. While John was waiting for the funding to come through he agreed to go to Proctor House where he could make a start on his rehabilitation. Within a few weeks the funding came through and I gave John a lift to Stockport railway station to put him on the train to Yeldall Manor. We sat in the mini bus together on the car park of the railway station eating some Macdonald hamburgers I had bought. John thanked me for all that we had done to help him and he promised to keep in touch. I told John that if things did not work out at Yeldall Manor that he could return to Proctor House. I gave him a big hug and prayed for God to bless his time at Yeldall Manor. We said our goodbyes and John gave me a big smile and a wave as he set off on his journey to Reading. I treated all the men and women in our care as I would my own children with a love that could only come from God. John was an individual person created by God just like every other resident in our care.

When we took residents in from off the streets of our cities we did not know what problems they had to overcome but like Jesus we offered them a new life. Some of them did need the specialist help of rehabilitation centres and we did everything in our power to steer them to the right places where they would receive the expert help that they needed. If we were to register our homes as care homes we would be prevented from helping the people that we took in off the streets of our towns and cities. Like Yeldall Manor we would have to go through a long drawn out process to obtain funding for the people we needed to help. Most of the people we took in were capable of looking after themselves in a physical way but needed help and guidance in decision making. The homeless people would never have been in a position to attend doctor's appointments, fill in forms for housing benefits if they had not been given a stable and supportive home like The New Life Centre to live in.

The inspection unit of the social services at Stockport made it very clear they were going to take The New Life Centre to court. Our solicitors made it clear that if we were prosecuted by Stockport Council the outcome could go any way. After much prayer we decided that we would carry on helping people and leave the outcome with God. We were not given any help or advice by anyone within the social services so I wrote a letter to them asking them to define what they considered personal care to be.

Our financial situation started to improve when we received a grant of £10,000 from a charitable trust that helped us meet all our financial obligations. We were also having discussions with this trust concerning further financial help towards the building extension and towards the salary of employing a full time co-ordinator. As we approached Christmas 1996 our future looked very uncertain but we put all our trust in God.

Chapter 37

"For to us a child is born, to us a son is given, and the government will be on his shoulders. And he will be called Wonderful Counsellor, Mighty God, Everlasting Father, Prince of Peace"

Isaiah 9 : 6

We decided that all our residents would share Christmas together at Proctor House where Ted and Maureen with the help of our other volunteers would look after them. This enabled me to spend Christmas with my own family so we made arrangements for all my children and grandchildren to be together on Christmas day. It was a very happy time and it made me realise how little time I had been spending with my family due to all the projects and missions I had been involved in. It was amazing to see how the Lord provided all the food for our residents at Proctor House. Different people had come along to donate items of food including two very large turkeys so it meant that Ted and Maureen did not have to buy one item of food over the Christmas period.

On New Year's Eve Jan had a lovely birthday surprise when our daughter Michelle gave birth to a beautiful healthy baby girl at Blackpool Victoria hospital. Jan and I were with Michelle throughout the birth giving her all the love and support that she needed. Jan helped the midwife in delivering Shannon Lee while I held the hand of Michelle and prayed that all would be well. It was not a time of looking back but in praising God for the life of a little baby girl that now had a life of her own. After Michelle and Shannon were settled in together back on the ward Jan and I made our way back home where we had a candlelight meal together. It was a special time as we thanked God for the birth of Shannon Lee and the good that had come out of a very difficult year. It was a nice way to end 1996 and welcome the new year of 1997. It reminded me that God always has the last word.

The start of 1997 began with good news from the charitable trust we had approached that they would give £20,000 per year for the next two years to enable our charity to employ a co-ordinator. This was the job that I had been doing for a number of years without any financial reward and it would be up to God if I was the person to be employed. We had various discussions with the trust how the position for co-ordinator was to be advertised and it would be left to the trustees to appoint the person they believed suitable for the job. The timing of this grant was perfect because I was being put under pressure by the employment service to find employment because I had been claiming unemployment benefit for a long period of time. The employment service had agreed that I could work for The New Life Centre on three months work training in the hope that I would be selected for full time employment. I wanted what was best for The New Life Centre and in my time of prayer with God I asked him to bring in another person if they could do a better job than I was doing.

It looked like our prayers for volunteers was being answered when I received a fax to say that Gemma and Eva had been granted a visa to come to England and that God had provided their air fares from Uganda. We decided that we would have a training course at Proctor House to give our volunteers an idea of what our ministry was all about just like I had undertaken in America. We had met lots of Christians who had volunteered to help out but many of them had created more of a problem than the people we had been called to help. I was amazed at how many Christians had come in who thought that they had all the answers and worked as a one man band. We decided that from now on we were not going to allow any Christians into the ministry if they could not work as part of a team within the structure of the working timetable and rules of the houses. We hoped that the training course would help prevent some of the difficult situations that had risen that created a lot of problems for Ted and Maureen. We had been forced on a number of occasions to ask volunteers not to come in anymore because of the problems they had created. This had always been undertaken in a loving and Godly manner but unfortunately some of the volunteers had bad mouthed The New Life Centre and spread many lies when reporting back to their own church. Some of our volunteers had started to form relationships with each other and our residents making me wonder if we were in competition with Blind Date.

On the 12th February Jan's mother died after a long battle against cancer. This was a very sad time for all the family especially for Jan who was very close to her mother. While Jan was comforting the rest of her brothers and sisters I received a fax to say that Gemma and Eva were on their way from Uganda and would be arriving at Heathrow airport on the 14th February at 6.20am. I was sure it was God's plan for them to be in England because many miracles had been undertaken on their behalf. All the letters I had written on their behalf to allow them to come to England seemed worthwhile as they shared in detail how God had undertaken for them. It had been a tiring drive through the night to Heathrow and the return journey back to Proctor House. When we arrived back Maureen was very upset because she had received some bad news about her daughter Julie who had to undergo major tests in hospital. Ted and Maureen welcomed Gemma and Eva but I felt uncomfortable about the situation as something did not feel right.

The following Tuesday it was the funeral of Jan's mother and this was the day that Ted and Maureen left the work at Proctor House. They both felt that they could not continue with the work especially Ted who was all burnt out. I knew how difficult a ministry it was because you had to give and give until sometimes there was nothing left to give. We were grateful to the local vicar at St. Chads for providing accommodation for Gemma and Eva until we could deal with the situation. This meant that the work at Proctor House could not continue and we had to concentrate on running Springfield House. I felt very sad for Ted and Maureen because they had given their all but we did not have enough responsible workers to help share the work pressures that Ted and Maureen had worked under. I think that this was the time when I thought that we might not be able to continue with the work at Stockport.

It was an answer to prayer when two Christians from Blackpool George and his wife Elizabeth offered to provide a home for Gemma and Eva. Jan made the suggestion that we should try and find another Christian organization to take over the running of Proctor House.

On the 24th February 1987 David Burgin and I met with the regional co-ordinator of Teen Challenge with a view of them taking over the lease of Proctor House. We did not care what name the work went under because of the need of so many people. We had also gone through so much hardship to keep Proctor House open and it would be sad if the work had to stop.

Chapter 38

"There is no fear in love. But perfect love drives out all fear"
1 John 4 : 18

On the 19th March we received the summons from Stockport Council to appear at Stockport Magistrates court to answer charges of running Proctor House as an unregistered residential care home. The trustees of The New Life Centre had decided that I was the person to be employed as ministry co-ordinator but I wondered if it would be a short term job with all the problems we faced. We did not have enough money in our bank to pay legal fees to defend the charge against our charity and it was agreed that I would defend The New Life Centre. In many ways I was looking forward to bringing out into the open the way that we had been treated by the local authorities especially agencies that were paid to care about the people we were trying to help, that was why there was so many sleeping rough on the streets. If they had cared I believed they would have been trying to help us and not close us down. We believed that we were making a stand for what was right before God and no-one knew the situation better than me as I had been involved with everything from day one.

At this time I needed a lot of help because of the severe pressure I was under as at times I felt so alone. I knew that God was giving me the strength that I needed on a daily basis but some days I felt completely drained. We had been unjustly and unfairly treated by many of the local agencies. This helped me to understand how Jesus must have felt when the same thing happened to him. Within a few weeks of Gemma and Eva arriving in Blackpool they decided with the help of the vicar from St. Chads to move on to another ministry that his daughter was involved in. I felt like the captain of a sinking ship where the other hands jumped overboard before they would help try and save the ship. Jan also had no help at the charity shop and had reached the stage where she felt that she could not carry on by herself.

The leaders of Teen Challenge had not made any positive moves to take over the lease of Proctor House so I wrote to the owners asking them if they would release us from our lease and take back Proctor House. I also wrote to the owners of the shop to see if they would release us from our lease just leaving us with Springfield House to concentrate on. The owners of Proctor House agreed to release us from our legal and financial obligations but the owners of the charity shop made it very clear that they would be looking to David Burgin and me to pay the rent if The New Life Centre could not meet its financial responsibility.

After Gemma and Eva had moved away God sent along a wonderful Christian from Scotland called Jane who had a heart for Jesus and the people we were helping at Springfield House. Jane was thrown in at the deep end but with the help of the Holy Spirit she settled in very quickly. Another volunteer called Mike came at the same time but within a few weeks he ran off with all the food money. It was still a difficult time as we continued to try and help people with our outreach soup kitchen and hostel in Blackpool. I was in my office when I heard the news come over the radio that the inquest was being held into the death of John who I had put on the train to Yeldall Manor a few months before. It was the first time that I knew that John was dead and I left my office to make my way to the inquest. It was a very sad day as I listened to the accounts of three young people who had all died from taking heroin who all lived in the Blackpool area. It was sad to hear the details of how they had died especially John who we had come to know and love. I felt an emptiness inside of me especially looking at his father and sister who had done so much to help the son and brother that they deeply loved. I could feel the pain that they were feeling and I was very angry that we were being stopped from helping people like John when no-one else really cared. I walked away from the inquest in tears after returning some of John's belongings back to his father that John had asked me to keep safe for him. John had written to me sending me a pawn ticket and asking me if I could get them out of the pawn shop before the ticket expired. They had been in my filing cabinet waiting for John to return not knowing that he had died a few days after writing to me. It was sad to think that all that John left behind could fit into a small brown envelope. It was something else that was brown and much smaller that had taken his life away. The fact that three people had died within the space of twenty four hours made me wonder if bad heroin was being sold by drug dealers.

I was determined that The New Life Centre would not close without a fight and that I would do everything in my power to keep it open. Our trial date at Stockport was set for the 8th May and we tried to continue with our work the best that we could. We made plans to bring Renato and his wife Anca, their daughter Roxane with Ana-Maria from a poor family Jan and I supported to England for a holiday. It was great news that Anca was now expecting a baby and that our prayers for her had been answered. It helped to take our minds off our own problems thinking about the needs of other people. Our daughter Donna had helped raise the money for their air fares by undertaking car boot sales with things we had been donated. We also received some gifts from other Christians who knew Renato to help towards the cost. We had great fellowship together and it was our pleasure and joy to look after them and give them a wonderful time. It was also our hope that Renato would receive some financial support from other Christians to help him develop his farm back in Romania. On the 15th April our Romanian friends returned to Romania whilst I concentrated on preparing the defense of The New Life Centre.

I spent hundreds of hours going through all the prosecution evidence and statements. I was very sad at the way that people had conspired against us. I felt very confident that God would vindicate us at court and that we would be cleared of the charge against us. The trial started on time on the 8th May with it being set for two days. I knew that God was giving me the ability to deal with the situation set before me. After outlining their charge the first of the prosecution witnesses gave evidence. I was able to cross examine each witness and I believed that I had got them to give answers that would prove that we were not guilty. The main area of charge was that we provided personal care for people in need of personal care. The head of the community drugs team and a doctor from Manchester agreed that they had never told any member of staff that the people they were seeing needed personal care. The prosecution alleged that by keeping hold of the resident's medicines in a locked filing cabinet was personal care. The case became very complicated and at the end of two days it was not over so the magistrates adjourned the trial until the 15th May.

I held on to the following scripture as our trial resumed on the 15th May. "The wicked lie in wait for the righteous, seeking their very lives; but the lord will not leave them in their power or let them be condemned when brought to trial" Psalm 37 : 32 - 33. I had called several witnesses on behalf of The New Life Centre including Ted and Maureen. Canon Noel Proctor M.B.E. and our chairman David Burgin. It was encouraging how each in turn was able to share what being a Christian involved. It was then my turn to give evidence where I shared in great detail about the work of The New Life Centre and about the people we were called to help. I provided evidence about the probation hostel in Stockport where two drug addicts had died from drug overdoses. I also provided evidence about a hostel in Manchester that had closed because two of the residents had died from taking prescribed drugs that had been prescribed for other residents. This showed the need for having a locked medicine cabinet to prevent people from stealing drugs from each other. Methadone was prescribed to addicts as a substitute for heroin but taken in large doses could be fatal. We had not had any of our residents dying from drug overdoses since we had been open that should have shown we were doing something that was needed. I had applied for a court order forcing the head of the social services inspection unit at Blackpool to give evidence. The court heard evidence that they did not consider that we needed to be registered as a care home and did not take the view of the inspection unit at Stockport. After giving my evidence it was now my turn to sum up our case as to why we were not guilty of the charge against us. I was able to bring out all the points that I believed proved we were not guilty especially the evidence of past residents of The New Life Centre. Some of the people were alive today because we had reached out a hand of love when they needed it the most. The magistrates then left the court to decide on the verdict.

Within an hour they had returned and the chairman of the bench said the following words, "We find the case proved" my heart sank and I felt that justice had not been done in that court room. The look of glee on the faces of Mike Jobbins and Janet Ranson made me believe that the devil had won a victory in that court room. Even though we had closed Proctor House the verdict had grave implications on any future work. The magistrates gave us a conditional discharge but ordered us to pay prosecution costs of £2000. All of us involved with the ministry believed we had received rough justice. David Burgin said to me the following words that I will never forget "Bob, I would rather be found guilty of caring than not caring and when we go to heaven I believe God will welcome us with open arms". As Jan and I made our way back to Blackpool we discussed the possibility of appealing against conviction to the Crown Court.

The Charity Commission was sent a newspaper cut out of the court case and they got in touch with us to find out why we had been prosecuted. I had been in touch with a Christian solicitor to seek a barrister's advice on the possibility of appealing to the Crown Court. I was advised that it would cost over £5000 to appeal and it was very likely we would lose our case. I had to make a decision there and then if we were to appeal because it was the last day for putting the appeal in at court. We did not have £5000 to fight the appeal and we had been instructed by the Charity Commission that we could not use central funds to appeal. I felt that I had no option but to say that we would not appeal against the conviction. As I left the barristers office and caught the train back to Blackpool I felt that my ministry at The New Life Centre was coming to an end.

Chapter 39

"I am confident of this: I will see the goodness of the Lord in the land of the living. Wait for the Lord, be strong and take heart and wait for the Lord"

Psalm 27 : 13 - 14

If ever I needed a word from God it was at this time and one of our supporters sent me a letter with the above words from God. I believed those words and wondered how long we could continue with everything going against us. I prayed to God for a clear understanding of why we had lost our court case and why we had not been able to appeal against conviction to the Crown Court. The owners of Proctor House agreed to release us from our commitment to the lease but wanted us to clear everything out of the house by the end of June. It was a very busy time as we cleared everything out of the house. We also emptied the charity shop of all donated goods so that could be closed down. We boxed everything up for Romania and donated them to a charity called J.O.Y. who we had worked with in the past. We received a telephone call from Renato in Romania to inform us that Anca had given birth to a healthy baby boy and they were giving him the name Robert Emmanuel after me. We needed some good news because it was a very sad time closing down Proctor House and the charity shop. We had put so much effort into keeping them open but without the support of local churches and Christians it was impossible to continue.

I wondered what the outcome was going to be now that we only had Springfield House to work with. The date for our appeal against the enforcement order served upon us had been set for the 15th July. I knew that I needed to get away from everything to spend time alone with God. I decided that I was going to go to the mountains of

Romania to seek God and prepare myself for the appeal hearing. On the 2nd July I had everything ready in my van so that I would be self sufficient in the mountains of Romania. I asked Jan to be patient with me and try to understand that I had to be by myself to seek God for answers to lots of questions. I knew that Jan was not happy about me going to Romania by myself as she could not understand why I had to go. Jan told me she could not put up with this life she was living any longer and she was leaving me and went to stay with our daughter Michelle. I told Jan that I loved her and to try and understand I needed this time alone.

Within two days of leaving Blackpool I had arrived in Romania with only one stop over in a hotel in Hungary. It was good to see Renato and his family again and baby Robert for the first time. I spent a couple of days visiting some poor families at Petresti to give them food and money that I had brought with me from England. I then found an ideal place near Renato's farm to pitch my tent and spend time alone with God. It was very quiet and peaceful as I reflected on everything that had happened since becoming a Christian. Suddenly a storm the like of which I had never experienced before came about. The lightening lit up the night sky and the cracks and noise of thunder was so loud it hurt my ears. The hail stones were very big and I was a bit concerned that they might come through the tent covers. It was like the experience that Elijah had with God on the mountain of Horeb. It was during a lull in the storm that God spoke into my heart concerning all aspects of my life and ministry.

God revealed to me where I had been drained by my ministry and what my family had suffered through all the turmoil we had gone through over the past seven years. The work had taken over time that should have been spent with the Lord and my family. I could hear God speaking into my heart telling me to let go of all the works I was involved in and to get close to him and my family again. I could feel the presence of God with all the love he had to give me. I knew at that moment that my ministry had come to an end with The New Life Centre and it was time for the door to be closed. The following day I visited a gypsy family where a young lady called Marta gave me a prophetic word from God confirming what God had revealed to me in the quiet of the storm. Renato was desperate for transport and I wanted to be back with my family as soon as possible so I decided to lend him my van and fly back to England. After praying with each other Renato took me to the railway station in Deva where I caught the overnight train to Bucharest and the plane back to England. In less than twenty four hours I was back in England with Jan and I explained to her everything that God had revealed to me. We both agreed that God came first but we needed to have time for each other. Jan agreed to give our marriage another chance and came back with me to our home in Cleveleys.

I informed David and Noel of my decision to give up my ministry and they both agreed it was time to wind up the New Life Centre. It was like a big burden had been lifted from off my shoulders as I attended the appeal hearing on the 15th July at Blackpool Town Hall. I knew that we were not going to win our appeal but God had put it on my heart to be a witness for him and not worry about the outcome. We were outnumbered 50 - 1 with some very influential people against us. It was sad to see so many people whose heart had been hardened. I felt very much like Daniel in the lion's den surrounded by lots of hostile people. I was able to cope with the situation because I knew that God was with me and that I was not alone. It was an opportunity to share what being a Christian was all about in front of a packed Town Hall. The appeal hearing lasted all day and at the end of it I felt that God was happy with the way I had presented the case for The New Life Centre. It was becoming very clear to me that we do not always receive justice in this world but sometimes we have to wait and be patient for God.

I informed Jane and the rest of the volunteer workers that we would not win our appeal as we made plans to find our residents suitable accommodation so that we could close down Springfield House. Jane moved back to Scotland and Jan and I spring cleaned Springfield House so that it could be handed back to the owner in good condition. It was agreed that we could donate the mini bus and caravan we had been using at Blackpool to Renato. Jan and I made plans to take the mini bus and caravan to Romania so that it would help Renato in his ministry.

During the last week of August we made the journey to Romania with the mini bus and caravan to hand them over to Renato. It was very tiring but we had a blessed journey as we talked about the many ways God had provided for us. We handed over to Renato the mini bus and caravan and I took back my own van that I had let him borrow. Renato was so happy to receive the mini bus and caravan and thanked God for everything. After spending a few days with Renato and visiting some poor families at Petresti we returned to England. As we entered Austria we hoped that we could find the hotel where we had met Cyril on our first mission to Romania way back in 1990. The roads had all changed but God knew what was on our heart and without any maps He directed us to the hotel we were looking for. It was a wonderful experience for us both as we remembered the goodness of our Lord. God had provided for us then and we believed that God would provide for us now even though we were giving up all our works and ministry.

Chapter 40

"Brothers, I do not consider myself yet to have taken hold of it, But one thing I do: forgetting what is behind and straining towards what is ahead. I press on towards the goal to win the prize for which God has called me heavenwards in Christ Jesus"

Philippians 3 : 13 - 14

Within a few days of arriving back from Romania we received the news that we had lost our appeal and that Springfield House could not operate as a hostel for homeless people. The local press and radio station could not wait to phone me and give me the news to see what our reaction was. I told them that it was very sad that a work that had benefited so many desperate people had been forced to close. I told them that the trustees had decided to close Springfield House before the outcome of the appeal because of the lack of support from within the community.

At first I felt that I had failed with the mission that God had called me to undertake until I realised all the people we had helped. God made it clear to me that it was faithfulness what counted and that I could leave the end results to him. I did feel that the bad guys had been allowed to win but realised that God's ways and purposes were different than the ways and thinking of man. I read a book by Charles R. Swindoll called "Laugh again" that blessed me very much. It was time for Jan and me to laugh again and enjoy the new life that God had given to us. I had forgotten what it was like to do things with my family and not to worry what was happening at the New Life Centre.

I believed that what we had experienced at Court and The New Life Centre would be used by God for his glory at a time and date that had not yet been revealed. God had put it on my heart to have twelve months out from ministry works so that I could get close to him and my family. It felt strange at first just walking arm in arm with my lovely wife Jan along the sea front at Cleveleys without a care in the world. As time went by I realised how much that we meant to God. We were more important to him than any ministry and what counted the most was our love for God. I still found that lots of people would still come up to us asking if we could do such and such a thing to help them, especially from within our own church. At first I found it hard informing them that we were having time out from all works. It soon became very clear that NO was an important word for a Christian as well as YES. I still don't think that we received the love and understanding from our Pastor or church that we needed. We were never approached or asked if we needed any help with all that we had gone through. As in the past God used individual Christians to give us the help and support that we needed.

    I started back in work and I made a start on writing this book with the spare time I had on my hands. In December 1997 I took Jan on a 23 day holiday to Hawaii stopping off for two days in San Francisco as it had always been her dream to go there. Just before we were due to depart we received news that David Burgin was in hospital after having a major operation to remove cancer from his colon. The operation had gone wrong and David suffered a massive loss of blood needing another five hour operation. We both went to see David in hospital and we were sad to see him on a life support machine unable to speak or move. We discussed cancelling our holiday but we knew there was nothing we could do for David except pray.

    We set off for Hawaii on the 11th December visiting San Francisco on route before travelling on to Hawaii. We had the time of our lives making up for all the times we had been apart in our lives. I swam with the turtles and obtained my Padi certificate for swimming under water. Jan went to see the island where Elvis Presley had made one of his films. We went all over the island and visited the memorial at Pearl Harbour where many people had lost their lives during World War 2. After two weeks in Hawaii we received the sad news that David had died and his funeral was going to take place on the 30th December. We still had one more week of our holiday to go but we decided to return to England so we could attend David's funeral and pay our last respects. David had been a very special friend to both of us and we were going to miss him very much.

Chapter 41

"I am the resurrection and the life. He who believes in me will live, even though he dies; and whoever lives and believes in me will never die. Do you believe this?"

John 11 : 25 - 26

We arrived back in England on the 30th December just in time to attend David's funeral and learned that my father was in hospital after coming very close to death. My mother wanted to keep the news from me so that our holiday was not spoiled but I was upset that I had not been informed. We attended David's funeral and then went to the hospital to visit my father who informed us that he had taken an overdose of tablets with a bottle of alcohol after having an argument with my mother. My father told us he was going to be discharged from the hospital the following day on Jan's birthday and he had nowhere to go. We told my father he could come back to Cleveleys with us until he found a place to live.

Jan and I had both been praying to God on what we were going to do with our lives after The New Life Centre had come to an end. It was Jan who shared a vision she had of building a home in Romania for homeless children. As Romania had always been close to my heart I agreed with her that it was something we could both do together. We prayed to God for a plan for undertaking the vision that Jan had and within a few days God revealed to me in a dream how everything could be undertaken.

The Charity Commission were still giving me a hard time because David had kept all the financial records on his computer and they gave me the responsibility of trying to finalize all the accounts of The New Life Centre before closing it down. I had cooperated with officials from the Charity Commission until they went to our accountants with a court order to remove the books and financial records that I had taken to the accountants for them to prepare the closing financial accounts. I believed that the Charity Commission suspected me or David of doing something wrong so I contacted a solicitor to act for me in my dealings with the Charity Commission. I was upset and angry at the way they had gone about things when I had been doing everything I could to put together the financial records of The New Life Centre especially with me having no dealings with the money side of things.

I knew that I had nothing to hide so it was not a problem to leave the Charity Commission to get on with looking through the books and records that they had removed from our accountants so that we could concentrate on the vision we both shared of building a home in Romania that would provide a loving home for at least forty homeless children. The first step was to share our vision with our Pastor from our church at Blackpool Christian Centre to see if he would be willing for us to undertake the vision through our church.

I met with our Pastor in early January 1998 to share the vision and how everything could be undertaken. We were given the green light so over the next three months we arranged a number of meetings in our church to share the vision and invite other people who might want to get involved. We also contacted our friend Renato in Romania to share the vision with him and to ask if he would be willing to work with us to help bring the vision into reality. In April 1998 we had a management committee of twelve people in England. Renato had brought together over twenty people in Romania to form a charity and undertake the vision we had for the children. It was during this month that my father died after suffering a relapse from an operation that had gone wrong. My life just seemed to be one long problem after another but I knew that Jesus was helping me get through each day. Jan and I had both visited my father in hospital just before he died and we both knew that it was going to be the last time we saw him alive. My father knew it as well as he told me that he had asked God to forgive him of all the sins he had committed and he was sorry for any pain or hurt he had caused to any other person. My father told me he was at peace with God and he was ready to be with Jesus and all those he had loved who had gone to be with Jesus before him. My father had hurt a lot of people while he was alive but for a number of years he had tried to do what was right and he told me he had repented for all the wrong he had done. My dad had helped me out on lots of occasions in my life and it was an opportunity for me to thank him for the many things he had done to help me especially for all the love he had shown me. I was so thankful to God that I had spoken those words to my dad because in the early hours of the following morning he passed away. My mum and dad loved each other very much and I was thankful that they had made up with each other before my dad died. They even made plans to go on holiday together while my dad was in hospital hoping that he would recover.

The day before the funeral I was hit with a bombshell from Jan who stated that she did not want my dad's ashes scattered on the grave of Mark that had always been my mum and dad's wish when they died. We had a very big argument about this and I could not understand why Jan was being this way. I was threatening to leave Jan when she told me that the reason she did not want this to happen was because Donna had told her my father had sexually abused her when she was a child. I could not believe what I was hearing and I remembered a time in the past when my sister Diane had asked me to find out if any of my children had ever been abused by my dad. I remembered asking Jan to talk with my children and after doing so she told me that nothing had happened to any of them. I passed this information back to Diane and left it at that. Now Jan was telling me that she had lied to me because Donna had told her to keep it secret from me. I talked with Donna but she would not tell me anything and just said she did not want my dad's ashes scattered on Marks grave. I was hurting so very much and did not know what to do because if my dad had been alive I would have confronted him about what I was now hearing for the very first time. My mum was heartbroken at my dad's death and I called my sister Diane and my brother Arthur for their help and advice. It was agreed we should go and talk with the vicar conducting the funeral service to tell him everything and ask for his advice. We were advised to wait until the funeral was over then talk with my mum and tell her what had happened. It was a day I will never forget as I went to my dad's funeral with so many unanswered questions in my mind knowing that I still had to face my mum and tell her things that would break her heart even more.

The day after the funeral I met with my mum with Arthur and

told her what Jan had told me and that my dad's ashes could not be scattered on the grave of Mark. I could feel all the pain and heartache my mum was feeling and at first she threatened to throw me out of her apartment for telling her lies. It was Arthur who managed to calm our mum down. Only God, my dad and Donna knew what had taken place but it was my mum who was paying the price. I knew that I had to go with the wishes of Jan and Donna but I wondered why they had waited for my dad to die before telling me. I asked Donna why she had gone to see my dad in hospital before he had died and she told me she wanted to see if he would say he was sorry to her for what he had done. I reminded Donna that she had been to see him on more than one occasion and had also had other times alone with my dad while she had been married to Steven. My mum telephoned Donna and asked Donna if she would come and talk to her but Donna refused.

After my dad's funeral and all the turmoil that followed it Jan and I worked harder than ever to help bring about the vision we both shared. With the money we received back from the holiday insurance for the loss of the last week of our holiday in Hawaii we were able to book a two week holiday to Egypt in early June. We both needed this holiday after all we had gone through and we managed to get it half price due to holiday makers being killed by terrorists the previous year and a lot of people being put off from going there. We had joined a house fellowship from our church at Val and Alan Dooley's home where we met once a week. We shared fellowship with a group of ten people including Sally, Tony and Daphne who were in contact with Christian prisoners in Egypt. Our house group had been praying for the release of these prisoners for a number of months because they had received unjust sentences from the courts.

Our holiday to Egypt was one where we were allocated our hotel on arrival and it was a very pleasant surprise to find we had been allocated the hotel Sheraton. I knew it was going to be a very busy time in the future for both of us so we spent lots of our days relaxing by the pool side in our hotel. Security was very tight because of the tourists that had been killed a few months before and the government wanted to make sure that it did not happen again. After getting used to the area we made plans to visit Kanater men's prison to visit the prisoners we had been praying for. We had made friends with some other people from England who were staying at our hotel and they asked if they could join us on the train journey to Cairo because they wanted to see the Pyramids and do other sightseeing. I think they also felt safe being with Christians who had no fear of anything. We agreed to travel together but made it clear that when we got to Cairo we would be going separate ways during the day.

Chapter 42

"The King will reply, "I tell you the truth, whatever you did for one of the least of these brothers of mine, you did for me"

Matthew 26 : 40

Because of the very high temperatures in the day we decided to get the overnight train to Cairo at a cost of £10 each. The train journey took about eight hours and when we arrived in Cairo it was early morning with the city alive with people. We made plans to meet our friends in the evening so we could both do the things we had come to Cairo for. We found a taxi driver who could speak some English and we hired him for the day for £30. We told him why we wanted to go to the prison at Kanater and our driver was a blessing sent by God. We only had the names of the prisoners we wanted to see but we had no visiting order or anything else that would allow us to enter the prison.

After a drive of about one hour we arrived at the prison and this was where our taxi driver took over. He spoke to the prison guards on our behalf and slipped a few Egyptian pounds into their hands. Our taxi driver explained that the prison guards had very little money to live on and this was the only way to get things done in Egypt. We waited in a very large room containing hundreds of woman and children who were waiting to see their loved ones. I could see that the prison was very basic and the conditions poor for all concerned. The prison guards had taken our camera but they allowed us to take in the large food hamper that we had brought with us from the Sheraton hotel. After waiting for about an hour we were taken into the prison to visit the men we had come to see. The prison guards were a bit rough with us and one of them emptied Jan's handbag all over the floor making sure she had not smuggled anything in that was not allowed.

Our passports were taken from us and then we were taken to a steel cage that measured about ten metres by four metres containing all the prisoners who were having a visit.

We had never met the prisoners we had come to see or even seen their photograph but right away we could see the Christian prisoners we had come to visit. The smiles on their faces made our journey worthwhile and we were able to give them the bible that Sally had sent for them. We also gave them the food parcel and it was easy to see they had not eaten such good food in a very long time. We told them about the plans we had for building a home in Romania for homeless children. After hearing about their plight in the prison we promised we would help them if we could. After praying together we left the prison making our way back with our taxi driver to Cairo to meet up with our friends. On our return journey to Cairo we had the opportunity of sharing our faith in Jesus Christ with our taxi driver at the same time thanking him and God for the way that we had been helped. We met up with our friends and we found a nice cheap hotel to spend the night before returning to the Sheraton hotel. Jan and I were both very hungry because we had given our food parcel to the prisoners at Kanater. We went in search of a good restaurant finding one at the Sheraton hotel in Cairo. I had learned a long time ago that we can't out give God and that night we had one of the best meals I can ever remember eating. After a good night's sleep we made our way back to the railway station in Cairo for another eight hour journey back to our holiday resort.

Many of the guests at the hotel knew of our plans to visit the prisoners so we had lots of opportunities of sharing how God had opened the door for us to visit the prisoners. It was a very happy time for Jan and I enjoying our holiday very much. On returning to England I contacted a number of voluntary agencies asking them to take up the case of the Christian prisoners in Egypt. One of these agencies was Christian Solidarity Worldwide who informed me that they would take up the cases of the prisoners we had visited. Even though our commitment was for building a home for homeless children in Romania we felt led to organise a charity dinner in Blackpool to help raise funds to fight for their release.

We then started to concentrate on raising the money for Romania where lots of people informed me they would like to help. Blackpool and the Fylde College were a great help with the staff and students preparing the drawings for the home we intended to build. While the drawings were being prepared Renato came up with the name of the home after blind Bartimaeus in the bible. Bartimaeus House soon became a name familiar with lots of people with the local papers giving us lots of free coverage and publicity. As Jan and I had made previous visits to Romania from our management committee we made plans to undertake an aid mission for December 1998 giving other members of the committee the opportunity of seeing for themselves the conditions for homeless children in Romania.

It was an opportunity to involve lots of schools and local people in our aid mission and within a few months we had collected enough aid to fill a twenty ton truck. While Jan and I were busy collecting all the aid Renato was busy forming the charity in Romania with the name of Asociatia Umanitara Bartimaeus. It was good to see the bank account growing with enough money to purchase the land where Bartimaeus House would be built. December 1998 came around very quickly and before we knew it a team of eleven people set off from Blackpool Christian Centre with a large truck loaded with aid plus a mini bus with all our team members. Before we left we had agreed that there would be no drinking of alcohol on this mission because of the bad road conditions we would be driving on. It was also because we had been informed that one of our team members had a drink problem. We elected our Pastor as the team leader but it soon became very clear that our Pastor was not a man who could handle confrontation.

Three of our team members were not Christians and it was not long before they started to consume large amounts of alcohol. This in itself created a lot of tension in our team and they started to find fault in everything that I had planned to do. Time and again God showed us that he was with us as we were able to overcome lots of difficult situations. The road conditions were the worst I had ever driven on as we made our way to Hateg in Romania. All our vehicles engines were frozen so we had to leave them parked up. We had to make the journey to Bucharest by train carrying some of the aid with us so we could visit the children who lived in the sewers. We arrived at Bucharest at 6.00am and we met two Romanians who worked with the street children by the names of Daniel and Liviu. As we arrived in Bucharest one of the members of our team who had been drinking very heavily and smoking like a chimney was arrested by the police in the railway station for his bad behaviour and given a fine. This same person ignored the advice Renato had given him not to change money with the street money changers and also ended up giving £80 for a handful of worthless paper.

Chapter 43

"Then he will say to those on his left, "Depart from me, you who are cursed, into the eternal fire prepared for the devil and his angels. For I was hungry and you gave me nothing to eat, I was thirsty and you gave me nothing to drink, I was a stranger and you did not invite me in. I was sick and in prison and you did not look after me."

Matthew 26 : 41 - 43

The sight of young children sleeping on the cold concrete floors of the underground stations was the first sight we were met with. From there we went down into the sewers to see children as young as two living in conditions that could only be described as hell. We handed out shoe bags filled with teddies and lots of goods donated by caring people in England but we knew that what these children needed more than anything was a loving home they could call home. All our team members had tears running down their cheeks and for some the sight was too much to take in. On a wall in one of the dark sewers one of the children had put up a poster showing Jesus Christ. The boy told us that Jesus was with him day and night pointing to the picture and in my heart I believed that Jesus was present in their situation.

After returning to Hateg from Bucharest we made plans to visit a few orphanages and poor families to distribute the aid we had brought from England. It was also an opportunity to meet with the Romanian committee that Renato had brought together to discuss the way forward with our plans. We looked at two plots of land that Renato had found that were for sale agreeing a price to buy one plot that we believed would be suitable for Bartimaeus House. Jan and I were very happy when it was time to leave Romania because of the constant problems with some members of our team. When the weather turned very bad some of our team wanted to leave Hateg at night time but I insisted that I would not leave until it was morning. This proved to be the right decision because by morning the road was good enough to drive on and we passed many vehicles that had slid off the road during the night.

    When we reached Hungary some of our team wanted to change the plans again and go it alone back to England. Our Pastor was already in discussion with the rest of our team when Jan and I arrived at the table. I made it very clear that we needed to stay together because if any vehicle broke down we would need the other vehicle to get help. After listening to me they decided we would stay together and after a good night's sleep we set off towards Austria. It was not long before I was proved right when the mini bus overheated and broke down on the motorway. After a short delay we carried on with our journey through Austria into Germany. This was when the conditions became very bad and the snow started to fall very thick. It was about 9.00pm and very dark except for the thick white snow falling all around. I knew from previous missions that if we left the motorway we would be in danger of being snowed in but most of the team members in the mini bus were insisting we left the motorway.

    I could hear the shouting and confrontations that were taking place in the mini bus because our Pastor had left his finger on the two way radio and I could hear everything taking place. I was in the truck with Jan and Michael leading the way but our Pastor insisted that we leave the motorway and when we did it soon became very clear it was not the right decision as both vehicles started to get stuck in the deep snow. It did not take long for everyone to agree we go back on the motorway and trust God to lead us to a hotel. After going back onto the motorway I saw a church in the distance and told Michael to come off at the next exit. Within a few minutes we had found a nice hotel where our hosts provided us with a hot meal before going to bed for a good night's sleep. We then made our way to France where we had planned to spend the last night of our mission before making the final leg of our journey back to England. We drove all through the day and found ourselves in a large traffic hold up that grid locked most of the roads in the area. I looked at the map and I found a way where we could leave the motorway and carry on with our journey. We arrived at the home of our friend Lydia in France on the border with Germany at about 10.0pm. This was when our Pastor informed me that the rest of the team were going to carry on back to England with the mini bus leaving Jan and I by ourselves with the large truck. I found it hard to believe that our Pastor would do such a thing after we had worked so hard to put the mission together and overcome all the problems we had faced. On the other hand Jan and I were happy to be by ourselves with the way that some of the team members had behaved.

Jan and I arrived back in England a day later than the rest of our team with a great deal of sadness at the way our Pastor had led the team mission. It soon became very clear to Jan and I that relations between us and our Pastor and his wife had become very strained. We had a quiet Christmas together at home at the end of 1998 but started to make plans to return to Romania in March 1999 to work on the building of Bartimaeus House. It was early January when we received news from Renato that the land we wanted to buy had gone up in price so they had decided not to proceed with the purchase. Renato told us about another plot of land that was for sale at Ciula Mica near to where he lived and he would try and get the owners to sell.

Chapter 44

"Ask and it will be given to you; seek and you will find; knock and the door will be opened to you. For everyone who asks receives; he who seeks finds; and to him who knocks, the door will be opened"

Matthew 7 : 7 - 8

Jan and I had been praying about giving up our rented bungalow and going to Romania in March as we believed the situation in Romania would only improve if we were present to oversee things. We did not have enough money to go but we asked God to provide for us if we were to give up our home and go to Romania. Once we had made the decision to go lots of problems started to go wrong with our mini bus that needed lots of money to put right. We found that cheques started to arrive from friends of ours that were enough to pay over £1000 for the repairs without taking any money from the Bartimaeus Romania bank account. Our friends in Switzerland asked us to call and see them on our way to Romania as they had some money they wanted to give to us. All this was confirmation that we were in the will of God in what we were doing. We informed our family and friends that we were taking a step of faith. We gave most of our large possessions away to our children but stored the things we wanted to keep in a shed at the bottom of Donna's garden. We were sad that our church did not even have a love offering or a prayer to send us on our way but by now we had learned to trust in God and not man. On the 31st March 1999 Jan and I set off with our mini bus loaded up with everything we would need. We were prepared to spend at least one year in Romania to help undertake the vision we had been given.

Our friends Cyril and Claudine in Switzerland were very pleased to see us. They made arrangements for us to stay in a nice hotel in

Basel. They took us out for lunch and Cyril gave us the equivalent of £4000 in Swiss Francs to help us undertake our mission. We arrived in Hateg after a five day journey where Renato had found us a nice apartment to rent for £100 per month. We paid three months rent in advance and settled into our new home very quickly. We then met with our Romanian committee to discuss the way forward with the purchase of land to build Bartimaeus House. The first thing that Jan and I wanted to do was see the land for ourselves. When we saw it we both knew right away that it was perfect for what we needed. Within four weeks we had purchased the land and commissioned the Romanian architect who was going to alter the drawings prepared by Blackpool and The Fylde College to Romanian specifications.

Things between Jan and I were not good as she believed that I was having an affair behind her back with a Romanian girl who was my translator. I tried to reassure Jan that I loved her and that I was not doing anything wrong. I was spending all my time with Jan and we went everywhere together but this was not the first time Jan had accused me of cheating on her. We both decided to have lessons from a teacher to learn the Romanian language but I think Jan was finding it hard to learn. I think a big part of her was missing our children and grandchildren back in England. In May we selected some of the workers to work on the land at Ciula Mica to help me put up fencing and build a concrete bridge for access onto the land. We were all very happy at the way things were going and we sent out monthly newsletters to our committee in England and supporters.

We sent a fax to our committee asking them to release some more money to us in Romania so we could carry on with what we were doing. It came as a big surprise to Jan and I when they informed us that they were not happy at releasing the money we had requested. We made it very clear that we would return back to England immediately if we had lost the support of our committee and if they did not trust us in what we were doing. Maybe I should have taken this as a sign of what the future had in store. Our committee soon released the money we had requested and our Pastor explained that various fractions had been taking place while we were in Romania. The main problem stemmed from a member of our committee who I had been sending faxes to. The faxes that I sent had not been passed onto the main committee who in turn thought I was not keeping them informed of what was taking place when I was in fact keeping them up to date.

By June we had reached the stage where there was nothing more we could do on the land until the architect had completed all the drawings and obtained all the planning and building permissions that we were going to need to build Bartimaeus House. As the fund raising was going very slowly Jan and I decided that it would be better if we both returned to England to help raise the money we were going to need.

We informed both committees of our decision to return to England and everyone agreed that this was the best way forward until we had the money we needed to build Bartimaeus House. We arrived back in England in early June at the home of our daughter Michelle who lived in Stockport. Michelle had suffered a break in while we had been in Romania when she was asleep with her two young children. Jan and I had both been very upset at this news and sad we had not been there to help her. Michelle was suffering from stress because the men who broke into her home had woken her by shining a torch into her face. We had no home of our own so we stayed with Michelle a short time while we prayed where to go.

We visited most of the housing associations in Stockport filling in application forms hoping we would be offered something to rent but we were told we were low priority. In early July Jan had to visit the doctor at Cleveleys and while we were in the town we noticed a sign in the butchers shop advertising a flat to rent. We decided to take a look at the flat and it was fully furnished with everything we needed. We still had some money left over so we paid the deposit and agreed to move into the flat the following day. The day after moving into the flat I noticed an empty shop to rent less than twenty metres from where we lived. I felt God saying to me that this shop would be our first charity shop for raising money for Bartimaeus House. I made some enquiries and it turned out that the butcher we rented our flat from also owned the empty shop. I went to speak with him and shared the vision we had of helping homeless children in Romania. The butcher explained that he was a Christian and that he was willing to let us rent the shop for £160 per week if we could pay three months rent in advance.

At our next committee meeting I put forward the plan of opening charity shops to raise money for Romania. I told them that Jan and I were willing to sign for the lease in our names and we would put up the money for the three months rent. They agreed for us to proceed with the legal formalities. Within two weeks Jan and I had fitted out the shop and we were ready to open. Local people supported us in a big way and the shop was full of donated items. Our first week's takings came to over £1200 and within the first month we had recouped all of our initial outlay.

We sensed a lot of resentment from certain members of our church because they had also opened a charity shop to raise money for the church that was situated in a bad place and only took about £300 per week. We tried to put this behind us and carried on working hard to raise the money we needed. I was unemployed so this gave me lots of free time to work on the vision we had been given. I was working over twelve hours a day writing to many different charitable trusts also speaking at lots of churches and schools trying to raise the money that was needed. Our house group was very supportive of what we were doing and we looked upon this fellowship as our real church. Val and Alan were also going through a very difficult time because Alan's cancer had returned and he was undergoing lots of treatment.

In August I was advised by a trusted friend to form Bartimaeus Romania into its own independent charity away from our church because he believed that our church wanted to claim Bartimaeus House for the Pentecostal movement. I was also advised by another good friend who worked for a large charity that we would need to be independent because of the large project we were undertaking. At our next management meeting I put forward the idea of forming our own independent charity. This was accepted by the committee and it was left to me to organise everything and undertake all the legal formalities. Our Pastor agreed we could carry on working under the charity number of our church while everything was undertaken.

The situation in our church was not getting any better with lots of people unhappy about the way our church was going. Val and Alan made a decision to leave the church and our Pastor telephoned me asking me to collect some books from Val and Alan that belonged to the church so he did not have to see them. I told my Pastor that I was not willing to do that and that he should go and see them himself and find out why they had wanted to leave our church. He became very angry with me and accused me of being a trouble causer and told me that I should consider leaving his church as well. He told me that he and his wife were now resigning from Bartimaeus Romania and that we should transfer everything from our church as soon as possible.

Jan and I still attended our church for the following weeks but we were praying for God to show us what to do. We did not want to leave the church because other people had left and we prayed the situation would change. This proved to be a false hope because when God gave me a word to speak at church I was obedient and started to share the word. God revealed to me that my Pastor would try and prevent me from sharing the word but I was to insist that I give it. I even wrote down on a piece of paper what my Pastor would do in the hope that I would be allowed to bring the word. As soon as I started to speak during open worship my Pastor told me to shut up and sit down. I refused to do so and I took the paper out of my pocket to show the members of our church what God had revealed to me. My Pastor told some of the church members from the gypsy community to get hold of me and physically eject me out of the church. My wife Jan left her seat and followed me out of the church. I could not believe what was happening and I wondered what my Pastor was afraid of. Lots of people in that church knew that things were wrong but not one person was prepared to stand up and ask the Pastor to let me bring the word so it could be tested. Jan and I returned home that Sunday morning and I went into my offices at the charity shop and typed out the words that God had given me to speak. I photocopied the paper and on the Sunday evening I returned to the church and handed a copy to everyone who would receive it. I knew that I had completed the task that God had put on my heart to do. It was also the last time we would go near that church. The following week we felt the backlash from our Pastor when he contacted the Charity Commission to inform them we were no longer working under the charity of the church.

I had already taken steps to register our charity with the Charity Commission so when they contacted me I was able to give them a full account of our situation. They informed me that it was not legal for us to work under the charity number of Blackpool Christian Centre and that our Pastor should have not allowed this in the first place. I was kept very busy writing endless letters to the Charity Commission who wanted to know everything about our plans to build Bartimaeus House. I would send them information they had requested and then I would receive another letter asking for information that I had already sent to them or they would ask for something else. I was asked to attend an interview at their office in Liverpool where they discussed in detail our situation. I knew that the work I was doing would be subject to strict investigation because of my dealings with the Charity Commission over The New Life Centre. I was not worried because I knew that all my dealings were honest and above board.

During this period I found myself working under a great deal of pressure especially as we had planned another aid mission to Romania for December 1999 that involved me in collecting all the aid. I found myself doing the work of about ten people and I knew that I could not continue at the pace I was going. Jan was also working very hard at the charity shop. I asked Jan to come with me to Romania so that we would not be separated. Jan insisted that she did not want to go and nothing was going to change her mind. I was also in negotiations for opening two more charity shops at Cleveleys and St. Anne's that would provide all the income that was needed for building and sustaining Bartimaeus House. At the same time it would enable all the key workers including myself to be employed by our charity.

Chapter 45

"Religion that God our Father accepts as pure and faultless is this: to look after orphans and widows in their distress and to keep oneself from being polluted by the world"

James 1 : 27

Everything seemed to be coming together and I had found a number of people who were prepared to sponsor Renato so that we could pay him £100 a month for working for our charity in Romania. We loaded up a twenty ton truck with all the aid we had collected for Romania and this was sent safely on its way. Our bank account was growing day by day and some large charitable trusts had made some large donations. Renato had been able to obtain most of the permissions we needed to build and we believed that by March 2000 we would be ready to start work on the foundations.

December 1999 came around very quickly and before we knew it Stephen, Sue, Alma. Bill, Brenda and I were on our way to Romania to meet up with Renato and Ica in Bucharest. Ica lived in Codlea near Brasov and we hoped that Ica would become one of the managers of Bartimaeus House when it was built. Jan and I had introduced Ica and Stephen to each other a few months before. Stephen had fallen in love with Ica and he hoped she would do the same. Bill and Brenda who were in their sixties were planning to stay long term in Romania. They had sold their home in England and were very excited at the prospect of going to Romania. We boarded the aeroplane at Manchester airport and had a trouble free flight to Bucharest via Amsterdam. When we arrived at Bucharest Renato and Ica were waiting to meet us with a mini bus and driver to take us to Hateg.

Alma, Sue and Ica were provided with accommodation at the home of Sorin and Nica Bistrian, Bill and Brenda at the home of the

Cotolan family and Stephen and I stayed at the apartment in Hateg that Renato used as the office for the charity in Romania. Everything worked out very well and we were kept busy distributing aid to many poor families and orphanages in the area. I did not realise it at that time but I was about to meet someone who would change my life in a very dramatic way.

The day started out very normal with us as busy as ever distributing donated aid to the orphanage at Pestianna where we put on a Christmas party for over one hundred children. I had the privilege of being Father Christmas and took great delight in being with the children and giving them all a Christmas present. In the evening we all had a meal with Sorin and Nica and at about 10.00pm Stephen and I walked home through the snow to the apartment where we were staying. We had a snowball fight on the way home and had a good laugh because of the electronic gadget that Stephen had brought with him from England that frightened dogs away at the press of a button. Stray dogs had always been a problem for us in Romania, especially Stephen who had once been bitten by one. We were like two young children in the way that we behaved and it felt good to let our hair down after giving so much of ourselves throughout the day.

When we arrived at our apartment I decided to clean my boots outside our front door of the apartment where we were staying. I noticed a Romanian lady aged about thirty five who was cleaning the front door of the apartment right next door to where we were staying. The lady tried to speak with me in Romanian and when she realised that I was from England she went inside to fetch her daughter who could speak a little English. They were both very friendly and I explained what we were doing in Romania, they explained to me that they were looking after the apartment while the owner was in Hungary. They invited Stephen and me in for a cup of coffee so I went and told Stephen.

We accepted their offer and went into their apartment. The lady was called Angela and her daughter was called Andreia. They both wanted to know all that we were doing in Romania. We then asked them about their own lives and they told us how difficult their own lives were and how they had no proper home of their own. They explained how both of them needed medication and at times they had no money to buy what they needed. Angela explained how she had a bad problem with her teeth and that she had an infection in her gums. Their story was very similar to lots of other Romanian people we had met and we went back into our apartment to pick up a box of aid and antibiotics to give to them.

They wanted to know what I looked like in my Father Christmas outfit and I went back into our apartment to dress up so they could see for themselves. Stephen happened to sneeze when I came back into their apartment and we all ended up laughing because of the way he frightened us all. We brought a lot of happiness into their lives and after about an hour we returned back to our own apartment. The following day we went to Pretesti to distribute aid and this time Renato played the role of Father Christmas. When Stephen and I returned home in the evening Andreia knocked at the front door of our apartment to ask how we were doing. Andreia explained that her mother needed some medication and they did not have enough money to buy any. I was able to give Andreia some more of the medicines we had brought from England and also some money for her mother. Andreia thanked us for helping them and told us how happy they were to receive the parcel of aid and clothes we had given them the previous night.

Andreia told us that she was fourteen years old and that in February it would be her birthday. She wanted to know what it was like in England and to travel through other countries. We both enjoyed the company of Andreia because she was so full of fun and happy to be with. I don't know what made me say it but I told Andreia that when I returned to Romania in February I would take her to Bucharest for her birthday. Andreia had lived in Romania all her life and had never once visited the capitol of her country. I knew that I would be going to Bucharest to visit the children who lived in the sewers and thought it would be a nice birthday present for Andreia.

Our last night in Hateg soon arrived and Renato called to pick us up in the mini bus to take us on our return journey back to Bucharest so we could catch our aeroplane back to England. I gave Angela and Andreia a small amount of money to help them buy some food for Christmas and any other medicines they might need. They were both sad that we were leaving and Andreia started to sing the song from Titanic "My heart will go on". I looked at the face of Andreia and I could see the tears running down her cheeks. I told her not to be sad and that in February we would be back in Hateg and would see her again. As we climbed into the mini bus Andreia gave me a kiss on the cheek as it is the Romanian custom to do so and we said goodbye.

As we made the overnight journey to Codlea we were all very happy to have completed a successful mission. We met the family of Ica in Codlea and after a two hour rest we continued on to Bucharest. We had saved lots of shoe bags filled with a teddy and goodies for the children who lived down the sewers in Bucharest and in the underground stations. Their situation had not changed since I had last visited the children and we were all sad to see the conditions they had to endure. They were very happy to receive the gifts we had brought with us from England but we knew that what they needed was a home of their own. In my heart I just wished that Bartimaeus House was completed so that we could offer some of the children we met a chance of rebuilding their lives. We took some photographs so we could show people back in England how the children had to live.

I finished the roll of film in my camera and I gave the camera to Renato so he could give it to Ana-Maria so she could take some photographs of her baptism that was going to take place in January. I asked Alma not to say anything to Jan about the camera because I knew that Jan thought something was going on between Ana -Maria and I. As we made our way back to Otopeni airport for our return flight back to England Alma told me she had something important to say. I wondered what it might be then she told me that she had seen the love I had for the people of Romania and had witnessed the sacrifice and commitment that Jan and I had made. She explained that her heart had been touched by God and that she wanted to bless Jan and I with a holiday and when we returned home she would give us £600 so we could take a holiday together.

Chapter 46

"Get rid of all bitterness, rage and anger, brawling and slander, along with every form of malice. Be kind and compassionate to one another, forgiving each other, just as in Christ God forgave you"

Ephesians 4 : 31 - 32

It was a good feeling to be back at home with Jan and we were both excited at the prospect of going on holiday for Christmas thanks to Alma. We looked around for a last minute holiday and we found a holiday for one week in Cyprus that left on Christmas day and returned the day after Jan's birthday. We should have been very happy on holiday but we were not and had a few disagreements. I think my mind was on the situation of the people in Romania that I had left behind only a few days before. I found it very hard to relax and switch off and it did not help when I got food poisoning and was ill for a couple of days. We saw in the New Year of 2000 from our hotel balcony and I could not help thinking how much money had been wasted throughout the world on fireworks when so many people were in need.

    We returned back to England and after a few days rest we re-opened the charity shop and made plans for returning to Romania so that I could select the builder for building Bartimaeus House. Bill and Brenda had given me £4000 to buy a mini bus for Romania and had also donated their old car to the charity shop for me to sell. I looked around for a suitable mini bus for Romania but I was not able to find a good one. I asked Jan if we should sell our mini bus to the charity for a nominal £2000 because we knew it was reliable and would be ideal for what was needed in Romania. We both agreed that this was a good idea and we put it to the management committee who agreed to purchase our mini bus. We tried to sell the old car that Bill had donated but without any success. When we agreed to sell our mini bus to the charity we decided to buy the car for ourselves for the £100 we were advertising it for. I put the money for the car into the charity shop and thought no more about it.

During the second week of January we made plans to go for a meal with Alma, Sue, and Stephen so we could share fellowship together and talk about our recent mission to Romania. We had a good time together until Alma let slip that I had given a camera to Ana-Maria. I knew by the look on Jan's face that I would be in for it when we returned home. The door of our apartment was barely closed when Jan accused me all over again of having a secret affair with Ana-Maria. I tried to explain that the reason I had not told her about the camera was because of the amount of times she had accused me of having affairs with her and also other females from our church. It led to a big row and in my heart I knew that I could not take much more of this from Jan.

Over the next two weeks I was very busy making plans for taking the mini bus to Romania and made sure that everything that needed repairing on the mini bus was undertaken. Stephen was also busy making plans for returning to Romania so that he could work with Renato on behalf of our charity. Stephen was going to spend a week with Ica's family at Codlea before going to Hateg to find out if Ica was still prepared to work for our charity in Romania. Jan and I agreed that it would be better for me to return to Romania before our wedding anniversary on the 1st February so that I would be back in England to oversee the legal formalities of opening two more charity shops we had planned to open. On the 28th January I took Jan out for a meal to celebrate our wedding anniversary and on our return home Jan started accusing me all over again of having an affair with Ana-Maria. I was not meant to leave for Romania until 3.0am but I could not take any more and left our apartment at 1.00am slamming the door behind me as I left.

I drove to Dover nonstop and at 9.00am I arrived safely at the port. I telephoned Jan on my mobile phone to try and make up with her and to tell her that I loved her but could not take much more of her accusations. After a three day journey I arrived safely in Hateg and met up with Renato and the other committee members of the charity from Romania. Renato had selected three builders as I had instructed him to do to prepare estimates for the building of Bartimaeus House. Over the next few days I was busy looking through the estimates and met with the builders to discuss various aspects of the building work with them. I met up with Andreia again who was very happy to see me. I told her that I was going to Bucharest to book my return flight back to England and if she wanted she was welcome to come with me as a present for her birthday. Andreia asked her mother Angela if it was alright for her to come with me and her mother agreed that she could go.

Over the next few days I saw a lot of Andreia and we started to enjoy each other's company a great deal. My feelings for Andreia started to turn from that of a friend to one of love (or was it lust?) and I could tell that Andreia felt the same way about me. We had a wonderful time together in Bucharest and this was where we told each other about our true feelings. I knew it was wrong to fall in love with a girl so young especially when I was already married and with the huge task I had undertaken for God to build a home for homeless children in Romania. I know that inside of my heart and mind a huge battle was taking place between the spirit and my flesh. On our return back to Hateg Andreia was with me in the apartment when I received a telephone call from Jan on my mobile phone. She told me that she knew that I was having an affair with either Angela or Andreia because she had opened a letter that had been sent to me by Andreia. I asked Jan to read the letter out to me over the telephone and when she did I knew that Jan had misinterpreted the letter. Jan told me that she was leaving me and that it was the end of our marriage. I pleaded with Jan not to do anything hasty but to wait until I returned home so we could talk things through. Jan told me to get with my bitch and that she was leaving me for good and closed the telephone.

I asked Andreia if she had wrote a letter and she told me that she had done so to thank me for helping her and her mother when I was in Romania at Christmas. The following day the committee members in Romania told me that people in Hateg were talking about the close relationship I had formed with Andreia and it would not be good for our charity. Renato explained that it was only a small town and that people would make things up even if it was not true. They advised me to break off all contact with Andreia but I knew in my heart that I could not do what they wanted me to do. On one hand I had started to fall in love with a beautiful young girl who had just turned fifteen and who I believed loved me the same way. On the other hand I had a beautiful wife who I loved who was constantly accusing me of having affairs and had left me. I knew that my mind was all mixed up and I did not know what to do for the best. After selecting the builder and making the contract with him for building Bartimaeus House I told Renato that I was returning to England to try and sort my personal life out. I asked him if I could write to Andreia through his home address because she did not have a permanent home of her own. On the journey back to England I tried to make some sort of sense out of what was happening in my life.

When I arrived back at our apartment in Cleveleys Jan was not there as she had told me and I noticed a letter that she had left for me to read. It was a copy of the letter Andreia had written to me and Jan had written a few words at the bottom telling me that I could have her. I made contact with Jan pleading with her to come home and let me explain all that had taken place. I still loved Jan and wanted to save our marriage but each time I contacted her I received a great deal of abuse. Renato telephoned me from Romania to inform me that it would be better if I helped Andreia and her mother move away from Hateg because of the way that people were talking. I told Renato that I would try and bring them to England because we would need people to help out in the charity shops we were going to open. I asked Renato to help them obtain passports and told him that I would send the invitations for them to come to England.

I now accepted that my marriage to Jan was over and I contacted a solicitor to apply for a divorce. Over the next four weeks I was very busy working at the charity shop and dealing with lots of paperwork in connection with the affairs of the charity. Even though I had accepted that Jan did not want to save our marriage I made several attempts for reconciliation. Each time I met up with Jan I came away with tears in my eyes because of the way she spoke to me. The legal formalities of opening one of the charity shops were almost completed and the money we needed for the first stage of the building works had now been raised. I had agreed with the builder to pay $50,000 for the first stage of the building work but decided that this was a large amount to give up front and informed him and our management committee in England that I was going to re-negotiate the contract so that the first stage payment for the building work would amount to $30,000. We had changed the money we had in our bank account into US$ ready for me to take to Romania but after re-negotiating the contract with the builder I was able to leave money behind in the bank and returned to Romania with $33,000 in cash to pay the builder, cover my expenses and to give Renato money for the expenses of the charity in Romania.

It was early March when I went back to Romania by aeroplane from Manchester airport and I asked Renato to meet me at Bucharest airport because of the large amount of cash I was carrying. Renato was waiting to meet me and we made our way across town to catch the train to Hateg. During the journey I received a telephone call from Brenda who was a trustee of our charity in England. She asked me what was going on in Romania with Andreia because she had spoken with Jan who had told her all sorts of things about me. I told Brenda that I would explain everything when I returned to England.

Renato had helped Angela and Andreia obtain their passports and the next step was to go to Bucharest to see the British Embassy to apply for their visa's to come to England. I went with them to the British Embassy in Bucharest but they were informed that they would have to attend a personal interview two weeks later where a decision would be made. As I would be back in England at the time of their personal interview I asked Renato if he would go with them. While I was still in Hateg I received news from England that Renato had opened and copied a love letter I had wrote to Andreia at his address and had sent it to Jan. By now Stephen and Ica were in Hateg and Stephen also had a copy of the letter I had written to Andreia. I was very angry and upset at the underhanded way that Renato and Stephen were behaving and I told them both how I felt. They each blamed the other person for opening the letter and it was difficult to work out who was telling the truth.

Everything was coming to a head and even though I knew my marriage to Jan was over I still had to decide on what to do concerning my relationship with Andreia. I knew that I could not have Andreia and also work for Bartimaeus Romania and that I had important decisions to make. I knew that if I was going to marry Andreia that I would have to wait until she was sixteen for our marriage to be lawful in England and I knew that lots of people would be against us. I told Renato that I would telephone him from England to let him know what decision I had reached and if I still wanted him to go to the British Embassy with Angela and Andreia so they could obtain their visa's to come to England. I also spoke with Jan on the telephone who told me that she would like to speak with me immediately upon my return from Romania at the home of my daughter Michelle.

After travelling for twenty two hours I arrived at my daughter's home to be met by my wife Jan and our three children Donna, Robert and Michelle. They had a copy of the love letter I had wrote to Andreia and they all made it clear to me that they did not approve of my relationship with a fifteen year old girl. My children told me that they accepted that my marriage to their mother was over and that if the girl I had met was older they could have accepted it but not with a girl so young. My children went on to tell me that if I continued with this relationship I could forget about ever seeing them or my grandchildren again.

I returned to Cleveleys knowing that I would have to make a decision one way or the other. On my return I met with Brenda and Eunice two trustees of our charity and explained the situation to them. They made it very clear that if I continued to see the young girl I had met in Romania that it could have serious affects on our charity and the work we had started in Romania. I told them that I was praying about the way forward and I would let them know at our next management meeting what I was going to do. I met up with Val and Rob who was the Pastor from the church I had started to attend and asked them to pray with me and for their advice. They both advised me to give up Andreia and concentrate on the building of Bartimaeus House.

On the 29th March I reached the decision to give Andreia up and I sent her a fax via Renato informing her that I was ending our relationship. I explained that I would have to give up my ministry and that my children and grandchildren would not want to speak with me again. I explained how the differences in our ages would turn lots of people against us and that I did not want to put her through that kind of pressure. I told Andreia that I would still help her and her mother financially but that it would be better all round if our relationship ended. Renato took Andreia to his apartment so that he could translate the fax and try and get them to understand why I was ending my relationship with Andreia. I informed Renato that I would telephone the British Embassy to cancel the appointment that had been made and that I would carry on with the building of Bartimaeus House.

On the 31st March 2000 I attended a meeting of the trustees where I also invited Jim Webber who I thought was a friend to discuss the possibility of him becoming a trustee of our charity. I had met with Jim on a number of occasions over the past few months to share with him in confidence the problems I was going through because of my relationship with Andreia so he knew all there was to know. I informed all the trustees that I had ended my relationship with Andreia before any real harm had been done and that by ending the relationship I believed I was doing the right thing and putting God and the children of Romania before my own desires. The trustees agreed that by the 14th April I should resign as a trustee and take up paid employment as Project Co-ordinator on a starting salary of £15,000 per year.

The following day I tore up the return flight ticket I had for Romania and sent off my passport to Swansea as proof of ID to apply for a new driving licence. In my heart and mind I had reached the decision to carry on with the ministry I had been given. On Tuesday the 4th April I received a telephone call from Stephen informing me that I needed to contact Renato urgently. Stephen was very upset and told me that all kinds of rumours were being spread around Hateg that I had forced Andreia to have sex with me. I managed to get hold of Renato who informed me that his wife Anca had been stopped by Angela outside of the main post office in Hateg demanding money from her. Renato told me that I would need to return to Romania and sort out these problems because he did not want to have anything more to do with it. He went on to explain that it was going to have very serious affects on our charity if the rumours that were going around were not brought to an end. I told Renato that I would return to Romania as soon as possible to try and resolve the problems that I had helped to create. On the 5th April I was out early collecting furniture that had been donated for our new charity store that we were about to open. When I returned to the charity shop and went into my office I was greeted by Carol Fowler and Eunice Forrest two trustees of our charity along with Jim Weber and Dave Thomas. Dave Thomas accused me of running an illegal charity and told me I was under investigation by the Charity Commission. Jim Webber told me that he had taken legal advice and told me that the trustees had dispensed with my services and that I should open a letter that was on my desk.

I opened the letter that was typed on official letter headed paper from our charity dated 4th April 2000. It read "Extraordinary Meeting Tuesday 4th April 2000". The letter informed me that I had been suspended forthwith as a trustee and that I should attend a meeting on the 25th April. I informed them that what they had done was not lawful and handed them a copy of the memorandum and articles of association pertaining to our charity. Carol Fowler told me to resign and Eunice Forrest asked me to give her the keys to the charity shop. I told them that I would not do anything without praying over the situation. I also advised them to see a solicitor and told Jim Webber and Dave Thomas that they had both told a pack of lies.

I left the charity shop and returned home to try and make sense of what had just taken place. Only five days before the trustees had agreed for me to carry on with my ministry and then they decided to hold an unlawful extraordinary meeting where they had not even bothered to contact all the trustees of the charity to form a quorum. I believed that Jim Webber and Dave Thomas had been working behind my back especially with the lies that they had told. After a night of prayer I decided that I would not accept their decision unless they called a lawful meeting. I wrote a letter to Eunice Forrest who was chairperson of our charity informing her of my decision and making it clear that if they held a lawful meeting I would attend and if at that meeting I did not have the support of the trustees to carry on with my ministry that I would resign. I asked them to hold the meeting after the 30th April to give me time to go to Romania and try and resolve the problems Renato had told me about.

Chapter 47

"If someone asks him, "what are these wounds on your body?" he will answer, "The wounds I was given at the house of my friends"

Zechariah 13 : 6

I managed to obtain an emergency passport to enable me to return to Romania on the 7th April. Before leaving I received a telephone call from my daughter Donna who was very distressed. Donna was five months pregnant and Donna and her husband Chris were both trustees of our charity. Donna told me that Jim Webber had telephoned her to say that I had stolen money belonging to our charity and had opened a secret bank account in Romania for transferring the stolen money. I tried to calm Donna down and explained that the bank account that I had opened in Romania was done with the approval and knowledge of all the trustees so that foreign currency could be deposited and withdrawn as it was needed. I told Donna that Renato and Nica had been given legal authority to use my account and that I had done nothing illegal. Donna did not believe me and she told me that she was resigning from the charity forthwith and so was Chris.

I was very angry at what Jim Webber had done and it was clear he wanted to frighten Donna and Chris to resign so he could get control of the charity. I wrote a letter to the trustees making it very clear that I was very upset at the way they were conducting their affairs and that I would take legal action against anyone who told lies about me. My heart was very sad at the way that people were behaving towards me when I had worked so hard to build the charity into a successful charity. I felt like all the love and hard work that I had given out had all been for nothing. I was being discarded like an old shoe and I was at a very low point in my life. My dear friend Alan had passed away while he was on holiday with Val in America and I remembered how much support he had given to Jan and I for the building of Bartimaeus House.

As I boarded my flight to Romania on the 7th April I knew in my heart that I had lost the support of everyone who was a trustee of Bartimaeus Romania. I wondered how they were going to carry on with the building of Bartimaeus House because I had been responsible for undertaking at least 80% of the work. I made my own way to Deva from Bucharest and telephoned Renato on the card telephone because my mobile telephone had been disconnected by the trustees without them even informing me. I arranged for Renato to pick me up at the railway station and on our journey to Hateg he brought me up to date with everything that had been taking place. I informed Renato that I was going to resign as a trustee from Bartimaeus Romania but before I did so I was going to help Andreia and Angela move away from Hateg. I explained that I was not going to discuss any details with him because of all the lies that were being spread about me and circulated back to England.

I made arrangements with Stephen and Bill to pick up the mini bus from them and I drove to Ciula Mica to inspect the work that the builder had started. I was very happy to see that the foundations had been installed but I wondered how far the work would proceed without me involved any longer. I met up with Andreia and Angela and we discussed all that had been happening while I had been in England. I was told that Renato and Anca had told lots of lies about me because they wanted to break up my relationship with Andreia. They informed me that Anca had told them that I had affairs with at least five other girls including Ana-Maria. Andreia explained how Stephen had put pressure on her to tell him the date I was returning back to Romania and I realised how he had been passing this information back to the trustees in England. I felt betrayed by Renato, Anca and Stephen and I told them face to face how I felt about them.

I telephoned the British Embassy to make a fresh appointment for Andreia and Angela to try and get their visa's to come to England. We discussed all the possibilities that were open to us and we agreed that the best thing for Andreia was for her to go and stay with her father Liviu who lived in Timisoara with his second wife Lica. From Timisoara we could go to the British Embassy in Bucharest and apply for their visas. We left Hateg on the 14th April with my mini bus loaded up with all my possessions from the apartment in Hateg and all the possessions that belonged to Andreia. We arrived in Timisoara at the home of Liviu and Lica after a five hour journey.

On Monday 17th April Angela, Andreia, Lica and myself travelled on the overnight train from Timisoara to Bucharest for a 2.00pm appointment at the British Embassy. Lica and I waited while Andreia and Angela had their personal interview and when I saw the look on their faces I knew that they had been refused a visa. On the refusal paper that they were given it stated that I was no longer a trustee of the charity and I was having a relationship with Andreia. They stated that they believed Andreia and Angela would not return to Romania if they were granted a visa but they could apply again in the future.

We decided that it would be best for Andreia to stay with her father and step mother in Timisoara while Angela returned to Hateg where she had a job. I boarded the return train to Timisoara with Andreia and Lica while Angela boarded a train to Deva. The train journey lasted for twelve hours and we were all cramped up in a small compartment where it was very hot. I became very ill after the train journey and I had to go to the hospital in Timisoara for emergency treatment. I was diagnosed as having pneumonia with a very bad chest infection. The way that Andreia looked after me showed me even more clearly that she really did love me.

I lay in bed trying to decide the best way forward with my life and asking God to show me what to do. Everybody was telling me to give up Andreia but even when I had decided to do so I was still being discarded like a worn out shoe, with many people stabbing me in the back. My wife and the trustees of the charity had made it very clear to me that I was not wanted anymore with my children threatening to disown me if I continued with Andreia. I thought about the love I had for Andreia and the love that Andreia had for me. I thought about the love I had for my children and grandchildren but I knew that I was entitled to try and find some happiness in my own life just like everybody else. God knew my heart and how hard I had tried to make things right with Jan and the trustees of the charity. I was convinced that God had forgiven me for where I had gone wrong because he had seen all the things that other people had done behind my back that had forced me into the situation I now found myself in. If my children really loved me I was convinced that one day they would forgive me because since becoming a Christian I had been a very good father to them. I knew that if I left Andreia it would break her heart and enough people had been hurt already by what had been taking place.

I talked everything over with Andreia and I asked her if she would marry me when I was divorced from Jan. Andreia did not hesitate to say yes even when I had told her how everybody would be against us being together. Andreia made it very clear to me that my age did not matter to her because she loved me very much. I told Andreia that I would return to England and finalise my affairs and return back to her as soon as possible. The mini bus had a major problem with the engine so I arranged for a friend of Liviu to carry out the repairs while I made plans to return to England. I booked a flight from Timisoara airport on the 25th April via Otopeni to Manchester.

On my return to Cleveleys I called into the charity shop with my resignation letter for the trustees of the charity and a list of expenses that I was owed by the charity that amounted to over £4000. I was met at the front door of the charity shop by a volunteer called Archie who informed me that I could not enter the charity shop to collect my personal belongings. He informed me that the police wanted to speak to me and that there was talk about me being a child molester. I told him that I would treat his remarks with the contempt they deserved and that I was more than happy to speak with the police if he could tell me who wanted to speak with me. Archie would not say who had made these comments to him and I was convinced they were words from his own heart and mouth. I contacted Cleveleys police but they had no information of anyone who wanted to speak with me.

I returned back to my home to sort out my affairs to prepare for leaving England for good. I telephoned Jan to let her know I was leaving and to see if there was anything she wanted from the home we had shared together. I met up with my mum to inform her of my decision and while I was with my mum in the car Donna telephoned me. Donna was screaming down the phone that she hated me and that she would never have anything more to do with me and I would never see my grandchildren again. I tried to explain why I was going back to be with Andreia but Donna was not in a listening frame of mind and closed the phone. I received a telephone call from the police who informed me that Jim Webber and Dave Thomas had made various allegations about me but the police had told them to get their facts and evidence before going back to the police. A few days later my front door bell rang and when I opened the door Jim Webber, Dave Thomas, Janice and Jim Mcvey were standing there like a lynching party.

Jim Webber shouted that he had come for the money and car I had stolen and that he wanted the computer I had in my home that belonged to the charity. I asked him to give me details of what he was alleging and told him I did not know what he was talking about. I told them that the police had told them to provide proof of what they were alleging and if it was true why were they there and not the police. I told them that the car belonged to me and was not registered in the name of the charity as I had paid £100 to the charity shop for the car when I had sold my mini bus to the charity. I invited Janice and Jim Mcvey into my home but told Jim Webber and Dave Thomas to wait outside as they were not welcome.

It was Janice's father Bill who had given me the car in the first place and she told me that if I had paid £100 for the car it was good enough for her and as far as she was concerned the car belonged to me. Jim and Janice told me that they were very unhappy about the way that Jim Webber, Dave Thomas and the trustees were behaving and it was not a good example of how Christians should behave towards each other. I broke down and started to cry because of the loving way they had behaved towards me. This had been the first time when I had witnessed anyone behaving in a Godly manner towards me. I told them that I did not want anything that belonged to the charity and that they could remove the computer from my home. I told them that I had been prevented from removing goods that belonged to me from the charity shop. While I was talking with Janice and Jim I noticed Jim Webber and Dave Thomas with big grins on their faces talking on a mobile telephone outside my front door. I was not really interested in what they were up to as I had already decided I would be making a new life for myself with Andreia and people could say or do what they wanted. I knew that God still loved me and knew the truth about everything and that was what counted to me. Jim and Janice left my home with the computer and placed it in the car of Jim Webber. The four of them stood talking for about twenty minutes and then I left my home to meet up with Val and Rob. As I got into my car Jim Webber shouted and told me to wait because a policeman was coming. I told him that the police knew where to find me if they wanted to speak with me. It became very clear that Jim Webber and Dave Thomas were very expert at spreading malicious rumours and getting gullible members of the trustees to believe them but the police who had more experience did not fall for their false accusations. The police never did call around to see me because I had never broken the law. It was clear to me that Jim Webber wanted control of the charity shop as I found out a short time later.

Chapter 48

"Love is patient, love is kind. It does not envy, it does not boast, it is not proud. It is not rude, it is not self-seeking, it is not easily angered, it keeps no record of wrongs. Love does not delight in evil but rejoices with the truth. It always protects, always trusts, always hopes, always perseveres"

1 Corinthians 13 : 4 - 7

I was very upset at the way certain people were treating me but I thanked God for the handful of Christians who had not turned their backs on me. I was still not fully recovered from my illness as I made plans to leave Cleveleys and return back to Andreia who was waiting for me. Some of my closest friends advised me against going back to Romania but I was hurting very badly and my heart was broken at the way those I had loved had rejected me. I just needed someone to show me some love and affection and the only person showing me that love was Andreia. I knew in my heart that I still loved Jan and I made one last attempt to make up with her. I knew that I had hurt her but she had also played a big part in pushing me away from her. I was also upset how easy it was for Jan to walk away from the charity that we had formed together when it had been her vision in the first place to build Bartimaeus House. I was still open to what God wanted and he knew I was prepared to save my marriage to Jan if that was also what she wanted.

   I called to see Jan but our meeting ended with me in tears because of all the hurtful things she said to me. I walked away from the pub where we had met knowing that our thirty years of married life was over. I spent a few days with my mum before my flight was due to leave for Romania. I had given all of my belongings to Jan and told her to sell what she did not want and to give my car to Michelle. My mum was one of only a few people who had not turned their backs on me and she told me that she wanted me to be happy. My mum was sad that my marriage was breaking up but she knew that I had tried my best to make things right with Jan. My mum said that if Jan had really loved me then she would have been able to forgive me and work at saving our marriage. I think I had realised when Jan had left me the last time that the flame of love that she once had for me in her heart was going out. On the 1st May 2000 I boarded a flight at Manchester airport with a return ticket to Timisoara not knowing if I would ever be using it. I was not sure if I would have any problems clearing immigration because of the underhanded ways that people connected with the charity were behaving. I was relieved when the customs officer gave me my visa for entering Romania.

Andreia, Lica and two other friends were waiting to meet me at the airport and they were very surprised at how quickly I had managed to return. All my worldly possessions were in one suit case and a small travel bag. I had withdrawn what money I had left in my bank account in England that amounted to about £2000 and I knew I would have to make this last for a very long time. I moved in with Andreia's family who were very happy to see me again. The mini bus repair bill came to £900 and I wrote a letter to the trustees enclosing a copy of the repair bill asking them to let me know how they intended to repay me. The same day I posted the letter I met up with Renato in Timisoara who showed me a fax he had received from Dave Thomas and Jim Webber who stated they were the appointed delegates of Bartimaeus UK.

The fax contained a lot of false accusations about Renato and accusing him of being in collusion with the builder. They stated that the builder was not a suitable contractor and that the builder had demanded money from them before completing the first stage. The builder was with Renato and he told me that what they had written was a pack of lies and he was considering taking legal action against the charity for breach of contract. The fax went on to say that Renato should donate the land and the unfinished building to Pastor Mircea Damean from the Pentecostal church. They also accused Renato of using charity money for his own expenses and not providing them with proper accounts for the money he had used.

I could not believe what I was reading but it became very clear to me that Jim Webber and Dave Thomas were out to destroy both

Renato and myself. I realised that they also wanted to take the charity over for their own plans when they had told Renato to give the land and unfinished building away. Renato told me that Jim Webber and Dave Thomas had visited Romania and told him that I had stolen money belonging to the charity. I was very angry at the way Jim Webber and Dave Thomas were behaving and also the trustees of the charity who were sanctioning all that was taking place. I wrote a letter to a reporter that I knew in Blackpool who worked for the Blackpool Gazette in the hope that she would bring out into the open the way that the trustees of the charity were behaving. I also wrote a letter to the trustees making it very clear to them if they did not use the money I had raised for building Bartimaeus House for that purpose I would take legal action against them when I returned to England.

The reporter that I wrote to had always printed good reports about the work we were undertaking in Romania and I was hoping she would help the work continue by printing the truth about what had taken place. Within a few days I received a telephone call from Jackie Morley from the Blackpool Gazette asking me lots of questions about my relationship with Andreia. She told me that she was going to print a story and that it was possible that some major national newspapers would get hold of the story and want to speak with me. Two days later my mobile telephone was red hot with all the calls from national newspapers wanting to talk with me. They were all focusing on my relationship with Andreia but I refused to speak with them all except a reporter from the Daily Mail who promised to print a fair report if I spoke to him.

I was very concerned about the effect that this would have on my family and friends but I was also concerned about the underhanded way that trustees of the charity were behaving back in England. I wanted the building of Bartimaeus House to continue and I hoped that the publicity would put enough pressure on the trustees that they would do what was right and continue with the work that the charity had been formed to undertake. The reporter told me that it would be better if they had a photograph of Andreia and I together because people would be able to see that she was not a little child that people were making her out to be. He informed me that some newspapers were making it out that I had found Andreia in the sewers as part of the work I was doing in Romania. The reporter offered to pay us £500 for the photograph and we both agreed it would be in our interest to let them have a photograph of us together. The reporter made arrangements for a photographer to meet up with us in Timisoara a few hours later who took several photographs of us together. Andreia always enjoyed having her photograph taken and she was not bothered in any way. I telephoned Jan to tell her that the newspapers were going to print a story and she was very angry with me. I tried to explain that it was my intention to try and bring out into the open all that was taking place with the trustees of the charity who were trying to destroy the work we had started.

The following day I spoke with my daughter Michelle who told me than the story was in all the newspapers and they were being hounded by reporters who wanted Jan to speak with them. Michelle told me that all my family was angry with me and they were all upset at the way the newspapers had printed the story. I spoke with Jan and advised her to give her side of the story so she could get some money to help her start her new life without me. I told her that the newspapers were making me out to be the bad guy and that most people would be on her side. Jan told me that she was going into hiding and that she did not want anything more to do with me and for me to stay out of her life forever.

I was very upset at the way that things had worked out. I had hoped a newspaper would do a proper investigation of everything that had taken place so the world could see all the good I had tried to undertake in Romania and that what Andreia and I had together was not the sordid picture that people wanted to paint. The only mistake I had made was to fall in love with a fifteen year old girl where in Romania it was legal to do so but not in England. It was a mistake I was prepared to rectify if the people I loved and worked with had been prepared to give me another chance. I felt like I had been forced into the situation I now found myself in because of the way that people had behaved towards me.

A week later Jackie Morley telephoned me again saying that allegations of fraud had been made against me to the Lancashire police who were investigating the complaint. She asked for my comments and told me that she had a duty to report the story and let the public know. She went on to tell me that Jim Webber had been reading this book I had been writing that was in my filing cabinet in the office at the charity shop and advised me to contact a solicitor. She told me that the opinion of a lot of people had changed against me for the better when they had seen the photograph of Andreia and me in the Daily Mail. She had also received some letters informing her of all the good work I had done in Romania. I told her that I had done nothing wrong and I was not afraid to speak with the police if they wanted to see me. I was not given any information about the allegations that had been made against me but I knew that Jim Webber and Dave Thomas had made a lot of false accusations against me before I had returned to Romania. I was convinced that they would be behind what was taking place in England especially after speaking with Renato and witnessing what they were capable of doing. I spoke with my good friend John Miles who had supported the work I was doing in Romania. John informed me that he had been contacted by Dave Thomas who wanted to know all about the money he had donated to Romania and that he had told John a lot of bad things about me. John informed me that he had told Dave Thomas that he had known me for a long time and I was not the person that Dave Thomas was painting me out to be.

Towards the end of May I wrote further letters to the trustees of the charity making it very clear that I was very upset at the way they were conducting their affairs and that I was prepared to take legal action against them if I had to. I also wrote letters to the Charity Commission and the British Embassy in Bucharest because of all the false accusations and information that had been passed on to them through Dave Thomas and Jim Webber. I found it very hard to understand why people who classed themselves as Christians could behave in such a way. I was so thankful of the personal relationship I had with God and it helped me to understand how Jesus felt when most of those he had loved and trusted treated him in the same way.

My life with Andreia's family started to go wrong when I refused to lend her step mother and father any more money. I had already helped them out by lending them money and giving them money for food. They had both been very friendly towards Andreia and me when everything had been going their way but the moment I refused to lend them any more money their attitude changed. At the end of May I was able to get my visa extended for a further two months and I was very relieved because I was concerned that I might be refused because of all the bad publicity that had been printed about me.

Andreia and I knew the time had come to leave Timisoara when Lica hit Andreia during an argument and her father did nothing to stop Lica from hitting his own daughter. I stepped in and told hold of the arm of Lica to make sure she did not hit Andreia again. They both made it clear that they would not be repaying the money I had lent to them. We both knew that they had only been using me for what they could get so we packed our belongings and returned to Hateg to stay with her mother Angela and the man she lived with called Nelu. We arrived back in Hateg on the 2nd June where Andreia and Angela were happy to be reunited. I had reached the stage where I was not bothered any longer what people thought about my relationship with Andreia because from now we were going to do what was best for us. Our love for each other was growing stronger everyday and we both wanted to be by ourselves so we could live our lives as man and wife. On the 9th June the trustees sent me a fax stating that the affairs of the charity were in the hands of their solicitor and the Charity Commission and that their solicitor would contact me in due course. They informed me that they did not wish to hear from me further and that it was finished. I wrote back stating I did not know what they meant by stating it was finished because as far as I was concerned it was far from finished.

Chapter 49

> *"Haven't you read" he replied, "that at the beginning the creator made them male and female," and said, " For this reason a man will leave his father and mother and be united to his wife, and the two will become one flesh? So they are no longer two but one. Therefore what God had joined together, let man not separate"*
>
> Matthew 19 : 4 - 6

Andreia and I discussed all the possibilities that were open to us in Romania as it was lawful for us to be together and to get married while she was fifteen with her mother's consent. We both believed that our future would be in England because in England I would be able to go back to work and earn enough money for us to survive. We could not get married anyway until my divorce with Jan was finalised and I was concerned that if I married Andreia before she was sixteen that our marriage would not be recognised as lawful in England. We both decided that we would live together in Romania as man and wife and we both prayed together that God would bless our relationship with each other as we looked for a cheap apartment to rent. We agreed to wait until Andreia was sixteen before getting married as we set a provisional date of the 10th February 2001 a day after Andreia turned sixteen for our wedding day. We hoped by then that my divorce would be finalised and that we would be free to marry with all the papers we would need. We also hoped that Renato would help me get my visa extended because in less than two months my visa was due to expire.

I spoke to my children over the telephone but only Robert and Michelle were prepared to talk with me. Donna made it very clear that she did not want me to contact her again but I told her that no matter what she thought about me that I still loved her and my grandchildren and that would never change. My mum was very supportive because she loved me and wanted me to be happy. My mum was not well off but she sent me some money to help me out and wrote letters on a regular basis. My mum also made regular telephone calls to check I was happy and in good health. She advised me to do what I believed was best and not to worry what people said as people could be very cruel. I knew that to be right because of the way that people had treated me.

On the 12th June Andreia and I found a cheap apartment to rent in Deva and I signed a lease for twelve months. It became a natural thing for Andreia and I to start sleeping together as we both loved each other very much. Andreia had been a virgin until meeting me and she made me feel like a teenager all over again. We enjoyed each other's company a great deal and we went everywhere together. We did not worry anymore about people seeing us arm in arm with each other because what mattered to us was our love for each other. Andreia made it very clear to me that for her I was beautiful and if we loved each other age did not matter. I knew that I felt the same way about Andreia and it was like starting out my life all over again.

I had a number of meetings with Renato and as the work on Bartimaeus House had come to a stop I asked him to return a generator and caravan that belonged to me. I was able to sell the generator for £600 and this helped me to pay the first five months rent on our apartment in Deva. The caravan had not been looked after by Renato so Nelu and Angela helped us to repair and clean it. We then had a short holiday to Balie Felix together to try and unwind from all the pressure we had been under. I started to see parts of Romania that I had not seen before where people had money to spend and lived in big houses. The camp site at Balie Felix was very beautiful and it had been established for more than one hundred years. All the swimming pools in the area obtained water from natural underground springs and the hot water they provided allowed for the swimming pools to be emptied every day. Everywhere we went we met young children begging on the streets and it was clear that the gap between rich and poor was getting wider as each day passed. Every town and village had its own share of people who had to survive from day to day not knowing where their next meal was coming from. I would have had to be very wealthy to be able to give money to everyone who asked me and I started to understand why so many people in Romania had hardened their hearts towards the poor.

We spent a wonderful four days at Balie Felix before returning home to Deva with our caravan. It had only cost me £10 for the camp site and it was one of the most relaxing holidays I had ever been on. The day before my birthday Andreia and I went to the pharmacy to buy a test kit to see if she was pregnant because her period was late. At first glance I thought it was negative because only one red line appeared but after about five minutes Andreia shouted to me with excitement that another red line had appeared giving a positive result. We had both planned to have children with Andreia making a joke that she would kill me if I did not make her pregnant with a baby boy but we were both surprised how quickly Andreia had conceived. We decided to buy another test from a different pharmacy to make sure it was not a mistake. The second test also proved positive and on my birthday the 17th July we went to the hospital in Hateg for Andreia to have a scan. It was no mistake and the doctor confirmed that Andreia was about four weeks pregnant.

We were both happy at the news especially me because I had been silently praying to God if I should return to England so that I could try and sort out all the problems that had developed back in England. I had asked God to forgive me for any sin that I may have committed with Andreia and I believed that God knew everything that had taken place and had forgiven me. I also believed that it would be an even greater sin to leave Andreia by herself now that she was expecting my child. For the first time in ages I was at peace with God and also myself as we started to make plans for our future together.

We both accepted that we would not be able to get married until my divorce came through and we would have to wait until Andreia was sixteen years of age. We knew that if we could get married on the 10th February 2001 it would give us about four weeks to try and get Andreia a visa so we could return to England as man and wife where our baby could be born. We were both concerned about Andreia giving birth in Romania because the conditions in the hospitals were not very good and there was a higher risk of fatality for both mother and baby. We knew we would have to put our trust in God because up to now everything had been against us. We both went out for a meal in Deva to celebrate my birthday and the news that we were expecting our first child. We decided to take our caravan for a week's holiday to Constanta because we knew it would be a long time before we had a chance of having another holiday together. The following day we left Deva at 5.00am for the 600 mile journey to Constanta. On the outskirts of Bucharest I missed the turning that would have bypassed the city and we ended up lost in the centre of Bucharest. It was one of the worst cities I had ever driven in for the lack of sign posts pointing the way to different places. After spending one hour driving around and getting nowhere I paid £2 to a taxi driver to lead us to the road we needed to be on. We were both thankful to be on our way again to Constanta.

    At about 2.00pm we stopped at the side of the road in a parking area to have some lunch that we had brought with us. It was a very hot summer's day and we both had our windows open to let in some fresh air. We both could hear the sound of hissing and when I looked outside I noticed the tyre on the caravan had a puncture. I was not concerned because I had a spare wheel and after using the toilet in the caravan I got the tools from the mini bus to change the wheel on the caravan. Within five minutes I had changed the wheel on the caravan and was ready to set off. As I got back into the mini bus Andreia asked me what I had done with her handbag from off the front seat of the mini bus. I told Andreia to stop larking around but it soon became obvious that Andreia was not joking.

    Not only was her handbag missing that contained both our passports, her identity card and money but also both of our mobile telephones that had also been left on the front seat. We were both sick to our stomach that someone had opened the front door of the mini bus while I had been changing the wheel on the caravan only a few metres away. We had not seen any other people or vehicles near us and it was clear that whoever it was had come from out of the woods. I picked up my hunting knife that Nelu had made for me and I told Andreia to wait inside the mini bus while I went into the woods. I could not see anyone and after about five minutes I returned to Andreia.

    We drove to a nearby café and we asked if we could use their telephone to call the police. They had no telephone in the café but some people who were eating a meal let us use their mobile phone to call the police. The police were not very helpful but informed us that we would need to go to the nearest police station to report the incident. The person who had let us use his mobile telephone charged us £2 for letting us use his phone. We drove on for about two miles until we found a police station where we were told that we would need to go to the main police station at Pantelimon to report what had taken place.

We were both upset at what had happened but I told Andreia that we should be thankful that my travel bag had not been stolen from off the back seat because that contained the bulk of our money. Only in the morning I had taken almost £200 in Romanian Lei from out of Andreia's handbag that she had been minding for me and placed it in my travel bag. On the short drive to Pantelimon we stopped at a garage to have the puncture repaired.

The police at Pantelimon were very sympathetic towards us and they informed Andreia that she would have to make a declaration in writing of all that had taken place. I now started to understand the way that the police worked in Romania because in England the police take the statement from you but in Romania it is the other way round. The police informed us that what had happened to us was a regular occurrence and that they had at least two cases a week of people being robbed in the same way. They only had six police officers for the whole town and it was not possible for them to track down the people responsible. After Andreia had made a written statement the police gave me a paper confirming that we had reported the incident to enable us both to have our passports replaced and also Andreia's identity card. It would mean that I would have to apply to the British Embassy in Bucharest for a replacement passport and Andreia would have to do the same thing when we returned back to Deva.

We considered cancelling our holiday but I told Andreia that we should not let the devil win and we should have our holiday. If all our money had been stolen we would have had no choice but we had come this far and I did not want to return home. I told Andreia that I was going to pray to God for our passports and her identity card to be found even if we did not get back the rest of our possessions. I made a quick prayer to God and asked him to help us get our passports back. After leaving the police station at Pantelimon we returned to the garage to pick up our repaired tyre. They showed us the tyre where it had been pierced with a sharp object and told us that it needed a replacement tyre. It cost us about £10 for a second hand tyre and we left the garage to go back to the place where the handbag had been stolen from.

Andreia told me that she had heard some voices on the other side of the road coming from the woods when the handbag had been stolen but I had only looked in the woods near to the side of the road where we had been parked. I told Andreia that I was going back into the woods and that she should stay in the mini bus with the doors locked. Andreia was frightened that I would come to some harm but I told her not to worry because God would protect me and I also had a very big knife. I went back into the woods like a hunter with my knife at the ready and very alert. The woods were very dense and it would have been easy to get lost. I tried to make a note of different markers so that I could find my way out of the woods very quickly if I needed to do so.

After searching for about ten minutes I noticed papers on the floor about twenty metres from where I was standing. I made my way through the bushes and trees and when I was about five metres away there was no mistaking the outline of a British passport. I was praying that everything would be intact and that all our passports and identity card would be found. It was clear that I was in the spot where the people responsible had emptied out Andreia's handbag to take the things that they wanted to keep.

I was very happy to find my passport and the important papers that had been inside that had been discarded by the thieves. I found Andreia's identity card holder but when I opened it her identity card had been removed. For some reason the thieves had wanted to keep the passport and identity card belonging to Andreia but not my passport. I was thankful to God that I had found my passport because I knew that it would have been a big problem to get it replaced. I returned to Andreia to give her the news that I had recovered my passport and we were both filled with mixed feelings about what had taken place. After a delay of about three hours we continued with our journey to Constanta where we arrived safely at about 10.00pm. We found a good camping site at Mamaia right next to the beach at a cost of £20 for the week. We were both tired after the journey and incidents we had endured and climbed into bed for a good night's sleep.

Chapter 50

"Then Peter came to Jesus and asked, "Lord how many times shall I forgive my brother when he sins against me? Up to seven times?" Jesus answered, "I tell you, not seven times, but seventy-seven times"

Matthew 18 : 21 - 22

We both tried to put behind us what had happened the previous day as we woke up with the sun shining out of a clear blue sky. It was a new day and we both wanted to enjoy our first holiday together at the seaside. Constanta was like visiting another country and for me it was just as good as Hawaii with beautiful clean beaches with everything you needed for a perfect holiday. We noticed that the cost of everything was 50% dearer than in other places in Romania but if we shopped in the markets it was possible to save money. We enjoyed ourselves in the sea where we went on a jet ski, banana boat, horse riding and spent many relaxing hours on a sun bed soaking up the sun. The bar prices on the beach were very expensive compared to what we had been used to paying but by European standards they were still very cheap at about £1 for a bottle of beer and 75p for a soft drink. In the evenings we went on the fun fair where we went on lots of rides together. I had experienced all the excitement of the fun fairs in England with living near to Blackpool but for Andreia it was her first time and she enjoyed herself very much. We both enjoyed ourselves so much we did not want our holiday to end. As a treat for Andreia I bought tickets to see her favourite pop stars called "Andre" who were performing a live concert in Constanta. It only cost £1 each for the tickets and for Andreia it was a dream come true. We went to see the dolphins and did lots of other things to make it a holiday to remember. We did everything that we wanted to do and we were both happy that we had continued with our holiday. I could feel my love for Andreia getting stronger as each day passed and I would kiss our little baby that was growing inside of Andreia's tummy every single night.

We were sad that our holiday had come to an end and we hoped that one day we would be able to return with our baby to the Savoy hotel that was situated right on the beach at Constanta. It was a very beautiful hotel that we took a look around to see all their facilities. It cost £50 a night to stay at the hotel but that was cheap for the facilities it had to offer. Only God knew if our dream would come true.

We left Constanta at 4.00pm after having a perfect holiday together. We decided we would find the bypass road around Bucharest but on our way towards Bucharest the large front window in the caravan shattered due to the bad road conditions. We were able to cover the broken window with a large sheet and we were thankful that the car travelling behind us had not been damaged. We continued with our journey finding the bypass road around Bucharest near the town of Pantelimon. It was a road I wished we had never found because the road surface was the worst I had ever driven on. We wondered if we would be able to get the min bus and caravan back home to Deva in one piece. It took us a long time to reach the motorway from Bucharest that led back towards Deva. We were both thankful when we reached the motorway and after a journey that lasted seventeen hours we arrived safely back at home.

One of my first jobs was to repair the window to the caravan and we decided that it would be better if we tried to sell it while it was still worth something. The caravan was worth about £700 and we took it to the local car market at Deva. We did not have any success so we advertised it in the local newspaper to try and find a buyer. While we were trying to sell our caravan we met up with Renato to see if he had been able to get my visa extended. Renato kept on coming up with different excuses of why he could not help me and it became very clear that I would not be able to have my visa extended before it expired on the 1st August.

I did not want to return to England and leave Andreia by herself especially with the fact she was expecting our child and she would need me by her side. I decided that I would stay in Romania without my visa and take things one day at a time. We went to the police to replace Andreia's identity card and to try and get her a replacement passport. We also had to obtain a new birth certificate for Andreia because the original had been stolen with her passport. It was a very complicated process trying to get her passport, birth certificate and identity card replaced but after a week Andreia managed to get a new identity card and birth certificate. The police informed her that she would have to wait for a paper to come from Bucharest before her passport could be replaced. It cost about £30 to pay for the replacement of the stolen items and I was surprised to find she had to pay a tax for losing her belongings when in fact they had been stolen.

We discussed the possibility of the police forcing me to leave Romania now that I had no visa and we decided we would go to Hungary if that situation arose. We wanted to be together at all costs. We hoped that I would be able to stay in Romania until we were married because we both did not like the thought of having to live in Hungary until I would be able to re-enter Romania again. I contacted the British Embassy to ask them to send me information on what I would need to do to marry a Romanian Citizen and to apply for a visa for Andreia to come to England when we were married. A few days later I received a letter giving me all the information that I needed to know. It was clear that we had lots of problems to overcome but we were going to face them together and take one day at a time.

I received a letter from my solicitor enclosing an affidavit for me to sign over my divorce with Jan. To save me having to go back to England to swear the affidavit I had the papers translated into the Romanian language and went to a Notary in Romania. It was now just a case of waiting for the Court in England to process my divorce that Jan was not going to contest. On the 6th August I made one last attempt for Renato to help me obtain the visa I needed but he informed me he was closing down the Romanian charity for a short time and he would not be able to help me. I was upset at this because Renato wanted my help to try and get the trustees in England to release the money that I had raised for the building of Bartimaeus House that were still in the bank account back in England.

I was also upset at the way the trustees were behaving as they had not made any attempts to contact me to resolve the issues that were still outstanding. I still had possession of the mini bus belonging to the charity and the charity owed me money and had possession of goods that belonged to me. It was sad to see the work on Bartimaeus House come to a stop as the builder was doing a good job and was well ahead of schedule with his work until Jim Webber and Dave Thomas started to interfere. The people who had been employed by the charity were now unemployed with many of them telling me how hard it was for them with no work and no income. They told me they were sorry I was no longer involved with the project and how good things were when I was leading the work. I decided to write the trustees another letter informing them of the situation and making it very clear that I was prepared to take any action that was open for me to make sure that justice was done.

    I wrote to a few close friends asking them if they were prepared to give me some financial help so that I could return to England and try and continue with the building of Bartimaeus House. I was prepared to form another charitable company to help raise the money that Renato needed if God opened the door for me. As far as I was concerned I had not broken any laws while I had worked for Bartimaeus Romania and it would only be a matter of time before I cleared my name. I knew that a lot of people had condemned me because of my relationship with Andreia but it was not the dirty sordid affair that people were making it out to be. In many ways people forced Andreia and I together because of the way we were rejected and only had each other's arms to fall into. We both wanted an opportunity to tell people our side of the story and that was when I decided I would continue writing this book to keep a record of all that had taken place.

    One of the main reasons I had not printed my book over two years ago was the fact that I had been advised by a very close friend to wait for a happy ending. He was a man of God and he remarked that it might put people off from becoming a Christian if they read my story and find out how hard it can be as a Christian and live for Jesus. I started to think about the advice I had been given and then realised that life is very hard and sometimes our lives do not have happy endings on this earth. It would have been nice if somewhere in this book I had been able to write that Jan and the trustees had forgiven me when I did wrong and that I had continued to work for Bartimaeus Romania. Maybe that would have been a happy ending but it was not to be. Jan and I were in the process of a divorce and the trustees of the charity had made it very clear that I was no longer a member of their team. I was also hearing news from England that the trustees were changing the name of the charity and had no intensions of completing the work we had started. It was clear that they were going to use the money that had been raised for building Bartimaeus House for another purpose. This confirmed to me that I was right all along about Jim Webber and Dave Thomas who had their own plans for the charity shop.

Andreia and I discussed how we were going to survive in Romania until we were married. We decided that we would start to buy second hand clothing and go to markets and small villages to sell them for a small profit. This would help the poor people out and at the same time it would give us a small income. It was not possible for me to obtain a proper job because my visa had expired and I would not be able to obtain a work permit without a visa. We had about £600 in Lei in a savings account in Timisoara that we were saving for our marriage and on the 9th August we decided we would return to Timisoara to withdraw the money so we could use it for trying to earn some money. Most of the people I had wrote to for help had refused to help me but two close friends did send me some money but it was not going to be enough to return to England at that moment in time. If I had stolen money belonging to the charity as Jim Webber and Dave Thomas were alleging I would not have had the money problems I was having. Our plans to earn a small income came to an abrupt end because the people in the villages were so poor they wanted everything for next to nothing. There was also a shop on every street corner trying to sell second hand clothes so they could earn a small income to survive.

I received a telephone call from Renato on the 10th August and he asked me to meet with him because he would try and help me obtain my visa. I was very surprised when Renato asked me for the equivalent of £400 so that he could re-open the charity in Romania and apply for my visa. Renato could have helped me before he closed down the charity but for some reason he chose not to do so. I told Renato and Anca that I had done everything I could to help him and what little money I had would be needed by Andreia and I to live on. I advised Renato to write one more letter to the trustees in England explaining how he had been forced to close down the charity because of their refusal to transfer the money to Romania that I had raised for Bartimaeus House. I also wrote another letter to the trustees making it very clear that I would take legal action against them if they continued to keep the money I had raised for

Bartimaeus House. I was very angry at the way the trustees had behaved but this was something I knew I had to leave with God because one day we all would have to give an account of our lives before the throne of God.

Chapter 51

"Do not judge, and you will not be judged. Do not condemn, and you will not be condemned, Forgive, and you will be forgiven. Give, and it will be given to you. A good measure, pressed down, shaken together and running over, will be poured into your lap. For with the measure you use, it will be measured to you"

Luke 6 : 37 - 38

Everything was still uncertain but Andreia and I decided that we would start to make plans for our wedding in the hope that my divorce would be finalised within the next three months. We set our wedding date for the 10th February a day after Andreia's sixteenth birthday. I wrote to my mum asking her to help me obtain certain papers that I would need to be married in Romania. At the same time we made a list of all the things we would need to do for our wedding and for applying for Andreia's visa. It helped to pass some time as we looked around for the most suitable restaurant for us to have our wedding reception. After looking at several places we found a nice restaurant very near to the Church in Hateg where we had decided to get married. Andreia was looking forward to her wedding day and could not wait for the day when she could put on her wedding dress and become my wife.

We both decided on the people we would invite to our wedding and it looked like we would be inviting about eighty people. My own guest list was very short because most of the people I knew had turned their backs on me and it made me realise how few friends I had. Of the few family and friends that had not completely rejected me I wondered how many would make the journey to Romania.

On the 17th August we both went to Hateg hospital for Andreia's monthly check up. The doctor was happy with Andreia's health and everything looked fine for our baby on the scanning machine. It was good the way the doctor explained everything to us and we were both happy and excited that we could see the heartbeat of our baby. It became very obvious to me that I had a big responsibility to Andreia and our baby whom I loved so very much. It was now my duty to provide for them the best way that I could but I knew that I would not be able to do so without help from God.

    It seemed that so many obstacles were still in our way to enable us to be married and then to apply for Andreia's visa so she could come to England as my wife before our baby was born. I was still praying to God almost every day and reading my bible. I was frightened that God might have deserted me because of being with Andreia but in my heart I still believed that God had forgiven me because of what was wrote in the scriptures of the bible. The more I read my bible the more convinced I became that the love of God was something very special and that he loved us even when we made mistakes and got things wrong. Andreia and I both decided that we would start attending church again on a regular basis because we wanted to get close to God and for him to lead us in the way we were to go.

    I decided to write to some Christian friends giving them an update on our situation but for the time being I decided that I would only tell three people that Andreia was expecting my baby. One of the important things I had to do was to try and find a job and a place to live in England for when Andreia became my wife. One of the conditions I had to meet for the British Embassy was to prove that I could support Andreia if she was to come to England. This was going to be very difficult for me because I did not want to return to England until we were married. I wrote to a Christian businessman I knew asking if he would be willing to help me. I did not want to give the British embassy any excuse to refuse Andreia a visa because if they did so I would not know what way to turn. I also knew that the only way I would be able to provide for Andreia and our baby was when we were back in England. I knew that when it was time for us to go to England we would be starting our lives at rock bottom so it did not really matter what part of England we returned to.

    What was important to us was that we could be together and our baby could be born in England. The only other way I could see of getting a job if my Christian friend did not help me was to form my own business again and become self employed. Nothing was going to be easy for us so the only thing we could do was to try our best and put all our trust in the Lord. My visa had now expired but I had not yet been stopped by the police. I still had the letter from the police at Pantelimon where my passport had been stolen if the police stopped me and asked to see my passport. All we could do was take one day at a time because nothing seemed certain for us no matter what way we looked at things. Even our wedding plans could only be made on paper because it was not possible to book anything until my divorce came through.

I was concerned about our money situation because what I had left was running out very fast and with no income it would not be long before we ran out of money. Our needs were met when we managed to sell our caravan for the equivalent of £500. I knew this money would not last for long and it was time to start making firm plans of returning to England so that I could make a start on rebuilding my life. We started to attend the Baptist church in Deva because we both wanted God to be at the centre of our lives. We were both able to pray about everything and I wrote letters to three Christian friends to ask for their help in returning to England.

It was early September and if Andreia and I were to get married in February I would need to have a place to live in England and a job to stand any chance of Andreia being issued with a visa to come to England. I was concerned at all the bad publicity and lies that had been printed in many newspapers about my relationship with Andreia and I wondered if any of this would have a detrimental effect on Andreia being issued with a visa when we were married. While I waited for replies to the letters I had sent we decided to visit some of the poor families that I had supported over a number of years. I felt by reaching out to others it would take our mind off our own problems.

We visited Petresti on the 14th September taking some food for one of the families who lived there. The family Hulei was very happy to see me and I explained to them why I had not been in touch for many months. They were very sad that my marriage had come to an end and even sadder at the way that people had behaved towards me. Viorica who was the mother from the family explained how desperate many families were who lived in that area and how they had asked Renato in January to contact me to see if I could help. I was sad to see lots of children without shoes and very little clothing. I knew that lots of aid was still at Renato's farm and I wondered why he had not distributed this aid to some of these poor families. We told the family Hulei that we would try and get some of the aid from the farm and return to Petresti very soon. It was good to see how friendly the Hulei family was towards Andreia and also Andreia towards them. It was good that Andreia had been able to translate everything that we wanted to talk about.

Andreia could understand how some of these families were suffering because she had been in that position many times herself. We were both angry and upset that the aid I had collected at Christmas had not been distributed to these poor families. On our return back to Deva we decided we would go and see Renato to get some aid for the families we had visited. Renato had agreed a few weeks before that I could have the aid in the barn for any poor families in need. We arrived at Renato's farm the following day at about 3.00pm. Renato and Anca were not at home and the grandmother told us they were in Hateg. I explained that I had called to collect some of the aid from the barn for some poor families at Petresti. I went into the barn and was shocked to see lots of the aid all over the floor of the barn. It looked like hundreds of the shoe boxes had been opened with Christmas cards from them scattered on the ground. Lots of boxes of clothing had been opened with some of the clothing on the dirty floor of the barn. I thought about all the hard work that had gone into collecting the aid and I was upset at the condition the aid was now in.

I collected four of the large drums and placed them in my mini bus and left a letter with the grandmother explaining the number of drums I had taken. We made our way back to Deva and after about one hour Renato telephoned me demanding that I returned the aid to his farm. I could not believe what I was hearing and Renato threatened to call the police if I did not return with the aid. I explained to him why I had taken the aid and told him that I would not return the aid and I was more than happy to go with him to the police if he wanted to take that action. I asked Renato to meet with me so we could discuss everything but he was not prepared to do so. I told him that I was returning to Hateg and I would meet with him at the police station.

On arriving at the police station in Hateg the police did not know anything about what was going on and they advised me to go to another police station that looked after the area where Renato lived. The police station was empty but about one hour later I received a telephone call from Renato informing me that Anca and he were at this police station. We returned to find the police station closed but they were standing about fifty metres away with a man they introduced as the chief of police. It was a very tense situation because I had no way of knowing if this man was the chief of police and I had no valid visa in my passport. I prayed with Andreia about this situation believing that God would undertake for us. The meeting with this policeman did not accomplish anything except he tried to make out that I was in the wrong for taking the aid from Renato's farm. I told the police the reasons for taking the aid and that I was the person who had collected all the aid in England with a promise that I would make sure it reached poor families and children in need.

I was more concerned about what was right before God than what Renato, Anca or the police thought about things. Anca asked me to sign a form of donation for the aid I had collected from their barn and I was more than happy to do this as the letter I left with the grandmother had confirmed. I told Renato and Anca in front of the police that I had taken photographs of what I had seen in their barn and I was thinking about making a statement to the press and TV stations about everything. We left this meeting very upset and angry about the way that Renato and Anca had behaved and they had not accomplished anything by calling the police. If anything the police did not want to get involved after I had threatened to contact the press and TV stations. Within ten minutes of leaving I received a telephone call from Renato informing me that I could take possession of all the aid left in the barn. I made arrangements to collect the aid the following Thursday as I made my way back home to Deva with Andreia.

It was a very quiet journey because I was thinking about all that I had done to help Renato and the people of Romania and the way that many people had now turned against me. I prayed about this situation all weekend and decided that I wanted an explanation from Renato and Anca on why the aid had been ransacked. I wrote them a letter and on the Monday morning I posted it through their letter box in Hateg. The following day I received a telephone call from Renato asking me to meet him in Deva. Renato said he was sorry for the way he had over reacted by calling in the police and he explained to me why all the bags for the children had been emptied with lots of the contents scattered on the ground. Renato explained that they were checking the shoe bags for any out of date sweets or chocolate and they did not have the time to put everything back in the bags. I decided that nothing would be gained by trying to take the matter any further. The main thing was that I was taking possession of the aid that was left and I could make sure that it reached the people it had been donated for.

I told Renato that I still wanted to help those in need in Romania and I still wanted to build a home for homeless children. It soon became clear that Renato had other plans for Bartimaeus House and he told me that he had changed the name of the charity in Romania. He promised me that if I formed a charity in Romania he would donate all the goods and money in England that I had raised for Bartimaeus House to the new charity. I knew that it would mean starting from the bottom all over again but this was a situation I had faced many times in the past.

On Thursday the 21st September I collected the aid from Renato's farm and took it to Andreia's grandparent's farm at Tustea for safe keeping. It took three journeys in my mini bus to transport the aid that was left. Renato told me he was sorry for the way he had behaved towards me and I accepted his apologies. Andreia and I spent the next few days sorting out the aid and making up the shoe bags that had been ransacked. We then made a visit to Petresti to distribute lots of aid to some very needy families. It was during this visit that I made my mind up to form another charity in Romania and England to carry on helping the people of Romania. On Monday 25th September Andreia was admitted into Hateg hospital with pains in her stomach due to lack of vitamins. I think the hard work of sorting out the aid had affected her and the doctor wanted her to rest and have some injections to help her.

We had made arrangements to meet a Romanian called Petru the following day who was going to help us form a new charity in Romania so I decided to keep the appointment. On the Tuesday I met with Petru and handed him a letter from Andreia explaining why she could not be present. I handed him the papers he had requested along with £225 as an advance payment for forming the charity. We made arrangements to meet again on the 20th October where I hoped that everything would be completed. This was the man who had formed the charity for Renato so I was confident that I could trust him to do a proper job. On returning to our apartment in Deva I contacted a company in England requesting that they form a new charitable company by the name of Humanitarian Aid International. I knew it was going to take most of what money we had left to form both charities but in my heart I believed that everything would work out. I received a letter from England informing me that the trustees of the charity in England had changed their name to C.A.R.E. trust. I wrote another letter to them giving them a final chance to pay me the money they owed me and return my personal belongings. I also contacted the Charity Commission informing them of everything and requested their help.

While Andreia was in hospital I wrote letters to a few friends in England asking if they would be able to lend me some money so I could rebuild my life back in England. I knew that it would not be possible for me to stay in Romania much longer as my money was running out very fast. After spending a week in hospital Andreia was allowed to come home. We both thanked God that everything was fine with her and our baby. We prayed about the way forward and we both agreed that I would need to return to England by myself to try and find a place for us to live for when we were married. I did not want to leave Andreia by herself for a long period of time especially with her being unwell. We also wanted to spend our first Christmas together and we agreed that I should return to England the first week of January 2001 for a three week period. I knew that I would need some financial help to pay a deposit on a home to rent and also cover other expenses we would have.

I had always had a desire to live in Cornwall and the town of Newquay would be as good a place as any for us to start our new life together. I waited patiently for my friends to respond to my letters asking for their help. The replies I received left me upset because of the way they all refused to help me. It was clear they had decided to reject me and most of them were still sitting in judgment of me. Only one friend and my mother were still showing me any love and kindness and both of them were not in a position to lend me any money. I was grateful to God for the love my mother and friend were showing to me and I prayed that God would soften the hearts of all my other friends who had rejected me.

I knew that in their eyes I was guilty of sinning against God but I asked them not to judge me but to leave that to God. No one knew better than me where I had let God down and I was still trying to put things right with God by trying to do what was right in the situation

I found myself in. It did not help my situation when I found out that Renato had contacted friends of mine in England telling them lies that I was selling the aid I had collected from his barn on the black market. I also found out that Jim Webber had contacted the Stockport express giving them another story that I was returning to England. The newspaper carried a story with the headlines "Charity worker in shock return" and printed a lot more lies about my relationship with Andreia. I wrote to the editor letting him know what I thought about his newspaper and invited him to do a proper reporting job by coming to Romania to find out the truth about everything. It just seemed like everyone was against me and I was heartbroken at the way people were behaving towards me.

I knew that I had to hand everything over to God because otherwise I would end up bitter and twisted. I prayed for all the people who had rejected me and had caused me so much pain. I prayed that one day the truth would come out and that people would get to know the real Bob Sutton who had given so much love to other people while I had been a Christian. I still had a desire in my heart to help other people even though I needed a lot of help myself. Andreia and I decided that we would continue to distribute the aid to those in need and at the same time to help a young girl called Ileana from Pestianna orphanage who had been in hospital with Andreia. The doctors found Ileana had a brain tumor and they were deciding if they needed to operate. Ileana had been rejected by her family and she had no-one to love or care for her. We started to let Ileana come to our home at weekends where we showed her a lot of love and care. Ileana was thirteen but only looked about ten years old. We enjoyed looking after her and it helped us to take our minds off our own problems.

In October we had to go to Bucharest to obtain papers so that Andreia could get her passport replaced that had been stolen. Everything was so complicated in Romania and it was easier to get a child from an orphanage than to overcome all the problems in obtaining a replacement passport. While we were in Bucharest we distributed some shoe bags to the homeless. We still found lots of homeless children and adults in Bucharest but most of the man hole covers had been sealed up to prevent them from sleeping down in the sewers and from where the underground heating pipes ran under the city. We found one old lady sitting on the edge of a man hole cover that had not been sealed up in the park opposite the main railway station. We gave her a shoe bag and some money and the tears in her eyes started to run down her cheeks. We felt sad at the hopeless situation she was in especially when we saw a policeman kick her like she was a dog telling her to move on.

Chapter 52

"Then Jesus declared, "I am the bread of life. He who comes to me will never go hungry, and he who believes in me will never be thirsty. But as I told you , you have seen me and still you do not believe. All that the Father gives me will come to me, and whoever comes to me I will never drive away"

John 6 : 35 - 37

We enjoyed our short time in Bucharest and returned to Deva with the papers we needed to obtain a replacement passport for Andreia. I found out that Renato had been unsuccessful in obtaining any financial help to continue with the building of Bartimaeus House and that he had plans to use it for another purpose. I wrote a letter to Renato asking him to donate the land and building to the charity I was forming so that I could complete the work I had started. I made it clear that I did not want to work with him but I still wanted to do something positive for homeless children in Romania. I knew that the plan God had given to me for building Bartimaeus House and raising all the money needed was a good plan and if God was still with me then the plan would still work. I knew that it would mean me starting from scratch all over again but I was prepared to do this if God wanted me to do so.

I was even prepared to let Renato keep the land and building if he wanted to do so with my prayers that it would be used to benefit people in need with all the hard work and sacrifice that had already gone into it. If I had to I was prepared to build another home to help homeless children if Renato did not want to donate the land and building to the charity I was forming. I still had an unanswered question in my heart, "Was it God who had prevented me from continuing the work on Bartimaeus House or was it the actions of so many unforgiving and judgmental people?"

By forming a new charitable company in England and Romania it would give me an opportunity of still doing something positive for children and people in need. I knew it would have been a lot easier for me to concentrate on my own life and problems but if God was with me and had forgiven me I was prepared to go down a more difficult road. All I could do was try my best but I knew that I would not succeed at anything without God by my side and leading me in the way forward.

In early November I received a letter from my solicitor informing me that my divorce to Jan had been granted by the court on the 30th September and that my divorce would be absolute by the 12th December. I had mixed emotions at this news, sadness that my thirty two years of marriage to Jan was over but happy that my divorce had come through in time to marry Andreia as planned on the 10th February when she would be sixteen. The month of November was a time when I could see things starting to come together. Both charitable companies had now been formed and I was in a position to have letter headed paper printed and to start working on a new profile with the vision for helping children and people in need.

I informed Renato he would have to let me know within a month if he was prepared to hand the land and building to the charity I had formed. If not I was going to prepare a profile with a vision for starting a new project that would not include the land and building already started at Ciula Mica. By now most of my money had run out but I was still at peace knowing that my future and that of Andreia and our baby were in God's hands.

As Christmas was fast approaching we decided that we would spend Christmas with Andreia's mother and Nelu in Hateg. They offered to let us stay with them for as long as we needed to and because of our shortage of money we decided to give up our apartment in Deva. We moved to Hateg a week before Christmas and we tried to make the best of things. We had a traditional Romanian Christmas where Nelu bought a full pig and I cooked dinner for us all. It was the nicest pork I had ever eaten. We also took Ileana from the orphanage to spend Christmas with us and although we were overcrowded we made the best of things giving Ileana a Christmas she would never forget. My mind was on the 6th January when I knew that I would be returning to England to try and organise everything for when Andreia and I were to be married.

Christmas and the New Year soon passed and it was time for me to return to England. I was able to buy my flight ticket very cheaply by returning from Budapest to Manchester via Amsterdam. I obtained my visa from the police at Deva on the 4th January after my papers arrived at the last moment from Bucharest. I had been without a visa for over five months and the police only fined me 750,000 Lei (£22) and gave me a six month visa free of charge. I felt that God was still with me as Jesus had promised and it was a big relief to know I had my visa.

I bought my train ticket from Deva to Budapest and at 3.30am on the 6th January Andreia and I kissed goodbye at the railway station where we both shed tears that we were parting. We had spent all our time with each other except for when Andreia was in hospital and we had grown so very close to each other. It was only going to be for three weeks but I did not want to leave her and I did not know what to expect when I arrived back in England. It was not a very pleasant train journey because something was making a loud banging noise from underneath the train and I was not able to sleep. After travelling for seventeen hours I arrived safely at Manchester airport where my mother was waiting to meet me. I was happy to see my mum again after being away for eight months and we had a lot of things to talk about. My mum had made arrangements for me to stay in the guest room at the sheltered accommodation where she lived and I was happy to be back in England again. One of the first things I had to do was to claim jobseekers allowance as I had no money and no job. I also made an application for a crisis loan and I was allowed £150 that I had to repay at £5 per week.

I needed money for a deposit for a home to rent and my sister Diane agreed to lend me £500 and my friend John Miles £400. My mum provided me with all my food and gave me £120 for our wedding present. I went to the bank to open a new bank account and I was very happy when I was offered a credit card with a limit of £1500. This meant I was able to put some money in my new bank account to show the British Embassy that I had money to provide for Andreia when we were married. The new charitable company that I had formed would be able to show that I had employment for when we would return to England as man and wife. I went to see my solicitor at Blackpool to pick up my divorce papers.

I then made my way to Cornwall to try and find a home to rent. It soon became clear that Newquay was not the place to start a fresh life with Andreia because I could not find a home to rent and it did not feel right. My sister had advised me to telephone my previous landlord asking for a reference so I decided to make the call. I was very surprised when he told me that he was willing to let me rent any property that they had available that would be suitable to my requirements. I had not contemplated on returning to Cleveleys but the more I thought about it the more it made sense. I also had unfinished business with the trustees of the charity shop who I planned to take to court for all the bad things they had done. I still had a few good friends who lived in the area and I knew that Andreia and I would need some help to rebuild our lives when we returned to England.

On Friday the 19th January I returned from Cornwall to my mums and told her that I would move back to Cleveleys so we could be near to her. I made plans to go to Cleveleys on the following Monday but on Saturday the 20th January I received a telephone call from Andreia to inform me that her waters had broken and that she had been admitted into Hateg hospital as an emergency.

I tried to reassure Andreia that everything would be fine and I prayed for her and our baby while we spoke on the telephone. After praying to God I felt a peace come over me that things would work out and I told Andreia that I would return to Romania as quickly as I could. I had done everything I had returned to England for and I had even issued a summons against the trustees of the charity in Cleveleys during the two weeks I had been in England. The only thing I had not done was to sign a lease for a home to rent so I bought a lease from a newsagent and filled in the details myself. I telephoned KLM to enquire if I could change my flight plans and I was very happy when they informed me that I could fly back to Budapest the following day at 6.15am for a charge of £68.

By 11.30pm on the Sunday evening the 21st January I was at the bedside of Andreia in Hateg hospital. We both cried when we saw each other and thanked God we were back together again. I was allowed to sleep at Andreia's side in the hospital bed while we waited for morning to arrive so we could speak with the doctor together. Although her waters had broken doctor Gavrish who was the doctor who had brought Andreia into this world wanted to wait a few more days before doing any operation to give our baby a better chance of survival. The doctor was the most experienced in Romania where he had delivered thousands of babies over the years and I had every confidence in him.

As we were not sure what was going to happen we decided to postpone our church wedding plans we had made for the 10th February and decided to get married at the Primar at Tustea where it would just be a ten minute ceremony. It was not what we wanted but we needed to take some pressure from us with what we were going through. I called to see Bill and Brenda who I had helped to come to Romania to ask if they would help me. I was hoping that they would lend me the money that I needed to pay the doctors and hospital for Andreia's operation but I was heartbroken when the door was slammed shut in my face. I wrote to some friends who had not completely deserted me and asked them to pray to God for Andreia and our baby. I also went to a nearby Monastery to pray to God and ask for his help. I spent time in prayer with God every day but on this day the 27th January it was filled with a lot of sadness with it being the anniversary of the death of my first son Mark. I had already experienced the grief of losing one of my children and I asked for God's mercy for Andreia and our unborn child. While I was at the Monastery I bought a small picture frame showing Jesus and I put it at the side of Andreia's head when I returned to Hateg hospital. I knew that I had done all that I could and I was at peace knowing that I had placed Andreia and our baby into the hands of my loving heavenly Father.

On Sunday the 28th January I was eating my breakfast at the home of Nelu when I received a telephone call from Andreia informing me that I had to come to hospital quickly as she was about to be taken into the operating theatre. I rushed to the hospital as quickly as I could and within five minutes I was at her bedside even if I was very much out of breath from running. Doctor Gavrish had called in from his home to see Andreia and decided it was time to do the operation. Andreia was extremely nervous with her hands and legs shaking with fear of what lay ahead. I tried my best to calm her down holding her hands and praying with her for God to take her fear away. Angela and Nelu also came to the hospital and we prayed together that everything would be alright for Andreia and our baby.

I wanted to be with Andreia but I was not allowed into the operating theatre and had to wait outside. I think I made a groove in the floor as I walked up and down silently praying to God over everything that was taking place inside of that theatre. It was only about fifteen minutes but it seemed like ages when one of the doctors came out to congratulate me on having a son. I asked about Andreia and our baby and was told that everything was fine and that our baby weighed 2.3kg. This was better than we had expected and our baby was taken by a nurse to be placed into an incubator. We were told that it would be at least another half hour before Andreia would be finished with and it was a big relief for us all when it was Andreia's turn to come out of the operating theatre and placed into a bed in the intensive care ward. My mind thought back to the time when I had brought incubators and hospital equipment from England to this hospital that had now been used for the benefits of helping those that I loved so very much.

I was so thankful to God that Andreia and our baby were alive and had come through the operation safely. I gave doctor Gavrish a big hug when he came to see me and I knew that he was happy with the knowledge that he had helped to save two lives. After seeing that Andreia was all right I went to take a look at our baby who was fast asleep in his incubator. He looked so beautiful and although tiny he was perfect in every way.

We decided to call our son David John Daniel after some men of God in the bible and after David Burgin and John Miles who had been an inspiration in my own life. I had committed my son David to God at that Monastery and I prayed that one day he would grow up to serve God in a mighty way. While Andreia was recovering in hospital I spent my time looking after her and organising everything for our wedding including the paperwork to obtain a birth certificate for David and have him included on Andreia's passport. Even though we were not yet married it was possible to have my surname entered on David's birth certificate so that his name was now David John Daniel Sutton. It involved me going to see a Notary and making a declaration that I was his father but it was worth the effort when I was given his birth certificate. I loved to watch Andreia feeding David from her breast as it was the most beautiful site for me to see the two loves of my life so close together. I arranged for a photographer to go to the hospital to take David's photograph so that I could go to the police in Deva to have him included in Andreia's passport. I then contacted a lot of people to re-arrange our wedding for the 17th February so that it would give Andreia and our baby time to get well and be discharged from hospital.

I just needed one more paper now from the registry office in England to enable our wedding to take place. On the 31st January my mum telephoned me to confirm that she had collected the certificate that I needed and it was in the post and on its way to me in Romania. For our wedding to take place on the 17th February I needed the certificate to arrive within one week but I was at peace knowing that God had undertaken for us in every way even if at times it was at the last moment. My love and faith in God was growing on a daily basis and even though I may have let God down so many times in my walk with him I knew that God had never forsaken me.

While I was solving all our problems Andreia's stepfather Nelu started to drink very heavily forcing me to look for somewhere else to live. With the help of Angela I found a Christian couple who were prepared to rent us their apartment in Hateg for £35 per month. It was a big relief knowing that I would not have to take Andreia and David to an environment where an alcoholic was living. I was very sad for Nelu because when he was sober he was a very good man but like most alcoholics he changed into a devil when drunk. I knew from experience that the only thing to do was to get away from him and pray that God would speak into his life. At times I felt like I was completely stressed out and that I could not take any more pressure but God gave me the ability to cope and peace came into my life once again.

Over the next few days Angela had talked some sense into Nelu and he stopped drinking. I think he had realised that he was in danger of losing the love and respect of the people who cared for him the most. David was growing bigger everyday and he was very beautiful. The doctors and nurses were very protective of David and it was only on the odd occasion that I was allowed to hold him in my arms. Andreia and I did not agree with the way that the doctors wanted to feed David by tube as we believed he was strong enough to be fed by Andreia through her breasts. We had to sign a form to prevent David from being fed by tube and we were very happy to see how fast he started to put on weight. The doctor told us that David would have to weigh 2.5kg before he could be released from hospital. We both prayed that David would soon reach that weight.

It was only a few days before our wedding date when Nelu asked if we would get married from his home and move back in until we were ready to return to England. The apartment that I had moved into was not suitable for Andreia or David so I agreed to move back in with Nelu. The 17th February was a very special day as Andreia was allowed to leave hospital and be married. The nurses had promised us that they would look after David for the weekend because after our marriage we had to go to Bucharest to see if Andreia would be given her visa to come to England.

When I saw Andreia in her wedding dress she looked like a princess and I could not believe we had overcome all the obstacles that we had overcome to get married. After a fifteen minute ceremony we were legally married and we drank champagne out of jam jars to celebrate. Our next stop was the Orthodox Church in Hateg to get married before God in a very special ceremony. It was our dream wedding coming true and I still found it hard to believe that we were now married.

The church service lasted for about one hour where we were married by a priest who had been very good towards Andreia and I. Afterwards we made our way to the restaurant in Hateg where we had booked our wedding reception. I was upset for Andreia that not one of her friends that she had invited had turned up except for one of her school teachers. At least all of Andreia's family from her mother's side was present but not her natural father. I had no family or friends to support me but I knew that God was with me and that was important to me.

Our wedding reception lasted until 6.00am the following morning and we had a wonderful time. The tradition in Romania was for all the wedding guests to give a gift of money but because they were all poor we stated that we did not want any of our guests to give anything we just wanted their presence. That did not stop them giving gifts of money and we received 6,500,000 Lei (£225) that was enough to pay for the settlement visa application on the 19th February. After leaving our wedding reception on the Sunday morning we slept for a few hours before making our way to the railway station for our overnight train to Bucharest and our appointment at the British Embassy.

I was praying that everything would work out because I could not bear the thought of having to return to England without Andreia and David. We arrived at the British Embassy for our appointment and I handed over £225 in Lei with the application form. When Andreia's name was called out we went into the booth for the interview. The man who interviewed us was very friendly and he asked if we had paid £225 for David's visa. We explained that we did not know that we had to pay for David but we were informed that he would need a visa also. I explained that we did not have another £225 and my heart started to sink. We were then informed that David might be able to obtain a British passport because I was his father. We then had to wait while a decision was made if a visa would be issued.

It was only a short wait when Andreia's name was called out again and the tears started to flow down my cheeks when we were informed that Andreia would be given her visa. We were also informed that if I returned to the Embassy with David's birth certificate and photograph he would be issued with an emergency British passport for £30. We left the British Embassy very thankful to God because all our prayers were being answered. It meant that I had to return to Bucharest but this was a small sacrifice to know that we could return to England as a family. I felt like we had been through the fires of hell to reach the stage we were now at and had overcome every single obstacle that had been put before us. I knew that we could not have done this if God had not been with us. It became very clear to me that even though people had falsely judged and condemned us for being together our God had not.

We both went to Hateg hospital on our return to give David lots of kisses and cuddles and hand some wedding cake to the doctors and nurses. Andreia was very happy as she showed everyone the visa stamp in her passport that would allow her to come to England. We dressed David as we waited for the doctors to sign the papers so he could be discharged from hospital into our care. We had bought a small Moses basket for David as we could not afford to buy a pram. The small wicker basket seemed very appropriate for David with all he had gone through already as like Moses he had been rescued from the jaws of death. We were two very proud parents as we left Hateg hospital with our little bundle of joy.

I returned to Bucharest for David's British passport and during the long train journey I thanked God for everything he had done for us. I was only at the Embassy for about two hours and I found it hard to take in when I was handed a British passport with the name David John Daniel Sutton printed inside with a lovely photograph of David. I made my way back to the railway station and caught the express train back to Deva.

The following Sunday we had a Christening service for David in the village church at Tustea attended by all the family members who had been at our wedding. It was also the time when Andreia would say her goodbyes to her family as we prepared to leave for England. It was a very special Christening and party that we had afterwards at the grandparent's home of Andreia who lived in Tustea. They only had a very simple house with two rooms and a toilet in the garden but we had a party we would never forget. I could see and feel the love that her family had not only for Andreia and David but also for me. We all shed a few tears as it was time to say goodbye not knowing when we would be returning. We went back to Hateg to load our mini bus with all our worldly possessions as we prepared to leave for England.

I went for a walk around the small town of Hateg by myself while I thought about all we had gone through in just over a year. I knew that I had a lot of love to give but I had been crushed in my spirit by all that had taken place. It was only by the grace of God I was still standing and still wanting to live my life as a Christian. I knew that a lot of arrows that had been shot at me by various people had hit me in the heart but I prayed to God that he would heal me and I would not end up bitter by all that had taken place. I loved Andreia so very much and I was hoping that the love she said she had for me was genuine. We both loved our little treasure with all our heart and we knew that he was a little miracle. As I walked past all the apartments where I had lived or stayed at with Jan I wondered where I would have been if Jan had not walked out on our marriage when I needed her the most. It was too late to change what had past and even though I had made some mistakes I did not regret being married to Andreia. I would have stayed with Jan if she had forgiven me for anything she thought I had done wrong but it did not happen. Now I had a very young and beautiful wife who I loved very much and a treasure from heaven that I would not swop for anything in this world. The scripture from Romans chapter 8 verse 28 came into my mind, "And we know that in all things God works for the good of those who love him, who have been called according to his purpose" I knew that God knew that I loved him with all my heart even if I got it wrong on many occasions. I knew that I would not stop loving any of my children no matter what they did wrong so I was confident that the author and creator of Love would never stop loving me.

Now it was time to look to the future and trust that God had everything worked out for our lives in England. I knew that there was a big age difference between Andreia and myself but we did not see it as we loved each other deeply and our little treasure from heaven. I was so thankful to God for all our answered prayers especially for David who made our family complete. I had gone through a divorce, birth and a marriage all within a few weeks.

Chapter 53

"Do not gloat over me, my enemy! Though I have fallen, I will rise. Though I sit in darkness, the Lord will be my light"

Micah 8 : 8

On the 1st march 2001 we set off for England in our mini bus with David in a Moses basket and just enough money to get us to England. We had no home to go to except for my mother who was living in sheltered accommodation in Stockport where they had a guest suite where family members of the residents could stay for short periods of time. We arrived safely at my mother's home three days after leaving Romania and my mum could not stop kissing David. We had all suffered in many different ways after my father had died and now my mum had someone to hold in her arms and make a big fuss of. It did not take long for the local press to find out we were back in England and they had photographers hiding in bushes so they could take photographs of us when we were not expecting it. They printed stories that contained lots of lies and we were contacted by the Richard and Judy show to ask if we would like to go on their programme and put our side of the story. We decided it would be the best thing for us to do because we were fed up of all the lies that were being printed about us. They agreed to pay our travelling expenses so we went down to London with David and appeared live on national television. We told how we had met and had fallen in love and how the people at Blackpool had taken over the charity shop and had stopped the work we was doing in Romania to help homeless children. I told all those watching that I loved Andreia and David very much and I was going to take the trustees to court for what they had done. We both felt that for once we had been given an opportunity to tell it how it was and not how many newspaper reports had printed lots of lies.

We had found a nice house to rent in Cleveleys where we had decided to live while I waited for the outcome of the court summons I had issued against the trustees of the charity I had formed that was now going by another name. I had to use up most of the money I had borrowed from John and Diane to pay the deposit and one month rent in advance. On the Saturday we were due to leave my mother's home and move to Cleveleys I put a 25p win heinz bet on at the bookies where I had picked six horses that were running that day. The bet cost me £14.25p and was all the money I had left in my bank account. I watched one of the horses on the television win at odds of 20-1 and I prayed that I would get a few more winners to go with it. I thought no more about the bet as we set off with our mini bus and all our possessions to our new home at Cleveleys. It did not take us very long to unpack as we did not have many things but we did have each other. I put the television on to see if it would work and all I managed to get was the teletext. I put on the horse results and I could not contain my excitement when I found out that I had 5 winning horses on my bet. I was jumping up and down saying to Andreia I had won a lot of money and thanking God. When Andreia asked me how much I said I did not know except it would be a few thousand pounds. When I sat down and worked the bet out I realised that after tax I had won over £7400.

For us it was a miracle as we now had enough money to buy the things that we needed for our home including beds to sleep on. I was able to repay the money that I had borrowed from John and Diane who was both surprised at how quickly I had repaid them. We decided to bring my mother-in-law Angela over from Romania so that she could help with David and be company for Andreia. I had enough money to buy a nice Ford Escort and we had no money problems. It was good to have Angela staying with us and it gave Andreia and I time for each other. When Angela arrived she told us that she had broken up with Nelu and asked if we could find her an Englishman to marry so she could have a better life. I told Angela that she should marry a person because she loved him not just for a better life. I had to laugh at the way Angela would walk with her eyes fixed to the ground looking for money that people had lost. I was amazed at how many times she would bend down and pick up pennies that no-one else had bothered to pick up. On some occasions she did find £5 and £10 notes and even a purse in the park that some child had probably lost. When we told Angela to hand them into the police she said that the money was a gift from God and now belonged to her. After staying with us for about three months Angela returned to Romania.

The case against the trustees was heard at Blackpool County Court and the Judge hearing the case found in favour of the trustees. I was upset at the outcome and did not believe that justice had taken place. I had represented myself and had proved that the charity shop was in my name and was opened for the Bartimaeus Charity in Romania but it made no difference to the Judge who I believed had been influenced by the fact I was now married to Andreia. At least it had given me the opportunity to prove that no money was missing from the charity that some of the trustees had told some newspaper reporters. I had done what I had told the trustees I would do and it was now time to move on and leave the past behind.

By November of 2001 our lease was due to expire and we decided to have a fresh start away from Cleveleys. We had changed our surnames to Williamson by deed poll so that no-one would trace us to where we moved. We looked in estate agents in Southport because it was near the sea side and we found a nice detached house to rent in Hesketh Bank about five miles from Southport. It was a nice feeling to have a fresh start where no-one knew anything about us and within a few days of moving we had settled into our new home. We decided to go to Romania for Christmas so Andreia could see her family and let them see how big and beautiful David was growing. It was a hard journey because of the weather and we ended up staying at the Deva Hotel in Romania because the conditions at the homes of family members were very basic. We had a happy time visiting all our family members and David was the star attraction where ever we went. It was while we were staying in the hotel that we talked about buying an apartment of our own so we could have a holiday home for whenever we went to Romania. I was so happy with my new family and I loved Andreia and David very deeply.

When we returned to England we decided to sell our car so we could buy an apartment in Romania that was on sale very cheaply. I sold my car for £3000 and with the money I had in the bank we had enough money to buy an apartment in Romania. I started back in work as a builder and advertised my services in the area where we lived. It did not take me long to get jobs as there was a shortage of good builders where we lived. We had joined the local church and got most of the people involved in making up shoe boxes filled with presents for the orphans and homeless children in Romania. We returned to Romania in the summer of 2002 and found a very nice apartment for sale in Deva for the equivalent of £5000. It had three rooms and a separate kitchen and bathroom and was everything we had wanted. Within a few days all the legal formalities had been completed and we both had our names on our own property. I was so thankful to God for the ways our fortunes had changed in the short time we had been married. We had a very happy holiday in Romania and we returned to England where we started to collect shoe boxes to take to Romania for Christmas. We also made plans to build a home in Romania for homeless children as I had never given up on the plans that had been stopped by the people who had taken over the charity I had formed in Cleveleys. I was working on a roof repair in Southport when Andreia came to see me waving a pregnancy test in her hands. I could tell by the excitement of Andreia that the test was positive before I had even got down off the roof. We were both overjoyed that Andreia was pregnant with our second child and I believed that God was pouring blessing after blessing into our lives. By the Christmas of 2002 we were back in Romania with over 2000 shoe boxes for children and a twenty ton wagon loaded with aid for poor families.

Our Church in Hesketh Bank had helped us in so many ways and we were a very happy family as we worked together reaching out to people in need. We had also involved Angela and the new man in her life called Lucica. We went to many of the schools and places that Andreia had known as a child and also the places where I had been helping families since 1999. We went to a village called Petresti where we visited lots of families including the family Hulei who had treated me so kindly every time I had called to see them. I felt like part of their family and they showered so much love on Andreia and David as well. Andreia started to bleed and we prayed that everything would be fine with our baby. We think it was the cold weather and all the travelling that had caused Andreia to bleed and we thanked God that everything was ok. We decided to buy a house in the country to help orphans and homeless children and be a base for taking aid to Romania on a regular basis. We found a house with lots of land for sale at Panc Saliste in Dobra for £6000 and within 3 days the house was in our name. We found an architect to draw up the plans to turn a very small house into one with seven large rooms that would be able to accommodate lots of children. We returned to England in early January where I continued working as a builder where I was being recommended because of my cheap prices and good standard of work I was doing. We arranged to bring Angela and Lucica to England for a few months so that Lucica could work with me and earn some money. It was good for me because Lucica was a very good worker and helped me with a lot of the heavy tasks. After a few months they returned to Romania and we were happy to be just the three of us again.

We did not stay three for very long when our beautiful daughter Naomi was born on the 9th July 2003. We were hoping that she would wait until my birthday but I think the excitement that Andreia had gone through just a few days before when she had auditioned for X Factor had been the deciding factor. The sadness that Andreia had suffered at being turned down by the X Factor judges was now replaced by the joy of the birth of Naomi. I had been with Andreia throughout the birth while the Pastor and his wife from our church had looked after David. I was so happy when the mid wife placed Naomi in my arms as soon as she was born and then into the loving arms of Andreia who breast fed Naomi right away. We both thanked God for a beautiful and perfect addition to our family and within three days Andreia and Naomi left hospital to be back at home with David and myself. I loved my family so very much and by Christmas of 2003 we were back in Romania at our apartment in Deva. We had Naomi baptized at the church where we had been married and we invited Nicoleta from the Hulei family to come and help Andreia with our children while we were in Romania. I had known Nicoleta and her family for many years without having any ungodly desires. For some reason I found myself being drawn to Nicoleta as I saw the way she was with my children and her gentle nature. I started to have nights out with Andreia and Nicoleta together while Angela looked after our children. I could see that Andreia and Nicoleta were also getting very close to each other and had become good friends. It was a day when Andreia and Nicoleta had been out shopping together when Andreia came home laughing and joking because some boys had jumped on the back of Andreia. I was upset that Andreia attracted boys so easily and we ended up having a row. I went out to the local club where I got drunk and ended up having my gold cross and chain stolen. When I came home Nicoleta opened the door for me and I ended up giving her a quick kiss.

I started to have strong desires for Nicoleta as the lust of my flesh stared to take control and when I tried to kiss her again a few days later she pushed me away and told me to think about Andreia and my children. I did not take no for an answer and a few days later when Andreia was out shopping I kissed Nicoleta again and this time she returned the passion I had for her. It was when I was taking Nicoleta back home to Petresti on our own that I stopped at the Deva Hotel and booked into a room. I tried making love to Nicoleta but was not able to do so because of the guilt I was feeling. I took Nicoleta back home to Petresti and returned back to Deva to be with Andreia, David and Naomi. I felt very bad about the feelings I had for Nicoleta knowing that I was married to Andreia with two beautiful children. I had everything a man could want and yet a part of me was prepared to risk losing all I had with Andreia. Maybe I should have gone for marriage counselling but I let the desires I had for Nicoleta get the better of me and a few weeks later I made love to Nicoleta for the first time. Nicoleta had been a virgin and I knew that it was important for a Romanian girl to marry the man who takes her virginity. I did not want my marriage to Andreia to end but I started an affair behind her back.

Chapter 54

"You shall not commit adultery"

Exodus 20 : 14

I only had a few chances to be with Nicoleta and this was when I would pick her up from Petresti or take her back home again after she had been staying with us to help with David and Naomi. We all had Christmas together and then it was time for Andreia and me to return back to England. We tried to get Nicoleta a visa to come with us to England and help look after our children but she was refused a visa at the British Embassy in Bucharest. We left Romania without her and I was very sad at leaving her behind as by now my feelings for Nicoleta had grown very strong. We had only been back in England for a week when Andreia received a telephone call informing her that her father Liviu was seriously ill in Timisoara hospital with heart problems. I made plans to return to Romania immediately and booked the ferry crossing for our mini bus. In less than three days we were in Timisoara where Andreia was very upset to see how poorly her father was. The Doctors told Andreia that smoking had caused much of the damage and he had to give it up or face an early death. I gave £200 to help towards the medical expenses knowing that in Romania a gift of money would help Liviu get the best care possible. While we were in Romania we met up with Nicoleta and I asked her if she would be willing to come to England without a visa and to see if we could get her into England. We also met up with Angela and Lucica and agreed to take them back with us to England to help them out and at the same time for Lucica to work with me. Our mini bus was full as we headed back to England and each time we crossed a border we hoped that Nicoleta would get through. After three days of travelling we arrived at Calais and drove onto the ferry boat to cross over the English Channel to England. My heart was beating very fast as I handed the passports to the customs officer hoping he would not count all the people in the mini bus. I felt relief when he told us to go and have a safe journey home.

When we arrived back home we sorted out the bedrooms where everyone would be sleeping. Nicoleta had the single room with Naomi, Angela and Lucica had the top bunk with David in the bottom bunk in the other bedroom, Andreia and I stayed in our own bedroom. I had landed a very big job where I needed to employ about eight workers and I was able to give Angela and Lucica work. I also paid Nicoleta some money each week for looking after Naomi and for a while we were one big happy family. I would sneak out of bed on some nights when Andreia was sleeping and get into bed at the side of Nicoleta. Andreia was a very sound sleeper and she did not notice that from time to time I had left the bed. It was towards the end of March when Andreia found out she was expecting our third child. I felt very guilty knowing that I was cheating on Andreia behind her back but by now I was also in love with Nicoleta. I wanted to tell Andreia that I had fallen in love with Nicoleta but I knew that if I had done so it would have broken her heart. I found myself torn between two beautiful girls that I loved and I did not know what to do.

One morning when I got up for work Nicoleta had come downstairs to make Naomi a bottle of milk, I took Nicoleta in my arms to kiss her and Lucica came into the kitchen and saw us kissing. I asked Lucica not to say anything to Angela or Andreia as it was just a friendly kiss. I decided to take Andreia away for a short holiday to see her Aunty Gabi who was working in Italy. We left Angela, Lucica and Nicoleta looking after David and Naomi while we went to Rome for a four day holiday. While we were on this holiday I caught a man stealing money from my pocket while we were on the underground train. I tried to get hold of the man who was a lot taller than me and ended up chasing him when he got off the train. I shouted at people to help me stop the thief but no-one bothered to help. I cornered the man and jumped on him pulling him to the floor but as I fell very hard onto the concrete floor I felt something crack in my chest and a very great pain. I had to let go of him and he ran off while I tried to pick myself up off the floor. Andreia came to help me and she told me I should have just let him go as he could have ended up killing me if he had a knife. It was the following day when we went to look at the

Vatican that the pain in my chest was unbearable and I had to go to hospital. The Doctors found out I had broken my ribs in three places and part of my rib case had come away inside my chest. I was in a lot of pain and was happy when the holiday was over and we returned back home. When we arrived home Nicoleta told me that Angela had slapped her face while we were away and was being very mean to her. I had an argument with Angela and Lucica over this who both denied doing anything to Nicoleta. We had more arguments over the next couple of weeks and Andreia and myself both told Angela and Lucica to leave. As they were leaving our house Lucica became very violent and started a fight with me. Lucica hit me full in the face and my nose was bleeding very heavily. David had witnessed what was taking place and Andreia telephoned the police and tried to stop my nose from bleeding. By the time the police had arrived Angela and Lucica had walked away from our home. Before walking away Angela told Andreia that something was going on between Nicoleta and me and that she should keep her eyes on me. I told the police that I did not want to press any charges against Lucica for assault but to make sure that he did not come near our home again. I knew that Angela and Lucica had over £2000 saved up while working for me and would have the means to go back to Romania. After the police had left Andreia told me what her mother had said but I told her she had only said that to cause problems between us.

    Life in our home was now very peaceful after Angela and Lucica had left and I was very happy living with both of the women I loved and my children. The peace did not last very long when the doorbell rang at 5.30am one morning in May 2004. It was the police and my life was turned upside down as they told me that my eldest daughter Donna from my marriage to Jan and my niece Amanda who was the daughter of Jan's sister Carol had made serious sexual allegations against me. I could not believe what I was hearing and was handcuffed and placed in a cage at the back of a police van like some kind of animal. Andreia and Nicoleta were also upset about what was taking place and I told them not to worry and I would contact them as soon as I could to let them know what it was all about. I was taken to Skelmersdale Police station at first where I contacted the duty solicitor. I was then driven to Stockport police station in Cheadle where I spoke with my solicitor. I was informed that Donna and Amanda had both made serious allegations against me of rape and indecent assault that dated back about twenty years and that the police wanted to interview me under caution. I told my solicitor that I had done nothing wrong and had nothing to hide and I was willing to be interviewed and answer any questions put to me. I was interviewed for about six hours and answered all the questions put to me. The police then informed me that I would be released on police bail while they conducted further enquiries and sent their file to the Crown Prosecution Service who would decide if I was to be charged or not. As soon as I left the police station I telephoned Andreia to let her know what had taken place and to tell her I was on my way back home.

I told Andreia and Nicoleta all that had happened and all about the allegations that had been made against me. Andreia knew how Donna had threatened me in the past when Donna had warned me she would have nothing to do with me and cut me off from seeing my grandchildren if I went to Romania to be with Andreia. The following morning the door bell rang and it was the police with Lancashire Social Services. They informed me that I could not stay at home where my children lived while the investigation was still ongoing and if I did not move out they would go to court and apply for emergency care orders on David and Naomi where they would be removed and placed into care. We were so angry at what we were being told and I felt like I was being treated like a convicted person before I had even been taken to court. We both decided that it would not be good for our children to be taken away and placed with strangers and agreed that I would move out while the police finished their enquiries. I was fortunate enough to have enough money to buy a second hand caravan and placed it on a caravan site near to where we lived where it had all the facilities I needed.

I wondered if all these bad things were happening to me because of committing adultery with Nicoleta and I had made God angry. I was very upset about all the allegations that had been made against me and it was hard for me going back to work with what had taken place. I had been placed on police bail for one month and it came as a great relief when my solicitor telephoned me to say that the police were not going to take any action against me. I asked my solicitor to inform Lancashire Social Services of the police decision and that I was going back home. The following day we received a visit from the Lancashire Social Services who informed Andreia and myself that they would like to do some work with our family to make sure that none of our children would be at risk. We both said that we understood their concerns and were willing to work with them. In July 2004 we went to Romania for our summer holidays and took Nicoleta back home to be with her family. I knew what I was doing with Nicoleta behind the back of Andreia was very wrong but I was deeply in love with them both. I had even made a joke when Andreia let Nicoleta try on her wedding dress that it would be nice if I had two wives. In my heart and mind I was serious and I wanted to tell Andreia the truth.

We went to Balie Felix for our holidays and stayed in a four star hotel where Nicoleta had her own room with Naomi, with Andreia, David and myself sharing another room a few doors away. It suited me because I could spend some time with Nicoleta when Andreia thought I was at the bar by myself having a quiet drink. When we returned back to our apartment in Deva Andreia caught me kissing Nicoleta and our secret affair was now no secret anymore. Andreia reacted as I knew she would do and shouted and screamed at us both to get out and leave. Andreia shouted that she should have listened to her mother and that we had both hurt her. I felt so sad knowing how much we had both hurt Andreia but a part of me was relieved that our secret was now in the open. It was with a sad heart that I took Nicoleta back to Petresti with my suitcase packed as well. Andreia started sending me bad text messages on my phone and I knew that I deserved what I was getting. I knew that Nicoleta was a few days late for her period and we went and bought a pregnancy test. We were both shocked as two red lines appeared on the test confirming that Nicoleta was also pregnant. Under normal circumstances I would have been happy but I knew that the situation for all three of us including our children had just got worse. I telephoned Andreia to tell her the truth about everything and that I still loved her if she would forgive me and have me back.

I knew that whatever way I went someone would end up getting hurt but I believed that Andreia needed me more than Nicoleta and I told Andreia I would give Nicoleta up if she would have me back. I was very surprised when Andreia telephoned me two days later to say she was willing to forgive me as she did love me and did not want to break up our family. I had the very hard task of telling Nicoleta that we could not be together even though I loved her very much.

Nicoleta cried and sobbed her heart out and my heart was breaking seeing the pain I had caused to all those I loved. I also had to talk with Stan and Viorica the parents of Nicoleta and explain what I had done. I thought they would be very angry with me but they were both calm considering the news I was giving them. I told Nicoleta and her parents that I would send money to Nicoleta every month to make sure she did not go short of anything for her or our baby. I had seen how Nicoleta was with David and Naomi to know that Nicoleta would make a perfect mother and I was determined that I would not run away from my responsibilities.

It broke my heart to leave Nicoleta behind carrying our unborn baby knowing how much I loved her and knowing how hard life would be for them in Romania. As we made our way back to England I talked with Andreia about why I had gone with Nicoleta in the first place and how hard it was for me to stop what I was doing. I was surprised when Andreia told me she felt sorry for Nicoleta leaving her behind and she wanted the best for Nicoleta even though we had both hurt her. I talked to Andreia about how happy we were when we were living together with Nicoleta and that a part of me wanted back what we had. Andreia told me that she had come to love Nicoleta herself and it was hard leaving her behind as she was losing her best friend as well. I promised Andreia that I would try and make things up to her for what I had done but in my heart I was also hurting for Nicoleta and our baby. I was working on a roof repair and at the same time I was pouring my heart out to God about all that had taken place. My telephone rang and it was Nicoleta informing me that she was in hospital bleeding and might be losing our baby. Nicoleta told me that I did not care what happened to her and our baby and it was breaking my heart to hear those words knowing just how much I did care. I cried out to God for him to show me what I should do. My phone rang again and this time it was Andreia who said the following, "I have been thinking all morning about being back together with Nicoleta and I would like us all to live together as a family and for you to have two wives" What I was hearing was an answer to my prayer to God and I rushed home to talk with Andreia about the telephone call I had from Nicoleta informing me she was in hospital.

I told Andreia that I would love her and Nicoleta both the same and be a good husband and father to my children. Andreia promised me that she would love me forever and never leave me. I knew from reading my bible that lots of Godly men in the past had more than one wife and from my own understanding it was never a sin with God for a man to have more than one wife. I knew in my heart that I was trying to justify with God what I was about to do and taking scriptures out of context. I even read the passage again where God had made provisions for the man with two wives so that the man treated his wives very fair. I told Andreia that I would talk with Nicoleta to ask if she would agree for me to have two wives and for all three of us to live together with our children. I also asked Andreia if she would also talk with Nicoleta so she would know we were both serious about what we were proposing to do. When I spoke with Nicoleta she said she would think about it and let me know. Andreia spoke with Nicoleta and she told me that she believed that Nicoleta was going to agree for us all to be together. The following day Nicoleta telephoned me and told me she was willing to give it a try and see how things worked out. I was so happy to know that I was going to be with both the women that I loved and all of my children. I had a wonderful picture in my mind of how it was going to be but I could not have been more wrong.

Chapter 55

"If a man has two wives, and he loves one but not the other, and both bear him sons but the firstborn is the son of the wife he does not love, when he wills his property to his sons, he must not give the rights of the firstborn to the son of the wife he loves in preference to his actual firstborn, the son of the wife he does not love"

Deuteronomy 21 : 15 – 16

I knew that I had sinned against God by committing adultery with Nicoleta just like King David had done with Bathsheba. I got down on my knees and prayed for forgiveness from God and also Andreia who I had hurt so deeply. If Andreia had not forgiven me or had insisted I leave Nicoleta in Romania then all our lives would have taken a different route. The fact was we all agreed to live as a family again but this time there would be no secrets. I wanted to treat Andreia and Nicoleta the same with no favorites as I loved them both very deeply. I wanted to provide for all their needs and those of all my children. I knew that God had described King David as a man after His own heart and that God was angry with him because Bathsheba was married to another man and King David had arranged for her husband to be killed so he could have Bathsheba as another of his wives. King David and Bathsheba were punished for their sin but when they repented God in his mercy forgave them and their son Solomon became the next king of Judah. What I failed to take into account was the sin that David committed had long term consequences on the lives of his children for many years.

We had agreed that we would go back to Romania for the wedding of the Uncle to Nicoleta called Marcel who was getting married in October 2004. It would give us a chance to see how we got on living together as a family and I could not wait to hold Nicoleta in my arms again. When we met up we talked about how we would do things living together as a family and how the sleeping arrangements would be. We spoke with the parents of Nicoleta and Andreia who all said we were mad and that it would never work. Maybe we should have listened to them but we did not and at the wedding of Marcel I was with the two women that I loved. They both looked so beautiful even though they were both pregnant and I was the happiest person in the world. Sadly my happiness did not last for long when I noticed Andreia could not take her eyes away from Dorin who was the younger brother of Nicoleta. Her eyes followed him everywhere as he waited on guests at the wedding and I knew that the promise that Andreia had made to me was being broken very quickly. After the wedding we went back to our apartment in Deva and we lived together while we waited for Andreia to give birth. We had planned for Andreia to give birth in Romania because of Doctor Gavrish who had delivered Andreia and David when they were born. We trusted Doctor Gavrish as he was a very experienced gynecologist and the best we knew. I went to the local car market and bought a brand new car for £8000 and had my personalised number plate BOB 28 on it. While I was at the auction I caught Andreia sending secret text messages to Dorin. It led to me having a very big argument with Andreia who denied anything was taking place with Dorin.

    I spent a lot of time organising building materials for the house at Panc and the workers that we needed to do the work. I started to have big doubts about Andreia as she was over friendly with lots of the male workers. I noticed that each time we went to Petresti that Andreia would not take her eyes off Dorin and I started to lose my trust in her. It soon came time for Andreia to give birth and on the 24th December 2004 I rushed Andreia to hospital in Hateg where Doctor Gavrish was waiting for us to arrive. I was happy to know that David and Naomi were in safe hands with Nicoleta and it meant I could stay with Andreia at the hospital. It was just before midnight when Andreia gave birth to a beautiful daughter who we called Victoria Elizabeth. It was a very difficult time because the placenta was stuck to the scar tissue after Victoria was delivered and it took all the skill of Doctor Gavrish to remove it. I was upset at seeing what Andreia was going through and I was praying all the time. I was so thankful to God when I knew that Victoria and Andreia were both fine and I took Victoria in my arms and gave her a big kiss.

Within a week Andreia left hospital with Victoria and we all lived at our apartment in Deva. Nicoleta had been a great help with David and Naomi and I could see the blessings from being one big family where we could help each other. My happiness did not last for long when Andreia told me that she did not want to share me with Nicoleta anymore and wanted Nicoleta to leave. It was so hard for me to tell Nicoleta and they very nearly came to blows. When I took Nicoleta back to her family at Petresti her mother and brother Dorin told me that Andreia had been after Dorin for ages. They told me that Andreia had bought Dorin a gold ring and some aftershave and all that had been going on behind my back. It was so hard knowing what to do for the best because I was taking Nicoleta back home when she had done nothing wrong and just because Andreia had changed her mind about sharing me with Nicoleta.

I wanted to end it with Andreia but I felt very guilty because I was the one who had cheated on her and made Nicoleta pregnant in the first place. I also loved my three children very much and I knew that they needed me more than Nicoleta did. I knew that Nicoleta had the love of all her family and that they would help her in lots of ways. I knew that I could not leave Andreia so we returned to our home in England leaving Nicoleta behind. We had only been back in England for a few weeks and my heart was breaking for Nicoleta knowing that I had left her behind when she was carrying my child. I spoke with Andreia about how hard it would be for Nicoleta giving birth in Romania with Doctors who might not be as experienced as Doctor Gavrish. I was talking with Nicoleta on the telephone and told her that I wanted to be in Romania for the birth of our son. We had been told by a gynecologist in Deva when we went for a scan that he was 99% sure our baby was a boy. I wanted to be there for the birth and not to leave Nicoleta alone. Andreia agreed to come back to Romania with me. Nicoleta was staying at our apartment in Deva because she had an argument with her mother.

When we arrived in Deva I asked Andreia if I could sleep with Nicoleta so I could talk with her in private about what help she expected from me when our child was born. Andreia told me that if I made love to Nicoleta that she would want to make love with Dorin. I agreed to this not thinking that I would make love to Nicoleta with it being so close to the birth of our baby. In the morning Andreia told me she had heard everything and now I had to agree for her to have Dorin. It was breaking my heart knowing how much I also loved Andreia to agree to this but Andreia was not going to change her mind. This was something that Andreia was not going to let go of but now it was time for Nicoleta to give birth. I had taken her to see Doctor Gavrish and asked him to deliver our baby. All the medical staff at the hospital knew I was married to Andreia and gave me lots of dirty looks. Doctor Gavrish was very understanding as I explained that I wanted Nicoleta and our baby to have the best Doctor and that was more important to me than being embarrassed in front of other people. Andreia was also by our side giving lots of moral support.

It was the 16th March 2005 when I was with Nicoleta in the operating theatre and Doctor Gavrish delivered our baby. I thought I was hearing things wrong when he said we had a beautiful baby girl in the Romanian language. When I was handed our new born baby there was no mistaking she was a girl. Nicoleta picked the name Bianca and I added Nicoleta as her middle name. I stayed with Nicoleta until she was moved into a small ward and I was so happy that they were both well. I had a very big sadness inside of my heart knowing that I would have to leave them behind and return to England. I loved then so very much and I did not believe that Andreia loved me like Nicoleta did. My heart was being torn into two pieces and I prayed to God that I would do the right thing. I thought about Andreia wanting Dorin and wondered if what she had for me was true love. Within a few days of Nicoleta leaving the hospital with Bianca I was hit with another bombshell from Andreia who told me she only wanted me and if I returned with her to England she would love me forever. At the same time Andreia told me she had given all her gold to strangers she had met who told her they could do magical things for her by praying over the gold. I could not believe that Andreia would trust complete strangers with over £1000 worth of gold presents I had bought for her and told her that the people would disappear. When I took Andreia to the apartment where she had met them and left her gold it was no surprise they were no longer there. I tried to break down the steel door with a big crowbar I had in my mini bus but I only succeeded in bending part of the door.

To make matters worse the police came and it turned out the people who had taken the gold had only rented the apartment and had given false identity cards. The owner of the apartment was now going to charge me with criminal damage and I had to pay over £150 for a new door so that the police did not charge me. I tried to understand where Andreia was coming from as she told me that she believed they could grant her a wish that I would stop loving Nicoleta and that I would leave Nicoleta so that Andreia could have her family back. I blamed myself for the situation we were in and it broke my heart again to have to tell Nicoleta that I would have to take her back to Petresti when I had hardly had any time with Bianca. My heart was broken yet again and so was Nicoleta as I told her that Andreia no longer wanted us to share. I knew that Nicoleta had done nothing wrong but I could not see any other way of doing things. After Nicoleta and Bianca had been at Petresti for a few weeks Nicoleta agreed to let me have Bianca at Deva for a couple of days. My heart melted when I held Bianca in my arms and I did not want to let her go. All four children were beautiful and I loved each one of them the same. I did not want to let any of them go and I told Andreia that I would agree for her to have Dorin from time to time if she agreed for me to have Nicoleta.

I was not surprised when Andreia accepted this proposal and she was very happy telling me that she would always love me and look after me forever. I knew it was going to hurt me to let the woman I deeply loved to have sex with a young man who had so many girls that I lost count and who I knew did not love Andreia. I could understand Dorin wanting to make love with Andreia but I was praying that he would not follow it through. Andreia telephoned Dorin first to meet us in Deva while Angela looked after David, Naomi and Victoria. A part of me was hoping that Dorin would not turn up but whatever Andreia said to him had the desired effect as he was in Deva within the hour. The three of us went to the restaurant where we used to go with Nicoleta. My heart was breaking as I thought of what was about to happen and I passed a note to Andreia saying that if she did not go through with it I would leave Romania with her and never go back for Nicoleta. Andreia looked at me and said that I could not change my mind now as it would not be fair on her. I think that was the moment when I knew that the love Andreia said she had for me was not genuine even though I wanted to believe that it was. I telephoned Nicoleta and asked her to meet me in Deva as I would not leave her again as I had given Andreia to her brother.

When morning arrived I think Andreia realised just how much she had hurt me as we sat down and had breakfast together. We took Dorin back to the bus station so he could go back to Panc where he was working on our home and we took Nicoleta back to Petresti. Within a few days the news filtered through from Panc that Dorin had been bragging to the other workmen of his conquest of Andreia. When some of the workmen said they did not believe him he waved the condoms around that he had used. It just confirmed to Andreia what I had told her about Dorin but only Andreia knew if it bothered her or not. I knew that I was torn between two genuine loves and no matter what way I went I was going to get hurt. I tried to get a visa for Nicoleta and Bianca to come to England and Andreia said she would pray for us. What we did not know was that Andreia had telephoned the British Embassy while we were on our way pleading with them not to grant them visas telling the embassy staff that she wanted to save her marriage. It cost me over £600 to apply for visas that we had no chance of getting once Andreia had made that telephone call. I thought I could put behind me what had taken place with Dorin and I returned to England without Nicoleta and Bianca. I soon realised that I was very wrong because now Andreia had formed a relationship with one of the other workers from Panc who also lived at Petresti called Danny. I had a bet on the horses so Andreia used this as an excuse to contact Danny. I also telephoned Nicoleta to see how her and Bianca were doing and this was something else that Andreia did not like. Andreia seemed to switch her affections between Dorin and Danny and I was never sure who she was with at any given time. I told Andreia that the only way I would be able to bring Nicoleta to England was if we got divorced and I married Nicoleta. I told Andreia that I would never stop loving her and that I would marry her again in the future. We agreed to return to Romania and get divorced and within 3 weeks of being in Romania our divorce was finalised in February 2006. I went again to the British Embassy and paid another £600 for visa applications only this time Andreia had told her family members to telephone the embassy and try to stop the visas being issued. I wasted the money again as we left the embassy in tears wondering why the visas had been refused. I had told the embassy that I would marry Nicoleta but because we were not actually married they used that as an excuse.

While we were in Bucharest Andreia went shopping with Nicoleta to help pick her wedding dress as we made plans to get married. I thought that things were working out as Andreia and Nicoleta talked together about the wedding with Andreia being a god parent. I bought myself a new suit and everything that was needed for the wedding. Andreia and I had to return to England because of the work I was doing. While we were back in England we had another big argument and Andreia called the police to have me removed from the house. I returned to Romania by myself in April so that I could get married to Nicoleta. While we were waiting for our wedding day to arrive we took Bianca with us for a short holiday to Balie Felix. We had a wonderful time together as we talked about our wedding that was only a few days away. It was the day before the wedding when Andreia telephoned me to say that she was sorry and loved me deeply and if I called off the wedding to Nicoleta I would never regret it. I still loved Andreia very deeply and I was thinking about David, Naomi and Victoria at the same time. I still felt guilty for breaking Gods commandment with Nicoleta and I agreed to call off my wedding. I telephoned Nicoleta to tell her that I could not go through with the wedding less than twenty four hours before we were due to get married. I made plans to return to England knowing that I had broken the heart of Nicoleta yet again.

Chapter 56

"Haven't you read," he replied, "that at the beginning the Creator made them male and female," and said, "For this reason a man will leave his father and mother and be united to his wife, and the two will become one flesh. So they are no longer two, but one. Therefore what God has joined together, let man not separate"

Matthew 19 : 4 - 6

I don't think I had been back in England for one week when I had a big argument again with Andreia who called the police out. I knew that I had made a big mistake not marrying Nicoleta and I telephoned to ask for her forgiveness and give me another chance. Nicoleta agreed to forgive me and I made plans to return to Romania while Andreia made plans to rent a house in Banks so she could have a fresh start. On the 27th May 2006 Nicoleta and I got married at Sebes with all her family present. It was a very beautiful wedding and I now had the certificate that was going to enable Nicoleta and Bianca to get the visa to come to England. While we were at the reception in the evening I received a telephone call from Andreia who was very upset. Andreia told me that she would like us all to be a family when we came to England and that she still loved me. The day after our wedding we were on our way to the British Embassy in Bucharest so that on the Monday morning we were first in line. We were so happy when this time we left the embassy with the visa stamps needed to gain entry into England. We stayed a few days in Romania so the family of Nicoleta had time to say their goodbyes to Nicoleta and Bianca. We set off for England in my mini bus on the 1st June 2006 and on the way Andreia telephoned and again asked me if we could all live together. I still loved Andreia very deeply and I knew that this way I could have both women that I loved and all my children under the same roof. I asked Nicoleta if she would give Andreia a chance for us all to be together and after a lot of persuading Nicoleta agreed but stated it would be the last time she would agree.

It was a good feeling as we drove through Europe together knowing that we had the visas that would allow Nicoleta and Bianca to live in England. It was not long before we arrived at our home in Hesketh Bank. We had agreed with Andreia that we would all talk together before we lived as a family again. I knew that Nicoleta was agreeing very reluctantly to share me with Andreia and this time I hoped that things would work out. We agreed to move in with Andreia at her new home in Banks but it was not long before Andreia was up to her old tricks. I was so happy taking all my four children out for the day while Andreia and Nicoleta had the day at Blackpool pleasure beach. I took my children to the beach at Southport and we had a marvelous time paddling in the sea. I then found out that Andreia had been back in touch with Dorin and we ended up having a big argument. It did not take much for Andreia to get angry even when she was in the wrong and she told me to leave with Nicoleta and Bianca. We went back to our home in Hesketh Bank while Andreia stayed in her house in Banks.

I was torn between Andreia and Nicoleta and when I had been apart from anyone of them I missed the one that I was not with. For a while I spent some days with Nicoleta and some days with Andreia but this arrangement did not last for very long. We agreed to get back together and go to Romania for the Christmas to see all our families. I also was going to do some work at Panc and meet with the builders. I thought we were happy again until I was going to work at Panc and Andreia gave me a letter to read. In the letter she told me she loved me but also had feelings for Dorin and asked me to share her with him. Andreia promised me anything I wanted if I agreed but I told her that I would not agree. When we went to Petresti Andreia tried everything she could to get Dorin to go with her but he refused because he did not want to come between us. Andreia then caused an argument with me and told me she was going to stay with her Uncle Lottery and his family for a few days. Andreia told me it was finished between us and I knew she was up to something. When I telephoned Andreia I could tell by her voice that she was lying to me about our children being poorly so I got a taxi to where she was staying. It was dark when I arrived and the front gate was locked. I had to climb over a 3 metre high wall to get into the garden and then I walked to where I knew Andreia would be sleeping. When I walked into the bedroom the first thing I could see was Andreia in bed with a man called Danny from Petresti and my children sleeping on chair beds.

I lost my temper and I went to where Danny was and punched him in the head. He ran out of the house very quickly while Lottery and Miehila came running into the room. All hell broke loose, it was only two days before Christmas and Andreia and her family made statements to the police and tried to get me in trouble for entering their home without permission and assaulting Danny. Nicoleta was at our apartment with Bianca and I telephoned her from the police station to explain what had happened. I told Nicoleta not to answer the door to anyone as I knew that Andreia would try and take control of the apartment. I was right about that as Andreia turned up banging on the door and threatening Nicoleta with all kinds of things if she did not open the door. I was kept at the police station all night and most of the following day before they let me go. It was Christmas Eve and thankfully we had bought everything we needed for Christmas. It was a Christmas I would never forget as all the presents I had bought for Andreia, David, Naomi and Victoria lay unopened under the Christmas tree. My heart was broken into pieces knowing that the woman that I loved and three of my children were with another man who was just a user of women. As Nicoleta, Bianca and I eat our Christmas dinner tears were flowing down my cheeks into my food.

We decided to take the Christmas presents for Andreia, David, Naomi and Victoria by taxi to where they were staying. It turned very nasty when Andreia came towards the taxi making lots of threats to Nicoleta. I told Andreia she was acting badly going from man to man because Dorin would not have her she threw herself at Danny. I hated Andreia as much as I loved her for what she did that Christmas and I made a plan to get her away from Danny. I knew that she did not love Danny and was just using him and that her real feelings were for Dorin. I asked Dorin to phone Andreia to say that he loved her and wanted her to come to him for the New Year at Petresti and be with all the family. When I phoned Andreia to ask her to come back to Deva she was very quick to dump Danny and come back believing that she would be with Dorin at the New Year. I was happy that

Andreia was back with my children but I was also hurting very deep inside my heart.

When it came to New Years Eve I watched Andreia spending hours in front of the mirror doing her makeup and putting on her sexiest clothes for Dorin. When we arrived at Petresti Andreia was all over Dorin but he kept ignoring her as he went from house to house with Danny dressed as a bear trying to get people to give them money. All the family was in on the bad trick being played on Andreia and watched her every move as she expected Dorin to go for her. Andreia had even bought a gold ring for Dorin and it was cutting my heart in two watching her lust after him. I thought of all the promises that Andreia had made on how she was going to treat me but it was just hollow words. I wished that I did not love Andreia so that I did not have the pain in my heart but now it was the turn of Andreia to feel the same way as Dorin told her that he did not love her. I knew that the reason I had done this was because I wanted to get Andreia away from Danny and at the same time to show Andreia that Dorin did not really love her. When I could see Andreia was upset I put my arms around her to offer her some comfort. If I had any sense I would have realised that it was over between Andreia and I but just like Samson I was blinded by love for a women who would keep on hurting me.

When we returned to England in early January it was not a pleasant journey as Andreia was sending lots of text messages to Danny. We lived together for a short period of time while Andreia tried to find another house to rent as the landlord wanted his house back in Banks. I still loved Andreia and from time to time we made love to each other. I still had lots of arguments with Andreia as she went between Dorin and Danny. It was just before Easter in 2007 when I made arrangements for Andreia and myself to go to Ellel Grange at Lancaster for Christian healing ministry. I had spoken with Andreia about us getting back together and having a fresh start then I caught her on the telephone with Danny. We had a massive argument with the police being called yet again to bring peace into the situation and Andreia ended up taking David, Naomi and Victoria to a hostel for the night. The following day I asked Andreia to come home with our children and I would not interfere in her life. I did not want Andreia or my children living in bad conditions and I was happy when they came back home. Andreia went to Ellel Grange for her healing ministry and I gave her a photo of our wedding to take with her with a letter telling her how much I loved her. Nicoleta and I looked after all our children and then it was my turn to go for healing ministry. The day I was leaving I had an argument with Andreia and in the heat of the argument I told her to leave my house. After I had calmed down I told Andreia I was sorry and she did not have to leave but to try and remember that I was badly damaged by all that had taken place between us and that was why I was going for healing ministry. I arrived at Ellel Grange knowing that I was badly damaged and needed a healing touch from God.

Chapter 57

"Come to me, all you who are weary and burdened and I will give you rest. Take my yoke upon you and learn from me, for I am gentle and humble in heart, and you will find rest for your souls. For my yoke is easy and my burden is light"

Matthew 11 : 28 - 30

I felt the presence of God as soon as I arrived at Ellel Grange and I had my own bedroom overlooking the garden at the side of the house. I met the members of my healing team and it was such a relief to be able to share all that had been taking place in my life. I phoned home before I went to bed to speak with Andreia, Nicoleta and my children to tell them how much I loved them. Andreia was very cold to me on the telephone and I could sense that something was not right. The following morning when I telephoned home Nicoleta answered the phone to tell me that Andreia had left with David, Naomi and Victoria at about 5.00am that morning and was on her way to Romania. I telephoned Andreia right away on her mobile phone and she answered it and told me she was on the plane and it was ready for leaving. I begged her not to go and not to take my children away from me and told her that Danny was not worth it. Andreia was cold and hard and told me she was never coming back.

I was in the right place at Ellel Grange where I received a lot of prayer over everything that had taken place and was happening in my life. I still found it hard to believe that Andreia had taken David and Naomi out of school to be with someone who went with any woman who would have him. After being at Ellel for three days I returned home to Nicoleta where the house seemed very empty without Andreia and our children. I was hurting in my heart and it was hard for me to concentrate on my work or anything else. I went with Nicoleta to look at a second hand Ford Galaxy that was for sale and I agreed to buy it for £3250. It was a lovely car and we decided to go on holiday to London for a short break hoping that it would help me get over losing Andreia and our children. I telephoned Andreia to find out she was living at Petresti in a rented apartment with our children and Danny. I told Andreia that I still loved and missed her and she told me the same. I was devastated that my children were living in such bad conditions and Andreia had used up all her money in the four weeks she had been in Romania.

I talked with Nicoleta about going back for Andreia and she told me that if I did I could take her and Bianca back to Romania and leave them there. It was early May 2007 and I drove Nicoleta and Bianca to Romania where I took them back to the parent's home of Nicoleta at Petresti. I had made arrangements to meet Andreia with our children at our apartment in Deva. I felt very bad at leaving Nicoleta and Bianca in Romania because I loved them so much and Nicoleta had not done anything to hurt me. I could not stop myself from what I was doing but I knew in my heart that I was very wrong to leave Nicoleta for Andreia. I was happy to see Andreia and my children and we resumed our relationship again. We left for England within a few days because I had left my work to go to Romania for them. It was a sad time for me as we drove back to England knowing I had left Nicoleta and Bianca behind.

I had only been back home with Andreia for a few days when Andreia found out that she had caught Chlamydia from Danny. I went to the hospital clinic for tests where I was given some medicine to kill the virus before the test results came back. I was very upset that Andreia had let Danny have sex with her without any condoms or without making sure he had no sexual deceases. Andreia told me that she had believed Danny when he told her he had no unprotected sex with anyone but I had warned her the kind of girls he had been going with at Panc. We continued to argue and I knew that I had made a very big mistake leaving Nicoleta to go back with Andreia.

Within two weeks I was flying back to Romania to reconcile with Nicoleta and told her I had found a nice house to rent in Ainsdale. I let Andreia take over the lease for our house in Hesketh Bank as I returned to England with Nicoleta and Bianca. I still found it very hard to get Andreia out of my heart and mind because I was seeing her on a regular basis when I picked my children up to have time with them. Andreia had started a college course to be a beautician and I helped her as much as I could. David and Victoria had behaviour problems that seemed to be getting worse. Andreia and I had tried to get specialist help for both of them and we worked very closely with the social services and education department. I was upset when I found out that Andreia was going out with a man she had met through her next door neighbour in Hesketh Bank as I still loved her even though we were not together. When her relationship with that man had broken down I talked with Andreia about coming to live with us as a family again at our home in Ainsdale.

During September we were all living together again as a family because Andreia could not cope by herself. As usual happy families did not last for long as Andreia went for a night out with friends from her college. Andreia left us looking after the children with a promise she would come home when the presentation night had finished. I was expecting Andreia home when she telephoned to say she was going onto a night club in Preston with some of her friends. This was not what we had agreed and it led to an argument with Andreia who closed her phone. By now I had lost all my trust in Andreia and I just believed she had met up with some men or was going in search of some men. Andreia could have asked for Nicoleta to go with her but it just showed me that Andreia only cared about her own pleasures and did not really care about keeping our family together.

David, Naomi and Victoria were very upset the following day as Andreia packed all their belongings into her car and moved back to Hesketh Bank. By November Andreia asked me to give our relationship another try but Nicoleta was having none of it and told me she would rather return to Romania before she would live with Andreia again. I still blamed myself for committing adultery with Nicoleta and why the things had gone wrong between Andreia and me. I knew that Andreia would not be able to cope with David, Naomi and Victoria by herself and I was hoping that things could get back to how they were before I had committed adultery with Nicoleta. In December I went to court with Nicoleta to allow her to take Bianca to live in Romania with me having regular access to Bianca when I was in Romania. I took Nicoleta and Bianca back to Romania and I returned to England and moved in with Andreia and our children at Hesketh Bank. Within a couple of weeks Andreia told me she thought she might be pregnant and went to the hospital for tests. While at the hospital Andreia started to bleed and the tests showed that Andreia had lost the baby and it might have been a false pregnancy. I felt trapped between the love I had for Andreia, Nicoleta and all my children and as Christmas approached my mind was thinking of Nicoleta and Bianca in Romania. I could not settle with Andreia and I told her that I was going to Romania to be with Nicoleta and Bianca.

I was going back and forth like a yoyo between Andreia and Nicoleta as I arrived in Deva with presents for Nicoleta and Bianca plus turkey and pork for our Christmas dinner. It was the 24th December and I arrived just in time to celebrate Christmas together. I was in a no win situation because as much as I was happy at being with Nicoleta and Bianca a part of me was unhappy at leaving Andreia, David, Naomi and Victoria behind in England. Life with Nicoleta was more peaceful than with Andreia because Nicoleta was more organised than Andreia and did not go chasing after men in the way that Andreia did.

In early January I returned back to England with Nicoleta and Bianca and in March it was the turn of Nicoleta to have a miss-carriage. My life was even more unsettled as I learned that Andreia planned to bring Danny to England. I took Andreia to court for shared residence of our children so that Andreia could not take them to Romania again without my permission. I could not bear the thought of Andreia living with Danny and my children when Andreia telephoned me and asked me to meet her at a pub in Ainsdale. Andreia told me she had broken things off with Danny and she believed that I should leave Nicoleta so we could get back together and give our children both their parents back. I told Andreia I would think about it and let her have an answer when I had decided what to do. I was having counselling because of all that had been taking place in my life but even that did not help me stay with any decision that I made. It was approaching the summer holidays and I talked with Nicoleta about what she would do if we were not together. I was hoping that Nicoleta would agree to share me with Andreia as we all drove to Romania for our summer holidays. I had moved back in with Andreia a few weeks before we left for Romania and Andreia told me she would talk Nicoleta round so that we could be a family again. This time Nicoleta was serious and she made it very clear that she did not want any more sharing.

I was very sad as I dropped Nicoleta and Bianca at Petresti and returned to Deva without them. I had made arrangements with Nicoleta to have Bianca for the month of August as part of my programme with Bianca so I was very happy when it was time to pick her up from Petresti. All my children were happy when they were together and we took them to Balie Felix for a holiday. When we returned from the holiday we spent the summer evenings in the square at Deva where everyone would relax having a drink or eating at one of the local bars. I telephoned Nicoleta to ask her if she would change her mind and share me with Andreia but she was having none of it. Angela told me that I should take Bianca with me back to England where she would have a much better life than in Romania. I watched my children as they played together and the way that they loved each other very much. Andreia told me that she loved Bianca as her own daughter and helped persuade me to take Bianca back to England without Nicoleta knowing. I told Andreia that Nicoleta was a good mother and I could never attempt to take Bianca from her but agreed that Bianca would have a better life in England as Bianca was settled at her pre-school in Ainsdale. I telephoned Nicoleta to ask if she had made a decision on if she was going to make her life in Romania or in England. Nicoleta told me she had not made her mind up and this helped convince me to return with Bianca so I could go back to court over the residence order.

I had the British passport belonging to Bianca and we had no problem getting through the Romanian border as all our family names were Sutton. As soon as we had arrived in Hungary I telephoned Nicoleta to let her know I was on my way back to England with Bianca to get the court order changed. This news made Nicoleta very angry towards me. I understood how she felt but told Nicoleta I was doing what I thought was best for Bianca as life in Romania would be very hard for her. Within two days of arriving back in England I had gone back to court for an emergency residence order that would prevent Nicoleta from taking Bianca back to Romania.

I spoke with Nicoleta on the telephone and arranged to pay for flight tickets so that Nicoleta could attend court and be with Bianca. It was never my intention to separate Bianca from her mother but to enable Bianca to stay in England where I could have regular contact with her. I was staying with Bianca at the home of Andreia in Hesketh Bank and Bianca had grown very close to Andreia during the five weeks we had all been together. I went with Bianca to meet Nicoleta at Manchester Airport when her flight arrived from Romania. As soon as I saw Nicoleta my heart melted as I still loved her and had missed her while we had been apart. I drove Nicoleta back to our home in Ainsdale while she held and kissed Bianca nonstop. I was happy that they were back together in England but I ended up arguing with Nicoleta as soon as we arrived in Ainsdale and I called out the police so that our argument did not get out of hand. The police said that one of us would have to leave so I left Nicoleta and Bianca together as I returned to Andreia at Hesketh Bank. It was about 11.00pm but I could not sleep as I was thinking about Nicoleta and Bianca.

Chapter 58

*"All night long on my bed I looked for the one my heart loves;
I looked for him but did not find him.*

Song Of Songs 3 : 1

I got out of bed very early and I told Andreia that I was going back to Ainsdale to talk with Nicoleta about the court case over Bianca. When I arrived in Ainsdale I asked Nicoleta to open the door and let me in. We talked about everything that had taken place and my reasons for bringing Bianca back to England. I was surprised how calm Nicoleta spoke with me and I was happy to see her after being apart for over 6 weeks. Within an hour of arriving back home I held Nicoleta in my arms and started to kiss her. We ended up making love together and now I had to tell Andreia that I was making my life with Nicoleta and Bianca. Andreia was very angry when I told her and she said that I had only used her to look after Bianca while Nicoleta was in Romania. I had not planned to get back with Nicoleta but my love for her was so strong and I could not resist her any longer. The month of September was a hard time for us all because Andreia was given a notice to quit her home in Hesketh Bank, we also went to court over Bianca where we agreed a shared residence order just in case we separated in the future. In November I moved with Nicoleta to a bungalow just around the corner from where we lived.

I started to settle down with Nicoleta even though I was still missing Andreia. I found it hard to get Andreia out of my heart and it did not help me that she was seeing other men. I continued to argue with Andreia over the telephone and we started to send bad text messages to each other. We were both as bad as each other and I could see our children were suffering to see us both argue. We had only been in our new home for a few weeks when Nicoleta found out she was pregnant. I was happy with the news until Andreia telephoned me and asked me to meet her for lunch. I made an excuse to Nicoleta and had lunch with Andreia. I listened as Andreia told me she had finished with Danny for good after finding out what kind of a person he really was and she wanted us to get back together for the sake of our children. I knew that David, Naomi and Victoria had suffered a great deal because of breaking up with Andreia and me going back and forth. I also knew that Andreia could not cope with our children by herself and that everything was getting on top of her. I was missing Andreia so much and I heard myself saying that I would come back to her and leave Nicoleta.

When I told Nicoleta that I could not leave Andreia to cope by herself and that I had to return to her Nicoleta accepted what I was saying in a calm manner. I told Nicoleta that I would be there for her and our baby but I was going to make my life with Andreia for the sake of David, Naomi and Victoria. I think that I was going out of my mind because I could not stay with either Andreia or Nicoleta for a long enough period without missing and returning to the one I had left. This time I believed it was going to be for good and I had Christmas with Andreia, my mum, David, Naomi and Victoria with Bianca joining us for Boxing Day. We had a lovely Christmas together and I tried everything to get Nicoleta to join us with Andreia saying she missed Nicoleta and Bianca and that it would be good if we could all be together again. Nicoleta would not agree and spent Christmas day alone with Bianca. When it was time for our children to go to bed the sound of Andreia shouting at our children gave me a headache. My telephone rang and it was Nicoleta asking me if I would go with her to the abortion clinic in Liverpool after Christmas. I could not sleep thinking about what I had driven Nicoleta to doing and I did not want a child of mine throwing in a dustbin at the abortion clinic.

I had gone back and forth between Andreia, Nicoleta and all my children for so long that I had lost count. All I knew is that no matter who I was with I had time with all my children and I loved them more than anything in this world. Maybe this would give me a reason to stay with Nicoleta once and for all even if my heart was broken by not being with Andreia anymore. I told Andreia that I could not live with myself if Nicoleta had an abortion and a big part of me believed that the love Andreia said she had for me would not last forever. I wondered how I would feel if Nicoleta had an abortion and then after a couple of years Andreia left me for another man. I had seen how easy it was for Andreia to switch her love from one man to another if that is what it was. When I told Andreia I was going back to Nicoleta to save the life of our unborn baby Andreia told me that Nicoleta was only doing this to get me back. Only Nicoleta knew if that was true but I knew that I loved Nicoleta as much as I loved Andreia and I loved my children the same. The life of my unborn child was precious and I returned to my home in Ainsdale the day after Boxing Day with Bianca. We had all four children with us in Ainsdale for New Years Eve while Andreia went with some friends to her own church. I enjoyed having all my children together and I was very happy that Nicoleta had me back and there was no more talk about abortions. I still had an empty hole in my heart where I was missing Andreia but I tried to put this to the back of my mind. Seeing my children playing and loving each other was a very precious sight.

Chapter 59

"Fix these words of mine in your hearts and minds; tie them as symbols on your hands and bind them on your foreheads. Teach them to your children, talking about them when you sit at home and when you walk along the road, when you lie down and when you get up."

Deuteronomy 11:18-19

We settled into our new home in Ainsdale and I looked forward to the times when I was not working so I had lots of time with Nicoleta and my children. It was always a hectic time when we had all four children together but my children loved each other very much and enjoyed each other's company. It was good the way that Nicoleta was very organised and we worked well together. We took our children on lots of outings so they would not get bored and we bought a yearly pass to the Safari park at Knowsley where we all loved to go. I think that Andreia enjoyed having a break from our children when it was my turn to have them every other weekend and on a Thursday evening. I know I enjoyed the peace when it was just Nicoleta, Bianca and I together even though I missed my children very much. I know that when it was time for our children to go to bed my energy levels would be depleted but I enjoyed reading their favourite story books, stories from the Bible and singing to them. It was so funny how they would always ask me to sing them one more song or one more story and sometimes they would argue about who's turn it was to choose the story. These were very precious times to me and I always finished bed time praying with my children. I loved them so very much but I also missed not having Andreia around who I also loved very deeply. When I left my children's room I would go and lie down next to Nicoleta and talk to our baby inside of her tummy and kiss her baby bump that was getting bigger by the day. I kept reminding myself of how much I loved my children and was silently praying for God to take the pain away I was feeling at not being with Andreia.

We made plans to travel to Romania for April so that Nicoleta could see her family for Easter knowing that we would not be able to travel to Romania during the summer due to our baby being due to be born in July. I was upset when Andreia told me she had met a man on the internet called Chipri who lived in Alba and would also travel to Romania at the same time as us to see her family and her new boyfriend. It hurt me knowing that Andreia had found a new man so quickly and it did not hurt her like it hurt me that we were no longer together. Andreia knew how to get to me and that is why she always made sure I knew she was with someone else. I made plans to travel in my mini bus with Nicoleta and Bianca while Andreia made plans to fly out with all her children to Bucharest where her mother was going to meet her and help her with our children.

I made plans to stay in our apartment at Deva so that I could do some work at Panc but Andreia was very angry at this saying that she wanted to stay in our apartment as it was half hers. I told Andreia that she knew we had booked our date for Romania before she had booked her date and that if she had wanted to stay in our apartment she should have booked different dates. Andreia knew that I needed to be near to Panc as I was still trying to finish the work. I was still spending all the money I worked for on Panc and it was nice to see the house taking shape after years of hard work. I made it clear that Nicoleta needed to stay where we had good conditions with being six months pregnant and she could stay with her family. I was upset when I found out that Andreia had left Naomi and Victoria with her family who lived in the mountains while she went off with David to stay with her new boyfriend in Alba. I ended up having a big argument with Andreia when I found out that Naomi had come out in spots all over her body and how quickly she had left Naomi and Victoria so she could go and have fun with her new boyfriend. I was not happy that she had David with her as he would see her sleeping with another man. I knew that Andreia was happy that I was upset because of the way she spoke to me on the telephone. I told Andreia that she was turning out like her own mother who had so many men in her life that she could not count them all or remember all their names. The fact that I still loved Andreia made it harder to accept that she would be in the arms of someone else when I loved her so very much. I could feel the pain deep inside of my heart welling up as I pictured her making love with someone else when I wanted it to be me.

I worked very hard at Panc putting in the central heating system and kitchen that I had brought from England trying to take my mind from what Andreia was doing. I missed my children but I had made it clear to Andreia before leaving England that I had come to Romania to work and while in Romania I would not be able to have my programme with my children. I did have David for one full day and I had a very special time with him at Panc where we went out shooting with an air rifle and pistol I had brought from England years earlier. My children all loved it at Panc and I was so sorry that we were split up as a family and I would have given anything for us all to be back together. Nicoleta worked with me at Panc during the day to clean the house after other workmen had put down the laminate on the floors. We then went out and bought some nice furniture and the house now started to look like a home. When I put the curtain rails up and curtains I could not wait to see my children's faces when they eventually got to stay in it. I had brought new beds and wardrobes from England with special bed covers for each of my children who would have their own special bedrooms. It was only going to cost about £5000 to install liquid gas tanks for the central heating system and a few minor jobs and Panc would be finished. I hoped that by the next time I went to Romania I would have the money to finish Panc so that it could be lived in. I knew that Andreia had wanted to put the apartment in her name and for me to have Panc so that we were no longer tied to each other. I also wanted the same but I was concerned that the land at Panc could not be put in my name because I was not a Romanian Citizen. With all the upset that was going on between Andreia and I we had given up on our plans for helping homeless children in Romania as we concentrated on our own problems.

We made plans to return to England and Andreia asked me if I would take David in the mini bus because the journey was so hard with all three of her children. I agreed to this request because I loved my children and I knew that it would be hard for Andreia. Before we left for England Andreia told me that she might be pregnant from her latest boy friend and the thought of it hurt me very much. I told her that this man would not want to take her on with three children who were not his and she had found another user. It did not take Andreia long to find out that all the promises he made of loving her were false as he rejected coming to England to be with her but went with his family to work in Spain. I don't know what it was but a big part of me still loved Andreia and wanted to be with her and she knew how to look at me with her eyes and get me interested in her. We talked about being back together and the thought of being with Andreia again was a very strong desire inside of me.

On the drive back to England I kept thinking about what to do as I was missing Andreia very much but I also loved Nicoleta and did not want to hurt her anymore. I had made plans to go away with my brother and sister to Budapest soon after arriving back in England and I hoped that during my time away I would be able to think more clearly on what I was going to do. While I was on holiday in Budapest I went into a church to pray to God over everything. I prayed that God would show me what to do as I was fed up of going back and forth between Andreia and Nicoleta especially for all the hurt and pain being caused to us all. I thought about everything that had taken place between us and I believed that David, Naomi and Victoria needed me the most. While I had been praying about everything I was in touch with Nicoleta and Andreia by telephone. Andreia also sent me picture messages of herself and children as they were getting ready to go out. When I looked at the photo my heart melted knowing how much I loved and missed them. I also looked at the photo I had of Nicoleta and Bianca knowing that I loved and missed them the same. I was praying that God would speak to me in a clear voice as I promised God I would be where he wanted me to be.

I knew that since committing adultery with Nicoleta my life had been a constant going back and forth between them both and no matter where I was I was unhappy at leaving the one that I also loved very deeply. My counsellor had helped me to understand that I had suffered great losses in my life and had suffered great emotional pain and that when the pain was great I dealt with it by running away and that was why I kept on returning to the one that I had left. I wish I could say that I heard God speak to me but I did not. I knew I could forgive Andreia for everything she had done to hurt me and that my love for everyone was equal. In my thinking I just believed that Andreia, David, Naomi and Victoria needed me the most so if I could get through the pain barrier and start all over again I believed that I should be where I was needed the most. When I spoke with

Andreia I told her that I would come back to her if she wanted me and we could court each other and see how we got on. As soon as the words left my lips I felt guilt and sadness knowing that when I returned to England I would have to tell Nicoleta and Bianca that I was leaving yet again.

My brother and sister could see how unhappy I was and both told me that I should make a decision and stick with it if I ever wanted to find my happiness again. It was very hard to tell Nicoleta and I told her I was going to sleep in a separate room during the week and go to Sunny Road at the weekends to be with Andreia and my children. When it was time to have my programme with Bianca she was happy to see David, Naomi and Victoria at the home of Andreia who by now had moved to Churchtown in Southport. I noticed that Andreia started to show me a lot of love and I thought that this was because I was only spending short periods of time with her and she was not taking me for granted anymore. I still helped Nicoleta with her shopping and going to hospital and doctors appointments and when I was not working I would take and collect Bianca from school.

Chapter 60

"Evil men do not understand justice, but those who seek the Lord understand it fully."

Proverbs 28: 5

When Andreia had moved to Churchtown in Sefton all the papers that were still relevant to our children in Lancashire were also transferred. Andreia and I were still working with the authorities concerning the behaviour of David and Victoria where we were trying to get them all the specialist help that they needed. Andreia, Nicoleta and myself had also attended a course to help us be better parents and to help us manage the difficult behaviour of David and Victoria that had been recommended by a social worker from Lancashire. It was during the month of June when Sefton social services got involved with Andreia when she had left her children playing in the garden of her home while she was doing some housework upstairs. The next door neighbour called them in when she saw David and Victoria playing with a knife or meat clever from the knife set from the kitchen. Andreia dealt with the situation right away but the neighbour still complained to the social services. When Kathrine Heath from the social services called she gave Andreia some advice including locking the knives away so the children had no access to them. When I called to her house Andreia told me what had happened and I bought a lock and chain and put the knives in a cupboard for the safety of our children. I thought that this was the end of the matter until a few weeks later when a bombshell hit me. Kathrine Heath wrote me a letter stating that she was re-opening the case from Lancashire concerning the allegation that had been made by Donna and Amanda in 2004 because she was not happy that Lancashire social services had done their job properly. The letter went on to say that they wanted me to leave the homes where I had been staying where all my children lived. I could not believe what I was reading and neither could Andreia or Nicoleta who had never been involved with the social services in Lancashire or Sefton. I wrote a letter to Kathrine Heath making it very clear I was not going to leave my homes as I had done this once before and had worked with Lancashire social services over these allegations in the past. Within a few weeks of that letter we all received a court order stating that Sefton were applying for care orders on all my children. We could not believe what was taking place and we had to instruct solicitors to work on our behalf.

I continued to stay with Nicoleta during the week while at weekends I stayed with Andreia. It was Andreia who asked if we should all stay at my home with Nicoleta due to give birth but Nicoleta did not agree. I could understand how Nicoleta was feeling because when all the children were together it was very noisy especially if the children were falling out with each other. We had our first court hearing over the care orders and we were very happy when the Recorder hearing the application did not order me to leave my home but asked Andreia and Nicoleta to make sure I was never alone with any of my children. I did not believe that what Sefton was doing was correct after Andreia and I had worked with social services in Lancashire for over five years and I believed that some kind of "witch hunt" was taking place. I found out that Sefton social services had a secret meeting behind our backs involving some of the staff from Victoria's pre-school. When we read the minutes from the meeting some of the staff made comments that we knew were a pack of lies.

On the 24th July 2009 Nicoleta was rushed into hospital with labour pains and I took Bianca to stay with Andreia so I could stay with Nicoleta at the hospital. After Nicoleta was settled in the labour ward I went out for a snack leaving my telephone number with the nurses. Nicoleta was hoping to have a normal delivery but I had only been out for a few minutes when my phone rang saying I should return to the hospital. The doctor was concerned because the heartbeat of our baby had slowed down and they wanted to do an emergency caesarean operation to bring our baby out. I prayed with Nicoleta that everything was going to be all right for both of them and put on the green gown looking like one of the doctors. This time we had been informed correctly concerning the sex of our baby as the doctors placed James in my arms who had lovely red hair, the lips of his mother but very much like me. I cut the cord from James and gave him lots of kisses and cuddles. I placed James next to Nicoleta so she could love and cuddle him to. I loved them so very much and my heart was still torn between Andreia and Nicoleta.

While Nicoleta was in hospital Andreia, David, Naomi, Victoria and Bianca came to see her. David had wanted a brother so very much and he could not stop kissing James. I spoke with Nicoleta about us all staying together while the matters with Sefton social services were still going on and to help Nicoleta until she was strong enough to look after herself. I was happy when she agreed because it meant that once again I would have all the ones I loved together under one roof. Sadly this situation did not last for long as when we appeared in front of Judge Dodds he made an order forcing me to move out of the home where my children lived. Nicoleta and I had been in front of this Judge once before when we had agreed to share residence of Bianca and he had a reputation of being a very strict Judge. We agreed that I would stay in the house in Ainsdale and both mothers and children would stay at the home in Churchtown. After a couple of weeks Nicoleta asked that we should change houses because she was finding it hard to use the buses for taking Bianca to school in Ainsdale.

Sefton legal team had asked the Court to have a "finding of facts hearing" concerning the allegation made by Donna and Amanda. Judge Dodds stated he was going to hear the case and also other allegations that had been made by staff at the preschool where Victoria had attended. The trial was set for the 11th November 2009 with a hearing listed for the 4th November 2009 to make sure everyone was ready for the main hearing. The Judge had set ten days for the hearing so we knew it was going to be a very long trial. After Andreia and Nicoleta being together with all the children for about four weeks they had a major fall out with Nicoleta phoning the police over the way that Andreia was behaving. I had to move out from the house at Churchtown so that Andreia could move back into her own house with her children. I had to go and buy a caravan like I had been forced to do in 2004 and live in it away from all the ones I loved.

Matters took a turn for the worse when we appeared at court on the 4th November 2004 and the Guardian acting for all the children stated she wanted David, Naomi and Victoria removed from Andreia and placed into care immediately. We could not believe what we were witnessing because Sefton had not made any such application and the Guardian had spent no time with Andreia or our children to witness why they had fallen out. We all opposed the application made by the Guardian who after a few hours had got Sefton to agree with her plan. I knew that I would have no chance before this Judge when he approved of the application and ordered David, Naomi and Victoria to be placed into the care of Sefton. My heart went out to my children and Andreia who then started to swallow lots of tablets in front of the Judge while he looked on. I could not believe what had taken place and I knew that we were all caught up in a system that was so cruel and unjust especially for the children they were supposed to protect and care for.

Things did not get any better as any contact I now had with my children had to be supervised at the family centre and on my first contact all my children grabbed hold of my arms and legs to try to stop me from leaving when it was time for me to go. My heart was breaking into pieces seeing how upset my children were and crying for me not to go. I hated all the people who had brought this situation about especially the people who were paid to care but were so hard and uncaring. I left the family centre with tears streaming down my face and praying to God about what was taking place.

When the finding of facts case started it was sad for me to hear Jan, Donna, Robert and Michelle say so many bad things about me that were not true. It was clear to everyone the hate that Donna had and none of them wanted to say anything good about me. I knew that God knew the truth about everything and how my life had changed since becoming a Christian in 1987. God knew how I had tried to help all my family in so many different ways when their lives were in a mess and all the other people I had reached out to in the name of Jesus. I knew the Judge was against me from the start by the amount of times he referred to the age of Andreia when we met and made love together in Romania. It was clear to everyone in court that the staff from the preschool was lying and even a witness confirmed this to be true but this Judge was not going to believe anything that was in our favour. It was no surprise to me on the 27th November 2009 when the Judge made findings against me believing Donna, Amanda and the preschool staff. It was a very bad Judgment and I knew he was so wrong in what he was reading out. When he finished reading his Judgment he made orders that I could not see my children and that I could not contact Nicoleta or Andreia. I was also ordered not to come within 100 metres of my home in Ainsdale.

I told my barrister that I wanted to appeal but he told me I would have to do the appeal myself as he did not believe I had any grounds for appeal. I could not believe that this Judge had so much power to force me apart from my wife and children when I had never been charged with anything by the police. I left court so sad with what had taken place and wondered why God had allowed all this to happen. Before I left the building I went into the court offices to ask for the appeal forms to lodge my own appeal.

I had no contact with Nicoleta and all I knew was that the social services had moved her, Bianca and James out of our home in Ainsdale. I had left a note for Nicoleta before the Judgment was made saying that I believed Dodds would make findings against me and not to give up on me. When we next appeared at court on the 4th December 2009 I read a statement from Nicoleta where she stated she accepted the findings of the Judge but Andreia was stating she did not accept them. I asked the Judge to relax the injunctions preventing me from having contact with Andreia and Nicoleta so we could talk over the telephone but he refused to do so. Sefton social services stated I had broken the injunction by putting a note in the home for Nicoleta so Dodds told them to make a formal application and he would deal with it. I told my barrister that I would not agree for this Judge to hear any application as he was biased against me and I would never get a fair hearing.

On the 23rd December we went back to court and I made the same application to have the injunction relaxed so I could talk on the telephone with Andreia and Nicoleta to sort out what we was going to do over everything in light of the findings of the Judge. I could not believe it when Dodds told Sefton and the Guardian to take careful note of what Andreia and Nicoleta were agreeing to. It soon became very clear that this Judge wanted to take Bianca and James from Nicoleta when Sefton and the Guardian then told the Judge they wanted to take Bianca and James into care. The Judge had told Nicoleta to think carefully about agreeing to have contact with me so Nicoleta and I told the Judge we would not ask him to relax the injunction if it put Bianca and James at risk of being taken away from their mother. It made no difference to this hard hearted Judge who removed Bianca and James from Nicoleta two days before

Christmas. After this cruel Judge made that order he removed the injunction that he had placed on me seeing Nicoleta but Andreia asked for the injunction on her to remain. I could not believe that any person could be so heartless as this Judge and the people who were involved in this case. My own barrister had never made any comments about this Judge but before leaving court he stated he was a "hard man" and to put in an appeal. I did not need him to give me that advice as I left court with my mum and Nicoleta who was completely heartbroken at having her children taken away.

Chapter 61

"Have mercy on me, O God, have mercy on me, for in you my soul takes refuge. I will take refuge in the shadow of your wings until the disaster has passed".

Psalm 57: 1

My heart and soul cried out to God about what was taking place as our nightmare continued. We were caught up in a system that had no heart for the children and people involved and it was only my faith in God that kept me from giving in. The following day on the 24th December Nicoleta and I took the Christmas presents for all our children to the family centre. We both had heavy hearts about what had taken place but at least we had each other for company when I had expected to spend my Christmas alone. I asked Nicoleta if she fancied going to London for a few days knowing that it would not be the same at home knowing all our children were with strangers. We knew that our children would be heartbroken as well especially James who had never left his mothers sight since he was born. I wondered how a Judge could be so hard hearted to take a five month old baby from his mother's arms two days before Christmas when everybody had accepted that Nicoleta was as near perfect a mother as any child could wish to have.

In the afternoon we got on the train leaving Preston for London to stay at the hotel we had booked for four days. I tried to occupy our time by booking to see a few shows and taking Nicoleta shopping to Oxford Street. On Christmas day as we sat in our hotel room missing our children so very much I worked on the appeal for Nicoleta. It was a very sad time for us both and the family centre made no contact with Nicoleta to let her know how our children were or when she could see them. When Nicoleta tried to contact the social worker she only got the answering machine. After four days in London we returned home to Ainsdale and I went direct to the Courts in Liverpool to hand in the appeal to the Royal Courts of Justice in London. I had spoken with Andreia and Nicoleta about the properties we owned in Romania and it was agreed we needed to sort things out once and for all. I was still concerned about Andreia because she was going on the internet sites meeting lots of men. We made plans to travel to Romania in February so that Nicoleta could purchase an apartment that was for sale at Petresti and Andreia to have the apartment in her name where I was going to have Panc in my name. Before we went to Romania we went back to court at Liverpool where Andreia asked for the injunction to be lifted on me so we could sort out our affairs in Romania. While we was at court I was very angry and upset when her legal team advised Nicoleta to withdraw her appeal to London as Judge Dodds would not like it and it would go against her. I shouted at Nicoleta in front of all the people in the courtroom not to listen to them as it was her right to appeal to London. I told Judge Dodds that what he was doing was wrong as it was he would had put the injunction in place when he got the barrister of Nicoleta to agree it was Nicoleta who had asked for it. Her barrister stated I had put in a homemade appeal against what he had done on the 23rd December 2009 that he did not believe had any chance of success. I left court very sad that Nicoleta was listening to bad advice and had given up a chance of getting her children back. It was about a week later when Nicoleta fell out with her solicitor and tried to get another solicitor to take her place. I told Nicoleta that she should never have agreed to withdraw her appeal to London as she had a chance of overturning what Dodds had done. I was very happy when I contacted the appeal court in London and they informed me that the appeal of Nicoleta had not been withdrawn and it would be heard at the same time as my appeal on the 11th March 2010.

 I contacted the Stockport Express and placed an advert to try and trace Lynn Swift who Donna had stated she stayed with when her mother Jan had given birth to Michelle. I knew that what Donna had told the court was a lie but the police had blanked out the name of Lynn Swift that prevented me from understanding who Donna was taking about in her statement until she gave evidence at court. I had forgotten about the advert until I received a telephone call from Simon Swift who was the youngest son of Lynn. I explained to him why I needed to trace his mother and if she could confirm that Donna did not stay with her when Michelle was born. I spoke with Simon a week later who told me that his mother was 100% certain that Donna had not stayed with her when Michelle was born but she did not want to get involved. I told Andreia and Nicoleta of the outcome who both told me not to give up.

We travelled to Romania to sort out our properties and cut our ties with each other so that the authorities could see that I was no longer connected to Andreia or Nicoleta. I was doing this for the benefit of my children in the hope that it would help Andreia and Nicoleta get their children back. I gave Nicoleta all the money that I had of £10,000 to purchase the apartment at Petresti where her family lived. I met up with Andreia and we went to see a Notary together. We found out that the land at Panc had not yet been registered in the name of Andreia and it was going to take months and cost over £500 to register the land in her name. We both agreed that it would be better if I had the apartment in my name and Panc was signed over to Andreia. I knew that Panc was worth over £100,000 and I thought about all the work I had done there but I knew I had done the work for my children's future. I told Andreia that I relied upon her to make sure my children benefited from Panc and not to let any of the men she went with take Panc from her and our children. We agreed that I could take all the furniture from Panc that Nicoleta had helped to buy and choose for her apartment at Petresti, while most of the furniture from the apartment in Deva could go to Panc. We wrote this agreement on a piece of paper that we both signed and then we completed all the legal formalities where Panc belonged to Andreia and the apartment belonged to me.

We were all happy as we knew that at last we were no longer tied to each other and we all had a property in our own names. It did not take Andreia very long to meet up with her latest find that she had met on the internet who lived at Criova in Romania. Andreia met up with me after she had returned from seeing him and bragged about how good he was in bed. I wondered what the Judge and social services would make of Andreia if they knew what I knew.

We returned from Romania and waited for our appeal to be heard in London at the Royal Courts of Justice. We were both very excited about this knowing we had a chance of turning around all the injustices that had taken place in Liverpool by Judge Dodds. We booked our hotel and travelled to London together but agreed from that moment that we would not let any of the authorities know we were together. It was very clear that they wanted to force a big wedge between myself, Andreia, Nicoleta and all my children so we learned from Judge Dodds that honesty did not pay. It was very overpowering at the appeal court as we waited to go before Lord Justice Wilson. We had been informed that we were only allowed twenty minutes each to put our case as we entered his court room. I gave all the reasons why the finding should be overturned and explained what Judge Dodds did when he took Bianca and James into care. After listening to my arguments the Judge refused my appeal but stated he would hear the appeal of Nicoleta in more detail and recommended she be granted legal aid to be represented at a new date set for the 29th March 2010 before himself and another Judge. I was very sad at losing my appeal but happy that he was going to look very closely at what had happened to Nicoleta. I also felt justified in arguing at court with the legal team of Nicoleta who tried to get her to withdraw her appeal and described what I had done as a "homemade appeal". Lord Justice Wilson asked for transcripts from the 23rd December to be supplied that I knew would show the injustices that had taken place. I was happy that Sefton and the guardian would now have to appear in London and for once were not getting everything their own way.

On the 29th March 2010 at the appeal court in London I thought things had changed for the better when Nicoleta won her appeal. Lord Justice Wilson and Judge Baron both agreed that Dodds had got many things wrong and set the 22nd April 2010 for rehearing what had taken place on the 23rd December 2009. Both appeal Judges gave examples to Sefton and the Guardian how they could have done things differently and given more help to Nicoleta. They highlighted the lack of contact they had given Nicoleta with her children especially James who was only five months old. I thought that at last we had found two Judges who were going to put things right. While we waited for the 22nd April to arrive the landlord of our home who was the Vicar from our local church gave Nicoleta a notice to quit because she could not afford to pay the full rent of £675 per month as Nicoleta was only receiving £550 per month in housing benefits. I had explained everything to him and how I had been forced to move out and rent my own flat. The social services had given Nicoleta no help what so ever and now the church who was supposed to represent God added to our problems. I wrote a letter to the Vicar telling him that his actions and those of his church were not Godly and I knew that one day they would have to give an account of their actions before God.

When we turned up at the appeal court in London on the 22nd April both appeal Judges gave a Judgment that slammed Judge Dodds and the actions of Sefton and the Guardian. They agreed that the hearing should be heard by Judge Baron on the 6th May 2010. When we turned up at London on the 6th May Judge Baron made it clear before the case started that she was not going to give Nicoleta her children back with an eviction notice hanging of her head. Sefton made lots of promises to the Judge of how they was going to help Nicoleta and give her more contact with her children and her legal team advised her to accept the amended care orders put by Sefton. I was so upset when Nicoleta agreed because what was taking place was so very wrong. Nicoleta had won her appeal against what Dodds had done but sadly was no better off. This was not justice and Judge Baron had changed her attitude from the 29th March. The Judge also put back in place the injunctions that prevented me from having any form of contact with Andreia and Nicoleta. I left court knowing that it was going to take a miracle to change our situation around.

I went back home to my flat and I turned on my computer and downloaded a copy of the Convention of Human Rights from the Court of Human Rights in Strasbourg, France. When I read it I knew that many of our human rights had been breached and I contacted my solicitor to ask for an expert opinion as I had been saying all along that what the courts had been approving and sanctioning was inhuman. I decided that I would put in 2 new appeals to London appealing against the injunctions that prevented me from having any kind of contact either direct or indirect with any of my children including Andreia and Nicoleta. By now I had become an expert at filling in the forms and I put together what I considered to be a very good appeal on human rights issues. While I waited to hear from the appeal court my solicitor was applying to the court in Liverpool so that I could have supervised contact with my children.

I decided to go back to Romania to do some work on my apartment and take a lot of things for the apartment Nicoleta had bought. We had court orders hanging over our heads that if broken and we were caught we could be sent to prison. I hated the unjust and cruel system we were caught up in and I saw no signs of it getting any better. When Judge Baron had rubber stamped what Sefton and the legal teams had agreed our case was sent back to be heard by Judge de Haas who was the senior family Judge at Liverpool. At least everyone had agreed that Judge Dodds should no longer deal with our case but I soon found out that this Judge was no different than Dodds. I spoke with Andreia and Nicoleta on the telephone secretly and when I met up with any of them I made sure that we were not seen by anyone. We all knew the risks involved but we had been forced into this situation by cruel and unjust people in authority. I had been saying all along that Dodds was not a fair or just Judge. The appeal court Judges who heard the appeal of Nicoleta both agreed that Dodds had got so many things wrong and yet they dismissed my appeal in less than twenty minutes. They also had not given Nicoleta her children back that showed me that the laws were barbaric and not civilised that had allowed this situation to take place.

    I only stayed a short time in Romania and returned back in time for our first appearance in front of Judge de Haas on the 15th July 2010. This Judge added another injunction that prevented Andreia or Nicoleta from having any form of contact with each other. Fifteen minutes before we went into court my legal team advised me they could no longer act for me because they were "embarrassed". This was because I had put in my appeal forms to London that I had never been advised of my human rights by any of my legal team. I told my legal team that I had wrote the truth as it was only when I downloaded a copy of the human rights convention that I understood what my human rights were. I had to represent myself and again the Judge got Nicoleta and Andreia to agree not to proceed with their application to have their children returned until all the "experts" had filed their reports. One of the experts had given Nicoleta a good report because she was telling them all the bad things they wanted to hear Nicoleta say about me but because Andreia did not do this the expert recommended that Andreia did not get her children back stating she would not be able to protect them and that Andreia might reconcile with me. These so called experts had got everything wrong because I was still in a relationship with Nicoleta that they thought was over and Andreia was in a relationship with at least two other men that I knew about. At least this Judge gave Andreia a chance by getting Sefton to agree to pay for Andreia to have specialist counselling over twelve sessions and for Helen Roberts to give another report to the court. I advised Andreia to say everything bad about me that she could think of and to do what Nicoleta had done to get them on her side. I told Andreia and Nicoleta that I would fight for justice at the Courts of Human Rights without involving them and for them to say what the experts wanted to hear and play them at their own game.

I was seeing Andreia on the odd occasion but realised that the only time that she wanted me was when she had problems to deal with or her latest boy friend had moved on. Andreia went back on her promise to let Nicoleta take her furniture from Panc when her family had turned up with a large van to collect it. Andreia had told her mother to change the locks. I was forced to take the car from Andreia that was registered in my name, refusing to give it back until Andreia had replaced the money that had been lost on the removal van and had handed over furniture that did not belong to her. It took about two weeks to resolve this conflict but eventually Andreia realised she had been wrong and everything was exchanged as we had agreed. I was sad that Andreia lost £300 but she had brought it on herself by listening to her mother.

When Nicoleta brought her brother Dorin to stay with her for about six weeks Andreia was lusting after him all the time. Nicoleta brought her brother to give Sefton the idea that she was alone and needed help and support. Andreia promised me everything if I would bring Dorin to her house so she could make love with him but I asked her why she would want someone who did not love her and just used her. I thought she had learned her lesson just after Christmas when she told everyone that Dorin was coming to England to make his life with her. Andreia had spent over £300 booking his flight tickets from Italy where he was working but when his family told him to dump Andreia he did what they had asked and did not come. It was only when Andreia was down that she would call me and ask me to meet up with her. I knew I was being used but sadly for me I still loved Andreia and I would be there for her. There were times when I got very angry and upset with Andreia when she threw me on one side to go with her latest lust. There were times when Andreia got worried she might have caught HIV from one of her men by having unprotected sex. I could not believe the risks that she was still taking knowing that the men she went with were going from woman to woman.

Chapter 62

"Bear with each other and forgive whatever grievances you may have against one another. Forgive as the Lord forgave you".

Colossians 3: 13

I wanted to get Andreia out of my heart and mind and I booked to go to Ellel Grange where Andreia had also booked for a healing retreat. I was going for healing because of all that had taken place in my life since the last time I had been there. I still loved Andreia and a big part of me still wanted her back even though she had been with other men. I knew that I was in a mess and was praying God would heal me and show me the way forward. I had lent Andreia over £400 to pay for leaflets to be printed and distributed for a cleaning business she had formed. I was happy to help her knowing that if she worked hard it would be a success and provide a good future for her and our children. I was going to let Andreia pay me back by giving me sex but at Ellel I told Andreia that she could keep the money as I wanted to do things the way of our Lord. I knew that she was giving sex free to men that were just using her but when I had ever made love to Andreia it was because that I loved her. I felt that God was doing a real work in my life as I dealt with many issues that I had never dealt with before. I knew that a lot of my anger and resentment of those in authority was being dealt with as I started to forgive all the people who had hurt me including family and friends. I knew how Jesus had felt when everyone betrayed him and falsely accused him before he gave his life on that cruel cross for the sins of the world. I knew that Jesus had died for all of my sins and I owed it to Jesus to forgive everyone who had hurt me.

After we returned from Ellel I started to attend church in Southport with Nicoleta but someone who worked for the social services attended the same church and made a report stating she had seen us on at least six occasions. We agreed from that moment that we could not be seen anywhere together because they would use it to stop her getting her children back. It was hard for me to come to terms with the way that even Christians had behaved towards us. I was hurting so much inside of my heart especially not being able to see my children or give them a kiss and a cuddle. I had a big argument with Andreia that resulted in her bedroom door being broken by me when she had formed a relationship with some Romanian men who were going shop lifting. I tried to warn Andreia about the people she was having a relationship with and she went from one bad relationship to another. I thought that after Ellel Andreia would change her ways but it did not last for long as she met another Romanian who was in London. I tried to help and advice Andreia but she now repeated what the authorities were getting her to accept and accused me of trying to control her life. I told Andreia that wild horses could not force her to do anything that she did not want to do and that she needed to take a long hard look at her own behaviour.

On the 22nd July 2010 I represented myself at Liverpool Court because I could not find another solicitor who was willing to take on my case due to all the work that had been done by my former solicitor. I was applying for supervised contact with my children but all the experts and those in authority were against me. I knew I was fighting a losing battle with people who were so set in their ways and who knew nothing about Gods justice but I was determined to go down fighting. I had prayed to God for wisdom and that I would not lose my temper as I put my case before the court. I was not surprised when the Judge refused to allow me contact with my children and stated that I could put questions to the so called "expert witness" in writing concerning indirect contact. I knew that the only chance I had of changing our situation around would be at the European Court of Human Rights. At least Judge de Haas stated that I had conducted my case with dignity and I was happy that she had noticed I was trying to deal with things in a proper manner.

I had received a letter from the Royal Court of Justice where I was given the date of the 2nd September 2010 for hearing my appeal against the injunctions I was appealing against. Lord Justice Wilson had insisted on taking the case. I prayed to God for wisdom in preparing my appeal for London and completing my appeal for the

ECHR in France. I went to London on the 2nd September knowing that I was fighting a losing battle because Lord Wilson had refused my previous appeal and stated that the findings of Judge Dodds could never be changed. I did not believe that Lord Wilson knew my Lord and savior who could change anything that he wanted to change. I already had my application prepared for the ECHR as I entered the court room of Lord Justice Wilson. I knew that God was with me as I spoke with wisdom and clarity explaining to the Judge the main points of my appeal. It was clear that the Judge was treating me with dignity and respect as he listened to everything that I had to say including reading the eleven pages of arguments that I had prepared. It came as no surprise to me when the Judge refused my appeals stating that the Judges were acting within the law. I knew that the laws they were working to were so unjust and the only chance of changing them would be in Europe. I returned back to Southport on the evening train knowing that Nicoleta was still behind me and waiting for me to return.

 The following day I completed the final parts of my application to the ECHR in France and photocopied all the documents I was going to rely on. I was very happy when I sent it off by International Signed for delivery and prayed it would reach its destination. I only needed to send the Judgment from Lord Wilson when it was completed and I had done everything that was in my power to do. I met up with my former solicitor who I was threatening to take to court for damages for no longer representing me and we reached an agreement where they agreed to take me back as a client. I was happy about this because I knew that they had been doing a good job on my behalf and I had no complaints with them. My mum had shown me a newspaper report of a barrister from Manchester who was an expert on human rights. I knew that if my application was successful in Europe I would need a good solicitor and barrister to represent me. My mum had never stopped believing in me and gave me lots of moral support. My mum was as upset as I was at having no contact with my children but she was very ill herself and rushed into Wythenshawe hospital. I witnessed another miracle as my mother was brought back to life when very near to death.

 My relationship with Andreia was getting worse as she treated me very badly when I tried to advise her about the men she was in relationships with. It seemed that Andreia only wanted to have contact with me when it suited her or when she had problems that she could not handle herself. Andreia had to sell her car because she was not handling her money properly and still wasted lots of money on her men and on things that she could have done without. It hurt me when I found out she was going to a lap dancing club to dance naked in front of men in the hope of earning lots of money. Andreia showed me all the sexy underwear she had bought in her hi5 photo album and I told her that what she was doing was not of God. I went to speak with the Pastor from her church asking him to talk some sense into Andreia and to try and help her with her financial problems. Andreia was telling me she was living her life as a Christian but I could not see it by her actions or the way she treated me. Andreia treated me nice for about a week when Alex had not contacted her from London. When he did contact her it was by letter from the prison where he was serving a prison sentence. It was clear that Alex was even lying about why he got sent to prison but Andreia believed what she wanted to believe. I told Andreia that she needed deliverance ministry at Ellel Grange for a spirit of lust was controlling her life as she went from man to man. It was during this conversation that Andreia told me that she had never really loved me and had gone with me for a better life. Andreia told me that the counsellor she was seeing had helped her to understand this. I now realised why I had felt the way I did years before when Andreia pushed me away a lot and I fell for Nicoleta.

    I told Andreia that I was not going to help her anymore and she would have to live with her own mistakes. When Andreia told me to go on her hi5 to look at photo's of my children I was angry and upset to see the men she had now met up with who had promised her earning of between £300 and £1000 per week selling sky packages. The photo's showed Andreia kissing her latest lust and where she had gone in the pubs or clubs with those she had now met up with. I tried to warn Andreia of the tricks that con artists use but she would not listen. Andreia also called my solicitor and left messages on her voice mail that I warned Andreia could backfire on her as she broke the injunction as well. It hurt me that Andreia told me to go on her hi5 to see my children only to see her with her latest lust. I wrote Andreia a number of letters informing her that what she was doing could affect her chances of getting her children back. I knew that if the social services knew everything that Andreia had been doing they would consider her an unfit mother.

The actions of Andreia helped to convince me that it was now time to let her out of my heart forever and to put the past behind me. I thanked God that I still had the love of Nicoleta and a hope for my future. I realised that the time I now had would be a time of getting close to God and dealing with all the issues that had caused me problems in the past. I knew that I had to give up gambling and any thoughts I had of being with Andreia again. I knew that I had to switch off from anything that Andreia did no matter how many men she went with. I knew that in Nicoleta I had everything a man could want if God made it possible for us to be together. This was going to be a time of healing for me and a time to write this book that I had first started over twelve years ago. I missed my children so very much and I was not happy at living my life where I was looking over my shoulder making sure that no-one was watching me if I saw Nicoleta. I bought all my children Christmas presents not knowing if they would know they were from me as I waited to go back to court over the indirect contact I had applied for. Even if I could not see my children I wanted them to know how much I loved them and that I was doing everything in my power to be able to see them. I knew that God knew the truth about everything and that my children were safe with me. God knew the real Bob Sutton not the one that Judge Dodds described in his Judgment. God knew how I had tried to change my life and ways after becoming a Christian in Strangeways prison in 1987 and all the people I had tried to help. God had seen all the bad things that people had done to hurt me over the years and how I had forgiven each and every one of them. God had seen how much love I had shown to Jan, Donna, Robert and Michelle after my release from prison and not the picture they painted at court about me. God had seen the love that I had for Andreia, Nicoleta and all my children and that when I had wanted two wives it was for the right reasons. God had seen how much pain Andreia had caused me as she went from man to man and threw me away like a used cloth when it suited her. God had seen all my broken promises to all those I loved and the pain I had caused to them. Only God knew if he was going to change my situation around but from this moment I knew that my life was secure in his hands. Yes I had forgiven everyone for everything they had done to hurt me as I prayed for God to forgive me of all my sins.

Chapter 63

"For I know the plans I have for you, declares the Lord, plans to prosper you and not to harm you, plans to give you hope and a future".

Jeremiah 29: 11

I knew that my hope was in God alone and that from this moment I would no longer be living in the past. I believed that my life was safe in the hands of God and that whatever God wanted to do with my life would be for the best. I could feel the Holy Spirit at work within me helping me to overcome lots of temptations to do things that caused me lots of unhappiness in the past. I still had a desire to gamble and I still had a desire to go back to Andreia but with the help of God I was overcoming these temptations on an hourly basis. It was helping me to write this book as I looked back on the past and the many miracles I had witnessed in my walk with Jesus. I knew that I had lost many battles in the courts over the years especially the ones with the authorities when I tried to run the New Life Centre. I wondered if God had let me go through all these experiences to prepare me for a time such as this. I knew that my life as a Christian had been a very hard and difficult walk and where I had let God down more times than I cared to remember. I also knew that God had never let go of my hand and had lifted me up when I was down. I knew that God still loved me and had not given up on me as I started to pray about the way forward as I looked to a future with Nicoleta and my children.

God knew that no matter what happened to me I would never stop loving him and that one day I would come forth as gold. I was thankful that I was in the hand of the potter who I knew was a God of love. I was thankful that my heart was filled with love and not hate especially with what man had tried to do to me. In some ways it helped me to understand how Jesus must have felt when all the ones he had loved betrayed him and turned their backs on him. I remembered how Jesus had reinstated Peter when Peter had denied him three times after promising Jesus he would follow him everywhere. It helped me to realise that even though I had failed Jesus more times than I cared to remember that Jesus loved me the same and he could do for me what he did with Peter. It brought tears of gratitude down my cheeks as I typed these words into my computer knowing that God had not finished with me just yet. I looked forward to my holiday to Marrakech with Arthur and Diane that was now only a few days away. I looked forward to spending Christmas with my mum believing that Nicoleta would be spending her Christmas with Bianca and James. I looked forward to the moments I was spending with Nicoleta praying that we would not be seen by anybody connected to the authorities. I was planning to make my life in Romania if God opened the door as I believed that it is where I could have a life with Nicoleta, Bianca and James when the care proceedings were finally over.

It was now the time to wait patiently on the Lord as the authorities completed their final care plans and I waited for my case to be heard at the ECHR in France. I also had to deal with the civil proceedings I had brought against Lancashire County Council who I believed to be negligent in all their dealing with my family when the allegations were first made against me in 2004. It was very wrong of Lancashire social services to let me believe the work they were undertaking with Andreia and myself cleared me for being with my family then Sefton state that what they did counted for nothing. I believed that we all had a strong case against Lancashire County Council where if we won could lead to all the members of my family receiving large amounts of compensation from what we had all gone through. I was thankful that God had given me the wisdom to deal with legal matters and I left the outcome in his hands.

I had a picture of living at my apartment in Deva with Nicoleta, Bianca and James with David, Naomi and Victoria coming to stay with us for holidays. I still hoped that one day I could work with my children to build them the tree house at Panc that we had talked about. I had a picture of seeing Andreia where I no longer had any desires for her and that it would not hurt me anymore to see her with another man. I had started to pray that Andreia would meet a Godly man to take care of her and our children. I hoped and prayed that we would be successful against Lancashire because that would enable Andreia to finish Panc and make her life in Romania where hopefully I could see my children on a regular basis. I still had plans to open an English chip shop takeaway and restaurant in Deva or another busy town in Romania if God opened the door. I always saw this as a way of providing the money we would need to live in Romania and where we could help poor families. God knew that I was prepared to sell my apartment if I had to do so and provide for my wife and children's future. I felt like a boxer who had been knocked down so many times but God had given me the strength to get back up and I was still in the ring fighting.

On the 1st November I went on holiday to Marrakech with Arthur and Diane hoping to get a break from all that was going on in my life. I kept in touch with Nicoleta and I was missing her very much. I found out from Nicoleta that Andreia had contacted her to say she was going to try and cause me lots of problems with Sefton because I had wrote letters to her. I knew that the letters I had written to Andreia was to try and advise her in a Christian way about the people she was associating with who were having a bad influence on her life. It hurt me that Andreia was deliberately trying to hurt me and cause me more pain after all that I had done to help her. It spoiled my holiday knowing that Andreia had gone back to her old ways when I was hoping she had learned from her past mistakes. It was nice to have some quality time with Arthur and Diane who I did not get to see a lot of but my mind was on Nicoleta and my children who I loved and missed so very much. I did not think that I was in the right frame of mind for a holiday as I was still grieving over the loss of Andreia. It was so hard knowing that I had to let her go because my love had been very real and genuine. It hurt me knowing that Andreia was going out of her way to cause me as much pain as she could but I knew from my past experiences that one day the sun would be shining in my heart and that God would bring me through these difficult times.

I prayed so hard to God that he would give me all that I needed so that I could handle things in a way that would be acceptable to God. I tried to explain to Arthur and Diane what I was going through but realised that they had their own problems to deal with. I sent Andreia some emails trying to explain to her that the only way we could get through our problems was by doing things our Lords way. I knew that

I was wasting my time when Andreia put her ex lust Alex back on her hi5 site. Andreia knew he was no good for her and our children and that he was not a Christian but the lust in Andreia had taken over her life once again. I was also informed by Nicoleta that Andreia had found another job that involved her taking her clothes off so that men could take pictures of her. It was clear that Andreia was going from bad to worse and she was blaming me for all the bad she was doing. I tried to advise Andreia as a friend would do but sadly her heart had grown very hard and cold. It hurt to know that the person I loved could behave in this way. I realised that the only good thing I could do for Andreia would be to pray for her and let her learn her lessons the hard way.

I returned from holiday feeling very sad in my heart and praying that God would come very near to me. I had so much love to give and yet I was forced apart from all the ones that I loved and I felt very crushed in my spirit.

Chapter 64

"Shadrach, Meshach and Abednego replied to the king, O Nebuchadnezzar, we do not need to defend ourselves before you in this matter. If we are thrown into the blazing furnace, the God we serve is able to save us from it, and he will rescue us from your hand, O king. But even if he does not, we want you to know, O king, that we will not serve your gods or worship the image of gold you have set up."

Daniel 3 : 16 - 18

I wanted to stay faithful to God no matter what the devil sent my way. I knew that God could see inside of my heart and feel the pain I was suffering. I believed that God could change my situation around and restore everything that had been taken away from me. God knew that even if he did not rescue me I would remain faithful to him and serve him in any way that I could. My relationship with God was getting better as each day passed and I found that God gave me the grace to carry on when at times I felt like throwing in the towel. I needed a good friend but sadly for me there was none to be found. I felt that Jesus was letting me know that he was all I needed and that if I did things his way I would come out a winner.

I learned that Sefton wanted to go to Romania to meet up with the family of Nicoleta, the child protection and see her apartment that I had bought for her. I was very curious as to what they would write in their final report that had to be in court by the 6th December 2010. I wondered if any injunctions could be enforced in Romania or if the Child Protection in Romania would want to get involved in something that had taken place in England. I had spoken with Nicoleta about us being a family again if none of our children were at risk of being taken away again. We talked about having a life together but none of us wanted to build our hopes up especially with all that had taken place. My life had been one long struggle overcoming problem after problem and I felt like the boxer who had been knocked down in every round. I kept reminding myself that I might be down but I am still in the ring fighting and I knew that I had a God of love and righteousness in that ring with me and on my side. I started to think about this book that I had stopped writing over twelve years ago and wondered if this is what God wanted me to finish.

I remembered twelve years ago sending copies of it to Christians that I loved and respected who told me that it might put people off from becoming a Christian if they read about the hard journey in my life. The more I thought about my book the more I realised that it could be a testimony of the love that God has for a sinner like me where God picked me up each and every time I fell or was knocked down in my life. I know that at times I was my own worst enemy like my teacher had written about when I was fifteen years of age. But at times I was also subjected to attacks from people who were controlled by the devil. I wanted everyone who read this book to know that my God is real and will never reject anyone who comes to him no matter what they have done wrong in their life. I was a sinner saved by grace and my God showed his love for me by sending Jesus to die in my place. I knew that my God had plans for my life that I could not imagine and all I had to do was trust in him alone. I had always been a man of action but now I was learning about waiting and being patient. I knew I was in the refiner's fire but with God in charge of the temperature I had nothing to fear. I felt God speaking into my heart letting me know he was in the flames with me and that I would come through them unharmed. I sobbed my heart out as I felt the love of God so near and so real. I told God that I wanted this book to be a witness for him that might help anyone reading it to put their trust and life in his hands. God was the potter and I was the clay and I knew that when God had finished his work that I would be fit for the kingdom of heaven. I felt like I was gold in the hands of God.

I felt that I had a purpose in my life again as I started to copy the only draft copy of my book that I had from twelve years ago into my computer. As I read my own book it helped my faith grow stronger as I was reminded of all the situations God had brought me through in the past. I hoped that my book would help anyone reading it understand all that I had gone through in my life and that serving

God and living by his word was the only way to find peace and happiness in this world. I had found my peace again and it would not be long before my happiness also returned. On the 11th November I met with my mum who had come for a week's holiday to Southport and it was so nice to have some special time with her. I let my mum read a copy of the application I had sent to the ECHR and she told me that a barrister could not have done a better job and if there was any justice left in this world I would overturn everything that had taken place over the child care issues. I told my mum that I believed that God had given me the ability to prepare my case so that no man got any of the credit if my application was successful. I realised how blessed I was to have such a loving mother who had stood by me through everything. My mum would tell me when I was wrong but even when I made mistakes my mum never stopped loving me. My mum was also hurting at not being able to see all her grandchildren who she loved so very much and I hoped that she would be alive to cuddle them when my children were no longer in the care of Sefton. I believed that Nicoleta would have her children with her for Christmas so I made plans to have Christmas with my mum and stay in the guest suite at the apartments where she lived for two days over Christmas. I was going to make sure that my Christmas this year was going to be different than the one I had last year even if I could not be with Nicoleta and all my children. I bought some nice toys for all my children and asked Andreia and Nicoleta not to tell my children they were from me so that Sefton did not find out I was still in contact with them. I did not like living this way but I could not accept what the courts and Sefton had done was justice in the eyes of God.

I thought back to how I prayed to God for a break in my life all those years ago when I sat on Marks grave before I was sent to prison. If I had not been sent to prison I may not have met God in the way that I had and I knew that what I had with God was more important than anything else in this world. God had forgiven me for every sin I ever committed because Jesus had paid the price for me on that cruel cross. I knew that the Bob Sutton who went to prison in 1987 died in that prison and the born again Bob Sutton became a new creation. I knew that all of my wives and children had loved the new me but I still had lots of character defects that God was still working on. I knew that God was going to complete the work he had started in me way back in 1987 not knowing if my book would have a happy ending in this world. One thing I was sure of was that my future life with God was secure and he had good plans for my life. As I wrote those words I could feel lots of burdens being lifted from off my shoulders. I had wrote another letter to Andreia to try and warn her about the men she was in relationships with but this time I did not give her the letter. I realised that she would not listen to anything I said to her so I decided that I would just pray for her and our children and leave everything in the hands of God. I trusted God with everything and all those I loved and I was not going to take the heavy load back that I had handed over to God.

Chapter 65

"Who is wise? He will realise these things. Who is discerning? He will understand them. The ways of the Lord are right; the righteous walk in them, but the rebellious stumble in them."

Hosea 14: 9

I did not see things getting any better with Andreia when on the 15th November she walked past me in Southport with the man called Alex that had been in prison only eight weeks before. When Alex got sent to prison Andreia showed me the letter he had sent to her from the prison and I was present when she spoke with him on the telephone telling him that now he had a prison record they could not be together. Andreia had me convinced that she wanted to walk with God and do things his way and when I saw it was all lies I exploded with anger. I told Alex that he was a bad influence and Andreia was putting him before her children. They both ran into the family centre and when they came out I told Alison that I was very unhappy that they stopped me from seeing my children and yet they could let Alex into the home where my children hoped to return. I told Andreia that what she was doing was evil and now I understood why her attitude had changed so badly towards me. Every time she had a man with darkness in his life she would treat me very bad.

It broke my heart to think that Andreia was putting her men before working hard to get her children back. I told Andreia that she could not play with the devil without paying a very heavy price. I knew that I was wasting my time and that the devil had a grip of her life yet again. All her statements that she was going to wait for God to send the right man into her life had now been thrown out of the window for a man that clearly had no respect for her or God. Andreia had told me about how he resisted going to church and would not wait to get married before having sex with her. Everything that Andreia learned at Ellel Ministries was thrown on one side for Alex. I telephoned my solicitor to seek advice on what I should do as I wanted my children returned to Andreia but was very concerned that she was going to give them the same life her own mother had given her. I knew that my children had been damaged because of the rows that I had with Andreia and the coming and going and they needed a stable life. I was convinced that they would never have this stable life while Andreia went from man to man and I was in a dilemma on what I should do. I told Andreia that she needed deliverance ministry to get rid of the Jezebel spirit that was controlling her life. Andreia ignored my advice and I knew that bad things would now come the way of Andreia for ignoring the ways of the Lord. It was clear that in all we had gone through Andreia had not learned anything.

I prayed so hard about what to do and I decided to go and see her Pastor Ian and his wife Christine from Farm Fellowship Church. I knew that Andreia had a lot of love and respect for them both as she referred to them as mum and dad. I told them both about the concerns I had for Andreia and I was happy to hear that they had similar concerns and Christine had spoken with Andreia the day before explaining similar things that I had wrote to Andreia about. I could not understand why Andreia was putting her relationship with Alex before her children and it was clear that Andreia was ignoring all the Godly advice she was being given. At least this time she could not say I was trying to control her life because her Christian mum and dad were telling her the same things. It was good to pray with Ian and Christian where they prayed for Andreia and I. I was happy that I could share the truth with other Christians who had a heart for the hurting and a heart for Jesus. After we had finished praying I knew that only God could get through to Andreia as I knew from past experiences that when Andreia had a lust for a man nothing could stand in her way from going for him. It hurt me to know that she was putting at risk her one chance of getting our children back that the Judge had given to her. It was clear that Andreia was not showing that our three children meant more to her than Alex. I had made arrangements to see my solicitor Sarah and I was more at peace about telling Sarah everything after meeting with Ian and Christine. It was also helping me to write this story of my life as I looked back on all the things that God had done in my life in the past. I knew that Alex could change if he repented of his sins and turned to Jesus but the way she had brought him from London with no money for his train fare did not give me much hope that God was in their relationship.

I wrote my last letter to Andreia hoping that God would speak to her before she lost our children for ever. I reminded her that the Judge had given her one chance only to show that she could protect her children. I knew only too well how the desires of the flesh had caused me to sin against God in the past and the bad consequences that resulted. The devil wanted to destroy all our lives and I prayed that God would intervene and turn everything around that was taking place. I loved my children so much and I would have given anything in this world to be a part of their lives. I had made lots of mistakes but I knew that I had learned from them and that I had a lot of Godly love and goodness to give to my children and anyone else I was in contact with. As I wrote those words I knew that I would have to show that to everyone including Alex. I knew it was not him that I hated but the evil spirits controlling his life.

On the 18th November I met with my solicitor and told her about all the contact I had been having with Andreia until she decided she did not want to see me anymore. I did not want any of this information passing on to Sefton or the Guardian because I believed that they would use it against Andreia. I was upset to find out that Andreia had told Sefton and the Guardian that I had been in touch with her making it look like I was the only one who had broken the injunction. It seemed that Andreia had forgotten to tell them how many times she had phoned me up for help and asked me to go out with her. I had tried to warn Andreia in my letters not to open up a can of worms where we could all end up the loser especially our children. I could not understand the mentality of Andreia because the first thing Sefton wanted to do was stop her having any more counselling but the director of her counselling service informed Sefton that Andreia should continue with her sessions. I had not done anything to hurt Andreia or to cause her any problems in getting our children back and all my letters were to try and get her to see that what she was doing with her men was not of God. There was a part of me that wondered if Andreia really wanted her children back or if she just wanted to have a single life with Alex. I asked my solicitor to write a letter to the solicitor for Andreia informing him of the full facts and not just the ones Andreia had given. I had a real concern that Sefton would apply to commit me to prison for breaking the injunction not to have contact with each other but they could not do that to me without also doing it to Andreia.

I knew that Andreia had contacted me for help on so many occasions since the injunction had been put in place and had wanted to have time with me when it suited her. The problem with Andreia was that each time she had a different man in her life she threw me on one side like a used cloth. I told Andreia the truth in all my letters and if Sefton did apply to commit me to prison I made up my mind that I would tell the truth and explain why I had broken the injunctions. I had never believed that anything that had taken place with Sefton or Lancashire had been justice but only God could rescue me now and turn my situation around. At least what Andreia was doing to try and hurt me showed me that she never really loved me and her lusts meant more to her than walking with Jesus and doing things his way.

On the 19th November I was at court over my civil claim against Lancashire County Council but Andreia and Nicoleta did not show up. I believed we all had a valid claim against them and I was shocked to be handed some papers by their barrister who was applying to have our claims struck out relying on legal arguments that had been tested in the House of Lords. If their argument succeeded it would mean than Andreia, Nicoleta and I would be denied the right to claim any damages even if Lancashire were negligent. The Judge adjourned the case to a new date to be set for a half day hearing to hear the application from Lancashire to strike out our claim. After reading their legal arguments and test cases I thought that I would lose before bringing any evidence. Then the words "Good Faith" jumped off the page and hit me in the face. All the cases involved authorities that had "acted in Good Faith" but I knew that what Lancashire had done was not in Good Faith. I downloaded legal definitions of "Good faith" and I realised that the evidence that I had would show that Lancashire had in fact acted in "Bad Faith" as many of the agencies and people employed by them had lied about lots of things to get Sefton to re-open a file that they had closed in 2008. As I started to write down my skeleton argument on why my claim should not be struck out I knew that I had an excellent chance of defeating their arguments in front of an unbiased Judge. One thing I knew was that even if I lost at the first hearing God had given me all the wisdom I would need to take my case to the appeal court in London. I thanked God for the wisdom he had given me as even though I did not fully understand the law I fully understood justice and the difference between right and wrong.

   I was praying continually to God about all that was taking place as I believed it would take a miracle to turn our situation around and give me my family back. I knew for the first time in years that if I had the chance to be with anyone it would be with Nicoleta, Bianca and James plus having David, Naomi and Victoria on a regular basis. I knew that now that Andreia had turned against me she was not going to do anything that would be in my favour especially now her life was joined to someone who did not even know Jesus. I was also prepared to accept not being with anyone if God did not turn my situation around because I trusted in God with all those I loved including my own life. The thought of never having my family back was a thought to painful to contemplate and I cried myself to sleep on many nights. I had to go to the doctor on lots of occasions because I was only sleeping for a few hours a night and I had wanted to see a counsellor. I think that God was trying to tell me something when I was informed that it would take several months on the waiting list to see a counsellor. The private counselling service given a contract by the health authority stated that I would need more sessions than they could provide after listening to what I had gone through. I realised that I was looking for help that God could give me so I opened up my heart to God and the tears flooded out on a regular basis.

   I knew that my Lord loved me with a very special love and that I could trust him with everything. God knew me better than any other person and he was the potter and I was the clay. I trusted that when God had finished with me I would shine like a very bright star and all my character defects would be removed. I felt at peace being able to pray for Andreia and Alex that they would do things Gods way and especially for them both to know and love Jesus like he deserved. I knew that I had failed God on lots of occasions even while I had been a Christian and that I had to remove the logs from my own eyes. This helped me to resist the temptations to do anything bad or sin against God.

Chapter 66

"But as for me, I watch in hope for the Lord, I wait for God my Saviour; my God will hear me. Do not gloat over me, my enemy! Though I have fallen, I will rise. Though I sit in darkness, the Lord will be my light".

Micah 7: 7-8

If ever I needed a word from God it was at this time because on the 25th November I was served with committal papers from the court because Andreia had applied for me to be committed to prison for breaking court injunctions not to contact her. This application was listed for directions from the Judge on the 29th November where the Judge was informed that Andreia had told her social worker on the 26th October that I had been in touch with her and because of this disclosure Sefton had got hold of all our telephone records. It was clear looking at the telephone records that Andreia, Nicoleta and I had all broken the court injunction not to contact each other. My heart was breaking for Nicoleta, Bianca and James as Sefton stated they no longer wanted Nicoleta to have unsupervised contact with her children at home but wanted her to have supervised contact at the family centre while all the contact was investigated. I could not believe that Andreia had given Sefton this information because she had been happy to have contact with me when it suited her.

I told my barrister that I hated this heartless system that was able to divide families and take children away from their mothers on the findings of a biased Judge who had finding made against him. I went on to say that I believed my God would put right all the wrongs that had been done against us all and that I was not frightened of going to prison for what I believed in. If the parents wanted to have contact with each other and that contact did not put the children in any danger then it was inhuman and against human rights to force the parents not to have contact with each other. I was praying silently in that court room for God to come and help us as our situation was now going from bad to worse. I had warned Andreia that if she contacted the social services to say we had been in touch with each other that she would end up opening a can of worms where Sefton would have a field day and there would be no winners. Like always Andreia ignored the advice I had given to her and now we were all going to suffer. The Judge set the new hearing date for the 16th March 2011 that was on the birthday of Bianca.

In my prayer time God had shown me a happy and unhappy ending to my story and asked me if I would still love him no matter what the outcome would be. God had shown me Stephen being stoned to death when he had done nothing wrong and having a love for God that was so special that he even asked God to forgive those who had stoned him with his dying breath. God then showed me Daniel in the lion's den and his three friends Shadrach, Meshach and Abednego being thrown into the blazing furnace for doing nothing wrong but on these two occasions God rescued them. I told God that I would trust him completely with the outcome and prayed that my life would be a testimony that would help other people reading my story come to know Jesus whatever the outcome. God knew that my prayer was to turn around all the injustices that had taken place against us in the courts that were still taking place as I was writing this book. The comfort that I took was that God knew the ending already but I had to wait upon my Lord. I prayed for Andreia, Nicoleta, David, Naomi, Victoria, Bianca and James asking God for his protection and to work for good through all that was taking place.

I was upset that the Judge would not even agree for my children to receive a Christmas card from me because the guardian of the children was against it. I had not seen or spoken with my children for over a year and Victoria had asked Andreia if I was dead during one of her contact meetings with our children. I had broken my heart writing the Christmas cards to my children and a birthday card for Victoria and now I was not allowed to give them to my children. I told my barrister that we were caught up in a heartless system with heartless people who had no real understanding of what harm they were doing to all of us. I told him that my children would grow up to hate the people and system that took them away from parents who loved them very much and who had never harmed them. All our lives were being destroyed because of allegations made against me that were never prosecuted by the police and dated back more than twenty years. I was also convinced that since Andreia had gone back to Alex she had changed for the worst and the devil was having a field day with all our lives. I believed from my past experiences with God that at the right time he would act on our behalf. I prayed for the power of the Holy Spirit in my life to help me cope and be a living witness for Jesus Christ. I wrote another letter to the European Court of Human Rights asking them to put my applications before the Judges as a matter of extreme urgency. I went to bed with a very heavy heart crying out to God to come quickly to our help or send angels to help us.

Chapter 67

"Therefore the law is paralyzed, and justice never prevails. The wicked hem in the righteous, so that justice is perverted. (The Lord's Answer) Look at the nations and watch and be utterly amazed. For I am going to do something in your days that you would not believe, even if you were told".

Habakkuk 1 : 4-5

If ever I needed a word from God it was now and when I read my bible after a very restless night the words from Habakkuk jumped off the page and sank deep into my heart. I shared the word with my true love who was also heartbroken at what was taking place. It hurt me that we had been forced apart by the Judge and now we all faced going to prison and all our children being put up for adoption. This had been the plan of Sefton all along and I knew that it was going to take a miracle from God to turn our situation around. I believed with all my heart that God was going to act on our behalf but I did not know how or when. For me this is what faith is all about and if God was not real then I would not want to live on this earth a moment longer. I decided to carry on writing this book even though my heart was very heavy. I also wrote to my solicitor asking if she could try and get me Pete Weatherby as my barrister as my mum had told me he was one of the very best and an expert on human rights issues. I hoped I could get him for the 16th March when we were next due back at court that just happened to be the birthday of Bianca. The present that Sefton and the guardian wanted to give her was to take her away from her mother and father who loved her so very much and place her and my other children for adoption with strangers. I believed that God would not let that happen and I needed to trust and be patient as I waited upon my Lord.

I continued to pray for Andreia, Nicoleta and all my children on a daily basis as I got closer to God. I knew that I had made lots of mistakes in the past that I was powerless to change. Writing this book helped me to understand just how many times I had let God down and had let the desires of my flesh get the better of me. I realised that I should not have committed adultery and then spent years going back and forth between Andreia and Nicoleta hurting all my children in the process. Now everyone that I loved had been taken away from me and only God could change my situation around. I decided that I was going to take all the blame for breaking the court injunctions and make a statement that I put pressure on Andreia and Nicoleta to keep in touch with me. I knew that God knew the truth about everything and he knew the real Bob Sutton that was not the bad man that everyone painted me to be. I found that I was now able to pray for Alex that God would touch his heart and that he would come to know Jesus as his Lord and Saviour. I wanted the best for Andreia and my children and if we were not meant to be together I hoped that she would find a Godly mad to share her life with who loved her and my children like I did. I also prayed for Jan, Donna, Robert, Michelle and their families on a daily basis with no bitterness in my heart. I could feel all my anger and bitterness melting away as I spent hours in prayer and reading my bible. I realised that if God was with me then no matter what the world threw my way I would be able to stand. If my legs gave way at any time I knew that my Lord would carry me in his loving arms because the love he had for me was so very special. I wanted to have the love that Jesus gave to me so that I could share it with other people. I had placed my loved ones and my own life in the hands of God and I believed with all my heart that they were safe in his loving hands and God would give us back what he knew was good for each and every one of us.

The 24th December was a very sad day for me as I remembered the birthday of Victoria knowing that I had not seen any of my children for over a year. The guardian of the children called Barie Beaumont had sent a report into the court stating that I should not be allowed to send a Christmas card to any of my children. I knew that this would be the outcome as soon as the Judge gave her the responsibility of making the decision because she had shown throughout the hearing that her heart was made of stone and she never did anything that would benefit my children. I wrote her a letter telling her that she had a hard heart and that when my children were old enough to know the truth about what had taken place they would hate the heartless system that had taken them away from their mothers who loved them very much and also me. I told the guardian to tell my children the full truth and not the half truth that she wanted to paint. I hoped my children would know that I loved them very much and I was still fighting to try and put right all the wrongs that had taken place.

    I had so much love to give my wife and my children and yet cold heartless people who did not even know me had forced me apart from all those that I loved. I cried out to God to send Angels to help me because I felt so alone in fighting the authorities with all the bad things that had happened. I felt the pain that Andreia, Nicoleta and all my children were feeling in being separated from each other and I wondered if God was going to help us and if so when it would be. I think that I was having a bad day with my heart torn into little pieces with everything that had taken place. I tried to remind myself that God was in control and the precious gift he had given us all at Christmas time with my Lord and Saviour Jesus Christ. I prayed so hard for God to give me my family back as the tears flowed down my cheeks. My wife and children were more important to me than anything in this world except for God and I knew that God knew that as well. I put the birthday card that I had wrote for Victoria in a safe place along with the Christmas cards for all my children hoping that one day I would be able to give the cards to them. At least my children would know how much I loved them by how hard I was fighting to be back in their lives.

    I received a telephone call from Andreia who was very drunk and she told me that Alex wanted to return to Romania but he had no money. It was clear that what I had tried to warn Andreia about was coming true because she had not done things in a Godly way. Andreia wanted to meet me but Alex had locked her in the house and was refusing to let her out. I could not believe that Andreia was letting this man control her life with all that the authorities had said about me. I had never known Andreia to drink alcohol not even at our wedding but living with an ungodly person was having a bad affect. I decided to pay for the flight and coach tickets so that Alex could return to Romania. I arranged to meet with Andreia the following day so that I could give her the tickets I had printed out from my computer. When I met with Andreia it was clear that she had not learned anything from all the things that had happened in her life. I still loved Andreia but in my heart I knew that she was just using me to try and hurt Alex because he had decided to leave her and return to Romania. I advised her to contact her Pastor from Farm Fellowship and return like the lost son who Jesus preached about. I told Andreia that I did not want the money back that I had paid for the tickets but wanted her to put our children before the desirers of her flesh. Andreia asked me to take her to London but I was not falling for what she wanted and told her I had made other plans that I was not going to change. While I was with Andreia it was sad to hear a Christian friend of Andreia telephone her and say I had only paid for the tickets for Alex so I could get back into her life. I made it clear to Andreia that I had learned from my past mistakes and that I only wanted what God planned for me to have. I had learned the hard way that when I sinned against God the devil came rushing in like a flood.

I was still not sure if Nicoleta truly loved me because since Bianca and James had been taken into care Nicoleta had been very cold towards me. We talked about this a lot and I tried to understand how much it was hurting Nicoleta and Andreia at being separated from all the children they loved so very much. I knew that God could see inside all our hearts and I was open to whatever God decided should happen with my life. It would have been very easy for me to take Andreia up on her offer to go to London with her but I had hurt Nicoleta enough in the past for giving in to my fleshly desires and this time I was determined to do things Gods way. I knew that Nicoleta had put her children first and they were more important to her than any man. I was hoping that Andreia would now put her children's needs before the desires of her flesh but only time would tell. I did not want to sin anymore and I just wanted one wife to love who would love me in return and all my children back. I believed that we had all paid a heavy price for the sins we had committed and now it was time to wait for God in His mercy to restore all what the devil had taken away. I thanked God for giving me the power to resist the evil desires of my flesh.

On the 30th December I was awake at 2.30am writing my legal arguments and statement for the hearing that was due to take place on the 3rd February 2011 where the legal team for Lancashire County Council was trying to have our claims struck out. I realised how much God had taught me through all the court cases I had been involved with over the years and I was very confident that they would not succeed if we had a fair Judge. I made it clear that I would never accept the findings of Judge Dodds who had findings made against him by the appeal court in London and the findings he made did not give Lancashire social services the right to act in Bad Faith or justify their own negligence. I also enclosed a copy of a letter that I had received from the European Court of Human Rights confirming they were looking into my complaints. I made it clear that God could nullify all what Judge Dodds presided over and show Lord Justice Wilson that what he said was a "Given Verdict" is not the end until God says so. I was at peace over everything and I knew that was because I had no hidden sins that had not been dealt with.

I turned up at Liverpool County Court on the 3rd February 2011 believing that I had a very strong claim against Lancashire County Council and I was happy to see that Andreia had also turned up to speak on her own behalf. Within 5 minutes of the case starting I knew that the Judge was against me as he was nodding his head in agreement with everything that the barrister acting for Lancashire was saying. The findings of Judge Dodds were mentioned and that the Law Lords in London had ruled that no local authority had any legal liability towards any parent if they had acted in Good Faith. I argued my case the best that I could but I knew everything I said was going to make no difference to a Judge who had already made his mind up. The hearing lasted for about three hours and we were asked to return to court the following day for the verdict. I knew in my heart what it would be and I went into the court office to ask for the appeal forms so I could make an appeal to London. On the 4th February we were back at court to hear the verdict where the Judge allowed the claims of Andreia, Nicoleta and I to be thrown out. Andreia and I asked the Judge for permission to appeal but as expected he refused and I left court knowing that justice had taken a back seat yet again.

That evening I thought long and hard about everything that had taken place and I realised that it would be pointless appealing to London knowing that the Judge in London would not change anything. I realised that it was time to let go and to let God change anything that he wanted to change. I started to throw away all the files and documents that I had accumulated since the court cases had started that filled a large rubbish container where I lived. It was also time to throw away all the building materials that I had kept in my apartment as I prepared for making a new life for myself in Romania. I only wanted to take to Romania what was really important and what I could not sell I threw away. I was praying that I could be back with Nicoleta, Bianca and James as a family but only God knew if this was going to take place. On the 7th February I received a telephone call from my mum who read a letter out to me that had been sent from the European Court of Human Rights. My heart sank as I heard the words that my appeal had been rejected and that I had no further right of appeal.

I told my mum that I needed some time to pray about what to do and I felt an emptiness inside of me knowing that I had exhausted all the legal channels I could go down and there was nothing else I could do to try and change things. I also felt I had no more fight left in me and felt very weak from all that I had suffered and gone through. I knew that Andreia and Nicoleta still had a fight on their hands to get their children back from Sefton and I was determined to do anything in my power to make sure our children would come back home to them. This was a time where I had to trust that God was in control and that God would work for our good through all things. I knew that God could see into the future and I still trusted that God had a good plan for all our lives. I was happy to know that Andreia was close to Jesus again and had opened up a web site called "Andreia, follower of Jesus" where she hoped to reach other lost people for Jesus. I still felt it was right to go to France and burn all my bridges in England even though I was not sure what was going to happen when I got there. I spoke with my brother and sister who both told me that I had to look to the future and not behind. Diane had booked a holiday for the three of us to go on in October to Turkey and I hoped by then that all the court cases had been finished with. I had placed my life and that of all my loved ones into the hands of God and I trusted that we were safe in His loving care.

Chapter 68

"Then Jesus declared, "I am the bread of life. He who comes to me will never go hungry, and he who believes in me will never be thirsty. But as I told you, you have seen me and still you do not believe. All that the Father gives me will come to me, and whoever comes to me I will never drive away".

John 6 : 35 – 37

I know that without God in my life I would have given up trying to fight all the injustices taking place a very long time ago. Some days I would feel very weak and inadequate but then I would pray and read Gods word to help me get through these times. Giving up my home in England seemed the right thing to do as I just wanted to have a new start with my life and go to France. My children were in danger of being placed for adoption because Sefton, the Judge and the Guardian did not want Andreia or Nicoleta to have any contact with me what so ever. I could not understand why one biased Judge had been given the power to destroy so many lives and for me true justice had gone out of the window and no longer existed in the child care proceedings. I had been denied any form of contact with all five of my children for over sixteen months and when I was refused permission to send them a Christmas and Birthday card it showed how far this heartless system was prepared to go. I had talked with Nicoleta about ways of making a living to support living in France if Nicoleta and myself were able to be together as a family in Romania. It was a friend of her father who planted a seed by asking Nicoleta if we could but a cheap tractor for him in England as second hand tractors in Romania were expensive and not very reliable. It did not take a lot of research to find a company in Bristol who were importing second hand tractors from Japan and selling them at reasonable prices. I got a picture right away of setting up a company in Romania to do the same thing as I believed there was a big market ready to tap into. I had just enough money left over to buy a car trailer and purchase my first second hand tractor but first I had to go to Romania and empty my van of everything that was packed into it.

Nicoleta could not look beyond getting her children back from Sefton and I knew that Andreia felt the same way. I agreed to give Andreia the deposit and bond to put down on another house because her landlord had given her a notice to quit. Sefton had broken the promise they had given to the Court of helping Andreia with her rent and I was the only person willing to give Andreia the money. It was clear that if Andreia did not have a three bedroom house that Sefton would use this as another reason to keep our children in care. Both Andreia and Nicoleta had to see Helen Roberts again so that she could give another so called expert report on why they both broke the injunction and contacted me by telephone. I wanted Andreia and Nicoleta to say all the bad things that they wanted to hear said against me and blame me for everything. I no longer cared what those in authority thought about me if the end result was my children being returned to the care of their own mother.

On the 28th February I met with my solicitor and gave her the statement I had prepared for the hearing listed for the 16th March but we still had not seen any of the statements from Sefton or the experts involved with the case. I had it on my heart for a long time to contact John Miles as I found that I was praying for him and his family on a regular basis. I was very sad to be given the news by John that his wife Liz had died from cancer the previous year. I told John that I had been praying for his family on a regular basis and I was there for him if he needed a shoulder to lean on. I missed the friendship that we had shared together over the years especially the adventures we had been on as we reached out to children and people in need. I knew what it felt like to lose so many people who I loved and not being able to see or hold my five children was like bereavement.

On the 4th March I went into an internet cafe to look at my emails and the letters sent to me from my solicitor. I was not happy at reading the report from Helen Roberts as she now talked about Andreia and Nicoleta seeing a rape counsellor. I just believed that things were being taken beyond the edge of reality and I wondered what they were going to come up with next. I was so happy to read the statement that Andreia had prepared for the court and I firmly believed that God had given Andreia wisdom and ability to prepare a statement that was good enough to have been prepared by a barrister. It was clear how much Andreia had learned from her child psychology course and from her training in ADHD. I was happy to know that Andreia was not prepared anymore for Sefton to keep her children in care and she was prepared to fight to get them back. It was clear that Sefton were not providing the proper help that David and Victoria needed and that their illness of ADHD was being ignored by everyone involved in the child care proceedings. I believed that the statement that Andreia had made would be the turning point of my children being returned to their mothers care and only a complete idiot and hard hearted Judge would be able to ignore what Andreia was saying.

On Sunday the 6th March I went to the Baptist Church to pray about everything and worship my Lord. It was Holy Communion and a special time to hand everything over to God as I prepared for a fresh start in France. After the service I went for a holiday to Romania and visited Tustea to see the Grand Parents of Andreia, then to Ciula Mica to see Renato and his family, and then back to Deva to see Angela and take a birthday present to Luciana who would be six years old on the Monday. I passed the Primar and church where I had married Andreia and the hospital in Hateg where David was born and all my memories came flooding back of when we were together. I also passed the ruins of the building that had been started at Ciula Mica that was supposed to be Bartimaeus House helping homeless children in Romania. I had so many regrets of things I had done wrong in the past but I knew that I could not change the past but I could learn from everything making sure I did not make the same mistakes in the future. I had a few butterflies in my stomach as I went to see people who had been a special part of my life not knowing how they would react. I was very happy to be welcomed with open arms everywhere I went but I did not get to see Renato who was at work when I called at his home. Anca telephoned Renato at work and let me speak with him and we made arrangements to meet up the following day after Anca had returned from taking Roxana to her college at Timisoara. I don't know what it was but after seeing everyone I felt like I was coming home after being away for a very long time. Robert and Roxane both told me they could not wait to get away from Romania but I told them that they could both make Romania into a very special country as England was not any better.

Chapter 69

"Yet the Lord longs to be gracious to you; he rises to show you compassion. For the Lord is a God of justice. Blessed are all who wait for Him!"

Isaiah 30 : 18

It was now time to give up my apartment in Southport and pack the last of my belongings into card board boxes ready for moving to Romania. I wanted to give Andreia and Nicoleta the best chance possible for getting their children back and I believed if I moved away from Southport and the UK the Judge would see I was not going to come between my children and their mothers. I had a plan of starting a new life in Romania but I did not want any of the authorities to know where I would be living as I knew they would want to interfere in my life wherever I was living. I told everyone I was going to move to France to be with my sister Diane and as soon as Sefton found out they told my solicitor they would notify the authorities in France that I was on my way. I could not understand how they had so much power to try and destroy all our lives when I had not been convicted of anything in a criminal court. I was not happy that Andreia had decided to bring Alex back from Romania and I also found out she had started to go back to the lap dancing club in Manchester to earn some money. I was very sad because I thought Andreia was walking with Jesus and she told me she would never go back to that club. I understood how hard it was for Andreia and I knew that she was lonely and had lots of financial problems because of what Sefton and the Courts had done to both her and Nicoleta.

I did not have a lot of money behind me but I decided to help Andreia and Nicoleta from the money I received from the sale of my van. I contacted their families through someone I knew in Romania so that Sefton would not know the money was coming from me and that I would not be in breach of the court injunction. I gave Andreia £800 towards the deposit for another home and £400 to pay for the final eight counselling sessions that Sefton were refusing to pay. I also gave £500 so that Nicoleta could pay for private counselling to show that Sefton had got things wrong and had not helped Nicoleta like they should have done. It was clear to me that we needed some counselling reports that were in our favour to counter the negative reports that had been given by the counsellor who worked at the courts on a regular basis. My own counselling reports showed that I was ready to move on with my life and make a fresh start away from England. I decided to have a few weeks with my mum before moving to Romania. I loved Nicoleta the mother of my children deeply and I still hoped that we might be able to be together away from the UK. We had both agreed that we would not be together if it put our children at risk of being adopted out.

I decided to leave my car parked up on the road near to where my mother lived and booked flight tickets to Romania that would allow me to come back to England for ten days on the 19th May 2011 and again for three weeks on the 15th July 2011 for the final days of the hearing at Liverpool court. My flight to Romania was booked for the 18th April and I had my last night in the arms of the woman I loved. I did not want the night to end and I held my sweetheart so close to me looking into her beautiful face while she was sleeping. I did not want the night to end and I hated the child care system that had been so barbaric and heartless in what it had done to all of us. It was a very sad and lonely drive back to my mum's home knowing that I would not see her again for at least a month.

On 18th April I said goodbye to my mum and set off on the bus to Manchester Airport for my flight to Romania. There would be no turning back as I set off to start my new life not knowing what lay ahead of me. I prayed to God about everything and put all my trust in my God who I loved knowing he loved me. I had a plan to set up a new business in Romania so that I could provide a future for my children and also to help poor people from any profits the business made. I was prepared to sell my apartment in Deva and use the money I received to start the business I was going to form. I travelled to Budapest and made my way by mini bus to Keleti railway station where I had a four and a half hour wait for my train that would take me to Deva in Romania. While at the railway station I met a Romanian lady by the name of Anda and we passed the time by talking to each other about lots of different things. I was hoping that Anda would help me learn Romanian and help me with setting up my business because she only lived about sixty miles from Deva and spoke perfect English. I asked Anda to pray about helping me and we exchanged telephone numbers. I was very excited because I believed God was showing me I was not alone and that he would provide for all my needs on this new journey.

After seven hours I arrived safely in Deva and said goodbye to Anda who was travelling on to Alba Iulia. After staying in Deva for a few days I decided to go and see some new friends I had made who lived in the town of Sibiu about 110km from Deva.

It was good for me to get away from Deva and to make new friends in Romania. I met up with Adrian who had a two year old daughter called Beatrice and his sister Elena who was twenty eight years old. I also met up with lots of their friends and I was made to feel loved and part of their family. Adrian and Elena had cared for an old man from England called James who had recently died in Romania at the age of seventy nine. They had looked after James for seven years in Romania and James had left the apartment he had bought in Romania and all his worldly goods to Adrian as a reward for looking after him. When Adrian showed me the wills that James had left I knew that James had made lots of mistakes in filling them in. James had made out eight wills from the pack he had bought in England when he only needed to fill in one of the forms. I showed Adrian where mistakes had been made and it was clear that James must have been confused with making out so many wills. I went to see the monument Adrian had made at the local cemetery and knew it was better than anything I had seen in England. I could feel the love that Adrian and his family had for James as I saw the photographs and video they had made together over the years. I believed God wanted me to help Adrian get the £5000 that was in the bank account belonging to James in Romania and any other money that might be in bank accounts in England or life insurance policies.

I advised Adrian to have the will translated and legalised by a Notary and to take this to the bank and ask for the money belonging to James. It was clear the will left everything to Adrian and as James had no other relatives I believed that James dying wish was for

Adrian to have everything. I wrote letters to the bank and private pension company in the UK asking if any other monies were owed to the estate belonging to James. I went to the Baptist Church on Easter Sunday with my new family I had met up with in Romania. It was like old times for me being welcomed into the homes of lots of people who wanted to meet me and make friends with me. I felt the love of God so near to me and I could sense that Elena and me were getting on very well.

    The next few weeks passed by very quickly as I found an Advocat in Deva to form a new company that I decided to call "David James and Daughters" after all of my children. Within two weeks my new company was formed and I went to the bank to open a new bank account for my business. I met up with Renato and Anca to find out if they would let me use their farm to store tractors. Things were falling into place very quickly and I felt that God had everything worked out even if I was not sure what the future held. I felt that I could be happy with a girl like Elena who seemed a very nice person with lots of good qualities. The 19th May arrived very quickly and it was time to return to UK where I had important meetings with my legal team. While I was in the UK I was able to get all the information I needed to deal with probate matters on behalf of Adrian who had given me power of attorney to act on his behalf. I also found myself back at Liverpool Court because Andreia and Nicoleta were applying for their mothers to have care of my children if the Judge refused to give my children back to their mothers care. I was given a copy of the final care plans that Sefton had for all my children and it broke my heart to read the evil plans they had made to adopt them out and even separate them from each other. I hated the evil and hard hearted people who had control of my children and I prayed that God would change the situation around. I had until the 13th June to prepare my final statement and I wanted the Judge to know the truth about everything that had taken place with her being a replacement Judge for the hard hearted and unjust Judge Dodds. I returned to Romania with my car on the 31st May so that I could visit different places while I waited for the final court hearings that were due to start on the 18th July 2011.

    It did not take me long to finish my statement and sent it to my solicitor by email and waited for her to reply. The money that I had taken with me to Romania was running out very quickly and I knew that my situation needed to change if I was going to survive in Romania. I placed free advertisements on the internet and local papers for the tractors I wanted to import from Japan to see if I could find buyers for them. In my mind I wanted to find ten people interested in buying a tractor from Japan and if I had ten people reply I was going to take that as a sign from God to commence importing tractors as soon as I had the money to do so. If I could not find ten people then I would look to open an English pub/restaurant as an alternative business.

For me I was not bothered what business I did if God was in it because I wanted to help poor people in Romania from any profits the business would make. I also wanted to have a business that my children could be involved with when they were older giving them hope for their future. On the 16th June I decided to go to Oradea to take a look at the town and to see if it would be a suitable place to live and start work. It was also an opportunity to stay two days at Balie Felix where I had many happy memories of holidays I had taken with Andreia, Nicoleta and my children. What I saw at Oradea convinced me that it would be a suitable place to live and work if God opened the door for it to take place. I knew from past experiences that it would be foolish to start anything in my own strength as I wanted to be in the will of God no matter what that would involve. I returned to Deva on the 18th June and waited for God to speak to me about the way forward in my life. On Sunday the 19th June it was Fathers day in the UK and I hoped my children would know how much I loved and missed them. It was not possible for me to speak to them because of the barbaric court injunctions so I just prayed that one day they would all know my love for them was very real. I also hoped they would know how hard I had fought the unjust things that had taken place against us all and the sacrifices I had made by leaving the UK to give them a better chance of being returned to their mothers care. I had a lot of sadness in my heart because of being separated from all the ones that I loved and wondered if my situation was going to improve and that of all my loved ones.

Chapter 70

" And you have forgotten that word of encouragement that address you as sons: My son, do not make light of the Lord's discipline, and do not lose heart when he rebukes you, because the Lord disciplines those he loves and punishes everyone he accepts as a son."

Hebrews 12 : 5 - 6

It was getting closer as each day passed to the date of the final hearing that would decide if my children were going to be returned to Andreia and Nicoleta. I was very happy when my mother telephoned me to say that Canon Noel Proctor MBE had wrote a letter to the Judge on my behalf. I had wrote to Noel, John Miles and Archie Barr asking if they would write a letter on my behalf to say what they knew about me because I was fed up of hearing the findings of Judge Dodds who stated I had spent a life time of wrong doing forgetting to mention over twenty two years of reaching out to people rejected by society. I was hoping that Judge De Haas would see a different person that that portrayed by Judge Dodds after reading the letter from Noel. I was sad that John and Archie had not done anything to help me as I thought we had been good friends and that as Christian brothers they would want to help. It was not for my benefit but my children because I wanted the Judge to understand that I was not a danger to my children and they should be returned to their mothers care. It helped me to understand how Jesus must have felt when all those closest to him had turned their backs on him when he needed them the most. I wrote a letter to Noel thanking him for his help and for being a very faithful man of God. I thanked Noel for the day he led me to Jesus explaining that without Jesus in my life I would have given up on life a long time ago. I also wrote a letter to John saying how sad I was that John and Archie had ignored my request for help.

I received a letter from my legal team who advised me against sending in my statement to the Court saying I should take a back seat and leave everything to the legal team of Andreia and Nicoleta. I was very surprised at their advice because my statement contained the full facts about all that had taken place and corrected lots of lies told by Sefton and the Guardian. My statement was also a record for my children on how hard I had fought at trying to overcome all the injustices that had taken place not just against me but also against them and their mothers. I also wanted Judge De Haas to know everything that had taken place and knew that none of the barristers would highlight where even the legal team for Nicoleta had failed her and were slated by Lord Wilson when Nicoleta had won her appeal at London. I had no confidence in any of the barristers as they were very timid in front of the Judge and even when the Judge got it wrong they never did anything about it. This was evident on the 23rd December 2009 when Lord Wilson stated that the legal team for Nicoleta could have appealed direct to London where her case would have been heard within a week instead of walking out of court and doing nothing about it. I knew that this was my only opportunity of telling everyone how I felt as I knew that if the Judge did not return my children to their mothers care that this case would go to the Royal Courts of Justice in London.

I instructed my legal team to send my statement to the court word for word informing them that I would put my trust in God in the outcome. I told them that if I did not put my statement in and my children were not returned to their mothers care I would regret it for the rest of my life. I did not care if the Judge turned against me for stating the true feelings I had about everything that had taken place and my first two sentences of my statement were. "Barbaric, heartless, uncaring, unlawful, unjust and inhuman are some of the words that best describe this child care system that ripped innocent children away from two mothers who were the best mothers that any children could wish to have. Some of my sentiments were backed up by lord Justice Wilson in the manner and way that HHJ Dodds removed Bianca and James from Nicoleta on the 23rd December 2009 two days before Christmas because she had been truthful to the court." I was at peace about everything knowing that I had done everything in my power to fight for Justice even though in my case justice had not prevailed. I was taking all the blame for breaking the injunction because I knew that what had happened against Andreia, Nicoleta and all my children was not their fault. Having my children returned to their mothers care was what was important to me even if it meant the Judge would send me to prison.

I was praying every day about all our situations not knowing what the future held except that God was in control. I still wanted to serve God and for my life to make a difference in this world and I was waiting patiently for God to act on my behalf and that of my loved ones. I was prepared for anything as long as God was by my side and leading me in the way forward. I only wanted what God knew was best for my loved ones and also for me even if it meant we could not be together. Finding a buyer for my apartment was very important if I was going to succeed with the business plans I had. I knew that I needed God to pour out his blessings from heaven if my situation and that of my loved ones was going to change. I re-read the statement I had sent into court for the final hearing and in my heart I believed I was doing the right thing by sharing my feelings about everything that had taken place.

The 15th July arrived and I was on my flight back to Manchester. I was happy to see my mum again as I settled into the guest room where I had planned to stay for the next three weeks. My 60th Birthday passed by very quietly as I enjoyed a meal at the local Chinese restaurant and went back home to share a bottle of Asti with my mum. Monday the 18th July soon arrived and I made my way to Liverpool Court for the first day of the ten days that had been booked for the final hearing. I was hoping that Sefton would agree to give my children back to Andreia and Nicoleta but this did not happen. On the Tuesday I had to go to the probate office in Manchester to sort out the certified will on behalf of Adrian and then go to Liverpool Court. On the Wednesday it was my turn to give evidence and I was in the witness box until the Friday morning. I tried to take all the blame for the contact we had with each other and it soon became very clear that Judge DeHaas was looking into everything in fine detail. I did not like the manner in which the barrister for Sefton was asking his questions and at one stage I was thinking about walking out of the witness box. If the barrister for Sefton missed asking a question about an important issue the Judge was very quick to ask the question and

I hoped this was not a sign that she was going to give my children to Sefton. The Judge came across as being very hard but there was something inside of me saying that she would look at things in a fair way and give my children back to their mothers care.

After day eight all the witnesses had given evidence and the Judge informed all the barristers that they should submit their final submissions by 10.00am the following morning. The Judge stated she would not give her decision until the 15th or 22nd August and that I could go back to France while she decided if she was going to take any action over the breach of injunction. It was perfect timing for the case to end because someone had died at the sheltered housing where my mother lived and the manager asked me to vacate the guest room where I was staying. I managed to book a flight back to France that was leaving Manchester airport on Friday morning the 29th July. All our barristers had done an excellent job and if there was any justice left and the Judge had a good heart I believed that my children would be returned to Andreia and Nicoleta. I told the Judge that when Mark had died and I was forced apart from my five children that my heart had been broken into a thousand pieces and I did not want Andreia or Nicoleta to suffer like I had done.

After spending a short time in France I travelled to Romania and arrived safely at Cluj airport and made my way by train to Deva. It had been a very long tiring journey and I was happy when I arrived at Deva railway station. On the Saturday I took the certified will to be translated into Romanian and legalised by a Notary. On the Sunday I went to the Monastery at Prislop near Hateg to pray and light candles for all my loved ones including Judge De Haas for God to touch her heart. On the Monday I made my way to Sibiu to give Adrian the certified copy of the will and we went to the bank together to set the wheels in motion for obtaining all the monies that James had left in the bank before he had died. It soon became clear that obtaining the money was not going to be a simple matter and we needed the help of a Notary that was going to cost Adrian about five hundred pounds. It was now just a case of waiting and trusting in God that all our situations were going to change for the better.

I received an invitation from a pastor of a small church at Petesti to go and speak and at the same time consider becoming a pastor of the church. I was available for anything God wanted me to do but I wanted to pray about everything and ask God to reveal his plan for my life. In all the problems I had gone through they had brought me closer to God and I was so thankful that I was not alone. After visiting Petesti and praying about everything I did not believe that God wanted me to move to Petesti or become a pastor of the church.

Chapter 71

" The troubles of my heart have multiplied; free me from my anguish."

Psalm 25 : 17

It was the 24th August 2011 and I had been informed by my solicitor to expect a telephone call from my barrister as Judge De Haas was going to hand down her judgement. I waited all morning for the call and when the phone rang it was Andreia crying down the telephone and I knew by her cries what the outcome was. I could not believe that yet another Judge was so cold and heartless as she approved plans to keep David, Naomi and Victoria in care and for Bianca and James to be adopted and even separated if they could not find placements for them to be together. I knew how both mothers would be feeling and I cried out to God and asked him why he was letting all the injustices continue. I tried to reassure Andreia that God was still on his throne and in control and not to give up hope. I knew that it was only God who had given me the strength to continue when everything had gone against me in the same court. It was not long afterwards when I received the telephone call from my barrister to confirm the same things and to inform me that Nicoleta had collapsed at court and had been taken to hospital by ambulance. I knew how much pain that both mothers would be suffering and my heart went out to them both especially Nicoleta who was so alone. I was praying and hoping that Andreia and Nicoleta would get their children back and it would be the end of court proceedings but my prayers were not answered that day and the fight for both mothers would continue.

My barrister advised me to leave it to both mothers to appeal but he could not tell me if their barristers were going to act for them or they had to do it by themselves. I knew that if the barristers did not give a legal advice that the Judge had made legal errors or had grounds for appeal that Andreia or Nicoleta would not receive legal aid and would have to do everything for themselves. I prayed that God would be close to both mothers of my children and surround them both with his love and protection. I was very sad when Andreia told me that the social worker called Paul had rushed as fast as he could to inform David of the outcome and had refused Andreia permission to be with David to comfort him. This again demonstrated the cold hard hearted people who had control of my children's lives. It was later the same day when I received a telephone call from Nicoleta informing me of what had happened. I knew how Nicoleta had felt when she told me that when the Judge told her the barbaric news of her judgement that her heart went very tight and she could not breathe. I asked both mothers if their barristers were going to appeal for them to London but none of them had been told anything.

I knew that they only had twenty one days for their appellant form to be received at the Royal Court of Justice so I informed both mothers I would prepare their appeals for them because I did not believe that their own barristers would help them. I knew in my heart that it would be very hard to get the appeal court to reverse the decision of Judge De Haas as it had been impossible for me to reverse what Judge Dodds had done to me. My barrister informed me that all the injunctions had now been lifted and that the Judge was not going to proceed with the breach of injunction that I had admitted to breaking. Nicoleta told me that she would have to give up the house she was renting because she would not be entitled to any benefits now her children had been removed and that Sefton were no longer going to help her with the shortfall in rent or to pay her what she had not been entitled to claim. I told Nicoleta that I was willing to come back to the UK to find a place to rent and help her stay in the UK while she waited for her appeal at London. I knew that I still loved Nicoleta very deeply but she had told me that it was hard for her because in some ways she blamed me for her children not being with her because all the findings were made against me. I could understand her feelings but I prayed that God would show her that real love does not blame and does not give up when persecution or troubles come our way.

Within forty eight hours I had downloaded the appellant's form on my computer and completed everything for both Andreia and

Nicoleta for their appeal to London. I received a telephone call from Adrian to inform me that he expected to be able to repay me the money he owed me within the next seven days so I took this as confirmation that it was right to return to the UK and it also felt right in my heart. I would need this money to start afresh in the UK as I had used up all the money I had while I had been staying in Romania without any income. I would have about £1600 in total to return to UK with plus my faith in God that was more precious than gold. Andreia informed me that she was going to write a letter to all the newspapers and TV stations to tell them how Andreia and Nicoleta had their children stolen from them by the Court in England. I told Andreia to do everything she could to try and get people on her side because what was taking place was done behind closed doors plus all the people who knew about this case said it was very wrong to punish the mothers and children for findings that were made against me. God had given me the wisdom to prepare all the legal documents even to the European Court of Human Rights if the Judge at London upheld the decision of Judge De Haas. I no longer had any confidence in any of the courts but my confidence in God would never be shaken and I knew he could change anything that he wanted to change in ways that we could never imagine.

For me I just wanted to be in the will of God no matter what he had planned for my life. I knew that if I was walking on the road he had mapped out for my life then no matter what came my way I would be able to handle it because God would be with me. It cost me over £300 to close my newly formed company down for up to two years and pay the cable contract for TV internet and telephone up to March 2012 as it had been signed for on a one year contract. I knew that I had become very close to Elena but I loved Nicoleta so very much and if it was the will of God for Nicoleta and me to be together it was what I wanted with all of my heart. I did not want to end up in a situation again where I loved two women at the same time and I kept a shield around my heart so that I would not fall in love with Elena unless God told me it was the right thing to do. I knew that I would have to go back to work in the UK but I did not have a problem with that while I had the strength to work. I wanted to show Nicoleta how much I loved her and that I would be there for her in her time of need. Nicoleta had told me that she did not want to get close to me because her children were her main priority and we had both agreed that if we could not be together so that Bianca and James could be back with their mother it was a sacrifice we were both prepared to make. I just wanted Nicoleta to see that if we did things through God and with love that all things were possible.

On Sunday 4th September at 1.00am I left Deva to make my way back to UK so that I could help Andreia and Nicoleta prepare their appeals for the Appeal Court in London. I did not have much money left and I decided to drive through the night just stopping for short breaks so I would not have to pay any hotel charges. I prayed to God about everything because I knew that only God could change our situations around. I told Nicoleta that I would help her in any way that I could and that I loved her very much. I wondered if it was the plan of God to put Nicoleta and me back together. I prayed a great deal as I made my way back to England talking to God about all my concerns and asking God to pour his blessings into the lives of all my loved ones including me. In less than thirty hours I arrived at the Ferry port in France and drove onto the Ferry that would take me back to Dover in England. I arrived in Dover at 9.00am and telephoned Nicoleta to ask if I could stay the night with her and talk about the way forward. We agreed to meet up later in the day where we went out for a meal together and talked about everything. I was sad about all that had taken place but happy to be with the girl that I loved once again.

I listened to Nicoleta as she told me how she felt and I knew what she was going through. I told her that I believed that if we loved each other and did everything Gods way that God would help us no matter what we had to go through. I told Nicoleta how sorry I was for everything I had done wrong in the past and that I would never hurt her again if she gave me a chance to prove I had learned from my mistakes. We were both single again and I wanted to show Nicoleta by my actions that I loved her very much and I would never hurt her again. I knew that trust was like building a brick wall where it became strong one brick at a time. The following day I received a telephone call from Adrian in Romania informing me that he had got the money from the bank in Romania that James had left him and that he had sent me a moneygram for the money he owed me. The money came at just the right time as I had almost used up the last of what money I had left.

I spent the next couple of weeks helping Andreia and Nicoleta prepare their appeals for London as both their barristers had stated they could find no grounds for appeal. When I read the judgment I found lots of points where the Judge had got things wrong and I started to list them so the Judge at London would be able to read them. Lots of people who knew Andreia and Nicoleta stated it was very bad what had taken place but sadly none of them did anything about it. There were no longer any injunctions in place but I made sure that I was never seen with Andreia or Nicoleta so that Sefton could not use this against them as they tried to get the findings of the Judge overturned. We all knew that it was going to be very difficult to win at London especially with none of the barristers who worked for us wanting to fight for us. We all agreed that if we lost at London we would fight on to the European Court of Human Rights. I thanked God that he had given me the experience of all that I needed to do for preparing all the appeals. I may have lost all my appeals but I was able to learn a great deal in the process that I now used for the benefit of Andreia and Nicoleta. We all lodged our appeals within the twenty one day period and now we waited to find out the date our appeal would be listed in London. I had requested for a stay of execution of the judgment of Judge De Haas pending the outcome of the appeal hearing to prevent Sefton from carrying out their plans to adopt Bianca and James. I had found a part of her judgment where the Judge had duplicated numbers in her judgment giving different findings at nineteen points and asked the appeal court to set aside her judgment and order a retrial. I was very surprised that none of the barristers had noticed these mistakes and it confirmed to me that they had never read her judgment in any detail as they had a duty to do. I did not know if the Judge at London would agree with me but at least it did show that there might be legal reasons for setting aside her very unjust judgment. Everything that I was doing I did with one eye on going to the ECHR as I believed they would look very closely at what had taken place.

    I had prayed to God on lots of occasions about being back with Nicoleta and hoped that Nicoleta would see that if we let love rule in our lives and do things Gods way that God could do wonderful things on our behalf. I knew that one of my prayers had been answered when Nicoleta told me that she was willing to give me a chance and be back in a relationship with me. I think that I realised at that moment why I had not been able to sell my apartment in Deva because God knew the timing was not right. We both knew that we would have to keep our relationship secret from Sefton and the Courts because they believed I was a very bad man and a danger to my children. We made plans to try and find a flat to rent in Manchester so we could be away from Sefton while we waited for a date from the Royal Courts of Justice in London for our appeal. I knew that I had done everything that I could do and that only God could change our situation around.

Chapter 72

" Your name will no longer be Jacob," the man told him. "From now on you will be called Israel, because you have fought with God and with men and have won."

Genesis 32 : 28

The 23rd September 2011 was a big turning point for me as I wrestled with God myself and talked with God about all that had been taking place. It was wonderful to know I could go into heaven with my spirit and talk with God knowing that Jesus was at his right hand side interceding on my behalf. I knew from reading the book of Job that sometimes we don't see the full picture and that trusting in God was very important. I knew that it was only because of Jesus that I was bold enough to speak with God and ask him why he had remained silent and not intervened on our behalf. I pleaded with God to help Andreia and Nicoleta to get their children back because they did not deserve what had happened to them. God knew everything and I asked God if he would remember all the good I had tried to do since becoming a Christian and do a miracle for Andreia, Nicoleta and all my children. When morning arrived I just believed that God was going to do something for us all.

   I was trying to find a place to rent and contacted the housing trust in Manchester and lots of housing associations to put my name down. I had changed my own name by deed poll so that it would be very hard for people to trace me when I found a place to rent. For me this was going to be a fresh start and this time I was determined to do things in a way that would please God. I was prepared to accept any plan that God had for my life because I knew that if I was in the will of God everything that God planned for me and all those that I loved would be good. It was now a time for patience as we all waited to receive a letter from London informing us the date our appeal would be listed. I wondered if we would get a fair judge and who it would be because I had been informed by my barrister that Lord Wilson had been promoted to the Supreme Court in London. I believed with all my heart that a fair and just Judge would give my children back to their mothers care but I had no confidence in anyone but God. I knew that God would only have to say the word and things would change for the better but only God knew if he was going to intervene on our behalf or if we would have to appeal to Europe. As I read the story of Joseph in my bible again it helped me to understand that sometimes we do not see the full picture of why bad things happen to us. I also wondered why God made Joseph wait two more years (Genesis 41:1) after the chief baker and chief cup-bearer had been released from prison before Joseph was set free. Only God knows the answer to that question and I just knew that I could only trust and believe that the purposes of God can be relied upon and that God can bring lots of goodness from the bad things that happen to us if we believe and have faith in him.

 I prayed that I would find a home to rent very quickly so that I could move all the furniture from the home that Nicoleta rented and start our life again in Manchester. I also wanted to go back into building work so I could earn a wage while we waited on God for what would happen at London. I knew that I could not open a restaurant in Romania unless I had the money so for now I was happy to go back into building work where God had given me lots of skills. Nicoleta also wanted to get a job while she waited to see if she would get her children back as Sefton had changed her contact with her children from five times a week to once a month. It was clear that Sefton were doing this to try and break the bond that existed between Nicoleta and her children and showed clearly the hard hearted people who had control of my children. Sefton were also doing the same to Andreia and her children for the same reasons. I was happy to hear that David had told Sefton that what they were doing was torture for him and his sisters and that he loved Andreia and me and that he wanted to have contact with me. I knew that my children would never stop loving me or forget all the good things I had taught them. David was only ten but he understood all what was taking place and he knew that the Judge was very bad in what she had done. It broke my heart to know that older boys in the care home were bullying David and teaching him to do bad things. David was led by an older boy to steal tools from a garden shed in an empty house that resulted in an official caution from the police for David. I knew that if David stayed in that care home much longer that he would be badly influenced and damaged in lots of ways. Naomi had threatened to kill herself if she was kept away from her mother any longer and Bianca had taken an overdose of medicines and cut off her hair when her social worker had told her one week before the final hearing had started that she was going to have a new mummy and daddy. Judge De Haas completely ignored all the bad things that had happened to my children whilst in the care of Sefton and I wondered if we would ever get a just Judge who would see things through honest and fair eyes.

It was good for me to be back at the home of Nicoleta but we made sure that we were not seen together and I was very careful not to be seen as I came and left her home. At least I had a roof over my head as I tried to find a home to rent in Manchester where Nicoleta and I could be together and away from Sefton. I knew that Nicoleta and Andreia were both very sad at what had taken place and I tried my best to encourage them and not to give up hope. Nicoleta decided to have a tattoo with the names of Bianca and James and booked the appointment for the 27th September and left a twenty pound deposit. On the day of the appointment Nicoleta started to have second thoughts because she was frightened of the needles. I decided that rather than lose the deposit that I would have the tattoo on my arm with the initials of David, Naomi, Victoria, Bianca and James on a scroll going through a red and blue heart. I knew that all my children would be happy to know I carried their names on my arm but more important than that I carried them around in my heart and mind. Not a day went by when I did not think about them and pray for them to God. I left the tattoo shop with a tattoo I had not planned to have and wondered how long it would be before my children got to see it with their own eyes.

Chapter 73

"Then Jacob said to Joseph, "I never thought I would see your face again, but now God has let me see your children, too!"

Genesis 48 : 11

When I read my bible there were times when certain scriptures jumped off the page and spoke right into my heart. I knew how Jacob had felt after thinking Joseph was dead and then years later not only did he get to see Joseph but the two grandchildren he did not know he had. I believed with all my heart that one day not only would I get to hold all my children in my arms again but the children that they would have. This encouraged me to keep my eyes on Jesus and to work at the plan I had to open a business that would help provide for their future and also poor people who were in need. My present circumstances were not very good but I trusted that God would help me as I walked in faith and did everything to improve my situation. I had a holiday booked to Turkey with Arthur and Diane that was all paid for and I decided to go on the holiday even though I did not have much money. It was an all inclusive holiday so I knew that I would have plenty to eat and drink. The holiday was booked for the 6th October for one week and I knew it would be good to have time with my brother and sister while I waited for God to act and for my situation and that of my loved ones to improve. My mum helped me in lots of ways and I was so grateful for all the love and support she gave to me.

I knew that God was with me in everything that I was going through and I was very happy to receive an offer from a Housing Trust of a one bedroom rented bungalow about a ten minute drive from where my mum lived. I went to look at the outside of the bungalow with my mum and Nicoleta and asked a neighbour if we could look inside to see the size of the rooms. We all agreed that the bungalow would be ideal for our needs and I telephoned the trust to inform them I would take up their offer and go and sign for it when I returned from the holiday to Turkey I had booked with Arthur and Diane. I had always wanted to live in a bungalow and I knew that we would make it into a very nice home. While I was getting ready to leave for Turkey on the 6th October Nicoleta received a letter from London to inform her that her appeal would be heard at the Royal Courts of Justice on the 1st December 2011. Now that Nicoleta knew her date for London she made plans to go and see her family in Romania for a couple of weeks in November as she had not seen them for a very long time. Sefton had already cut the contact she was having with Bianca and James from five times a week to once a month. I told Nicoleta I would travel with her to Romania so she was not alone but I was sad in my heart that her family was blaming me for all what had happened to Bianca and James. I could understand why they felt this way and I just prayed that God would change everything. We both agreed that I would stay in Deva while Nicoleta went to her apartment at Petresti to be near her family and have time with them.

I went on holiday to Turkey with Arthur and Diane and it was a time to relax and think about all that was taking place. The holiday was all inclusive so even though I did not have much money I had everything that I needed. It helped me to be able to talk with Arthur and Diane who gave me some good advice. I knew that if I did everything right before God that he would undertake for me and my loved ones. I bought some bead bracelets in Turkey for all my children with their names wrote on them saying that mum loved them. I knew if I had wrote my name that Sefton would have taken them from them and I also did not want Sefton to know I was in touch with both mothers. I knew my children would be happy to wear them and when they read this book they would know how much I loved them. Within a few days of returning from Turkey I signed the lease for the bungalow I had been offered and with the help of Nicoleta it was fully decorated with new carpets fitted before we left for Romania on the 3rd November.

While I was in Romania I received a telephone call from Andreia informing me that Nelu had died and she was coming to Romania for his funeral that had been arranged for the 11th November. I went to the funeral with Andreia and her mother Angela and on the way we spoke about the way that Nelu had given his life to Jesus and asked God to forgive all his sins a few months before he had died. When we arrived at the cemetery in Hateg where Nelu was going to be buried Andreia started to get very upset. I told Andreia to remember it was just his body and that his soul and spirit were now with Jesus. It was the custom in Romania for the body to be placed in an open coffin so that people could pay their last respects and say goodbye before the lid was sealed. When we looked at Nelu we could see him very clearly in a new suit with shirt and tie under the white lace that had been placed to cover his body. I asked Andreia if she could see that Nelu had a smile on his face and Andreia told me she could see him smiling and took it as a sign that he was happy and with Jesus. Andreia then started to read from psalm 23 and I placed flowers on the grave where I had wrote the verses from Revelation 21 : 4. After the funeral we went to a local restaurant where the daughter of Nelu had arranged for food and non alcoholic drinks to be served. While at the restaurant Andreia told me of her plans to marry Alex and asked me to lend her the original papers and translations of our divorce that she needed for the Registry Office in England. When we returned to Deva I took the papers to Andreia and told her that I wished her the best for her marriage to Alex and that I prayed she would get our children back at London.

On the 20th November I made my way to Cluj Airport where I had arranged to meet Nicoleta who had spent all her time with her family while she had been in Romania. Our flight was not due to leave until 6.00am and then it was delayed for an hour due to the bad weather. I had missed not being with Nicoleta and I was sad that her family blamed me for our children being in the care of Sefton and that I was not welcome at Petresti. Nicoleta did not want her family to know that she was still with me so I had to hide until they left the airport. I told Nicoleta that she should tell her family the truth and how I had done everything I could to help her change the situation for our children, fighting all the injustices that had taken place. I knew that I had to leave everything with God knowing that my life and the lives of all my loved ones were in his loving hands. It was a very hard journey back to Manchester and I told Nicoleta that I did not want to travel this way again and that I would not hide anymore from her family. Within 3 days of arriving home we had moved all the furniture from the home of Nicoleta to my bungalow. I had to borrow £750 from my sister Diane so that I could pay for the removal van and buy a new gas stove. It was a relief for us both to be away from Sefton and to be settled in our new home where we hoped no one would ever find us. On the 30th November we set off to London for our appeals that had been listed for the 1st and 2nd of December in front of Lord Justice Thorpe at the Royal Courts of Justice.

Chapter 74

" I also noticed that under the sun there is evil in the courtroom. Yes, even the courts of law are corrupt! I said to myself, "In due season God will judge everyone, both good and bad, for all their deeds."

Ecclesiastes 3: 16

I knew in my heart that the Judge at London was not going to change all the injustices that had taken place and that the only hope we had would be at the European Courts of Human Rights. We had to go through the appeal to qualify for going to ECHR and I told Nicoleta and Andreia not to expect to win at London. I wanted the Judge to know that God was in control no matter what he decided. It came as no surprise when Nicoleta phoned me up on the 1st December to tell me the Judge had refused her appeal. I sat up most of the night writing out what I wanted to say to the Judge and to involve God in my arguments. When it was my time before the Judge on the 2nd December I told him that as the courts recognise almighty God that I wanted to involve God in my arguments and I quoted the above scripture to him. I asked Lord Justice Thorpe how it can be called justice when all the findings were made against me and yet the court punishes two innocent mothers and five innocent children for things that had nothing to do with them. I spoke for about fifteen minutes and Lord Justice Thorpe listened very carefully to what I had to say. I told the Judge that I was asking nothing for myself but to change the injustices so that my children could be with their own mothers who were the best two mothers in this world. It did not take the Judge long to reject my appeal and back up every bad thing that HHJ De Haas had done in her judgement.

I was very sad when I left The Royal Courts of Justice and I prayed that God would stay very close to us all. I had already started work on the application to the ECHR for Nicoleta and Andreia so I was prepared for the outcome. I knew that the laws in England and Wales over children matters gave too much power to one Judge who had the power to destroy so many lives. The word Barbaric was the best description I could find to describe the manner and way the people running the system had set out to destroy all our lives. I telephoned Andreia to tell her the news and to expect the same result when she went before the same Judge on the 7th December the day after she was getting married to Alex.

We spent our last day in London visiting the British Museum as we waited for our train that was due to leave London at 10.00pm. I could feel all the pain that Nicoleta was going through knowing that she would not be with her children at Christmas for the third year running as I shared the same pain. I prayed silently for God to give us the strength to carry on and to do things in a way that was pleasing to him. I knew it was important to get back into fellowship with other Christians and to try and find a church where we could worship God together. When we arrived back home I went on the internet to search out churches in our area and found that The Lighthouse Church was only a five minute drive away from where we lived. I prayed that God would speak to us and heal all the pain in our hearts. It was no coincidence when the Pastor spoke about all the people who were going through adversity just like the women who suffered years of bleeding who Jesus healed. I could feel the presence of Jesus so close to me as the Pastor preached and as the tears flooded down my cheeks from the pain deep within my heart. I knew that healing was taking place and it was the same again the following week as we both returned to the same Church. It had been a long time since I had been to church two weeks running and I had Nicoleta at my side who I loved very much. Our financial situation was the worst it had been for over ten years and I knew that I would have to start from rock bottom all over again if we were to survive and make something of our lives. I wanted to help other people in need but I knew that I also had to do something to help ourselves get back into a position where we could also help other people.

I knew that God had given me lots of skills and that I could start up a building business again using all the knowledge I had gained over the years. I contacted my printer Simon in Blackpool and asked him to send me some prices for printing 10,000 leaflets so that I could let people know what I had to offer. I talked with Nicoleta about making plans for the future and trusting in God for everything. Nicoleta also wanted to try and find a job and I knew that if we both worked that we would be able to improve our financial situation. I still held on to my dream to open a business in Romania but for now it was time to get back into work in England. While I waited for my printer to do my leaflets I worked on the application for Nicoleta and Andreia for the ECHR. When Andreia telephoned me on the 7th December to inform me that Lord Justice Thorpe had refused her appeal I knew that we only had one chance left at Europe to try and change things.

I worked hard preparing the application forms for Nicoleta and Andreia and I thanked God that he had given me the wisdom to do everything. I wanted all my children to know that I had done everything in my power to try and change the injustices that had taken place and no matter what happens in their life never stop believing in God or give up in trying to do what is right. I also had the daily battles with my own flesh in giving up things that I knew were not good for me or would prevent God from blessing my life. I think gambling was a very big temptation because I needed some money but I knew from past mistakes that if I won some money by gambling it would not be long before I gave it all back with more besides. I was able to borrow £500 from my mum and I decided to use this to pay for my leaflets and letter headed paper to be printed. I talked with Nicoleta about the way forward and asked her to trust in God for everything. My car had developed a fault and I did not know if I should try and sell it or try and get the fault repaired. I had already spent £160 on the car trying to repair the problem and I prayed that God would show me what to do for the best. It was the birthday of Nicoleta on the 8th December and I made her a cooked breakfast and let her stay in bed while I did all the work. I would have liked to take her on holiday as a nice surprise but I knew that for now those kinds of thoughts would have to be put on hold.

I took my car to the garage and had to spend £200 having a new part fitted and I was still not happy with the way it was running. I placed an advert in the Auto Trader to sell the car for a reduced price of £3000 and I was happy to sell it for £2900 to the first person who called to see it. I had lost 0ver £2000 on the car but I was grateful to have some money to go and buy another car. We looked at a number of cars before we found one that we were happy with. We had spent a full day looking at cars that were in very bad condition and we walked for miles in the freezing cold trying to find the right car. I was praying silently to God asking for his help as we made our way home on foot after another wasted journey. We had both given up hope of finding a car that Friday as we went to the bus station to enquire about the timetable for Nicoleta to be able to travel to Southport by bus for the following Monday to see Bianca and James for the last time before they were placed for adoption. When we arrived home we decided to go on the internet and take another look for a car. It was about 6.00pm in the evening and we found a Fiat Punto that was 6 years old and had only done 30,000 miles. The car had been advertised for £2000 and we agree a price of £1700 with the seller over the telephone on condition the car was in the condition described and shown in the photographs. Within two hours of making the phone call we had tested the car and completed the sale and were the proud new owner of a car in much better condition than the one I had sold. We also had £1200 over from the sale that would help me start in business again. We were both thankful to God for having a car again that would mean we could go to church on Sunday and I could take Nicoleta to Southport to see Bianca and James. My mum was also happy knowing we would be able to pick her up on Christmas day and have the day together as planned at our home.

On the Saturday evening I could not sleep and I was praying to God about everything and I felt that I needed to write a letter to Judge Dodds and Judge De Haas for the way they had taken all my children into care. I wrote a very truthful letter quoting the scripture from Ecclesiastes 3 : 16 and asking both judges to think about the evil and barbaric judgments they had both given and how 5 innocent children would not be with their mother this Christmas. I asked them if they knew, loved and feared almighty God and told them I would pray that they would get to know Jesus Christ. I wrote that the law should be changed to prevent single judges from having the power that they had to destroy so many lives and that all contested cases should be tried by an independent jury especially when so many lives are at stake. I let them know I would never give up trying to overturn the injustices that had taken place in both their court rooms and that I would put my trust in God no matter what took place.

As we made our way to the Lighthouse church on the Sunday morning I spoke with Nicoleta about us both keeping close to Jesus and trusting in God for what we were both going through. I could feel the presence of God so close as we shared fellowship with lots of other Christians at our new church. I prayed for God to help Nicoleta on the Monday knowing that she would be seeing Bianca and James for the last time for many years unless she won her appeal to the ECHR. I thought about the Panorama TV programme we had watched on BBC 1 a few days before that was all about the child care system in the UK and showed children being adopted and taken away from in some cases perfectly good parents. We were both sad to hear that over 65,000 children were in care in the UK and since the baby P scandal there had been a 40% rise in the number of children taken into care. I wondered if God was going to use the appeal of Andreia and Nicoleta to let judges in Europe see and change what was taking place in the UK. As these thoughts and prayers were made the tears were flooding down my cheeks as I could feel the pain that Nicoleta was going through. I also felt God healing the pain in my own heart that I had carried with me for a long time and setting me free to live again for Jesus. It felt so good to be back in a living church and I knew that God was going to do a mighty work in our lives for what we were going through. We both decided to go back to church on the Sunday evening for the carol service and nativity play especially when we were told that Pastor Paul was going to do a rap.

We were both happy to be back in the house of God at 6.00pm and to worship God and thank God for the precious gift of his only son Jesus Christ. We were blessed in many ways and I was happy to see Nicoleta laughing again as Pastor Paul did his rap and the children performed their nativity play. I just knew that the only safe place for Nicoleta and me to be was close to Jesus and to live our lives in a way that would be pleasing to God. We both had broken hearts that needed a healing touch from Jesus and I could feel the healing balm from Jesus taking effect as we worshiped God in that very holy and anointed place.

It was Monday morning the 19th December 2011 as we made our way down the motorway to Southport where Nicoleta was seeing Bianca and James for the last time. I hated the system and heartless people who were in control of my children and had ripped them out of the loving arms of the best two mothers in this world. At least

Andreia would get to see her children because they were in foster care but the authorities had plans to adopt Bianca and James as they were intent on breaking the very strong loving bond between them. There is no other word than Barbaric to describe what the authorities in the UK were doing to all my children and both mothers. I knew that Jesus did not want me to hate but I would be lying if I said I did not feel this way and I prayed that God would take away my hate and fill me with his love. I was thankful to God when Nicoleta told me she had a wonderful time with Bianca and James and had let them open their Christmas presents at the family centre. Bianca told her mother that as soon as she was old enough she would go to Romania to be with her. As we made our way back home to Manchester I could feel the pain Nicoleta was feeling as the tears ran down both our cheeks once again. I told Nicoleta to think positive and to work for our children's future and trust that God will bring us through and in His timing our children will come home again. I told Nicoleta we should keep our eyes on Jesus and do everything in our power to live for Jesus in every area of our lives. We still had the appeal to the ECHR to complete and send to Europe and I knew from my own experience with God that sometimes miracles do take place. The most important thing I had learned was to keep on trusting and loving God no matter if our prayers were answered or not. With that in mind I wrote a Christmas card to Canon Noel Proctor MBE thanking him for the day he led me to Jesus Christ in that strip cell in Strangeways prison so many years before. I knew that once again I was starting my life from rock bottom but with God on our side there was only one direction we could go and look and that was upwards.

On the 20th December we went to Blackpool to pick up all the leaflets and letter headed paper that had been printed to advertise my new building business that I planned to start in January 2012. I believed that God would bless all our efforts and I looked forward to the day I would start delivering them and posting them through people's letter boxes. I knew that I had to forgive all the people who had brought so much pain into my life and the lives of Andreia, Nicoleta, David, Naomi, Victoria, Bianca and James if I was to be forgiven by God for all the people I had hurt in my life. I also did not want to have any barrier that would come between God and I that would prevent God from blessing my life. I talked with God about my feelings and I forgave everyone who I had bad feelings against and asked God to replace any hate that I had with a godly love for that person.

I knew that God understood and knew everything about me and that with his help I would become the person he intended me to be. My life had been one long battle after another and I wanted to experience the peace of God that Jesus had spoken about when he was on this earth. I knew that this would only come about by being in complete obedience to God in every area of my life and surrendering all to him. After making that prayer I felt burdens being lifted from me that I had been carrying around with me for a long time. Now it was time to draw very near to God and trust him completely with everything. I reminded myself of all the trials and tribulations that God had brought me through to date.

On Christmas day I woke Nicoleta with a kiss and we opened the presents and cards we had bought each other. I had bought Nicoleta a gold locket and inserted two photographs of Bianca and James knowing that she could keep it close to her heart all the time. The amazing thing for me was knowing that Nicoleta had bought the same lockets for Bianca and James with photographs of them when they were together. We both wished a happy Christmas to our children and a happy birthday to Jesus as we remembered what Christmas was all about. After having breakfast we got ready and made our way to our new church so we could celebrate Christmas with other believers. It was a very special time and although we had missed watching our children open their Christmas presents we watched all the children from our church who had brought one of their special presents to show everyone at church. All the way through the service I felt the love of God so very close to me and I prayed that God would be close to Nicoleta, Andreia and all of my children. I had a picture in my mind of David, Naomi, Victoria, Bianca and James opening their Christmas presents and I prayed that Jesus would be with them through everything. After the service had finished we called to pick my mum up and took her back to our home where we had Christmas day together. We played chess and cards together and then I cooked our Christmas meal that we were all ready to eat by the time it was on the table. I told Nicoleta and my mum that one day in the timing of God our children will come back home and we had to trust in God through everything. As I spoke those words I knew God was telling me to let go of everything that would prevent me from having a perfect relationship with God. After taking my mum back home and watching some TV. together it was time for bed. While Nicoleta was sleeping I thought about everything that Jesus did not want in my life and I knew I had to break all contact with Elena Farcas who had wanted to have a relationship with me. I knew that I had hurt Nicoleta in the past going between her and Andreia because my heart had been torn between them both and I did not want that to happen again. When the morning arrived I told Nicoleta that I wanted to live my life for Jesus and love her with a sincere love where after God she and our children would take over my heart. I then wrote the letter to Elena informing her that I would be making my life with Nicoleta and breaking all contact with her. As I wrote the letter I could hear Jesus speaking into my soul and telling me that what I was doing was the right thing to do and that he would help me resist the evil desires of my flesh as I stayed close to him. I knew the lessons from the past had been very painful but I also knew that the future was going to be brighter because I had learned from my mistakes.

Chapter 75

"Consider it pure joy, my brothers, whenever you face trials of many kinds, because you know that the testing of your faith develops perseverance. Perseverance must finish its work so that you may be mature and complete, not lacking anything."

James 1 : 2 – 4

I had read that scripture many times but for the first time I really understood what James was trying to teach people. I had endured many trials in my own life but I realised that through them all God had been doing a work in my own life and that through them all my faith was growing stronger, also my relationship with God was getting closer. Even though I had been in the refiner's furnace I had not been destroyed but refined just like pure gold. I could feel the bad things that God was helping me remove from my life, things like hate, lust, unforgiveness and anger just to name a few. I found myself praying for all the people including the Judges involved in the child care system who I had hated for tearing my family apart. I prayed that they would all come to know Jesus and experience the love and forgiveness that I had experienced in my own life. I shared with Nicoleta all the things that I had learned hoping that Nicoleta would also trust in God for everything in her life and what was happening to our children.

On New Year's evening we had a family meal together with my mum and after taking my mum back home Nicoleta and I sat quietly watching television waiting for 2012 to arrive. We were both missing our children very much and my heart went out to Nicoleta as I saw the tears running down her cheeks. I felt the same pain in my own heart and I prayed that God would be close to us all especially our children. I received a text message from Andreia wishing us all a happy new year and I sent one back to her and Alex. We were all trusting that Jesus would change things for the better in 2012 and I really believed 2012 was going to be the year of the Lords blessing on all our lives. As we watched the people of London seeing in the New Year and the wonderful firework display I promised Nicoleta that one year we would all be there with our children to see in the New Year. I did not know what year it would be but I believed that the vision God had given me with Nicoleta and my children would come about.

It was soon the 1st January 2012 and I started off my new year by going to church at the Lighthouse to worship God. Nicoleta was not feeling very well so I left her resting in bed and hoping she would soon recover. At church I received confirmation from God through the worship and sermon from Pastor Dele that God was with us and our lives were going to be blessed in 2012. The sermon was all about having a vision from God, writing our story as a legacy for our children and God answering our prayers that we had waited a long time to be answered. It was all about trusting in our God to undertake the impossible and I knew that this is what I had been doing for years. I thought about the appeal to the ECHR I was preparing for Andreia and Nicoleta, the vision to open a business in Romania so I could help people in need and the business I had just opened in the UK and all the leaflets I had printed ready to distribute. I believed with all my heart that God was with me in everything and that all I had to do was do the things God had given me the wisdom to do and trust God with the end results. The tears flowed down my cheeks as I thought about everything Jesus had done for me on that cruel cross and the difficult times he had brought me through so far. I was so thankful to God that he loved me so much especially knowing how many times I had failed or let him down. I was happy to start 2012 with a renewed heart and spirit to serve God with all my heart and to be the person that would bring glory to his name. I could not wait to go back home and share with Nicoleta all that God had spoken to my heart about while I was at church. It was the first day of a new year and I was very excited knowing that God was with us and the best was yet to come. I wanted this book to be a testimony for Jesus and to encourage other people especially my loved ones to know that only through Jesus Christ could we ever have a new life. I knew that the last chapter of this book would be finished when the appeal to ECHR had been concluded and then I would start book number 2 to let everyone know what happened after that. The only thing I was sure of was that my story would have a happy ending if not in this book but in book number 2.

It did not take long before the devil had a go at me when my car was broken into while we were sleeping and my Sat Nav was stolen. The thief had used some kind of tool to force open the passenger door lock and trigger the automatic door locking mechanism to get into my car. I did not let the devil take my peace away and I prayed that the thief would come to know Jesus. I knew from my past experiences of working at The New Life Centre how drugs and alcohol could destroy a person's life and drive them into a life of crime. I was sorry that I had left my Sat Nav in the car and it prompted me to take out home insurance to cover any future incidents that might take place. I had a £250 excess to pay on my car insurance policy to I decided not to claim for the damage to my door as I could not afford to pay the excess. At least the door locks still worked and the damage to the door lock was not very severe. I soon put this incident behind me and at church the following Sunday God spoke so clearly into my heart through the worship ministry and teaching from Pastor Paul. I was so happy to be in the house of the Lord to worship God with other believers of Jesus. The word was so clear that God was going to do mighty things in 2012 for those who loved God and put all their trust in Him. We were all challenged to change by 1% and to be a bright light for Jesus. I thought about how God was changing me as each day passed into the likeness of his son, and this was the plan of God for all those who would come to know Jesus. I knew that I fell far short of being anything like Jesus but at least God knew I was willing to let him change me and after all God was the potter and I was the clay. That in itself helped me not to get discouraged when I knew how much more work God had to do in my life to change me into the likeness of his Son.

On the 11th January the judgment from the 1st December came through from London so Nicoleta and I spent the morning numbering all the papers and packing the two files containing the papers with an application form for the European Court of Human Rights in Strasbourg. The files contained 678 pages for the Judge in Europe and we prayed over the parcel before taking it to the post office. Lord Justice Thorpe had acknowledged in his judgment that injustices had taken place against Nicoleta and her children but he still did nothing to change the injustices. We prayed that God would find a Judge who could see the injustices that had taken place and the breach of Human Rights and would be willing to change things for all my children. I spoke with Andreia on the telephone and asked her to let me have her judgment when it arrived from London so her papers could also be sent to Europe. I knew that Andreia was at least one week behind Nicoleta and maybe a few days more because of the Christmas and New Year holidays when the courts were closed. I knew that I had done everything in the wisdom that God had given to me and Lord Justice Thorpe had stated in his judgment that the case of Nicoleta was impeccably prepared. Only God could change the situation for Andreia, Nicoleta and all my children. I trusted in God completely that he would work for our good through everything that was taking place and I had a peace in my heart that nothing was going to take away.

It was now time to start distributing the 10,000 leaflets for my new building business and to get rid of the excess fat I was carrying in my body. We decided to work for about two hours a day when it was not raining and we were able to distribute about two hundred leaflets per hour between us. At least this way we could pick the areas we wanted to work and also make sure that every leaflet was distributed. It was going to take about fifty hours of work to distribute all the leaflets and about five weeks of work but I knew that any one leaflet could bring me a job to help me get back into a good financial situation so I could repay my sister and mother the money I had borrowed from them.

On Sunday the 15th January we were at our church together when God spoke a very powerful word into my heart through the worship team and preaching from Pastor Alex Robertson. I had been praying for Alex that God would give him a powerful anointing and my prayer was answered. God had seen all the injustices that had taken place and how lots of people had wrote me off and had not given me any credit for all the good I had done in my life from becoming a Christian. God was going to raise me up to do wonderful things in the name of Jesus and my name was being talked about in Heaven. My past was exactly just that and I had a future because of what Jesus had done for me on that cruel cross. The tears of gratitude and love for Jesus rolled down my cheeks as I believed that Jesus had a plan for my future and also my loved ones. I also understood that the words being preached were also meant for other people in our church who may have gone through difficult times and I thanked God for speaking words through Pastor Alex that I had longed to hear. God knew I was serious about living the rest of my life for Him and dealing with every sin or bad habit in my life that would come between the relationship I had with Jesus. I believed that the plan I had for opening a business in Romania would come into being when it was the right timing from God. I felt at peace over everything and I trusted that God would bless the new company I was just starting in Manchester and that God would help me get the work I needed to have. Knowing that my life and the lives of my loved ones were in the hands of God gave me the confidence that everything was going to come good.

On Saturday the 28th January I attended the men's conference at my church and the next day the BBC broadcasted a live service from our Church that reached one and a half million people. It felt good to be part of a church where good things were taking place and for the first time in ages I felt my happiness coming back. I felt God telling me to be a member of the Gideon 300 at our church who would give £20 a month to support the ongoing expenses so that our church could stay where it was. My own financial situation was the worst it had been in over ten years but for me I was taking a step of faith and letting God know I trusted in him and that money would be in my bank to pay the standing order every month.

I knew that God was healing me from all the hurt and rejection I had suffered and Pastor Paul confirmed this while he was preaching. The teaching from the book of Daniel made it clear that God was able to change our situation at any time he wanted to and that he was in the blazing furnace with me and my loved ones just like he was with Shadrach, Meshach and Abednego. I loved and trusted in God with all my heart and even if my prayers were not answered in the way that I had wanted them answered my love of God would never change. I was so grateful for what God was doing in my heart and life and for leading me to The Lighthouse. It was like being back at Heaton Chapel Christian Church the first church I attended after leaving prison in June 1988. Looking back I realised the journey I had been on had more valleys and mountains than anyone could imagine but God had been with me every step of the way no matter what I was going through. I knew that my life was starting from scratch all over again and God was giving me yet another opportunity to get it right and do things his way. This time I knew that I was not going to let anything or anyone come between Jesus and me.

I met a man called Jeff at church who had known me from The New Life Centre even if it did take him a while to figure out where he had met me before. I just asked Jeff not to believe everything he may have read in a newspaper or what people may have said badly about me as God was doing a mighty work in my life. When I arrived back home from the Sunday service a message was on my phone informing me I had been given my first job to do where I would earn about £200 that was followed by another message informing me I had my second job to do where I would earn about £1000 undertaking central heating work. I thanked God for giving me these jobs knowing that my faith in filling out the standing order when I owed my sister and my mother money had been rewarded by God. The feeling I had in my heart was of so much love for my Lord Jesus who knew exactly what I was going through including all those that I loved.

It felt good to undertake my first jobs for the new company I had formed even if my body hurt from using muscles that had not been used in a long time. I had been able to open a new business bank account and the first cheque that I paid in was enough to pay my sister Diane the £750 I had borrowed from her. I knew that my life was secure in the hands of God and I trusted that God would be with me each step of the way. My time was spent delivering leaflets, pricing up jobs and working on jobs that I had been given. It had been over one month since posting the papers to the ECHR in Strasbourg and Nicoleta had not had any letter confirming they had been received so I sent a letter to the court asking if they had been entered into the court files. I knew that God could raise up a Judge in Strasbourg to change the situation for Nicoleta, Andreia and all my children if it was the will of God and I prayed for this to happen every day. I prayed for a Judge to see all the injustices that had taken place who had the wisdom and courage to change all that had taken place. I knew that it would not change my situation but even if the Judges decided that I deserved all that had happened to me the same thing could not be said about Nicoleta, Andreia and all five of my children. I believed with all my heart that one day all of my children would come back to me and my God who I loved and trusted with all my heart knew the exact date that it would take place. For me I just needed to trust, believe and do the things in my life that would honour my Lord Jesus. With that in mind I decided to take the first steps of joining the men's fellowship group at Church following on from the Manpower conference I had attended. I joined a group of about twenty men who all wanted to be used by God to reach a lost and hurting world. From this meeting a group of us joined David King the following Saturday morning to walk the streets of Salford praying for the people who lived in the area as God touched our hearts.

On Thursday the 16th February Andreia gave me the judgment that had been sent from London so I could finish the file that I had prepared for the European Court of Human Rights in Strasbourg. It only took me about an hour to finish everything and hand it back to Andreia so she could sign it and send it on its way. I knew that only God could change the situation that we were all in as there was nothing more we could do except to pray and trust in God no matter what the outcome would be. I talked with Nicoleta about having a short holiday in Blackpool with my mum and on the 19th February we went to the Cliffs for a five night break. We all enjoyed the break but when I saw lots of other families with their children it broke my heart knowing that all my children were in care and not with their own families. I missed my children so very much and I knew that Nicoleta felt the same way without her saying one word. The five days went by very quickly and it was time for us to return to Manchester. I had another job to start on the 5th March so I had lots of things to organise. On the Sunday morning we went to our Church and Pastor Dele spoke on how God was able to do anything that God wanted to do. I agreed with everything that our Pastor spoke about and I was praying silently for God to tell a Judge in Strasbourg to overturn all the injustices that had taken place against all my children, Andreia and Nicoleta. I was singing praises to my Lord with tears running down my cheeks with gratitude for all that God had done for me by sending his one and only son Jesus to pay the penalty for all my sins on that cruel cross. I knew that even if none of my prayers were ever answered again that what Jesus had done for me was something that deserved my eternal praise and thankfulness.

Chapter 76

" For I know the plans I have for you," says the Lord. " They are plans for good and not disaster, to give you a future and a hope. In those days when you pray, I will listen. If you look for me wholeheartedly you will find me. I will be found by you," says the Lord. " I will end your captivity and restore your fortunes."

Jeremiah 29 : 11 – 14

This was my daily reading from The UCB Word For Today on Tuesday the 28th February. I needed to read those words again as I had received news that David was being badly abused in the care home where he had been placed by Sefton since removing him from Andreia in November 2009. I advised Andreia to go to a solicitor, the police and contact the Guardian solicitor to see if they can do anything about what was taking place. I told Andreia that we had to pray and trust that God would work for all our good with what was taking place. It broke my heart thinking about how this barbaric child care system and the cold heartless people running it had taken my children who I loved so very much from the best two mothers than any child could wish to have. It was only by praying that I could overcome the bad thoughts I had of wanting to harm the people who I believed had been evil in the actions they had taken that resulted in my children being in care and being abused.

    On Sunday the 4th March Nicoleta and I became official partners of our church The Lighthouse where along with other people we were called out to the front of our church to be welcomed and prayed for by our pastor and other leaders from our church. I felt at peace in my heart because I believed that I was where God wanted me to be at least for this moment in time. The following Sunday our pastor informed us all how the church had been broken into and the safe and both his passports had been stolen. I knew how Pastor Paul was feeling and I prayed that God would be close to him and work for good through all that had taken place. I even found myself praying for those who had broken into our church because I knew that their lives were being controlled by the devil.

One the 16th March it was the birthday of Bianca who was now seven years old and Nicoleta had made a special birthday card for her and also enclosed a gift of money. I was sad that my name could not go on the card so that the social services would not know that I was in contact with Nicoleta but I knew that one day my children would know the truth about everything. On Sunday the 18th March it was mother's day and I bought a card and flowers for Nicoleta and my mum. I also told them both I would cook a meal for them both as a way of letting them know how important they are and how good a mother they both were. My heart was breaking during the Sunday service when all the mothers were asked to stand up so Pastor Paul could pray for them all. Nicoleta stayed sat in her chair because we had decided not to let anyone know what we were going through and to stop people from asking difficult questions on why our children were not with us. I knew that God understood what we were both going through and I prayed that God would be very close to us both. I knew that all my children would have wrote cards to Andreia and Nicoleta but sadly the so called carers in charge of Bianca and James had made no effort to send a card to Nicoleta. Pastor Alex spoke about having unity in our church and that was where God would pour out his blessings. I agreed with everything that Alex spoke about and I believed that our church was full of godly people who would understand our situation if they knew what we had been going through. I was happy that Nicoleta decided to buy a ticket to attend a ladies fellowship meeting at our church for Saturday the 24th March that was called "The Overcomers". I prayed that through that meeting that Nicoleta would meet some godly people to come along side of her and help her grow close to Jesus. I knew from my own life that only Jesus could meet all our needs and help us overcome situations that would break most people who did not know or have a personal relationship with Jesus. When Pastor Paul stated that we write our vision in ink but our plans in pencil I could identify with what he was saying. I still had my vision deep inside my heart but for now my plans were in pencil not knowing when God would call us to move on and return to live and work in Romania.

My plans changed overnight when we talked about setting up a business that would help people and provide work for Nicoleta and lots of other people. We knew there was a great need in the UK for carers to look after elderly people and those with special needs. We talked and prayed about setting up a business that would provide carers for people in their own homes so that they would not have to go into a residential care home or nursing home. We knew lots of people in Romania who would make ideal carers who would be very happy to come to the UK and do a job where they would be well paid. I was amazed how quickly everything came together and within two days we had formed a limited company, employed a company to design our web site and contacted my printer to design leaflets and letter headed paper for our new business. We were both excited at the prospect of starting a new business that we dedicated to God and prayed that God would be the head of our company and at the centre of everything we wanted to do. We both had a desire to serve God with our lives and to help other people who were in need. We did research on the internet and found companies doing a similar work but they were charging a lot more money for their live in carers than we planned to charge our clients.

We prayed that the business would be a success because we knew how many people would benefit from what we wanted to do. Giving up my building business was something that I would be happy to do as I was finding it harder now that I was sixty years of age. The main thing is that I was at peace with whatever God wanted for our lives but deep inside my heart I could sense that God was going to do a remarkable work in and through our lives. We talked about donating some of the profits from our business back to God to help orphaned children in Romania and India, poor families and also old people in Romania who were homeless. We knew that we were living in a hurting and suffering world and we wanted God to use us to reach out and help a difference.

Chapter 77

"So now I am giving you a new commandment: Love each other. Just as I have loved you, you should love each other."

John 13 : 34

This was the scripture we decided to have at the top of our advertising leaflets, letter headed paper and web site. We wanted our business to reflect Jesus and by obeying that commandment we believed that our business would be a very bright light in our dark and hurting world. We attended the Easter services at our church and it was a time to reflect on the love that God has for each and every one of us. Pastor Paul preached on being planted, rooted and sorted in a church and I knew that Nicoleta and I had been planted at The Lighthouse Church for a good reason. Pastor Paul showed some photographs of his recent missionary journey to India and shared about the faithfulness of the Pastors in that Country. On bank holiday Monday I joined the men from the church who were meeting for prayer that was led by Pastor Alex. We were only a small group of seven men as some of the men were on holiday or away at conference. It was a very special night for me as I felt God saying to me I should ask my Christian brothers to pray for our new business that we had dedicated to God and for the Judge at Europe to change all the injustices that had taken place against Andreia, Nicoleta, David, Naomi, Victoria, Bianca and James.

It was the first time I had felt able to share my burdens with anyone else but I did not go into all the details with it being a long story to share. I realised that I was amongst a small group of men who really loved Jesus and Pastor Alex made the effort to come to church when he was full of a cold. When our prayer meeting was over Patrick came up to me and advised me to share my burdens with Pastor Dele and ask the prayer warriors from our church to pray about the situation in the hands of the Judges at Europe. Patrick told me about the amazing answers to prayers that were taking place because faithful people were praying to God. I believed it was time to share my burden with Godly people and as soon as I arrived home I sent an email to Pastor Dele outlining some of the problems and also sent him a copy of this unfinished book for him to read. I lay in bed with my arms around Nicoleta telling her that I had shared our burdens with some of the men from church and also with Pastor Dele because we needed our Christian brothers and sisters to pray to God as it was our only chance at Europe to change the injustices that had taken place and for all my children to return home to Andreia and Nicoleta. The tears rolled down my cheeks as I could feel the pain that Nicoleta was suffering with not seeing her children from December 2011. I sensed that something was happening in heaven that was going to bring great blessings into our lives that we in turn could be a blessing to other people. I was at peace knowing that God was in control of our situation and we were safe in His loving care.

On the 11th April Nicoleta received an email from Sefton informing her that the social worker who was responsible for Bianca and James had not given the birthday card and present to Bianca that Nicoleta had sent for the birthday of Bianca who was seven on the 16th March. It was so sad to know that the people in charge of our children could be so cruel and heartless and I wondered how Bianca must have felt on her birthday thinking that her mother had forgot her so quickly. It had been over three months since Nicoleta had last seen her children on the 19th December but we were pleased to read that they had not found any adoptive parents for our children as there plan was to separate Bianca and James from each other. My heart was breaking at what was taking place especially to see the tears running down the cheeks of Nicoleta knowing that of all the loving care she had spent on the birthday card for Bianca had been for nothing. I told Nicoleta that we should send a copy of the email and birthday card to the European Court Of Human Rights so the Judge reading all the papers could see the cold heartless people who had control of our children and the human rights being broken. The only word I could think of to describe the actions of the so called carers was inhumane. I was putting all my trust in God that he would intervene on behalf of Andreia, Nicoleta and all my children. I went on the internet to see a video of a recent case that had been heard at the ECHR against the United Kingdom that had taken place in the grand chamber in front of at least twenty judges. The case involved an animal rights charity concerning television advertising and I wondered if the cases of Nicoleta and Andreia would go before the grand chamber of judges. In the letter we wrote to the ECHR to be included in the papers for Nicoleta it stated that the judge had the power to change all the injustices that had taken place and to put the cases before the grand chamber. I knew from my own failed application to the ECHR that one judge again had decided my outcome and I prayed that God would find a judge with a good and honest heart who was prepared to change all the bad things that had and were still taking place. Andreia had informed me she was no longer prepared to give me any information about David, Naomi and Victoria who I believed she was seeing every two months. I was sad at this decision by Andreia who I felt had used me when it suited her and now that things were working out for her I was surplus to requirements. I wrote Andreia a letter and sent it to her by email and I told her I would leave her and her decisions in the hands of God.

I was busy undertaking all the problems associated with forming a new company and dealing with all the government departments. I was informed that if we were to be exempt from VAT we would need to register with a care regulating body. I thought about all the problems we had faced at The New Life Centre and prayed I would not have to go through that all over again. I decided to hand that burden over to God and it was a problem we would only have to face if our new company was a success and we had clients who needed a live in carer. I was also doing estimates for the new building company and undertaking jobs as we were given them to do. I thanked God for giving me the ability to cope and I was learning to take life one day at a time. I was informed on the 12th April that I needed to have a Colonoscopy on the 19th April to check that everything was good in that area of my body. I had a few symptoms that my doctor was concerned about that had gone away over the past few weeks but I decided I would go ahead with the test on the advice from Nicoleta and my sister Diane. In my heart I was at peace over everything and my life was secure in the hands of God who I knew loved me with an everlasting love. I also knew that God had given doctors the gift of healing people through modern day medicines and I was thankful to be in the UK where free treatment and tests were available for me. I knew that all the plans that I believed God had put on my heart to do required that I be fit and healthy so now was a good time to have the test even if it was the last thing I wanted to do.

While I was waiting for the Colonscopy test I was asked by Jeff Stoker from our church if I could help collect a commercial kitchen that had been donated for the charity in Romania. It would mean travelling to Leicester but I was happy to help knowing how hard Jeff worked for the charity. I was used to waking up early and I was happy to be part of a small group of people who had also given their time up to help. I was amazed to see kitchen equipment that would have cost about £30,000 to install that was in excellent condition. Within six hours we had dismantled everything and loaded it onto the large truck that Jeff had organised. Jeff treated us all to our lunch from McDonalds and we had a great time of fellowship together. It felt good doing something that would help the children of Romania and being a member of a church that was working in India and Africa as well. It was also a good time to get to know some of the other members of my church and talk with them one to one.

On the 20th April Pastor Dele came to our home and we were able to share with him everything that had taken place. It was the first time we had talked with anyone about what had been taking place in our lives and I believed that God had ordained for this meeting to take place. When Pastor Dele told Nicoleta and me that God had ordained this meeting and was the plan of God for our lives I believed that God was at work on our behalf. When Pastor Dele told us that Jesus had forgiven us and we had to look to the future I knew that a representative of God was with us. Pastor Dele prayed for us before leaving and I believed that great and marvellous things were about to take place.

I did not think it was a co-incidence that our new company was going live on the internet at about the same time Pastor Dele was at our home. It made a big difference to have a man of God praying for us and our children and to know that very soon over twenty prayer warriors from our church would also be praying for our situation.

Chapter 78

"Observe the requirements of the Lord your God, and follow his ways. Keep the decrees, commands, regulations, and laws written in the Law of Moses so that you will be successful in all you do and wherever you go."

1 Kings 2 : 3

On Monday evening the 23rd April Nicoleta was sent an email from her family in Romania with a copy of the letter sent from the European Court of Human Rights that was dated 10th April 2012. The letter stated that on the 3rd April a single judge (V.A. De Gaetano assisted by a rapporteur) decided to declare inadmissible the application lodged by Nicoleta. The Court had found that the admissibility criteria set out in Articles 34 and 35 of the convention have not been met. This decision is final. It is not subject to an appeal either to the Grand Chamber or to any other body. The Registry is unable to provide you with any further details concerning the Single Judge's decision.

The letter sent to Nicoleta was word for word as the one I had received in 2011 from the ECHR and from the same Judge. We were broken hearted knowing that we had exhausted all legal options and we could do nothing more to try and get our children back and overturn all the injustices that had taken place. I wrote a letter to the President of the court and the Registrar to ask for one reason why the application had been refused. It seemed that the only cases that went before the Grand Chamber were if you were a terrorist or an animal as those were the only cases that got any media coverage. We read Articles 34 and 35 and basically it seemed like one Judge had the power and authority to throw out any application without giving any reasons. We told the Judge that Justice had been thrown out of the window and that the application made by Nicoleta deserved to be looked at by the Grand Chamber of Judge's and not just one Judge. The application had been thrown out before the prayer warriors from our church had become involved but we did not know it at that time. Pastor Dele phoned to talk with us and we told him the bad news we had just received. It was good to hear Pastor Dele inform us that God could do anything to change our situation around and work in ways we had never thought or dreamed could happen. It was good for us to know that we were not alone and that Godly people from our church would still be praying into our situation.

I did not understand why God had allowed all these injustices to take place but my love and faith in God was still very strong. I knew that lots of bad things had happened to Jesus when he lived on this earth and that Jesus had never done anything wrong and was without sin. I could not say that about myself but what I could say was that I understood how Jesus must have felt when he was unjustly treated by all those he had come to save. I also knew that I had been forgiven by God for every single thing I had done wrong in my life and for every sin committed by me because of what Jesus did for me on that cross by paying the price and penalty for my sin and that I was washed clean by the blood of the Lamb. If none of my prayers were ever answered again by God I had plenty to thank God for in giving His precious Son Jesus as a living sacrifice so that my relationship with God could be restored. I believed that God had a special plan for all our lives and I trusted in God completely. I was able to say like Jesus "Not my will but your will God for my life and for those of my loved ones."

I felt the pain that Nicoleta was feeling and I held her close in my arms trying to reassure her that God had everything under control. I told Nicoleta that we could still work for our children's future at the businesses we had started and at the same time help lots of people.

Looking back over my life I knew I had made many mistakes and committed lots of sins that I could never change. I also knew that I had been forgiven by a God of love who never once let go of my hand or given up on me when most people had. I was reminded by Pastor Dele that God could change any situation and we just needed to trust in our living God that one day our children would return home. It made a big difference having Pastor Dele at our home who gave us lots of Godly advice and prayed with us. We were happy to hear that over twenty people would be praying into our situation from our church.

We had lost our legal fight to try and get our children back from Sefton Borough Council but we would never give up on our children or ever stop loving them. I knew that I had forgiven all the people who had hurt me and I knew that I had tried to make things right with all the people I had hurt in my life. The Bob Sutton who entered Strangeways Prison in 1987 died and a new creation left prison in June 1988 after being born again when I was led to Jesus Christ by Noel Proctor the prison chaplain. My walk with Jesus is full of many ups and downs with lots of twists and turns. Up to now I have been down more times than I can count but thanks be to God that each time I was down the power of God in my life helped me to get back up. So once again a new beginning is in front of Nicoleta and me with the past behind us. We are walking in victory because we know that our God is for us and that we are more than conquerors through Jesus Christ. We are going to work for our children's future and wait for the day they will come back home to us. It is my prayer that everyone reading this book will know Jesus Christ in a personal way and never give up on life no matter what problems you may face. I hope you will also read my second book as I work towards the day all of my children come back home to me. I will leave you with the scripture God gave to me that I believe will come true.

"Look around you and see, for all your children will come back to you. As surely as I live." Says the Lord, "they will be like jewels or bridal ornaments for you to display."

If you like a happy ending you will enjoy reading my second book
When Tested I Will Come Forth as Gold